The Book of Enoch

Messianic Prophecy Edition

Time-Capsule to the Last Generation

Including:

"Who Really Wrote the Book of Enoch?"

The Book of Enoch

Messianic Prophecy Edition

Time-Capsule to the Last Generation

The Five Scrolls
Attributed to the
Biblical Enoch

Lost for More than 1,000 Years but
Found Preserved among the
Jews and Christians of Ethiopia

R. H. Charles Translation Included

Featuring:
"Who Really Wrote the Book of Enoch?"

by R. I. Burns

SageWorks Press
2017

Cover concept: P. Burns
Cover composition: M. DeRaud

First Snowfall print edition, December 2017.
San Francisco, CA USA
ISBN: 978-057819869-9
ASIN: B0776K4TTN

www.TheBookofEnoch.info

Thanks to:

My first love in this world, my wife
Who helped me with researching, editing,
Proofing, and beautifying this book and
Who fascinates me with her fascination for God.

To Daniel in the UK,
and Ann in Florida,
who have been my friends in cyberspace
who helped me understand the Book of Enoch.

Dedication:

This book is dedicated to
The Last Generation
Who will be living in the Day of Tribulation

Enoch, the seventh from Adam, *prophesied, saying, "Behold, the Lord comes with ten thousands of His holy ones, to execute judgment on all and to convict all the ungodly of all their deeds of ungodliness that they have committed in such an ungodly way, and of all the harsh things that ungodly sinners have spoken against Him."*

Letter of Jude 1:14-15

"Behold! He cometh with ten thousands of His holy ones to execute judgment upon all, and to destroy all the ungodly: and to convict all flesh of all the works of their ungodliness which they have ungodly committed, and of all the hard things which ungodly sinners have spoken against Him."

Book of Enoch 1:9

The Book of Enoch
Table of Contents

Who Really Wrote the Book of Enoch?

Appendices

Index of Tables, Graphs, and Inserts

Preface

What the Book of Enoch Offers Today's Reader

The *Book of Enoch* has much to offer readers today. In it you will find:

- Messianic prophecies fulfilled by the coming of Jesus Christ
- End-time prophecies to be fulfilled at the return of Jesus Christ
- A promise of blessing to readers of the book in the last days
- Clarification and insight into difficult passages of the Bible
- An outline of God's salvation plan from creation to eternity
- Vivid descriptions of the future blessings for believers
- Insight into the nature of the spiritual warfare in today's world

About This Edition

The translation being used for this edition of the *Book of Enoch* was published a century ago by R. H. Charles. Amazingly, the readability and vivid style of Charles' translation still holds up after more than a century.

Print copies of R. H. Charles original work used Roman numerals for chapters and verses. The use of Roman numerals for chapter and verse numbering has been eliminated here. It is hoped the use of traditional numbering of chapters and verses will encourage the use of quotes and passages from the *Book of Enoch* in books, articles and Biblical studies, and will render this edition a useful reference tool. Readers will no doubt find it easier to refer to Enoch 105:2, rather than Enoch CV:II! Also, the text has been set to single-column-paragraph style to help the reader differentiate between narration, dialogue, and the versified, poetry sections.

The *Book of Enoch Messianic Prophecy Edition*, introduced here for the first time, is fully cross-referenced to the Bible. Biblical references are printed fully in the footnotes in order to quickly assist the reader, to see the thoroughly Scriptural character of the *Book of Enoch*. Explanatory notes are provided for difficult passages.

It is hoped the notes, articles, and study aids in this edition, will help the reader to find the *Book of Enoch* a source of blessing and encouragement. May the *Book of Enoch* receive its proper recognition as the legacy of Israel and the heritage of the Church so that many may discover its stunning testimony to Jesus Christ, delivered as it was before His first appearing and in anticipation of His return.

R. I. Burns
September 28, 2009

Introduction

The Bible tells us precious little about the Biblical figure known as Enoch. In Genesis 5:24, we read, "Enoch walked with God, and he was not, for God took him." In the Epistle to the Hebrews, it says, "By faith Enoch was taken up so that he should not see death, and he was not found, because God had taken him. Now before he was taken he was commended as having pleased God" (11:5). Finally, in Jude 1:14, we discover, "Enoch, the seventh from Adam, prophesied." Jude proceeds then to quote a passage from the *Book of Enoch.*

Why would Jude, one of the inspired writers of the New Testament quote from a book not found in our Bible and call it prophecy? Does the *Book of Enoch* agree with or contradict the Bible? It is hoped this volume will assist the reader to get closer to the answers to these and other questions.

The *Book of Enoch,* is sometimes referred to as *1 Enoch* or *Ethiopic Enoch,* (because the only complete copy of the book in an ancient language is an Ethiopic one). In ancient times the book was referred to as the *Book of the Words of Enoch* (pp. 234-235). I think a better title than all these might be the *Revelation to Enoch* or the *Apocalypse of Enoch,* since that better describes the book's contents.

The *Book of Enoch* began as a set of smaller books which circulated as independent scrolls. Eventually, these smaller books were combined into The *Book of Enoch,* which we have today. Despite the composite nature of the *Book of Enoch,* there is a certain logical arrangement to it. For instance, the first chapter of the first section and the last chapter of the last section share common themes. Consider too, the first chapter opens with a message to the generation who will be living at the end of time, who are said to be alive when God comes to tread upon the earth. It is Jude who interprets this vision for us. Jude says this passage should be understood not just as poetic imagery but as a vivid vision of God coming to earth as Messiah at the Second-coming of Jesus Christ.

The *Book of Enoch Messianic Prophecy Edition,* is presented here as a study edition of the *Book of Enoch.* For the purposes of this edition, it is assumed the *Book of Enoch* is the legitimate writings of the Biblical Enoch. For a detailed defense of this position, the book, *"Who Really Wrote the Book of Enoch?"* is being introduced in print here for the first time. There, detailed evidence is brought forth to the reader, arguing the *Book of Enoch* is indeed the authentic writing of the Biblical Enoch.

In the *Book of Enoch Messianic Prophecy Edition,* passages which are believed to contain messianic prophecies have been marked with a " ✡ " symbol. This symbol indicates a footnote is included which shows how the passage can be understood Messianically.

Introduction to the Book of the Watchers

Title ~ The first of the five scrolls which became the book we now refer to as the *Book of Enoch*, is commonly called the *"Book of the Watchers."* The title came about because the major role played by a group of angels called 'Watchers' in this section.

Authorship ~ The *Book of the Watchers* is written in the first-person as the Biblical Enoch, (see verses 1:1-3 and 12:2). The Hebrew form of Enoch's name is "Hanoch", which means "dedicated." The Bible describes Enoch's dedication in these words, *"Enoch walked with God."* (Genesis 5:24) In the *Book of the Watchers*, we are told Enoch's writings were entrusted to his son Methuselah, and Methuselah's grandson, Noah. It is possible these descendants of Enoch updated certain portions of the book. However, the book's internal style and arrangement argues for a single author for most of it.

Date ~ Beginning in chapter 14, the *Book of the Watchers* contains a lengthy description of one of Enoch's dream-visions which he received soon after being called by God to the role of prophet. Chapters 6-10, record events which occurred both before and after Enoch's time on earth. In Enoch 106:13, Enoch states the earlier events were revealed for him in a vision. It is possible the later events were similarly revealed to him in a vison, and written down by him before they occurred. This would place the writing of the entire book before Enoch was translated to heaven, which would be more than six centuries before the flood of Noah's day.

Major Theme ~ *"But ye- ye have not been steadfast, nor done the commandments of the Lord" (Enoch 5:4).* The operation of the fixed order of nature, sun, moon, and stars is contrasted with the actions of men and of angels. Unlike the ungodly, the natural world fulfills the purposes for which it was assigned by God. God has determined to put an end to ungodliness and establish in the midst of humanity a godly people, (later referred to as the "plant of righteousness" Enoch 93:5), from which godliness will finally flourish and spread throughout the earth.

THE BOOK OF THE WATCHERS

Background ~ The world of Enoch's day found itself in the throes of a deepening crisis brought about by the activities of certain evil angels, their offspring, and a complicit humanity. The subjugation of humanity at that time is portrayed here in the most extreme terms. In response, God declares his decree to punish the ungodly and cleanse the earth by means of a flood. In chapters 10 and 11, using language similar to passages in the Old Testament prophets, the coming of the Messianic Age is foreseen; here God introduces his promise to set up his kingdom on earth which will inaugurate a golden age for humanity, while repudiating all that was out of order in Enoch's day. The Messianic Age will stand as God's answer to the 1,000-year *misrule* of the Watchers and their offspring.

Purpose ~ According to Enoch 1:1-3, the purpose of *The Book of the Watchers* is to become a blessing for those living in the future "day of tribulation." The manner in which this is to be realized begins to crystallize as one combines the message of *The Book of the Watchers* with the four books which follow it. It is the claim of this book to be a kind of time-capsule to the last generation, the relevance of which is said only to be fully realized by the generation living at the end of the age.

The *Book of Enoch*, its writer claims, will have a role to play in the last days. This fact may partly explain the *Book of Enoch's* diminished importance within the Church for the past 2,000 years; its time had not yet come. This may also partly explain why there is an increased interest in the book in these times; it is as if the book is being positioned to play an increasing role in our world as the end of the age draws nearer.

Synopsis ~ In chapter 1, Enoch, a contemporary of the first man, Adam, sends a message across the millennia dedicating his book to the last generation who will be living at the end of the age.

In chapters 2 to 5, Enoch gives a short summary of his burden as prophet for his own generation. *"Ye have not been steadfast"*, decries the prophet. The generation of Enoch's day is contrasted with the fixed order of creation. The Watchers and sinful humanity have abandoned the plan of God for their lives and have instead perverted their ways.

In chapters 6-11, we are given the broad, sweeping overview from start to finish of the crisis before the flood. We see how the situation began, how it progressed, and how it would be resolved.

In chapters 12-13, we are given the first of two flashbacks. Here Enoch retells in greater detail, part of the story he has just related in chapters 6-11. Enoch describes how he was called to the role of prophet, receiving commission from the Lord to take God's word of reprimand to the angels who sinned. Enoch describes his call, his ministry, and his message.

In chapters 14-36, we have the second of two flashbacks. Here again, Enoch retells the events of the dream-vision he related in the previous section but in greater detail.

~~~~~~~~~~~~~~~~~~~~~~~~~~~~~~

Outline ~

I. Overture (1:1-5:9)
- A. Dedication to earth's last generation (1:1-3a)
- B. God's kingdom to come (1:3b-9)
    1. The righteous delivered, ungodly removed (1:8)
- C. The prophet's burden (2:1-4:1)
    1. The godly blessed, the ungodly cursed (5:1-9)

II. Kingdoms in Contrast (6:1-11:2)
- A. The Passing Era of Watcher misrule (6:1-10:16a)
    1. Watcher Descent (6:1-7)
    2. Monstrous Births (7:2)
    3. Human Subjugation (7:1-8:4)
    4. Angelic Intercession (9:1-11)
    5. Judgment (10:1-16a)
- B. The Coming Era of Messianic rule (10:16b-11:2)
    1. Divine Descent (1:4)
    2. Human Deliverance (10:17)
    3. Global Liberation (10:16b)
    4. Righteous Births (10:17)
    5. Blessings (10:18-11:2)

III. 1st Flashback: Enter Enoch the Prophet (12:1-13:10)
- A. The call of Enoch (12:1-4a)
- B. The ministry of Enoch (12:4b-13:10)

IV. 2nd Flashback: Message and Vision of Enoch (14:1-36:4)
~~~~~~~~~~~~~~~~~~~~~~~~~~~~~~

THE BOOK OF THE WATCHERS

The Book of the Watchers

Dedicated to the Last Generation

1 The words of the blessing of Enoch, wherewith he blessed the elect and righteous, who will be living in the day of tribulation,[1] when all the wicked and godless are to be removed. 2And he took up his parable[2] and said, Enoch a righteous man, whose eyes were opened by God, saw the vision of the Holy One in the heavens, which the angels showed me,[3] and from them I heard everything, and from them I understood as I saw, but not for this generation, but for a remote one which is for to come. 3Concerning the elect I said, and took up my parable concerning them:

> ***Enoch and the Last Days***
>
> The *Book of Enoch* claims to be writings of the Biblical Enoch. The Epistle of Jude quotes the *Book of Enoch*, with the preface, "Enoch, the seventh from Adam, prophesied." In so doing, Jude is telling us something about Enoch which the rest of the Bible does not; Enoch was a prophet. How did Jude know Enoch was a prophet? Undoubtedly it was by inspiration of the Holy Spirit who also lead Jude to quote from the *Book of Enoch*. Is the *Book of Enoch* truly the writings of Enoch? If true, that would make it the oldest book in the world! If so, that makes the book's claims more incredible, for, in this passage the writer claims to be writing a book for the last generation who will be alive when God sets up his kingdom on earth. Could the *Book of Enoch* be the world's oldest book written for the world's last generation?

The Second Coming of Christ

The Holy Great One will come forth from His dwelling,[4] ✡
4And the eternal God will tread upon the earth, even on Mount Sinai,[5]

---

[1] **"He blessed the elect who will be living in the day of tribulation"**; what is stated in the *Book of Revelation* is also found in the *Book of Enoch*. John writes, "Blessed is the one who reads aloud the words of this prophecy, and blessed are those who hear, and who keep what is written in it, for the time is near." (Revelation 1:3) John's blessing to his readers is tied to the nearness of the end times. Enoch sends blessings to his readers in the last generation. Both Enoch and John thus pronounce blessings upon their readers living in the last days.

[2] **"He took up his parable"**; The use of the word "parable" here and elsewhere in the *Book of Enoch*, is unusual and should probably be understood as synonymous with "oracle" or "prophecy". In this verse, the Dead Sea Scrolls have a word which is better translated "oracle" than "parable".

[3] **"Which the angels showed me"**; both Enoch and John say they received their revelations through angels. **Revelation 1:1-2**, The revelation of Jesus Christ, which God gave him to show to his servants the things that must soon take place. He made it known by sending his angel to his servant John.

[4] ✡ **"The Holy Great One will come forth from His dwelling"**; introduced here for the first time is a theme which recurs throughout the *Book of Enoch*; at some future period, God will personally come to earth as judge and deliverer. The passage should not be simply understood as a theophany, since according to Jude 1:14-15, this part of Enoch is a prophecy of the 2nd-coming of Jesus Christ. **Hosea 5:15**, I will return again to my place, until they acknowledge their guilt and seek my face, and in their distress earnestly seek me. **See: Enoch 25:3, 52:9, 77:1, 90:15,18,20, 91:7, 100:4**

[5] **"The eternal God will tread upon the earth, even on Mount Sinai"**; as we see here before the law was given to Moses at Sinai, that mountain was already part of a growing tradition. Sinai is here prophesied to have importance in the end times; it will be one of four mountains that figure prominently in the triumphal return of Christ, along with Mt. Paran in Jordan, the Mount of Olives, and Mt. Zion, in Israel, see **Isaiah 63:1, Zechariah 14:4, and Psalm 68.**

And appear from His camp
And appear in the strength of His might[6] from the heaven of heavens.

[5]And all shall be smitten with fear,
And the Watchers[7] shall quake,[8]
And great fear and trembling shall seize them unto the ends of the earth.

[6]And the high mountains shall be shaken,
And the high hills shall be made low,
And shall melt like wax before the flame.[9]

[7]And the earth shall be wholly rent in sunder,[10]
And all that is upon the earth shall perish,
And there shall be a judgment upon all men.

[8]But with the righteous He will make peace,
And will protect the elect,
And mercy shall be upon them.

And they shall all belong to God,[11]
And they shall be prospered,
And they shall all be blessed.

And He will help them all,
And light shall appear unto them,
And He will make peace with them.[12]

Micah 1:3-4, Behold, the Lord is coming out of his place, and will come down and tread upon the high places of the earth. And the mountains will melt under him, and the valleys will split open, like wax before the fire, like waters poured down a steep place.

[6] **"In the strength of His might"**; **Ephesians 6:10**, Be strong in the Lord and *in the strength of his might.*

[7] **"The Watchers"**; the description here of angels as "Watchers" is found in Enoch only in *The Book of the Watchers*, where it is used 15 times. The term is used for both fallen and holy angels. This title is repeated in Daniel 4 where it is used in the following three verses. **Daniel 4:13**, I saw in the visions of my head as I lay in bed, and behold, a watcher, a holy one, came down from heaven. **Daniel 4:17**, The sentence is by the decree of the watchers, the decision by the word of the holy ones. **Daniel 4:23**, The king saw a watcher, a holy one, coming down from heaven.

[8] **"The Watchers shall quake"**; **Isaiah 24:21**, On that day the LORD will punish the host of heaven, in heaven, and the kings of the earth, on the earth. They will be gathered together as prisoners in a pit; they will be shut up in a prison, and after many days they will be punished. **Luke 21:26**, The powers of the heavens will be shaken. **Enoch 13:3, 102:2**

[9] **Enoch 1:3-6**, is apparently copied in a shortened form in **Micah 1:3-4**, Behold, the LORD is coming out of his place, and will come down and tread upon the high places of the earth. And the mountains will melt under him, and the valleys will split open, like wax before the fire, like waters poured down a steep place. **Psalm 97:5**, The mountains melt like wax before the LORD, before the Lord of all the earth. **Enoch 52:6**

[10] **"The earth shall be wholly rent in sunder"**; **Isaiah 24:1,3,19**, Behold, the LORD will empty the earth and make it desolate, and he will twist its surface and scatter its inhabitants. The earth shall be utterly empty and utterly plundered; for the LORD has spoken this word. The earth is utterly broken, the earth is split apart, the earth is violently shaken.

[11] **"They shall all belong to God"**; **Malachi 3:17**, They shall be mine, says the LORD of hosts, in the day when I make up my treasured possession.

[12] **"He will make peace with them"**; **Isaiah 40:1-2**, Comfort, comfort my people, says your God. Speak tenderly to Jerusalem, and cry to her that her warfare is ended.

"Behold, the Lord comes with ten thousands of his holy ones" ~ Jude

[9]And behold! He cometh with ten thousands of His holy ones[13]
To execute judgment upon all,
And to destroy all the ungodly:

And to convict all flesh
Of all the works of their ungodliness
which they have ungodly committed,
And of all the hard things[14] which
ungodly sinners have spoken against Him.

Enoch and the Second-Coming

Enoch 1:9 is quoted in the Epistle of Jude. Per St. Jude, this part of Enoch is to be fulfilled by the 2nd-coming of Christ at the end of the age. The message of Enoch's book is to be specifically applicable to those living in a future "day of tribulation", (v1). His book is not being written for his own generation according to verse 3, but for "a remote one, which is for to come". More detail about this future event is found in verses 3-9. Whatever one believes about the *Book of Enoch*, what the book claims for itself is incredible on the surface of it. This book purports to be a kind of time-capsule to the last generation!

The Burden of the Prophet Enoch

2 Observe ye everything that takes place in the heaven, how they do not change their orbits, and the luminaries which are in the heaven, how they all rise and set in order each in its season, and transgress not against their appointed order.[15]

[2]Behold ye the earth, and give heed to the things which take place upon it from first to last, how steadfast they are, how none of the things upon earth change, but all the works of God appear to you. [3]Behold the summer and the winter,[16] how the whole earth is filled with water, and clouds and dew and rain lie upon it.

3 Observe and see how in the winter all the trees seem as though they had withered and shed all their leaves, except fourteen trees, which do not lose their foliage but retain the old foliage from two to three years till the new comes.

---

[13] **Jude 1:14-15**, It was also about these that Enoch, the seventh from Adam, prophesied, saying, "Behold, the Lord comes with ten thousands of his holy ones, to execute judgment on all and to convict all the ungodly of all their deeds of ungodliness that they have committed in such an ungodly way, and of all the harsh things that ungodly sinners have spoken against him."

[14] **"All the hard things which ungodly sinners have spoken"**; **Malachi 3:13**, Your words have been hard against me, says the LORD. **Enoch 5:4, 27:2**

[15] **"They transgress not against their appointed order"**; The fixed order of creation is a theme throughout the book. This fixed order is contrasted with the sinning angels and mankind who routinely transgress God's laws. **Enoch 72:1, 101:1**

[16] **"Behold the summer and the winter"**; **Genesis 8:22**, While the earth remains, seedtime and harvest, cold and heat, summer and winter, day and night, shall not cease.

4 And again, observe ye the days of summer how the sun is above the earth over against it. And you seek shade and shelter by reason of the heat of the sun, and the earth also burns with glowing heat, and so you cannot tread on the earth, or on a rock by reason of its heat.

5 Observe ye how the trees cover themselves with green leaves and bear fruit: wherefore give ye heed and know with regard to all His works, and recognize how He that liveth for ever hath made them so. [2]And all His works go on thus from year to year for ever, and all the tasks which they accomplish for Him, and their tasks change not, but according as God hath ordained so is it done. [3]And behold how the sea and the rivers in like manner accomplish and change not their tasks from His commandments.

[4]But ye- ye have not been steadfast,
nor done the commandments of the Lord,
But ye have turned away and spoken proud and hard words[17]
With your impure mouths against His greatness.
Oh, ye hard-hearted, ye shall find no peace.

[5]Therefore shall ye execrate your days,
And the years of your life shall perish,
And the years of your destruction
shall be multiplied in eternal execration,
And ye shall find no mercy.

[6]In those days ye shall make your names
an eternal execration unto all the righteous,
And by you shall all who curse, curse,
And all the sinners and godless shall imprecate by you.

And all the elect shall rejoice,
And there shall be forgiveness of sins,
And every mercy and peace and forbearance:
There shall be salvation unto them, a goodly light.
And they shall inherit the earth.[18]
And for all of you sinners there shall be no salvation,
But on you all shall abide a curse.
[7]But for the elect there shall be light and joy and peace,
And they shall inherit the earth.[18]
And for you the godless there shall be a curse.

[8]And then there shall be bestowed upon the elect wisdom,
And they shall all live and never again sin,

Blessings of the Righteous

Joy
Forgiveness
Mercy
Peace
Forbearance
Salvation
Divine Light
Inheritance of the Earth
Wisdom
Life
Sinlessness
Longevity
Eternal Gladness

---

[17] **"Hard words"; Enoch 1:9, 27:2**
[18] **"They shall inherit the earth"**; **Matthew 5:5**, Blessed are the meek, for they shall inherit the earth.

Either through ungodliness or through pride:
But they who are wise shall be humble.

[9]And they shall not again transgress,
Nor shall they sin all the days of their life,
Nor shall they die of (the divine) anger or wrath,
But they shall complete the number of the days of their life.

And their lives shall be increased in peace,
And the years of their joy shall be multiplied,
In eternal gladness and peace,
All the days of their life.

Crisis in the Days of Jared: The Descent of the Watchers

6 And it came to pass when the children of men had multiplied that in those days were born unto them beautiful and comely daughters.[19] [2]And the angels, the children of the heaven, saw and lusted after them, and said to one another: "Come, let us choose us wives from among the children of men and beget us children."

> ***Understanding Genesis 6:1-4***
>
> Within Judaism before the destruction of the temple in 70 AD, the common understanding of Genesis 6:1-4 was the angels, the heavenly sons of God, lusted after the daughters of humankind and conspired to break God's law; they left their assigned place in heaven, and took human wives. These angels sinned, defiling themselves by sexual relations with women in order to beget children who turned out to be gigantic and monstrous. This event is mentioned in Jude 1:6 and 2 Peter 2:4. Here, Enoch tells the story in greater detail than Moses in Genesis 6.

[3]And Semjaza, who was their leader, said unto them: "I fear ye will not indeed agree to do this deed, and I alone shall have to pay the penalty of a great sin."

> *"The angels left their proper dwelling" ~ Jude 1:6*

[4]And they all answered him and said: "Let us all swear an oath, and all bind ourselves by mutual imprecations not to abandon this plan but to do this thing."

[5]Then swore they all together and bound themselves by mutual imprecations upon it. [6]And they were in all two hundred; who descended

---

[19] **"The children of men had multiplied"**; Enoch 6, shares a number of remarkable similarities with Genesis 6. If the *Book of Enoch* was truly produced by the Biblical Enoch, that could make it the source for Moses' account. **Genesis 6:1-4**, "When man began to multiply on the face of the land and daughters were born to them, the sons of God saw that the daughters of man were attractive. And they took as their wives any they chose. Then the LORD said, "My Spirit shall not abide in man forever, for he is flesh: his days shall be 120 years." The Nephilim were on the earth in those days, and also afterward, when the sons of God came in to the daughters of man and they bore children to them. These were the mighty men who were of old, the men of renown." For a fuller examination of Genesis 6:1-4 see page 189.

in the days of Jared[20] on the summit of Mount Hermon,[21] and they called it Mount Hermon, because they had sworn and bound themselves by mutual imprecations upon it.

[7]And these are the names of their leaders: Samiazaz, their leader, Arakiba, Rameel, Kokabiel, Tamiel, Ramiel, Danel, Ezeqeel, Baraqijal, Asael, Armaros, Batarel, Ananel, Zaqiel, Samsapeel, Satarel, Turel, Jomjael, Sariel.[22] [8]These are their chiefs of tens.

> ***"Took unto themselves wives"***
>
> In Enoch 6:2, the Watchers construe their action as "marriage". However, God refers to the offspring of these unions as "bastards" and the "children of fornication" (Enoch 10:9). An aspect of the Watchers' sin can be seen as redefining marriage to their liking. They sought to lend an air of legitimacy to their actions but God viewed it as a perversion, justifying judgment. In Ephesians, 5:29-32, Paul implies the range of human expression between men and women in marriage was intended by God as a rich metaphor from which we should draw analogy to the closeness possible between humankind and God. Paul sees marriage as a dim shadow of the surpassing reality which exists between Jesus Christ and His Church indwelt by the Holy Spirit. It's not surprising then, Satan and the evil angels tried then, as they do now, to subvert the true meaning of marriage.

The Watchers Redefine Marriage

7 And all the others together with them took unto themselves wives, and each chose for himself one,[23] and they began to go in unto them and to defile themselves with them,[24] and they taught them charms and enchantments, and the cutting of roots, and made them acquainted with plants. [2]And they became pregnant, and they bare great giants, whose height was[25] three thousand ells:[26] [3]Who consumed all the acquisitions

---

[20] **"Descended in the days of Jared"**; if the prolonged span of life detailed in the genealogy in Genesis 5, is taken in a straightforward manner, then the crisis which Enoch says began "in the days of Jared" and which ended at the flood of Noah's day, spanned a period of about 1,000 years; it was the millennium of Watcher misrule. **Enoch 106:13**

[21] **"They descended on the summit of Mt. Hermon"**; a parallel can be drawn between this angelic imposition of themselves as lords of humanity and the earlier rebellion of Satan who desired to be like God. Mt. Hermon is literally, *"in the far reaches of the north"* of the land of promise, and was used as a *"mount of assembly"* for the Watchers. **Enoch 54:6** tells us in so doing the Watchers were becoming subject to Satan. **Isaiah 14:13-14**, You said in your heart, "I will ascend to heaven; above the stars of God I will set my throne on high; I will sit on *the mount of assembly in the far reaches of the north*; I will ascend above the heights of the clouds; I will make myself like the Most High." **Enoch 86**

[22] **"Satarel, Turel"**; This list is supposed to mention 20 angels, but there are only 19 names. One of the names was lost from the text of Ethiopic Enoch. This passage is recovered in the Dead Sea Scrolls which shows the angel Tummiel coming between Satarel and Turel.

[23] **"Each chose for himself one"**; This language seems to imply the Watchers were monogamous. However, the Dead Sea Scrolls clarify the text for this verse. The Aramaic reads *"all took for themselves women, from all they chose"*. The Watchers were polygamous. The passage also removes human co-operation in these marriages. The Watchers took whatever women they desired. These forced marriages were in fact rape.

[24] In **Enoch 39:1-2**, there is described another future (in Enoch's day) descent and fall of angels. When taken with **Enoch 6-10**, **18:13**, and **21:3**, there are no less than four separate occurrences of angelic corruption described in the *Book of Enoch*.

[25] **"Whose height was..."**; Verse 2 should be corrected in favor of the Greek fragment for this passage which says nothing about the stature of the giants, "And they conceived from them and bore to them great giants. And the giants begot Nephilim, and to the Nephilim were born Elioud- and they were growing in accordance with their greatness," Nickelsburg/Vanderkam.

[26] **"Three thousand ells"**; an "ell" is an ancient unit of measurement. The precise value of this measurement has been lost to history. Regardless, this part of the Ethiopic text should

of men.[27] [4]And when men could no longer sustain them, the giants turned against them and devoured mankind. [5]And they began to sin against birds, and beasts, and reptiles, and fish, and to devour one another's flesh, and drink the blood.

[6]Then the earth laid accusation against the lawless ones.[28]

Doctrines of Demons

8 And Azazel taught men to make swords, and knives, and shields, and breastplates, and made known to them the metals of the earth and the art of working them,[29] and bracelets, and ornaments, and the use of antimony, and the beautifying of the eyelids, and all kinds of costly stones, and all coloring tinctures.

[2]And there arose much godlessness, and they committed fornication, and they were led astray, and became corrupt in all their ways.

---

be corrected in favor of the Greek fragment, as noted above. This passage does not tell us how tall these giants were.

[27] **"Who consumed all the acquisitions of men"**; this passage and the one following outlines the increasing depravity of the Watcher offspring, and their subjugation of mankind. The reader should take note this narrative section uses a high degree of time-compression in relating the story. The oppressive kingdoms of the children of the Watchers seems to have taken centuries to reach the peak of their power and depth of their degradation. The children of the Watchers here are the group to whom Moses later referred as, "the mighty men who were of old, the men of renown", and whom Enoch repeatedly calls, "the kings, the mighty, the exalted, those who rule the earth", as in **Enoch 62:9**.

[28] **"The lawless ones"**; in the New Testament, the term "lawless one" is reserved uniquely for the coming final Antichrist. In Enoch, the term is used to describe the reprobate offspring of Watcher-human breeding. When Jesus said, "Just as it was in the days of Noah, so will it be in the days of the Son of Man" (Luke 17:26), does this hint at the unnatural birth of earth's final Antichrist who will be one of the illegitimate fallen offspring of the angels? If so, in New Testament times, the term "lawless one" may have become an idiom for the offspring of these angelic-human unions. **2 Thessalonians 2:8-9**, "Then *the lawless one* will be revealed, whom the Lord Jesus will kill with the breath of his mouth and bring to nothing by the appearance of his coming. The coming of *the lawless one* is by the activity of Satan with all power and false signs and wonders." On a related note, in a book found among the Dead Sea Scrolls which scholars refer to as *"The Genesis Apocryphon"*, there is indication the term "the mystery of wickedness" was also used to refer to the offspring of Watcher-human unions, a term which is also found in 2 Thessalonians 2.

[29] **"Made known to them the metals of the earth and the art of working them"**; here the Watchers pass on the technology of metallurgy to mankind. Not all that the Watchers taught was evil in substance. However, the Watchers leveraged their superior knowledge to introduce certain technologies to mankind in advance of their natural discovery by mankind over the course of time. The Watchers caused human development to be accelerated but also corrupted. The Watchers corrupted that which might have had positive application for humanity. What could have been the normal course of mankind's discovery and creative innovation under God was diverted to one under the direction and tutelage of the evil angels.

Azazel in the Bible and in Enoch

Among the fallen angels, the role of Azazel is unique. Azazel is said to have taught warfare to mankind, and to have encouraged promiscuity and fornication. As a result of Azazel's influence, *"there arose much godlessness, and they committed fornication, and they were led astray, and became corrupt in all their ways."* In 10:8, we read, *"The whole earth has been corrupted through the works that were taught by Azazel: to him ascribe all sin."* Azazel's negative influence upon humanity is said to be so notable, he is singled out for special judgment among the angels. He is bound in the abyss in the wilderness before the rest of the angels; civil war is then incited among the Watcher offspring who are then destroyed by the very devices of war Azazel introduced to humanity. Azazel is also mentioned in Leviticus 16; there a goat is drawn by lot for sending to Azazel in the wilderness. The sins of the people are first symbolically laid upon the goat which is then sent. In sending off the people's sins on the goat to Azazel in the wilderness, a picture is presented akin to sending the trash out to the garbage dump. The temporary nature of Israel's sacrificial system is also here illustrated, for just as Azazel awaits the judgment of God, so too the sins of the people awaited the yet-future lamb of God, Jesus Christ, who once for all takes away the sin of the world.

[3]Semjaza taught enchantments, and root-cuttings, Armaros the resolving of enchantments, Baraqijal taught astrology, Kokabel the constellations, Ezeqeel the knowledge of the clouds, Araqiel the signs of the earth, Shamsiel the signs of the sun, and Sariel the course of the moon.

[4]And as men perished, they cried, and their cry went up to heaven...

The Faithful Angels Entreat God

9 And then Michael, Uriel, Raphael, and Gabriel looked down from heaven and saw much blood being shed upon the earth, and all lawlessness being wrought upon the earth. [2]And they said one to another: "The earth made without inhabitant cries the voice of their cryings up to the gates of heaven. [3]And now to you, the holy ones of heaven, the souls of men make their suit, saying, 'Bring our cause before the Most High.'"

[4]And they said to the Lord of the ages: "Lord of lords, God of gods, King of kings, and God of the ages, the throne of Thy glory standeth unto all the generations of the ages, and Thy name holy and glorious and blessed unto all the ages! [5]Thou hast made all things, and power over all things hast Thou: and all things are naked and open in Thy sight, and Thou seest all things, and nothing can hide itself from Thee.

[6]"Thou seest what Azazel hath done, who hath taught all unrighteousness on earth and revealed the eternal secrets which were preserved in heaven, which men were striving to learn: [7]And Semjaza, to whom Thou hast given authority to bear rule over his associates. [8]And they have gone to the daughters of men upon the earth, and have slept with the women, and have defiled themselves, and revealed to them all kinds of sins.

[9]"And the women have borne giants, and the whole earth has thereby been filled with blood and unrighteousness. [10]And now, behold, the souls

> ***"Michael, Uriel, Raphael, and Gabriel"***
>
> Here we are introduced to four of the seven angels who figure prominently throughout the book, Michael, Uriel, Raphael, and Gabriel. The remaining three are Raguel, Saraqael and Remiel, who are all mentioned in chapter 20. Traditionally, these seven have been referred to as archangels. Michael is referred to as an archangel in Jude 1:9. In Enoch, Michael and Uriel (also called Phanuel) are called archangels. Michael, Uriel, Raphael, and Gabriel are mentioned most frequently throughout the book and in chapter 40 are shown to have an especially close role in relation to the throne of God. The Book of Revelation also shows a group of seven angels who figure prominently in doling out the judgments of God on earth, in similar fashion to Enoch 10.

of those who have died are crying and making their suit to the gates of heaven, and their lamentations have ascended: and cannot cease because of the lawless deeds which are wrought on the earth.

[11]"And Thou knowest all things before they come to pass, and Thou seest these things and Thou dost suffer them, and Thou dost not say to us what we are to do to them in regard to these."

God's Judgment Begins

10 Then said the Most High, the Holy and Great One spake, and sent Uriel to the son of Lamech, and said to him: [2]"Go to Noah and tell him in my name 'Hide thyself!' and reveal to him the end that is approaching: that the whole earth will be destroyed, and a deluge is about to come upon the whole earth, and will destroy all that is on it. [3]And now instruct him that he may escape and his seed may be preserved for all the generations of the world."

[4]And again the Lord said to Raphael: "Bind Azazel hand and foot, and cast him into the darkness:[30] and make an opening in the desert, which is in Dudael, and cast him therein. [5]And place upon him rough and jagged rocks, and cover him with darkness,

Angels on Assignment	
Uriel ("Light of God")	*"Go to Noah and reveal!"*
Raphael ("God Heals")	*"Bind Azazel and heal!"*
Gabriel ("Hero of God")	*"Proceed against the bastards!"*
Michael ("Who is like God?")	*"Bind Semjaza, and his associates!"*

and let him abide there for ever, and cover his face that he may not see light. [6]And on the day of the great judgment he shall be cast into the fire. [7]And heal the earth which the angels have corrupted, and proclaim the healing of the earth, that they may heal the plague, and that all the children of men may not perish through all the secret things that the Watchers have disclosed and have taught their sons. [8]And the whole earth has been corrupted through the works that were taught by Azazel: to him ascribe all sin."

---

[30] **"Bind Azazel hand and foot, and cast him into the darkness"**; compare the near word-for-word allusion to this passage in **Matthew 22:13,** Then the king said to the attendants, "Bind him hand and foot and cast him into the outer darkness. In that place there will be weeping and gnashing of teeth."

[9]And to Gabriel said the Lord: "Proceed against the bastards and the reprobates, and against the children of fornication: and destroy the children of fornication and the children of the Watchers from amongst men: and cause them to go forth: send them one against the other that they may destroy each other in battle: for length of days shall they not have. [10]And no request that they make of thee shall be granted unto their fathers on their behalf; for they hope to live an eternal life, and that each one of them will live five hundred years."

Seventy Generations from Methuselah to Jesus

[11]And the Lord said unto Michael: "Go, bind Semjaza and his associates who have united themselves with women so as to have defiled themselves with them in all their uncleanness. [12]And when their sons have slain one another, and they have seen the destruction of their beloved ones,[31] bind ☼ them fast[32] for seventy generations[33] in the valleys of the earth, till the day of their judgment and of their consummation, till the judgment that is for ever[34] and ever is consummated. [13]In those days they shall be led off to the abyss of fire: and to the torment and the prison in which they shall be confined for ever.[35] [14]And whosoever shall be condemned and destroyed will from thenceforth be bound together with them[36] to the end of all generations. [15]And destroy all the spirits of the reprobate and the children of the Watchers, because they have wronged mankind. [16]Destroy all wrong from the face of the earth and let every evil work come to an ☼ end: and let the plant of righteousness[37] and truth appear: and it shall prove a blessing; the works of righteousness and truth shall be planted in truth and joy for evermore.

---

[31] **"Their beloved ones"**; the offspring of the Watchers. **Enoch 10:12, 12:6 and 56:3-4**

[32] **"Bind them fast"**; **2 Peter 2:4**, God did not spare angels when they sinned, but cast them into hell and committed them to chains of gloomy darkness to be kept until the judgment. **Jude 1:6-7**, The angels who did not stay within their own position of authority, but left their proper dwelling, he has kept in eternal chains under gloomy darkness until the judgment of the great day.

[33] ☼ **"Seventy generations", Enoch 10:12**, pinpoints exactly the generation of the birth of Jesus Christ. The sinning angels are to be bound in the abyss for 70 generations from the days of Methuselah. According to **Luke 3:23-38,** from the days of Methuselah to the birth of Jesus Christ were 70 generations. The final judgment of the Watchers and their children is to take place by the One born seventy generations from Methuselah. Jesus Christ will sit on the throne of God's glory to pass judgment on the devil and his angels and their offspring. **Enoch 55:3-4**, "I will cause My chastisement and My wrath to abide upon them, saith God, the Lord of Spirits. Ye mighty kings who dwell on the earth, ye shall have to behold Mine Elect One, how he sits on the throne of glory and judges Azazel, and all his associates, and all his hosts in the name of the Lord of Spirits." (See page 156 for a fuller explanation).

[34] **"Till the judgment that is forever"**; **Enoch 16:1, 55:4**

[35] **Enoch 62:1-16**

[36] **"Will from thenceforth be bound together with them"**; both Enoch and the Bible teach that even though people will indeed end up in hell, the abyss of fire was *not* created for mankind. **Matthew 25:41**, Then he will say to those on his left, "Depart from me, you cursed, into the eternal fire prepared for the devil and his angels."

[37] ☼ **"The plant of righteousness"** is a reference to the godly lineage to be traced from Noah to the patriarchs and beyond. The term is messianic in its implications because from this "plant of righteousness" sprung Jesus Christ the messiah; Jesus is the reason the plant inherits the quality of righteousness. **Enoch 10:16, 84:6, 93:2+5+10**

The Coming Messianic Kingdom

[17]"And then shall all the righteous escape,
And shall live till they beget thousands of children,
And all the days of their youth and their old age
Shall they complete in peace.

[18]"And then shall the whole earth be tilled in righteousness,[38] and shall all be planted with trees and be full of blessing. [19]And all desirable trees shall be planted on it, and they shall plant vines on it: and the vine which they plant thereon shall yield wine in abundance, and as for all the seed which is sown thereon each measure of it shall bear a thousand, and each measure of olives shall yield ten presses of oil. [20]And cleanse thou the earth from all oppression, and from all unrighteousness, and from all sin, and from all godlessness: and all the uncleanness that is wrought upon the earth destroy from off the earth. [21]And all the children of men shall become righteous, and all nations shall offer adoration and shall praise Me, and all shall worship Me.[39] [22]And the earth shall be cleansed from all defilement, and from all sin, and from all punishment, and from all torment, and I will never again send them upon it from generation to generation and for ever."

11 "And in those days I will open the store chambers of blessing which are in the heaven, so as to send them down upon the earth over the work and labor of the children of men. [2]And truth and peace shall be associated together throughout all the days of the world and throughout all the generations of men."

Enoch's Call to Ministry

12 Before these things Enoch was hidden, and no one of the children of men knew where he was hidden, and where he abode, and what had become of him. [2]And his activities had to do with the Watchers,[40] and his days were with the holy ones.

---

[38] **"Then shall the whole earth be tilled in righteousness"**; in Enoch 10:16b-11:2, in language which reminds us of the Old Testament prophets, the coming ideal age of Messiah is contrasted to the passing age of Watcher-Nephilim misrule. Both the Messianic and Watcher eras last a millennium. In the *Book of the Watchers*, the idea of the Messianic Age is introduced, in the *Book of the Parables*, the Messiah Himself is revealed.
[39] **"All nations shall worship me"**; the coming universal worship of the true God is centrally located on the prophetic timeline. It will come about during the Messianic Age with the worldwide worship of Jesus, the Messiah. **Isaiah 45:23**, By myself I have sworn; from my mouth has gone out in righteousness a word that shall not return: To me every knee shall bow, every tongue shall swear allegiance. **Philippians 2:9-11**, God has highly exalted him and bestowed on him the name that is above every name, so that at the name of Jesus every knee should bow, in heaven and on earth and under the earth, and every tongue confess that Jesus Christ is Lord, to the glory of God the Father. **Enoch 48:5**
[40] **"Enoch's activities had to do with the Watchers"**; We might say something similar about Daniel the prophet. **Daniel 4:13**, I saw in the visions of my head as I lay in bed, and behold,

[3]And I, Enoch was blessing the Lord of majesty[41] and the King of the ages, and lo! the Watchers called me- Enoch the scribe- and said to me: [4]"Enoch, thou scribe of righteousness,[42] go, declare to the Watchers of the heaven who have left the high heaven, the holy eternal place, and have defiled themselves with women, and have done as the children of earth do, and have taken unto themselves wives: [5]'Ye have wrought great destruction on the earth: And ye shall have no peace nor forgiveness of sin:' [6]and inasmuch as they delight themselves in their children, the murder of their beloved ones[43] shall they see, and over the destruction of their children shall they lament, and shall make supplication unto eternity, but mercy and peace shall ye not attain."

Enoch's First Address to the Watchers

13 And Enoch went and said: "Azazel, thou shalt have no peace: a severe sentence has gone forth against thee to put thee in bonds: [2]And thou shalt not have toleration nor request granted to thee, because of the unrighteousness which thou hast taught, and because of all the works of godlessness and unrighteousness and sin which thou hast shown to men."

[3]Then I went and spoke to them[44] all together, and they were all afraid, and fear and trembling seized them.[45] [4]And they besought me to draw up a petition for them that they might find forgiveness, and to read their petition in the presence of the Lord of heaven. [5]For from thenceforward

---

a Watcher, a holy one, came down from heaven. **Daniel 4:17**, The sentence is by the decree of the Watchers, the decision by the word of the holy ones, to the end that the living may know that the Most High rules the kingdom of men and gives it to whom he will and sets over it the lowliest of men. **Daniel 4:23**, The king saw a Watcher, a holy one, coming down from heaven and saying, "Chop down the tree and destroy it, but leave the stump of its roots in the earth."

[41] **"Enoch was blessing the Lord"**; What was to become the common experience of both Israel and the Church, is here at a much earlier time the experience of Enoch. Enoch receives the call of God while worshipping. In the *Book of Acts*, the call to mission for Barnabas and Saul came while in worship too. **Acts 13:2,** While they were worshiping the Lord and fasting, the Holy Spirit said, "Set apart for me Barnabas and Saul for the work to which I have called them."

[42] **"Enoch, thou scribe of righteousness"**; here, as in 15:1, Enoch is called a "scribe". That Enoch was a writer of books is found in 14:1, 39:1-2, 68:1, 72:1, 82:1, 92:1, 93:1, 100:6, 104:11-13, and 108:1+10.

[43] **"Their beloved ones"**; the offspring of the Watchers, see **Enoch 10:12, 12:6** and **56:3-4**.

[44] **"I went and spoke to them..."**; this is the first of two prophesies of God's judgment to the Watchers. The second is in 13:9-10. Later, Jesus' first of two prophesies to the same group is mentioned in 1 Peter 3:18-20. Christ's second proclamation occurs at the last judgment when He is seated on the Great White Throne. In this way the Watchers have two witnesses prophecy against them twice, Enoch and Jesus. **1 Peter 3:18-20,** Christ also suffered once for sins, the righteous for the unrighteous, that he might bring us to God, being put to death in the flesh but made alive in the spirit, in which he went and proclaimed to the spirits in prison, because they formerly did not obey, when God's patience waited in the days of Noah.

[45] **"Fear and trembling seized them"**; in Enoch and the Bible, the evil angels and the demons are characterized by fearfulness toward God. In contrast, the child of God seeks to cultivate the fear of the Lord, which is an attitude of respect that leads to godly living. **James 2:19**, You believe that God is one; you do well. Even the demons believe- and shudder! **Enoch 1:5, 102:2**

they could not speak with Him nor lift up their eyes to heaven for shame of their sins for which they had been condemned. [6]Then I wrote out their petition, and the prayer in regard to their spirits and their deeds individually and in regard to their requests that they should have forgiveness and length.

"Visions Fell Down Upon Me!"

[7]And I went off and sat down at the waters of Dan, in the land of Dan,[46] to the south of the west of Hermon: I read their petition till I fell asleep. [8]And behold a dream came to me, and visions fell down upon me,[47] and I saw visions of chastisement, and a voice came bidding me to tell it to the sons of heaven, and reprimand them.

Enoch's Second Address to the Watchers

[9]And when I awaked, I came unto them, and they were all sitting gathered together, weeping in Abelsjail, which is between Lebanon and Seneser, with their faces covered. [10]And I recounted before them all the visions which I had seen in sleep, [48] and I began to speak the words of righteousness, and to reprimand the heavenly Watchers.[49]

Enoch Recounts His Dream-Vision

14 The book of the words of righteousness, and of the reprimand of the eternal Watchers in accordance with the command of the Holy Great One in that vision. [2]I saw in my sleep what I will now say with a tongue of flesh and with the breath of my mouth: which the Great One has given to men to converse therewith and understand with the heart. [3]As He has created and given to man the power of understanding the word of wisdom, so hath He created me also and given me the power of reprimanding the Watchers, the children of heaven. [4]I wrote out your petition, and in my vision it appeared thus, that your petition will not be granted unto you throughout all the days of eternity, and that judgment has been finally passed upon you: yea your petition will not be granted unto you. [5]And from henceforth you shall not ascend into heaven unto all eternity, and in bonds of the earth the decree has gone forth to bind

---

[46] **"At the waters of Dan, in the land of Dan",** either the place-name "Dan" was already in use in ancient times, or scribes of a later date felt no reluctance to update this place name in the text in order to preserve the record of its geographic location for a later generation. In Genesis 14, centuries before the Tribe of Dan settled in the area, the place name Dan is used. **Genesis 14:14**, When Abram heard that his kinsman had been taken captive, he led forth his trained men, born in his house, 318 of them, and went in pursuit *as far as Dan*.

[47] **"Visions fell down upon me"**; **Numbers 12:6**, Hear my words: If there is a prophet among you, I the LORD make myself known to him in a vision; I speak with him in a dream.

[48] **"I recounted before them all the visions which I had seen in sleep"**; what Enoch recounted before them all is found in chapters 14-36.

[49] **1 Corinthians 6:3**, Do you not know that we are to judge angels? How much more, then, matters pertaining to this life!

you for all the days of the world.[50] [6]And that previously you shall have seen the destruction of your beloved sons and ye shall have no pleasure in them, but they shall fall before you by the sword. [7]And your petition on their behalf shall not be granted, nor yet on your own: even though you weep and pray and speak all the words contained in the writing which I have written.

Come Up Here!

[8]And the vision was shown to me thus: Behold, in the vision clouds invited me and a mist summoned me, and the course of the stars and the lightnings sped and hastened me, and the winds in the vision caused me to fly and lifted me upward, and bore me into heaven.[51] [9]And I went in till I drew nigh to a wall which is built of crystals and surrounded by tongues of fire:[52] and it began to affright me. [10]And I went into the tongues of fire and drew nigh to a large house which was built of crystals: and the walls of the house were like a tessellated floor made of crystals, and its groundwork was of crystal. [11]Its ceiling was like the path of the stars and the lightnings, and between them were fiery cherubim, and their heaven was clear as water. [12]A flaming fire surrounded the walls, and its portals blazed with fire. [13]And I entered into that house, and it was hot as fire and cold as ice: there were no delights of life therein: fear covered me, and trembling got hold upon me. [14]And as I quaked and trembled, I fell upon my face.

The Vision of the Great Glory

[15]And I beheld a vision, And lo! there was a second house,[53] greater than the former, and the entire portal stood open before me, and it was built of flames of fire. [16]And in every respect it so excelled in splendor and magnificence and extent that I cannot describe to you its splendor and its extent. [17]And its floor was of fire, and above it were lightnings and the path of the stars, and its ceiling also was flaming fire. [18]And I looked and saw therein a lofty throne: its appearance was as crystal, and the wheels

---

[50] **"The decree has gone forth to bind you for all the days of the world"; 2 Peter 2:4**, God did not spare angels when they sinned, but cast them into hell and committed them to chains of gloomy darkness to be kept until the judgment. **Jude 1:6-7**, The angels who did not stay within their own position of authority, but left their proper dwelling, he has kept in eternal chains under gloomy darkness until the judgment of the great day.

[51] **"Bore me into heaven";** here for the first time Enoch is caught up into heaven for the purpose of receiving revelation. This occurs again in **Enoch 39:3**. The last time is recounted in **Enoch 70:1-4**, which tells us the details of Enoch's final catching away, as mentioned in Genesis 5:24 and Hebrews 11:5. In total, Enoch makes two excursions into heaven before his translation. After his translation, he makes two excursions back to earth in **Enoch 65** and **106**. **Hebrews 11:5**, "By faith Enoch was taken up so that he should not see death, and he was not found, because God had taken him." **Genesis 5:24**, "Enoch walked with God, and he was not, for God took him."

[52] **"Tongues of fire"; Enoch 71:5**

[53] **"There was a second house, greater than the former"**; Enoch enters into a house in heaven where he beholds the glory of God. When instructed to build a tabernacle in the wilderness, Moses was told to build everything according to a pattern which was shown him upon the mountain. The earthly tabernacle represented a heavenly reality which is here described by Enoch.

thereof as the shining sun,[54] and there was the vision of cherubim. [19]And from underneath the throne came streams of flaming fire[55] so that I could not look thereon. [20]And the Great Glory[56] sat thereon,[57] and His raiment shone more brightly than the sun[58] and was whiter than any snow. [21]None of the angels could enter and could behold His face by reason of the magnificence and glory,[59] and no flesh could behold Him.[60] [22]The flaming fire was round about Him, and a great fire stood before Him, and none around could draw nigh Him: ten thousand times ten thousand stood before Him,[61] yet He needed no counselor. [23]And the most holy ones who were nigh to Him did not leave by night nor depart from Him.

The Great Glory

"Great Glory" evokes a sense of awe and terror. It is a powerful word picture magnifying the beauty, splendor, radiance and greatness of God. The Hebrew word for glory connotes something "heavy" or "weighty". In all the universe the Great Glory is the most significant and weighty One, above and over all. Enoch finds Him enthroned in heaven; He will later come to earth's highest mountain to be seated on His sapphire throne. (Enoch 18:8, 25:3)

[24]And until then I had been prostrate on my face, trembling: and the Lord called me with His own mouth, and said to me: "Come hither, Enoch, and hear my word."

[25]And one of the holy ones came to me and waked me, and He made me rise up and approach the door: and I bowed my face downwards.

Enoch Hears the Voice of God

15 And He answered and said to me, and I heard His voice: "Fear not, Enoch, thou righteous man and scribe of righteousness:[42] approach

[54] **"The wheels thereof as the shining sun"**; **Ezekiel 1:16**, As for the appearance of the wheels and their construction: their appearance was like the gleaming of beryl. And the four had the same likeness, their appearance and construction being as it were a wheel within a wheel.

[55] **"From underneath the throne came streams of flaming fire"**; **Daniel 7:10**, A stream of fire issued and came out from before him.

[56] **"The Great Glory"**; "Great Glory" is found twice in the *Book of Enoch* in 14:20 and 102:2-3. Great Glory seems synonymous with Majestic Glory in 2 Peter 1:17. Other similar names found both in Enoch and the Bible are: God of Glory, King of Glory, Lord of Glory. Father of Glory, and Spirit of Glory are also related names which are found only in the New Testament. Taken together, this symphony of names perfectly harmonizes to present to our attention the Father of Glory, Lord of Glory and Spirit of Glory, the Holy Trinity of Glory, (See Appendix III).

[57] **"The Great Glory sat thereon"; Revelation 4:2**, At once I was in the Spirit, and behold, a throne stood in heaven, with one seated on the throne.

[58] **"More brightly than the sun"**; **Matthew 17:2**, He was transfigured before them, and his face shone like the sun, and his clothes became white as light.

[59] **"None of the angels could enter and could behold His face"; 1 Timothy 6:15-16**, Who dwells in unapproachable light.

[60] **"No flesh could behold Him"**; **Exodus 33:20**, He said, "you cannot see my face, for man shall not see me and live."

[61] **"Ten thousand times ten thousand"**; **Daniel 7:10**, A thousand thousands served him, and ten thousand times ten thousand stood before him. **Revelation 5:11**, I heard around the throne and the living creatures and the elders the voice of many angels, numbering myriads of myriads and thousands of thousands. **Enoch 40:1, 60:1, 71:8, 71:12**

hither and hear my voice. [2]And go, say to the Watchers of heaven, who have sent thee to intercede for them: 'You should intercede for men, and not men for you:[62] [3]Wherefore have ye left the high, holy, and eternal heaven,[63] and lain with women, and defiled yourselves with the daughters of men and taken to yourselves wives, and done like the children of earth, and begotten giants as your sons?[64] [4]And though ye were holy, spiritual, living the eternal life, you have defiled yourselves with the blood of women, and have begotten children with the blood of flesh, and, as the children of men, have lusted after flesh and blood as those also do who die and perish. [5]Therefore have I given them wives also that they might impregnate them, and beget children by them, that thus nothing might be wanting to them on earth. [6]But you were formerly spiritual, living the eternal life, and immortal for all generations of the world. [7]And therefore I have not appointed wives for you; for as for the spiritual ones of the heaven, in heaven is their dwelling.[65]

The Origin of Evil Spirits

[8]"And now, the giants, who are produced from the spirits and flesh, shall be called evil spirits upon the earth,[66] and on the earth shall be their dwelling. [9]Evil spirits have proceeded from their bodies; because they are born from men and from the holy Watchers is their beginning and primal origin; they shall be evil spirits on earth, and evil spirits shall they be called. [10]As for the spirits of heaven, in heaven shall be their dwelling, but as for the spirits of the earth which were born upon the earth, on the earth shall be their dwelling. [11]And the spirits of the giants afflict, oppress, destroy, attack, do battle, and work destruction on the earth, and cause trouble: they take no food, but nevertheless hunger and thirst,[67] and cause offences. [12]And these spirits shall rise up against the

---

[62] **"You should intercede for men, and not men for you"**; **Hebrews 1:14**, Are they not all ministering spirits sent out to serve for the sake of those who are to inherit salvation?

[63] **"Ye left the high, holy, and eternal heaven"**; **Jude 1:6**, The angels did not stay within their own position of authority, but *left their proper dwelling.*

[64] **"Begotten giants as your sons"**; **Genesis 6:4**, There were giants in the earth in those days; and also after that, when the sons of God came in unto the daughters of men, and they bare children to them. (KJV)

[65] **"Therefore I have not appointed wives for you; for as for the spiritual ones of the heaven, in heaven is their dwelling"**; in Matthew 22:30 and Luke 20:34-36, Jesus speaks of the normal state of affairs in Heaven. In the gospels, there is no marriage in heaven, and the *Book of Enoch* does not contradict this. In fact, the *Book of Enoch* here teaches the same thing as **Matthew 22:30**, "For in the resurrection they neither marry nor are given in marriage, but are like angels in heaven. **Luke 20:34-36**, And Jesus said to them, "The sons of this age marry and are given in marriage, but those who are considered worthy to attain to that age and to the resurrection from the dead neither marry nor are given in marriage, for they cannot die anymore, because they are equal to angels and are sons of God, being sons of the resurrection."

[66] **"Shall be called evil spirits on earth"**; despite the Church's history of speculation on this subject, it remains a fact that nowhere in the Bible is the origin of evil spirits explicitly explained. Fallen angels are never equated with "demons" or "unclean spirits" in the Bible. Only in the Bible of Ethiopian Orthodoxy do we find this description of the origin of unclean spirits.

[67] **"They take no food, but nevertheless hunger and thirst"**; it is a notable fact that unclean spirits seem to desire to remain en-fleshed by indwelling human hosts. In this way are they attempting to vicariously fulfill the desires of the carnal nature? **Matthew 12:43**, When the

children of men and against the women, because they have proceeded from them.

16 "From the days of the slaughter and destruction and death of the giants, from the souls of whose flesh the spirits, having gone forth, shall destroy without incurring judgment- thus shall they destroy until the day of the consummation,[68] the great judgment in which the age shall be consummated, over the Watchers and the godless, yea, shall be wholly consummated.

[2]"And now as to the Watchers who have sent thee to intercede for them, who had been aforetime in heaven, say to them: [3]'You have been in heaven, but all the mysteries had not yet been revealed to you,[69] and you knew worthless ones, and these in the hardness of your hearts you have made known to the women, and through these mysteries women and men work much evil on earth.'

[4]"Say to them therefore: 'You have no peace.'"

Enoch's First Sojourn Through the Cosmos

17 And they took and brought me to a place in which those who were there were like flaming fire,[70] and, when they wished, they appeared as men. [2]And they brought me to the place of darkness, and to a mountain the point of whose summit reached to heaven. [3]And I saw the places of the luminaries and the treasuries of the stars and of the thunder,[71] and in the uttermost depths, where were a fiery bow and arrows and their quiver, and a fiery sword[72] and all the lightnings. [4]And they took me to the living waters, and to the fire of the west, which receives every setting of the sun. [5]And I came to a river of fire in which the fire flows like water

---

unclean spirit has gone out of a person, it passes through waterless places seeking rest, but finds none.

[68] **"Thus shall they destroy until the day of the consummation"**; **Matthew 8:29**, They cried out, "What have you to do with us, O Son of God? Have you come here to torment us before the time?" **Luke 8:30-31**, Jesus then asked him, "What is your name?" And he said, "Legion," for many demons had entered him. And they begged him not to command them to depart into the Abyss. **Enoch 10:12, 55:4**

[69] **"Mysteries had not yet been revealed to you"**; Here, and in numerous Bible verses the limited nature of the knowledge of the angels is emphasized. **Matthew 24:36-37**, But concerning that day and hour no one knows, not even the angels of heaven. **1 Peter 1:12**, Things into which angels long to look. **Job 15:15**, Behold, God puts no trust in his holy ones, and the heavens are not pure in his sight.

[70] **"Those who were there were like flaming fire"; Hebrews 1:7**, He makes his angels winds, and his ministers a flame of fire. **Hebrews 13:2**, "Do not neglect to show hospitality to strangers, for thereby some have entertained angels unawares." That angels *can be* winds (spirits) and fire does not mean they cannot have physical bodies. Both Old and New Testaments testify to this fact.

[71] **"The treasuries of the stars and of the thunder"**; **Job 38:22**, Have you entered the storehouses of the snow, or have you seen the storehouses of the hail?

[72] **"A fiery sword"; Genesis 3:24**, At the east of the garden of Eden he placed the cherubim and a flaming sword that turned every way to guard the way to the tree of life.

and discharges itself into the Great Sea[73] towards the west. [6]I saw the great rivers and came to the great river and to the great darkness, and went to the place where no flesh walks. [7]I saw the mountains of the darkness of winter and the place whence all the waters of the deep flow. [8]I saw the mouths of all the rivers of the earth and the mouth of the deep.

18 I saw the treasuries of all the winds:[74] I saw how He had furnished with them the whole creation and the firm foundations of the earth. [2]And I saw the cornerstone of the earth:[75] I saw the four winds[76] which bear the earth and the firmament of the heaven. [3]And I saw how the winds stretch out the vaults of heaven, and have their station between heaven and earth: these are the pillars of the heaven. [4]I saw the winds of heaven which turn and bring the circumference of the sun and all the stars to their setting. [5]I saw the winds on the earth carrying the clouds: I saw the paths of the angels.

The Seven Mountains

[6]I saw at the end of the earth the firmament of the heaven above. And I proceeded and saw a place which burns day and night, where there are seven mountains of magnificent stones, three towards the east, and three towards the south. [7]And as for those towards the east, one was of colored stone, and one of pearl, and one of jacinth, and those towards the south of red stone. [8]But the middle one reached to heaven like the throne of God, of alabaster, and the summit of the throne was of sapphire.[77] [9]And I saw a flaming fire.

The Bottomless Pit

[10]And beyond these mountains is a region the end of the great earth: there the heavens were completed. [11]And I saw a deep abyss, with columns of heavenly fire, and among them I saw columns of fire fall, which were beyond measure alike towards the height and towards the depth. [12]And beyond that abyss I saw a place which had no firmament of the heaven above, and no firmly founded earth beneath it:[78] there was

---

[73] The Mediterranean Sea

[74] **"I saw the treasuries of the winds"**; these "treasuries" are also called "chambers" in **Enoch 41:4**.

[75] **"The cornerstone of the earth"; Job 38:4+6**, Where were you when I laid the foundation of the earth? *Who laid its cornerstone?*

[76] **"I saw the four winds"**; **Revelation 7:1**, After this I saw four angels standing at the four corners of the earth, holding back *the four winds* of the earth, that no wind might blow on earth or sea or against any tree.

[77] **"The summit of the throne was of sapphire"**; **Ezekiel 1:26**, There was the likeness of a throne, in appearance like sapphire; and seated above the likeness of a throne was a likeness with a human appearance.

[78] **"No firmly founded earth beneath it",** in other words, a bottomless pit. The Greek word used by John in Revelation for "bottomless pit" is "abyssos" which can be translated as abyss. **Rev. 9:1-2**, And the fifth angel blew his trumpet, and I saw a star fallen from heaven to earth, and he was given the key to the shaft of the bottomless pit. He opened the shaft of the bottomless pit, and from the shaft rose smoke like the smoke of a great furnace, and the sun

no water upon it, and no birds, but it was a waste and horrible place. [13]I saw there seven stars[79] like great burning mountains, and to me, when I inquired regarding them, The angel said: [14]"This place is the end of heaven and earth: this has become a prison for the stars and the host of heaven. [15]And the stars which roll over the fire are they which have transgressed the commandment of the Lord in the beginning of their rising, because they did not come forth at their appointed times. [16]And He was wroth with them, and bound them till the time when their guilt should be consummated even for ten thousand years."

19 And Uriel said to me: "Here shall stand the angels who have connected themselves with women, and their spirits assuming many different forms are defiling mankind and shall lead them astray into sacrificing to demons as gods,[80] here shall they stand, till the day of the great judgment in which they shall be judged till they are made an end of. [2]And the women also of the angels who went astray shall become sirens."[81]

[3]And I, Enoch, alone saw the vision, the ends of all things:[82] and no man shall see as I have seen.

---

and the air were darkened with the smoke from the shaft. **Rev. 9:11**, They have as king over them the angel of the bottomless pit. His name in Hebrew is Abaddon, and in Greek he is called Apollyon. **Rev. 11:7**, The beast that rises from the bottomless pit will make war on them. **Rev. 17:8**, The beast that you saw was, and is not, and is about to rise from the bottomless pit and go to destruction. **Rev. 20:1**, Then I saw an angel coming down from heaven, holding in his hand the key to the bottomless pit and a great chain.

[79] **In Enoch 18:13** and **21:3**, Enoch describes other angels who sinned and were punished before the event in the days of Jared. In 18:13, their sin is described as having "transgressed the commandment of the Lord in the beginning of their rising, because they did not come forth at their appointed times." The angel volunteers this information about these angels who sinned. **Enoch 39:1-2**, describes another group of sinning angels who are yet future in Enoch's day.

[80] **"Sacrificing to demons as gods"**, **1 Corinthians 10:20**, What pagans sacrifice they offer to demons and not to God. I do not want you to be participants with demons. **Rev. 9:20**, The rest of mankind, who were not killed by these plagues, did not repent of the works of their hands nor give up worshiping demons and idols of gold and silver and bronze and stone and wood, which cannot see or hear or walk.

[81] **"Shall become sirens"**; R.H. Charles deferred to the Greek for this passage. Per Olson, verse 2 should be corrected in favor of the Ethiopic for this passage, "And the wives of the angels who went astray will have peace." Per Olson, the unfortunate wives of the Watchers were victims and this passage assures they will not share the Watchers' punishment. Knibb also has, "will become peaceful."

[82] **"I, Enoch, alone saw the vision, the end of all things"**; **1 Peter 4:7**, *The end of all things* is at hand; therefore be self-controlled and sober-minded for the sake of your prayers.

The Seven Watcher Archangels

20 And these are the names[83] of the holy angels[84] who watch.[85]

[2]Uriel, one of the holy angels, who is over the world and over Tartarus. [3]Raphael, one of the holy angels, who is over the spirits of men. [4]Raguel, one of the holy angels who takes vengeance on the world of the luminaries. [5]Michael, one of the holy angels, to wit, he that is set over the best part of mankind[86] and over chaos. [6]Saraqael,[87] one of the holy angels, who is set over the spirits, who sin in the spirit. [7]Gabriel, one of the holy angels, who is over Paradise and the serpents and the Cherubim. [8]Remiel, one of the holy angels, whom God set over those who rise.

The Angels Who Watch	
Uriel:	*"Light of God"*
Raphael:	*"God Heals"*
Raguel:	*"Friend of God"*
Michael:	*"Who is like God?"*
Saraqael:	*"Command of God"*
Gabriel:	*"God My Hero"*
Remiel:	*"Thunder of God"*

Other Fallen Angels

21 And I proceeded to where things were chaotic. And I saw there something horrible: [2]I saw neither a heaven above nor a firmly founded earth, but a place chaotic and horrible. [3]And there I saw seven stars[88] of

[83] Compare this list of angels with the angels listed in chapter 40.

[84] **"These are the names of the holy angels"**; in Enoch and John's Revelation, seven angels are featured prominently throughout. In Enoch their names are listed, in John they are not. **Revelation 8:6**, The seven angels who had the seven trumpets prepared to blow them. **Revelation 15:1**, I saw another sign in heaven, great and amazing, seven angels with seven plagues, which are the last. **Revelation 21:9**, Then came one of the seven angels who had the seven bowls full of the seven last plagues.

[85] **"The holy angels who watch";** in Enoch, the heavenly creatures "who watch" are the angels, i.e. "the Watchers". The designation "Watcher" is not reserved for the fallen angels, but here is used for "holy angels", i.e.: angels who are not fallen. Other heavenly creatures in Enoch, the Cherubim and Seraphim, are referred to as "those who sleep not", in other words, they never rest from worshipping God. See **Enoch 39:12 and 40:2**.

[86] **"Michael is set over the best part of mankind"** the *best part of mankind* is synonymous with "God's people"; later and in other ancient Jewish literature, Michael is shown having a special commission to protect Israel, as in **Daniel 12:1**, At that time shall arise Michael, the great prince *who has charge of your people*. **Revelation 12:7**, War arose in heaven, Michael and his angels fighting against the dragon. And the dragon and his angels fought back, but he was defeated, and there was no longer any place for them in heaven. **Revelation 12:13**, And when the dragon saw that he had been thrown down to the earth, he pursued the woman who had given birth to the male child.

[87] Nickelsburg/Vanderkam and Olson have "Sariel".

[88] **"There I saw seven stars"**; in Enoch 18:13, and 21:3, Enoch describes other angels who sinned and were punished before the event described in Enoch 6. In 21:3, their sin is described as having "transgressed the commandment of the Lord". The angel speaking with Enoch seems unwilling to reveal more. **Enoch 39:1-2**, describes another group of sinning angels who are yet future in Enoch's day.

the heaven bound together in it, like great mountains and burning with fire.[89]

[4]Then I said: "For what sin are they bound, and on what account have they been cast in hither?"

[5]Then said Uriel, one of the holy angels, who was with me, and was chief over them, and said: "Enoch, why dost thou ask, and why art thou eager for the truth? [6]These are of the number of the stars of heaven, which have transgressed the commandment of the Lord, and are bound here till ten thousand years, the time entailed by their sins, are consummated."

[7]And from thence I went to another place, which was still more horrible than the former, and I saw a horrible thing: a great fire there which burnt and blazed, and the place was cleft as far as the abyss, being full of great descending columns of fire: neither its extent or magnitude could I see, nor could I conjecture.

[8]Then I said: "How fearful is the place and how terrible to look upon!"

[9]Then Uriel answered me, one of the holy angels who was with me, and said unto me: "Enoch, why hast thou such fear and affright?"

And I answered: "Because of this fearful place, and because of the spectacle of the pain."

[10]And he said unto me: "This place is the prison of the angels, and here they will be imprisoned for ever."[90]

22

And thence I went to another place, and he showed me in the west another great and high mountain and of hard rock. [2]And there was in it four hollow places, deep and wide and very smooth. How smooth are the hollow places and deep and dark to look at!

[3]Then Raphael answered, one of the holy angels who was with me, and said unto me: "These hollow places have been created for this very purpose, that the spirits of the souls of the dead should assemble therein, yea that all the souls of the children of men should assemble here. [4]And these places have been made to receive them till the day of their judgment and till their appointed period till the period appointed, till the great judgment comes upon them."

---

[89] **"Like great mountains and burning with fire";** here, and in Revelation 8:8, this imagery is idiomatic for fallen angels. **Revelation 8:8**, The second angel blew his trumpet, and something like a great mountain, burning with fire, was thrown into the sea, and a third of the sea became blood.

[90] **"The prison of the angels"**; Enoch's is the oldest book to inform us hell was not originally intended for humankind, but rather fallen angels. **Matthew 25:41**, Then he will say to those on his left, "Depart from me, you cursed, into the eternal fire prepared for the devil and his angels."

A Visit to Sheol

[5]I saw the spirits of the children of men who were dead, and their voice went forth to heaven and made suit. [6]Then I asked Raphael the angel who was with me, and I said unto him: "This spirit- whose is it, whose voice goeth forth and maketh suit?"

[7]And he answered me saying: "This is the spirit which went forth from Abel, whom his brother Cain slew, and he makes his suit against him[91] till his seed is destroyed from the face of the earth, and his seed is annihilated from amongst the seed of men."

[8]Then I asked regarding it, and regarding all the hollow places: "Why is one separated from the other?"

[9]And he answered me and said unto me: "These three have been made that the spirits of the dead might be separated.

And such a division[92] has been made for the spirits of the righteous, in which there is the bright spring of water.

[10]And such has been made for sinners when they die and are buried in the earth and judgment has not been executed on them in their lifetime. [11]Here their spirits shall be set apart in this great pain till the great day[93] of judgment and punishment and torment of those who curse for ever and retribution for their spirits. There He shall bind them[94] for ever.

[12]And such a division has been made for the spirits of those who make their suit, who make disclosures concerning their destruction, when they were slain in the days of the sinners.[95] [13]Such has been made for the

---

[91] **"He makes suit against him"**; here the spirit of Abel makes suit to God until Cain's "seed is destroyed from the face of the earth". Abel's prayer was answered at the flood of Noah's day as all of the seed of Cain were then destroyed. The souls under the altar in Revelation 6, similarly make suit to God for vengeance on those who killed them; their prayers are to be fulfilled by the return of Christ to earth. In our time, however, the blood of Jesus, speaks a better word than the blood of Abel, for it speaks of the mercy God extends toward sinful humanity in Jesus Christ. **Hebrews 12:24**

[92] **"A division has been made"** In the *Book of Luke*, this is referred to in the words "a great chasm has been fixed". **Luke 16:26**, And besides all this, between us and you a great chasm has been fixed, in order that those who would pass from here to you may not be able, and none may cross from there to us.

[93] **"The great day of judgment"**; **Jude 1:6**, He has kept in eternal chains under gloomy darkness until *the judgment of the great day*. **Enoch 54:6**

[94] **"He shall bind them"**; **Matthew 22:13**, Then the king said to the attendants, "Bind him hand and foot and cast him into the outer darkness. In that place there will be weeping and gnashing of teeth." **Enoch 10:4**

[95] **"They were slain in the days of the sinners"** is a reference to the martyrs of the faith; **Revelation 6:9-10**, When he opened the fifth seal, I saw under the altar the souls of those who had been slain for the word of God and for the witness they had borne. They cried out with a loud voice, "O Sovereign Lord, holy and true, how long before you will judge and avenge our blood on those who dwell on the earth?"

spirits of men who were not righteous but sinners, who were complete in transgression, and of the transgressors they shall be companions: but their spirits shall not be slain in the day of judgment nor shall they be raised from thence."

[14]Then I blessed the Lord of glory and said: "Blessed be my Lord, the Lord of righteousness, who ruleth for ever."[96]

23 From thence I went to another place to the west of the ends of the earth. [2]And I saw a burning fire which ran without resting, and paused not from its course day or night but ran regularly. [3]And I asked saying: "What is this which rests not?"

[4]Then Raguel, one of the holy angels who was with me, answered me and said unto me: "This course of fire which thou hast seen is the fire in the west which persecutes all the luminaries of heaven."

The Mountain of the Lord of Glory

24 And from thence I went to another place of the earth, and he showed me a mountain range of fire which burnt day and night. [2]And I went beyond it and saw seven magnificent mountains all differing each from the other, and the stones thereof were magnificent and beautiful, magnificent as a whole, of glorious appearance and fair exterior: three towards the east, one founded on the other, and three towards the south, one upon the other, and deep rough ravines, no one of which joined with any other. [3]And the seventh mountain was in the midst of these, and it excelled them in height, resembling the seat of a throne: and fragrant trees encircled the throne. [4]And amongst them was a tree such as I had never yet smelt, neither was any amongst them nor were others like it: it had a fragrance beyond all fragrance, and its leaves and blooms and wood wither not for ever: and its fruit is beautiful, and its fruit resembles the dates of a palm. [5]Then I said: "How beautiful is this tree, and fragrant, and its leaves are fair, and its blooms very delightful in appearance."

[6]Then answered Michael, one of the holy and honored angels who was with me, and was their leader.

25 And he said unto me: "Enoch, why dost thou ask me regarding the fragrance of the tree, and why dost thou wish to learn the truth?"

---

[96] **"Blessed be my Lord, the Lord of righteousness, who ruleth for ever"**; here Enoch pauses to praise God. Enoch blesses God for his justice in His disposition of humankind after death. This is the first of three doxologies in this section of the book. These three doxologies can be found in **Enoch 22:14, 27:5 and 36:4**.

[2]Then I answered him saying: "I wish to know about everything, but especially about this tree."

The Tree of Life

[3]And he answered saying: "This high mountain[97] which thou hast seen, whose summit is like the throne of God, is His throne, where the Holy Great One, the Lord of Glory, the Eternal King, will sit, when He shall ✡ come down[98] to visit the earth with goodness. [4]And as for this fragrant tree no mortal is permitted to touch it till the great judgment, when He shall take vengeance on all and bring everything to its consummation for ever. [5]It shall then be given to the righteous and holy. Its fruit shall be for food to the elect:[99] it shall be transplanted to the holy place, to the temple of the Lord, the Eternal King.

[6]"Then shall they rejoice with joy
and be glad,
And into the holy place shall they enter;
And its fragrance shall be in their bones,
And they shall live a long life on earth,
Such as thy fathers lived:

And in their days shall no sorrow or plague
Or torment or calamity touch them."[100]

"Its fragrance shall be in their bones"

"On either side of the river, is the Tree of Life with its twelve kinds of fruit, yielding its fruit each month. The leaves of the tree were for the healing of the nations" Rev 22:2

[7]Then blessed I the God of Glory, the Eternal King, who hath prepared such things for the righteous, and hath created them and promised to give to them.

---

[97] **"This high mountain"**; **Isaiah 2:2-3**, It shall come to pass in the latter days that the mountain of the house of the LORD shall be established as the highest of the mountains, and shall be lifted up above the hills; and all the nations shall flow to it, and many peoples shall come, and say: "Come, let us go up to the mountain of the LORD, to the house of the God of Jacob, that he may teach us his ways and that we may walk in his paths." For out of Zion shall go the law, and the word of the LORD from Jerusalem.

[98] ✡ **"He shall come down to visit the earth";** here Enoch restates the language of **Enoch 1:3-4**, "The Holy Great One will come forth from His dwelling, and the eternal God will tread upon the earth, even on Mount Sinai, and appear from His camp, and appear in the strength of His might from the heaven of heavens." Earth's final judgment will come about when God "shall come down" to earth. In the Epistle of Jude we are told Enoch saw this will be accomplished by the second coming of Jesus Christ. **Enoch 1:3, 25:3, 52:9, 77:1, 90:15,18,20, 91:7, 100:4**

[99] **"Its fruit shall be for food to the elect"**; **Rev. 2:7**, To the one who conquers I will grant to eat of the tree of life, which is in the paradise of God. **Rev. 22:2**, Through the middle of the street of the city; also, on either side of the river, the tree of life with its twelve kinds of fruit, yielding its fruit each month. The leaves of the tree were for the healing of the nations. **Rev. 22:14**, Blessed are those who wash their robes, so that they may have the right to the tree of life and that they may enter the city by the gates.

[100] **"In their days shall no sorrow touch them"**; **Rev. 21:4**, He will wipe away every tear from their eyes, and death shall be no more, neither shall there be mourning, nor crying, nor pain anymore, for the former things have passed away. **Rev. 22:3**, No longer will there be anything accursed, but the throne of God and of the Lamb will be in it, and his servants will worship him.

26 And I went from thence to the middle of the earth, and I saw a blessed place in which there were trees with branches abiding and blooming of a dismembered tree. [2]And there I saw a holy mountain, and underneath the mountain to the east there was a stream and it flowed towards the south. [3]And I saw towards the east another mountain higher than this, and between them a deep and narrow ravine: in it also ran a stream underneath the mountain. [4]And to the west thereof there was another mountain, lower than the former and of small elevation, and a ravine deep and dry between them: and another deep and dry ravine was at the extremities of the three mountains. [5]And all the ravines were deep and narrow, being formed of hard rock, and trees were not planted upon them.

[6]And I marveled at the rocks, and I marveled at the ravine, yea, I marveled very much.

27 Then said I: "For what object is this blessed land, which is entirely filled with trees, and this accursed valley between?"

The Day of Judgment

[2]Then Uriel, one of the holy angels who was with me, answered and said: "This accursed valley is for those who are accursed for ever: here shall all the accursed be gathered together who utter with their lips against the Lord unseemly words and of His glory speak hard things.[101] Here shall they be gathered together, and here shall be their place of judgment. [3]In the last days there shall be upon them the spectacle of righteous judgment in the presence of the righteous for ever: here shall the merciful bless the Lord of glory, the Eternal King. [4]In the days of judgment over the former, they shall bless Him for the mercy in accordance with which He has assigned them their lot."[102]

[5]Then I blessed the Lord of Glory and set forth His glory and lauded Him gloriously.[103]

28 And thence I went towards the east, into the midst of the mountain range of the desert, and I saw a wilderness and it was solitary, full of trees and plants. [2]And water gushed forth from above. [3]Rushing like a

---

[101] **"Of His glory speak hard things"**; **Jude 1:14-15**, Behold, the Lord comes with ten thousands of his holy ones, to execute judgment on all and to convict all the ungodly of all their deeds of ungodliness that they have committed in such an ungodly way, and of all *the harsh things that ungodly sinners have spoken against him.* **Enoch 1:9, 5:4**

[102] **"He has assigned them their lot"**; **Daniel 12:13**, But go your way till the end. And you shall rest and shall *stand in your allotted place* at the end of the days.

[103] **"I blessed the Lord of Glory and set forth His glory and lauded Him gloriously"**; here Enoch pauses to praise God. Enoch praises God for the blessings which are to come to his people. This is the second of three doxologies in this section of the book. These three doxologies can be found in **Enoch 22:14, 27:5 and 36:4.**

copious watercourse which flowed towards the north-west it caused clouds and dew to ascend on every side.

29 And thence I went to another place in the desert, and approached to the east of this mountain range. [2]And there I saw aromatic trees exhaling the fragrance of frankincense and myrrh, and the trees also were similar to the almond tree.

30 And beyond these, I went afar to the east, and I saw another place, a valley full of water. [2]And therein there was a tree, the color of fragrant trees such as the mastic. [3]And on the sides of those valleys I saw fragrant cinnamon. And beyond these I proceeded to the east.

31 And I saw other mountains, and amongst them were groves of trees, and there flowed forth from them nectar, which is named sarara and galbanum. [2]And beyond these mountains I saw another mountain to the east of the ends of the earth, whereon were aloe-trees, and all the trees were full of stacte, being like almond-trees. [3]And when one burnt it, it smelt sweeter than any fragrant odour.

The Garden of Righteousness

32 And after these fragrant odours, as I looked towards the north over the mountains I saw seven mountains full of choice nard and fragrant trees and cinnamon and pepper. [2]And thence I went over the summits of all these mountains, far towards the east of the earth, and passed above the Erythraean Sea[104] and went far from it, and passed over the angel Zotiel. [3]And I came to the Garden of Righteousness,[105] and saw beyond those trees many large trees growing there and of goodly fragrance,[106] large, very beautiful and glorious, and the tree of wisdom whereof they eat and know great wisdom. [4]That tree is in height like the fir, and its leaves are like those of the Carob tree: and its fruit is like the clusters of the vine, very beautiful: and the fragrance of the tree penetrates afar.

[5]Then I said: "How beautiful is the tree, and how attractive is its look!"

[6]Then Raphael the holy angel, who was with me, answered me and said: "This is the tree of wisdom, of which thy father old in years and thy aged mother, who were before thee, have eaten, and they learnt wisdom and

---

[104] The Red Sea

[105] **"The Garden of Righteousness"; Enoch 32:3, 60:8+23, 61:12, 77:3**

[106] **"Many large trees growing there and of goodly fragrance"; Genesis 2:9**, And out of the ground the LORD God made to spring up every tree that is pleasant to the sight and good for food. The tree of life was in the midst of the garden, and the tree of the knowledge of good and evil.

their eyes were opened,[107] and they knew that they were naked and they were driven out of the garden."

Enoch Receives the Geocentric Calendar Book

33 And from thence I went to the ends of the earth and saw there great beasts, and each differed from the other; and I saw birds also differing in appearance and beauty and voice, the one differing from the other. And to the east of those beasts I saw the ends of the earth whereon the heaven rests, and the portals of the heaven open. [2]And I saw how the stars of heaven come forth, and I counted the portals out of which they proceed, [3]and wrote down all their outlets, of each individual star by itself, according to their number and their names, their courses and their positions, and their times and their months, as Uriel the holy angel who was with me showed me.[108] [4]He showed all things to me and wrote them down for me: also their names he wrote for me, and their laws and their companies.

34 And from thence I went towards the north to the ends of the earth, and there I saw a great and glorious device at the ends of the whole earth. [2]And here I saw three portals of heaven open in the heaven: through each of them proceed north winds: when they blow there is cold, hail, frost, snow, dew, and rain. [3]And out of one portal they blow for good: but when they blow through the other two portals, it is with violence and affliction on the earth, and they blow with violence.[109]

35 And from thence I went towards the west to the ends of the earth, and saw there three portals of the heaven open such as I had seen in the east, the same number of portals, and the same number of outlets.

36 And from thence I went to the south to the ends of the earth, and saw there three open portals of the heaven: and thence there come dew, rain, and wind. [2]And from thence I went to the east to the ends of the heaven, and saw here the three eastern portals of heaven open and small portals above them. [3]Through each of these small portals pass the stars of heaven and run their course to the west on the path which is shown to them.

---

[107] **"Their eyes were opened"**; **Genesis 3:6-7**, So when the woman saw that the tree was good for food, and that it was a delight to the eyes, and that *the tree was to be desired to make one wise*, she took of its fruit and ate, and she also gave some to her husband who was with her, and he ate. Then *the eyes of both were opened*, and they knew that they were naked.
[108] **"Uriel the holy angel who was with me showed me"**; Per 33:3-4 both Enoch and the Archangel Uriel, wrote down some of the information regarding the Geocentric Calendar, which is not recounted here but later starting with chapter 72.
[109] **"And they blow with violence"**; **Job 38:22-23**, Have you entered the storehouses of the snow, or have you seen the storehouses of the hail, which I have reserved for the time of trouble, for the day of battle and war?

Enoch Concludes Retelling his Dream-Vision

[4]And as often as I saw I blessed always the Lord of Glory,[110] and I continued to bless the Lord of Glory who has wrought great and glorious wonders, to show the greatness of His work to the angels and to spirits and to men, that they might praise His work and all His creation: that they might see the work of His might and praise the great work of His hands and bless Him for ever.

---

[110] **"As often as I saw I blessed always the Lord of Glory"**; here Enoch pauses to praise God. He blesses God for both the wonders of creation as well as God's on-going work in the cosmos. This is the third of three doxologies in this section of the book. These three doxologies can be found in **Enoch 22:14, 27:5** and **36:4.**

Introduction to the Book of the Parables

T*itle*** ~ Chapters 37-71, of the *Book of Enoch,* comprise the section called the *"Book of the Parables."* This section gets its name from Enoch 68:1, where Noah refers to it by that title. Sometimes this section is referred to as *"The Book of Similitudes"* ; a *similitude* is another word for a parable. In Enoch, the term *parable* signifies a *prophecy* or *oracle*; one might well refer to this section as, *"The Book of the Oracles."* In it, Enoch describes a dream-vision, in which he receives three oracles.

A*uthorship*** ~ According to Enoch 37:1-2, the book is written in the first-person by the Biblical Enoch. However, beginning with chapter 60, we have a section written in the first person by Noah, the great-grandson of Enoch. According to Enoch 68:1, the *Book of the Parables* was given by Enoch to Noah, who then added the book's final eleven chapters. Noah's section serves as corroboration, a second witness to many of the same things which Enoch saw in heaven in the early part of this section.

D*ate*** ~ Chapters 37-59, are the record of Enoch's second dream-vision after being called to the office of prophet. Enoch's portion may have been written as early as six centuries before the flood. Chapters 60-71, record revelations received by Noah. Noah's portion was likely written sometime shortly before the flood.

M*ajor Theme*** ~ *"Ye mighty kings who dwell on the earth, ye shall have to behold mine Elect One, how he sits on the throne of glory and judges Azazel and all his associates, and all his hosts in the name of the Lord of Spirits."(Enoch 55:4)* This book is dominated by the pervasive presence of the Son of Man, the Messiah who will judge the angels and their children.

B*ackground*** ~ The worldwide crisis which came about due to the fall of the angels and their offspring, began to deepen in the earthly lifetime of Enoch. The flood of Noah's day would be to cleanse the earth of the legacy of the sins of that generation. However, the final judgment of that generation is to take place at a future time after the establishment of the kingdom of God on earth. In chapters 1-36, of the *Book of the Watchers*, the subject of the future final judgment of the Watchers and their beloved children was introduced; in the *Book of the Parables*, Enoch now shows the manner in which that judgment will be carried out: God's Messiah, the Son of Man is to be seated on the throne of God's glory. God gives his Messiah authority to execute judgment, because he is the Son of Man, and he will be the righteous judge of the Watchers and *their offspring*-- called here, *the kings and the mighty and the exalted and those who rule the earth.* (Enoch 55:4, 69:27, John 5:27)

Purpose ~ According to Enoch 37 and 38, the book's purpose is to stand as a record of the indictment against the generation of Enoch's day, and is written for those who will *"come after"*, that is, the last generation mentioned in 1:1-3. The *Book of Enoch* itself is thus to have a role to play in the unfolding events of the last days.

Synopsis ~ The *Book of the Parables* is the record of the second dream-vision received by Enoch subsequent to his call to ministry. Here, Enoch relates three oracles received by him in the dream-vision.

~~~~~~~~~~~~~~~~~~~~~~~~~~~~~~

Outline ~

I. Dedication (37:1-39:2)
- A. Dedication to those who will come after (37:1-5)
- B. The timeframe for which the vision is: (38:1-39:2)
  - a. When the congregation appears 38:1
  - b. Sinners judged and removed 38:1
  - c. The Righteous One appears 38:2
  - d. Light upon the righteous 38:2
  - e. Mercy withdrawn from sinners 38:6
  - f. When angels sin again and have offspring 39:1

II. Enoch's Second Vision (39:3-69:29)
- A. The First Oracle: Concerning the dwelling-places of the righteous (38:1-44:1)
  - a. They will dwell with the God's Elect One 39:6
  - b. Sinners will be expelled from there 41:2
  - c. Wisdom dwells there 42:1-3
- B. The Second Oracle: concerning those who deny the Lord (45:1-57:3)
  - a. They will have no inheritance 45:2
- C. The Third Oracle (58:1-69:29)
~~~~~~~~~~~~~~~~~~~~~~~~~~~~~~

The Book of the Parables

Dedication to Those Who Will Come After

37[111] The second vision which he saw,[112] the vision of wisdom- which Enoch the son of Jared, the son of Mahalalel, the son of Cainan, the son of Enos, the son of Seth, the son of Adam, saw. 2And this is the beginning of the words of wisdom which I lifted up my voice to speak and say to those which dwell on earth: Hear, ye men of old time, and see, ye that come after, the words of the Holy One which I will speak before the Lord of Spirits.[113] 3It were better to declare them only to the men of old time, but even from those that come after we will not withhold the beginning of wisdom. 4Till the present day such wisdom has never been given by the Lord of Spirits as I have received according to my insight, according to the good pleasure[114] of the Lord of Spirits by whom the lot of eternal life has been given to me.

5Now three Parables were imparted to me,[115] and I lifted up my voice and recounted them to those that dwell on the earth.

The First Oracle:
The Coming of the Righteous One

38 The first parable.[116]

---

111 ***"The Book of the Parables"***; This book gets its title from **Enoch 68:1**, where Noah, after receiving the book from Enoch, refers to it by that name. In fact, *The Book of the Parables*, becomes a book of dual-authorship after Noah writes its concluding chapters, 60-71. In chapter 71, Noah recounts his own Enoch-like journey into heaven and reports seeing many of the same details Enoch had reported seeing in chapters 14-36, among them a heavenly house of crystal and fire. The *Book of Genesis* infers a unique similarity and connection between Enoch and Noah when it reports of both men, they *"walked with God"*. However, one man was raptured to heaven, the other was required to remain on earth in order to save all the living through the flood. Both men's walks delivered them from the coming judgment, one by removal one by passing through.

112 **"The second vision which he saw"**; **Enoch 1:1-2, 92:1, 108:1**

113 **"Lord of Spirits"**; this is a title for God found in Enoch only in the *Book of the Parables*, where it occurs 84 times. This title seems to be echoed in the following verses: **Numbers 16:22,** "O God, the *God of the spirits of all flesh*, shall one man sin, and will you be angry with all the congregation?" **Numbers 27:16,** "Let the LORD, the *God of the spirits of all flesh*, appoint a man over the congregation." **Hebrews 12:9**, Shall we not much more be subject to the *Father of spirits* and live?

114 **Luke 12:32**, Fear not, little flock, for it is *your Father's good pleasure* to give you the kingdom. **Enoch 39:9, 48:7, 49:4**

115 **"Three parables were imparted to me"**; the three "parables", or oracles, are found in **Enoch 38:1, 45:1, 58:1**

116 **"The first parable"**; The use of the word parable here and elsewhere in the *Book of Enoch*, is uncommon and should probably be understood as synonymous with "oracle" or "prophecy". In Enoch 1:2, the Dead Sea Scrolls have an Aramaic word which translates as "oracle" rather than "parable".

When the congregation of the righteous shall appear,[117]
And sinners shall be judged for their sins,
And shall be driven from the face of the earth:[118]

[2]And when the Righteous One shall appear[119] before the eyes of the ✡ righteous,
Whose elect works hang upon the Lord of Spirits,
And light shall appear to the righteous and the elect who dwell on
the earth,

Light Shall Appear
The Shekinah glory of God will shine on the faces of God's people.

Where then will be the dwelling of the sinners,
And where the resting-place of those who have denied the Lord of Spirits?
It had been good for them if they had not been born.[120]

[3]When the secrets of the righteous shall be revealed and the sinners judged,
And the godless driven from the presence of the righteous and elect,
[4]From that time those that possess the earth
Shall no longer be powerful and exalted:[121]
And they shall not be able to behold the face of the holy,
For the Lord of Spirits has caused His light to appear
On the face of the holy, righteous, and elect.[122]

[5]Then shall the kings and the mighty perish[123]
And be given into the hands of the righteous and holy.

---

[117] **"The congregation of the righteous shall appear", Romans 8:19**, The creation waits with eager longing for the revealing of the sons of God. **Enoch 46:8, 53:6, 62:8, 104:2**
[118] **"Shall be driven from the face of the earth"; Matthew 25:41**, Then he will say to those on his left, "Depart from me, you cursed, into the eternal fire prepared for the devil and his angels."
[119] ✡ **"The Righteous One shall appear";** this title for Messiah is found twice in the *Book of the Parables* and once in the *Book of the Preaching of Enoch*; it is also found in the Old and New Testaments. In **Enoch 92:3** the resurrection of Jesus Christ, the Righteous One is prophesied. **Isaiah 53:11**, By his knowledge shall the *Righteous One*, my servant, make many to be accounted righteous, and he shall bear their iniquities. **Acts 3:14**, You denied the Holy and *Righteous One*, and asked for a murderer to be granted to you. **Acts 7:52-53**, They killed those who announced beforehand the coming of the *Righteous One*, whom you have now betrayed and murdered. **Acts 22:14**, The God of our fathers appointed you to know his will, to see the *Righteous One* and to hear a voice from his mouth.
[119] **Enoch 53:6, 92:3**
[120] **"Good for them if they had not been born"; Matthew 26:24**, Woe to that man by whom the Son of Man is betrayed! It would have been better for that man if he had not been born.
[121] **"Shall no longer be powerful and exalted"; 1 Corinthians 2:6**, The rulers of this age, who are doomed to pass away.
[122] **"Caused His light to appear on the face of the holy";** the Shekinah glory of God will be seen on faces of His people. (See footnote to Enoch 106:4) **Daniel 12:3**, And those who are wise shall shine like the brightness of the sky above; and those who turn many to righteousness, like the stars forever and ever. **2 Corinthians 3:18**, And we all, with unveiled face, beholding the glory of the Lord, are being transformed into the same image from one degree of glory to another.
[123] **"Then shall the kings and the mighty perish"**; throughout the *Book of the Parables*, a group being singled out for judgment is "the kings and the mighty and the exalted and those who rule the earth", (Enoch 62:9). This group is a major focus of the *Book of the Parables*,

[6]And thenceforward none shall seek for themselves mercy
from the Lord of Spirits
For their life is at an end.

A Future Descent of Watchers

39 And it shall come to pass in those days that elect and holy children[124] will descend from the high heaven, and their seed will become one with the children of men.[125] [2]And in those days Enoch received books of zeal and wrath, and books of disquiet and expulsion.

And mercy shall not be accorded to them, saith the Lord of Spirits.
[3]And in those days a whirlwind carried me off from the earth,[126]
And set me down at the end of the heavens.

[4]And there I saw another vision, the dwelling-places of the holy,
And the resting-places of the righteous.

[5]Here mine eyes saw their dwellings[127] with His righteous angels,[128]
And their resting-places with the holy.

And they petitioned and interceded and prayed for the children of men,
And righteousness flowed before them as water,

And mercy like dew upon the earth:
Thus it is amongst them for ever and ever.

---

and are mentioned in 38:5, 46:4, 53:5, 54:2, 55:4, 62:1,3,6,9, 63:1,12, and 67:8,12. In Enoch 56:3-4, they are referred to as the "beloved ones" of the Watchers, which identifies them as the Watchers' offspring who oppress mankind in Enoch 7. (See also 10:12, 12:6 and 14:6). This is the same group who will be written about at a later time by Moses using terminology similar to Enoch's in these words, "These were the mighty men, who were of old, men of renown". (Genesis 6:4) The *Book of the Parables*, informs us these Watcher children had ruled the earth of their time, and they are destined at some future time to be finally judged by the Son of Man, seated on the throne of His glory. This saga, which began in the *Book of the Watchers*, with the prophesy of Enoch 10:12, that the final judgment of the Watchers and their children is to take place 70 generations from Methuselah, is fleshed-out here as we are shown their condemnation consummated at the judgment seat of Jesus Christ.

[124] **"Elect children"**; **1 Timothy 5:21**, In the presence of God and of Christ Jesus and of the *elect angels*.

[125] **"Their seed will become one with the children of men"; Enoch 39:1-2**; Here, in Enoch's time, an as-yet future descent and fall of angels is described. This passage, taken with **Enoch 6**, **18:13**, and **21:3**, describe no less than four separate occurrences of angelic corruption in the *Book of Enoch*.

[126] **"A whirlwind carried me off from the earth"**; here for the second time Enoch is caught up into heaven. On this occasion, as in **Enoch 14:8**, it is for the purpose of receiving revelation. Enoch's final journey is recounted in **Enoch 70:1-4**, which tells us the details of Enoch's last catching away, as mentioned in Genesis 5:24 and Hebrews 11:5. In total, Enoch makes two excursions into heaven before his translation; after his translation, he makes two excursions back to earth in **Enoch 65** and **106**. **Hebrews 11:5**, "By faith Enoch was taken up so that he should not see death, and he was not found, because God had taken him." **Genesis 5:24**, "Enoch walked with God, and he was not, for God took him."

[127] **"Mine eyes saw their dwellings"**; **John 14:2**, In my Father's house are many rooms. If it were not so, would I have told you that I go to prepare a place for you?

[128] **"Their dwellings with His righteous angels"**; **Enoch 104:6**

The Elect One of Righteousness

[6]And in that place mine eyes saw the Elect One[129] of righteousness and ✡ of faith,
And righteousness shall prevail in his days,
And the righteous and elect
Shall be without number[130] before Him for ever and ever.
[7]And I saw his dwelling-place under the wings[131] of the Lord of Spirits.
And all the righteous and elect before Him
shall be strong as fiery lights,
And their mouth shall be full of blessing,

And their lips extol the name of the Lord of Spirits,
And righteousness before Him shall never fail,
And uprightness shall never fail before Him.

[8]There I wished to dwell,
And my spirit longed for that dwelling-place:[132]

And there heretofore hath been my portion,
For so has it been established concerning me before the Lord of Spirits.

"Holy! Holy! Holy!"

[9]In those days I praised and extolled the name of the Lord of Spirits with blessings and praises, because He hath destined[133] me for blessing and glory according to the good pleasure[134] of the Lord of Spirits. [10]For a long time my eyes regarded that place, and I blessed Him and praised Him, saying: "Blessed is He, and may He be blessed from the beginning and for evermore. [11]And before Him there is no ceasing. He knows before the world was created what is for ever and what will be from generation unto generation. [12]Those who sleep not[135] bless Thee: they stand before Thy

---

[129] ✡ **"The Elect One"** is synonymous with "Chosen One" as in Luke 9:35 below; this title for Messiah in Enoch, is found only in the *Book of the Parables*, where it occurs 16 times. This title is echoed in **Luke 9:35**, And a voice came out of the cloud, saying, "This is my Son, my Chosen One; listen to him!". **Isaiah 42:1**, Behold my servant, whom I uphold; mine Elect, in whom my soul delighteth. (KJV) **Luke 23:35**, The people stood beholding, and the rulers with them derided him, saying: He saved others; let him save himself, if he be Christ, the Elect of God. (Douay)

[130] **"Without number"; Revelation 7:9-10**, After this I looked, and behold, a great multitude that no one could number, from every nation, from all tribes and peoples and languages, standing before the throne and before the Lamb.

[131] **"Under the wings of the Lord"**; **Psalm 61:4,** Let me take refuge under the shelter of your wings! **Psalm 91:4**, He will cover you with his pinions, and under his wings you will find refuge; his faithfulness is a shield and buckler.

[132] **"My spirit longed for that dwelling-place"**; **Philippians 1:23**, My desire is to depart and be with Christ, for that is far better.

[133] **"He hath destined me for blessing and glory"**; **1 Thessalonians 5:9**, God has not destined us for wrath, but to obtain salvation through our Lord Jesus Christ.

[134] **Luke 12:32**, Fear not, little flock, for it is *your Father's good pleasure* to give you the kingdom. **Enoch 37:4, 48:7, 49:4**

[135] **"Those who sleep not",** in Enoch the various types of heavenly creatures are divided into two groups, those "who watch", who are the Watcher angels, and those "who sleep not", the

glory and bless, praise, and extol, saying: 'Holy! Holy! Holy, is the Lord of Spirits: He filleth the earth with spirits.'"[136] 13And here my eyes saw all those who sleep not: they stand before Him and bless and say: "Blessed be Thou, and blessed be the name of the Lord for ever and ever."[137] 14And my face was changed;[138] for I could no longer behold.

40 And after that I saw thousands of thousands and ten thousand times ten thousand,[139] I saw a multitude beyond number and reckoning, who stood before the Lord of Spirits.

The Four Presences

The Four "Presences"	
Michael ("Who is like God?")	*"Blesses the Lord of Spirits for ever"*
Raphael ("God Heals")	*"Blesses the Elect One and the elect ones"*
Gabriel ("Hero of God")	*"Intercedes for those who dwell on earth"*
Phanuel ("The Fear of God")	*"Fends off the satans"*

2And on the four sides of the Lord of Spirits I saw four presences, different from those that sleep not,[25] and I learnt their names: for the angel that went with me made known to me their names, and showed me all the hidden things.

3And I heard the voices of those four presences as they uttered praises before the Lord of glory. 4The first voice blesses the Lord of Spirits for ever and ever. 5And the second voice I heard blessing the Elect One[140] and the elect ones who hang upon the Lord of Spirits. 6And the third voice I heard pray and intercede for those who dwell on the earth and supplicate in the name of the Lord of Spirits. 7And I heard the fourth

---

Cherubim, Seraphim and Ophanim. They "sleep not" means they never cease or rest from worshipping God. **Enoch 39:17, 40:2**. This is echoed in **Revelation 4:8**, "Day and night they never cease."

136 **"Holy, holy, holy"**; The writings of Enoch, the Old Testament and the New Testament, all contain mutually complementary descriptions of God's throne room. **Isaiah 6:3**, One called to another and said: "Holy, holy, holy is the LORD of hosts; the whole earth is full of his glory!" **Revelation 4:8**, The four living creatures, each of them with six wings, are full of eyes all around and within, and day and night they never cease to say, "Holy, holy, holy, is the Lord God Almighty, who was and is and is to come!"

137 **"Blessed be the name of the Lord for ever and ever"**; **Psalm 113:2**, Blessed be the name of the LORD from this time forth and forevermore!

138 **"My face was changed"**; **Matthew 17:2**, He was transfigured before them, and his face shone like the sun. **Exodus 34:29**, Moses did not know that the skin of his face shone because he had been talking with God. **Enoch 106:2**

139 **"I saw thousands of thousands"**; **Daniel 7:10**, A thousand thousands served him, and ten thousand times ten thousand stood before him. **Revelation 5:11**, I heard around the throne and the living creatures and the elders the voice of many angels, numbering myriads of myriads and thousands of thousands. **Enoch 14:22, 60:1, 71:8, 71:12**

140 **"The second voice I heard blessing the Elect One"**; **Luke 9:35**, And a voice came out of the cloud, saying, "This is my Son, my Chosen One; listen to him!". **Isaiah 42:1**, Behold my servant, whom I uphold; mine Elect, in whom my soul delighteth. (KJV) **Luke 23:35**, The people stood beholding, and the rulers with them derided him, saying: He saved others; let him save himself, if he be Christ, the Elect of God. (Douay)

voice fending off the satans [141] and forbidding them to come before the Lord of Spirits to accuse[142] them who dwell on the earth.

[8]After that I asked the angel of peace who went with me, who showed me everything that is hidden: "Who are these four presences[143] which I have seen and whose words I have heard and written down?"

[9]And he said to me: "This first is Michael, the merciful and long-suffering: and the second, who is set over all the diseases and all the wounds of the children of men, is Raphael: and the third, who is set over all the powers, is Gabriel: and the fourth, who is set over the repentance unto hope of those who inherit eternal life[144], is named Phanuel."[145]

[10]And these are the four angels of the Lord of Spirits and the four voices I heard in those days.

The Mansions of the Holy

41 And after that I saw all the secrets of the heavens, and how the kingdom is divided, and how the actions of men are weighed in the balance.[146] [2]And there I saw the mansions of the elect and the mansions of the holy,[147] and mine eyes saw there all the sinners being driven from thence which deny the name of the Lord of Spirits, and being dragged off: and they could not abide[148] because of the punishment which proceeds from the Lord of Spirits.

---

[141] **"Fending off the satans and forbidding them to come before the Lord"**; the theology of Satan before the Christian era, allowed for the existence of many "satans", a word which simply means "adversary"; see Enoch 40:7, 53:3, and 69:4,6. Nevertheless, the existence of a leader, simply referred to as "Satan" was also acknowledged, see Enoch 54:6. No matter the spiritual adversary arrayed against the child of God, these enemies are mere creatures who should be "fended off", "forbidden to come" and forbidden to "accuse" God's people.

[142] **"To accuse them who dwell on earth"**; **Revelation 12:10**, And I heard a loud voice in heaven, saying, "Now the salvation and the power and the kingdom of our God and the authority of his Christ have come, for the accuser of our brothers has been thrown down, who accuses them day and night before our God. **Zechariah 3:1**, Then he showed me Joshua the high priest standing before the angel of the LORD, and Satan standing at his right hand to accuse him.

[143] Compare with angels listed in chapter 20.

[144] **"Those who inherit eternal life"**; **Hebrews 1:14**, Are they not all ministering spirits sent out to serve for the sake of those who are to *inherit salvation*? **Matthew 19:29**, And everyone who has left houses or brothers or sisters or father or mother or children or lands, for my name's sake, will receive a hundredfold and *will inherit eternal life.*

[145] Here and throughout the *Book of the Parables*, the archangel Uriel is given the name Phanuel.

[146] **"The actions of men are weighed in the balance"**; **Daniel 5:27**, You have been weighed in the balances and found wanting.

[147] **"I saw the mansions of the holy"**; **John 14:2**, In my Father's house are many rooms. If it were not so, would I have told you that I go to prepare a place for you?

[148] **"They could not abide"**; **2 Thessalonians 1:9**, They will suffer the punishment of eternal destruction, *away from the presence of the Lord* and from the glory of his might.

[3]And there mine eyes saw the secrets of the lightning and of the thunder, and the secrets of the winds,[149] how they are divided to blow over the earth, and the secrets of the clouds and dew, and there I saw from whence they proceed in that place and from whence they saturate the dusty earth. [4]And there I saw closed chambers out of which the winds are divided, the chamber of the hail and winds, the chamber of the mist, and of the clouds,[150] and the cloud thereof hovers over the earth from the beginning of the world. [5]And I saw the chambers of the sun[151] and moon, whence they proceed and whither they come again, and their glorious return, and how one is superior to the other, and their stately orbit, and how they do not leave their orbit, and they add nothing to their orbit and they take nothing from it, and they keep faith with each other, in accordance with the oath by which they are bound together. [6]And first the sun goes forth and traverses his path according to the commandment of the Lord of Spirits, and mighty is His name for ever and ever. [7]And after that I saw the hidden and the visible path of the moon, and she accomplishes the course of her path in that place by day and by night- the one holding a position opposite to the other before the Lord of Spirits.

And they give thanks and praise and rest not;[152]
For unto them is their thanksgiving rest.
[8]For the sun changes oft for a blessing or a curse,
And the course of the path of the moon is light to the righteous
And darkness to the sinners in the name of the Lord,
Who made a separation between the light and the darkness,[153]
And divided the spirits of men,
And strengthened the spirits of the righteous,[154]
In the name of His righteousness.

---

[149] **"The secrets of the winds"**; here they are called "the secrets of the winds", in v.4 they are referred to as "closed chambers", and in 18:1, "treasuries". As one might expect from ancient literature, some language seems archaic and difficult to decipher for modern readers. "Secrets" seems to be a case in point. For comparison, consider the archaic usage of certain words in **Job 36:29-30**: Can anyone understand the spreading of the clouds, the thunderings of his pavilion? Behold, he scatters his lightning about him and covers the roots of the sea. See also **Enoch 11:1, 17:3, 18:1, 41:4-5, 59:1, 60:12,15,18-21, 59:1-3, 69:23,** and **71:4**.
[150] **"The chamber of the clouds"**; **Psalm 104:3**, He lays the beams of *his chambers* on the waters; he makes the clouds his chariot; he rides on the wings of the wind. **Deuteronomy 28:12**, The LORD will open to you *his good treasury*, the heavens, to give the rain to your land in its season and to bless all the work of your hands. **Psalm 33:7**, He gathers the waters of the sea as a heap; he puts the deeps *in storehouses*. **Jeremiah 10:13** and **51:16**, When he utters his voice there is a tumult of waters in the heavens, and he makes the mist rise from the ends of the earth. He makes lightning for the rain, and he brings forth the wind from *his storehouses*.
[151] **"The chambers of the sun"**; **Psalm 19:4-6**, In them he has set a tent for the sun, which comes out like a bridegroom *leaving his chamber*, and, like a strong man, runs its course with joy. Its rising is from the end of the heavens, and its circuit to the end of them, and there is nothing hidden from its heat.
[152] **"They give thanks and praise and rest not"**; **Psalm 19:1**, The heavens declare the glory of God, and the sky above proclaims his handiwork. **Psalm 148:3**, Praise him, sun and moon, praise him, all you shining stars!
[153] **"Who made a separation between the light and the darkness"**; **Genesis 1:4**, God separated the light from the darkness.
[154] **"The spirits of the righteous"; Hebrews 12:22-23,** You have come to Mount Zion and to the city of the living God, the heavenly Jerusalem, and to innumerable angels in festal

9For no angel hinders and no power is able to hinder; for He appoints a judge[155] for them all and He judges them all before Him.

The Personification of Wisdom

42 Wisdom found no place where she might dwell;[156]
Then a dwelling-place was assigned her in the heavens.

2Wisdom went forth to make her dwelling among the children of men,
And found no dwelling-place:

Wisdom returned to her place,
And took her seat among the angels.

3And unrighteousness went forth from her chambers:
Whom she sought not she found,
And dwelt with them,

As rain in a desert
And dew on a thirsty land.

43 And I saw other lightnings and the stars of heaven, and I saw how He called them all by their names[157] and they hearkened unto Him. 2And I saw how they are weighed in a righteous balance according to their proportions of light: I saw the width of their spaces and the day of their appearing, and how their revolution produces lightning: and I saw their revolution according to the number of the angels, and how they keep faith with each other.

3And I asked the angel who went with me who showed me what was hidden: 4"What are these?"

---

gathering, and to the assembly of the firstborn who are enrolled in heaven, and to God, the judge of all, and to *the spirits of the righteous* made perfect.

155 **"He appoints a judge for them all"**; **John 5:22**, The Father judges no one, but has given all judgment to the Son. **John 5:27**, And he has given him authority to execute judgment, because he is the Son of Man. **Enoch 69:27**

156 **"Wisdom found no place where she might dwell"**; the personification of wisdom can be found in Enoch and the *Book of Proverbs*. Wisdom is portrayed here as a woman who seeks and fails to woo the sons of men into an intimate relationship with herself. **Proverbs 1:20-23**, Wisdom cries aloud in the street, in the markets she raises her voice; at the head of the noisy streets she cries out; at the entrance of the city gates she speaks: "How long, O simple ones, will you love being simple? How long will scoffers delight in their scoffing and fools hate knowledge? If you turn at my reproof, behold, I will pour out my spirit to you; I will make my words known to you. {**See also Proverbs 3:13-18, Proverbs 8:1-5, Proverbs 8:17-21**} **Job 28:12-14**, But where shall wisdom be found? And where is the place of understanding? Man does not know its worth, and it is not found in the land of the living. The deep says, 'It is not in me,' and the sea says, 'It is not with me.'

157 **"He called them all by their names"**; **Psalm 147:4**, He determines the number of the stars; he gives to all of them their names.

And he said to me: "The Lord of Spirits hath showed thee their parabolic meaning: these are the names of the holy who dwell on the earth and believe in the name of the Lord of Spirits for ever and ever."

44 Also another phenomenon I saw in regard to the lightnings: how some of the stars arise and become lightnings and cannot part with their new form.

The Second Oracle

45 And this is the second Parable[158] concerning those who deny the name of the dwelling[159] of the holy ones and the Lord of Spirits.

[2]And into the heaven they shall not ascend,
And on the earth they shall not come:
Such shall be the lot of the sinners
Who have denied the name of the Lord of Spirits,
Who are thus preserved for the day of suffering and tribulation.[160]

☼ [3]On that day Mine Elect One[161] shall sit on the throne of glory[162] ☼
And shall try their works,[163]
And their places of rest shall be innumerable.

And their souls shall grow strong within them
when they see Mine elect ones,
And those who have called upon My glorious name:
[4]Then will I cause Mine Elect One to dwell among them.[164]

---

158 **"The second parable"**; The use of the word parable here and elsewhere in the book is uncommon and should probably be understood as synonymous with "oracle" or "prophecy". The Dead Sea Scrolls have "oracle" in the place of "parable" in Enoch 1:3. The three "parables" are found in **Enoch 38:1, 45:1, 58:1**

159 **"Who deny the name of the dwelling"; Revelation 13:6**, It opened its mouth to utter blasphemies against God, blaspheming his name and his dwelling, that is, those who dwell in heaven.

160 **"The day of suffering and tribulation"**; **Revelation 3:10**, The hour of trial is coming on the whole world, to try those who dwell on the earth.

161 ☼ **"Mine Elect One";** Elect One is synonymous with "Chosen One" as in **Luke 9:35**, And a voice came out of the cloud, saying, "This is my Son, my Chosen One; listen to him!". **Isaiah 42:1**, Behold my servant, whom I uphold; mine Elect, in whom my soul delighteth. (KJV) **Luke 23:35**, The people stood beholding, and the rulers with them derided him, saying: He saved others; let him save himself, if he be Christ, the Elect of God. (Douay)

162 ☼ **"Throne of glory"**; **Matthew 25:31**, When the Son of Man comes in his glory, and all the angels with him, then he will sit on his glorious throne.

163 **"Shall try their works"**; **1 Corinthians 3:13**, Each one's work will become manifest, for the Day will disclose it, because it will be revealed by fire, and the *fire will test what sort of work each one has done.*

164 **"Then will I cause Mine Elect One to dwell among them"**; **Revelation 21:3**, Behold, the dwelling place of God is with man. He will dwell with them, and they will be his people, and God himself will be with them as their God.

And I will transform the heaven
and make it an eternal blessing and light:
[5]And I will transform the earth and make it a blessing: [165]

And I will cause Mine elect ones to dwell upon it:[166]
But the sinners and evil-doers shall not set foot thereon.

[6]For I have provided and satisfied with peace My righteous ones
And have caused them to dwell before Me:

But for the sinners there is judgment impending with Me,
So that I shall destroy them from the face of the earth.

Enoch Sees the Son of Man

46 And there I saw One who had a head of days,[167]
And His head was white like wool,[168]
And with Him was another being
Whose countenance had the appearance of a man,[169] ✡
And his face was full of graciousness,[170] like one of the holy angels.

[2]And I asked the angel who went with me and showed me all the hidden things, concerning that Son of Man,[171] who he was, and whence he ✡ was, and why he went with the Head of Days?[172] [3]And he answered and said unto me:

---

[165] **"I will transform the earth"**; **Isaiah 35:1-2**, The wilderness and the dry land shall be glad; the desert shall rejoice and blossom like the crocus; it shall blossom abundantly and rejoice with joy and singing.

[166] **"I will cause Mine elect ones to dwell upon it"**; **Matthew 5:5**, Blessed are the meek, for they shall inherit the earth.

[167] **"Head of Days"**; this name of God is translated "Ancient of Days" in Richard Laurence's translation; in Enoch it occurs 11 times only in the *Book of the Parables*. "Ancient of Days" is found in Daniel 7:9, below. "Head" here is used in the sense of a source or origin point of a thing, as in a river head. God is the "head of days", the source of or creator of "days", i.e. *time*.

[168] **"His Head Was White Like Wool"; Daniel 7:9**, As I looked, thrones were placed, and the Ancient of Days took his seat; his clothing was white as snow, and the hair of his head like pure wool.

[169] ✡ **"Whose countenance had the appearance of a man"**; Enoch's 'Son of Man' has the appearance of a man by reason of the incarnation of Jesus Christ.

[170] **"His face was full of graciousness"**; **John 1:14**, We have seen his glory, glory as of the only Son from the Father, *full of grace and truth*.

[171] ✡ **"The Son of Man"**; this title for Messiah is found in Enoch only in the *Book of the Parables*, where it occurs 16 times. This title is echoed throughout the four gospels in the New Testament, where Jesus Christ is the Son of Man.

[172] **"He went with the Head of Days"**; **Daniel 7:13**, I saw in the night visions, and behold, with the clouds of heaven there came one like a son of man, and he came to the Ancient of Days and was presented before him.

This is the Son of Man who hath righteousness,
With whom dwelleth righteousness,
And who revealeth all the treasures of that which is hidden,[173]

Because the Lord of Spirits hath chosen him,
And whose lot hath the pre-eminence before the Lord of Spirits in uprightness for ever.

[4]And this Son of Man whom thou hast seen
Shall raise up the kings and the mighty from their seats,[174]
And the strong from their thrones

And shall loosen the reins of the strong,
And break the teeth of the sinners.[175]

[5]And he shall put down the kings from their thrones and kingdoms
Because they do not extol and praise Him,
Nor humbly acknowledge whence the kingdom
was bestowed upon them.[176]
[6]And he shall put down the countenance of the strong,
And shall fill them with shame.

And darkness shall be their dwelling,
And worms shall be their bed,[177]

And they shall have no hope of rising from their beds,
Because they do not extol the name of the Lord of Spirits.

[7]And these are they who judge the stars of heaven,
And raise their hands against the Most High,
And tread upon the earth and dwell upon it.

And all their deeds manifest unrighteousness,
And their power rests upon their riches,

And their faith is in the gods which they have made with their hands,
And they deny the name of the Lord of Spirits,

---

[173] **"Who revealeth all the treasures of that which is hidden"**; **Colossians 2:2-3**, Christ, in whom are hidden all the treasures of wisdom and knowledge.
[174] **"Shall raise up the kings and the mighty from their seats",** in other words, they are former kings, now powerless, and brought before the judgment throne of Jesus Christ. **Luke 1:52**, He has brought down the mighty from their thrones.
[175] **"Break the teeth of the sinners"; Psalm 3:7**, Arise, O LORD! Save me, O my God! For you strike all my enemies on the cheek; you break the teeth of the wicked.
[176] **"Whence the kingdom was bestowed upon them"**; **Romans 13:1**, There is no authority except from God, and those that exist have been instituted by God.
[177] **"Worms shall be their bed"**; **Isaiah 66:24**, And they shall go out and look on the dead bodies of the men who have rebelled against me. For their worm shall not die, their fire shall not be quenched. **Mark 9:47-48**, Thrown into hell, where their worm does not die and the fire is not quenched.

[8]And they persecute the houses of His congregations,[178]
And the faithful who hang upon the name of the Lord of Spirits.

The Souls of Those Who Had Been Slain

47 And in those days shall have ascended
the prayer of the righteous,[179]
And the blood of the righteous[180] from the earth
before the Lord of Spirits.[181]
[2]In those days the holy ones who dwell above in the heavens
Shall unite with one voice
And supplicate and pray and praise,
And give thanks and bless the name of the Lord of Spirits
On behalf of the blood of the righteous[70] which has been shed,
And that the prayer of the righteous may not be in vain
before the Lord of Spirits,
That judgment may be done unto them,
And that they may not have to suffer for ever.
[3]In those days I saw the Head of Days when
He seated himself upon the throne of His glory,
And the books of the living[182] were opened before Him: [183]

---

[178] **"They persecute the houses of His congregations"; Acts 8:1**, There arose on that day a great persecution against the church in Jerusalem, and they were all scattered throughout the regions of Judea and Samaria. **Galatians 1:13**, For you have heard of my former life in Judaism, how I persecuted the Church of God violently and tried to destroy it. **Enoch 38:1, 53:6, 62:8**

[179] **"Shall have ascended the prayer of the righteous"**; The passage foresees the vindication of all the righteous whose blood was shed upon the earth. **Revelation 8:3-4**, Another angel came and stood at the altar with a golden censer, and he was given much incense to offer with the prayers of all the saints on the golden altar before the throne, and the smoke of the incense, with the prayers of the saints, rose before God from the hand of the angel.

[180] **"The blood of the righteous"; Lamentations 4:13**, This was for the sins of her prophets and the iniquities of her priests, who shed in the midst of her *the blood of the righteous*. **Matthew 23:35**, So that on you may come all the *righteous blood* shed on earth, from the blood of innocent Abel to the blood of Zechariah the son of Barachiah, whom you murdered between the sanctuary and the altar. **Enoch 47:2+4**

[181] **Revelation 6:9-11**, When he opened the fifth seal, I saw under the altar the souls of those who had been slain for the word of God and for the witness they had borne. They cried out with a loud voice, "O Sovereign Lord, holy and true, how long before you will judge and avenge our blood on those who dwell on the earth?" Then they were each given a white robe and told to rest a little longer, until the number of their fellow servants and their brothers should be complete, who were to be killed as they themselves had been.

[182] **"The books of the living were opened before Him"; Psalm 69:28**, Let them be blotted out of the *Book of the Living*; let them not be enrolled among the righteous.

[183] **Daniel 7:9-10**, As I looked, thrones were placed, and the Ancient of Days took his seat; his clothing was white as snow, and the hair of his head like pure wool; his throne was fiery flames; its wheels were burning fire. A stream of fire issued and came out from before him; a thousand thousands served him, and ten thousand times ten thousand stood before him; the court sat in judgment *and the books were opened*. **Revelation 20:11,12,15**, Then I saw a great white throne and him who was seated on it. From his presence earth and sky fled away, and no place was found for them. And I saw the dead, great and small, standing before the throne, *and books were opened*. Then another book was opened, which is the *Book of Life*. And the dead were judged by what was written in the books, according to what they had done. And if anyone's name was not found written in the *Book of Life*, he was thrown into the lake of fire.

And all His host which is in heaven above and His counselors
stood before Him,
4And the hearts of the holy were filled with joy;

Because the number of the righteous had been offered,
And the prayer of the righteous had been heard,
And the blood of the righteous[70] been required[184] before the Lord of Spirits.

An Inexhaustible Fountain of Righteousness

48 And in that place I saw the fountain of righteousness ☆
Which was inexhaustible:[185]
And around it were many fountains of wisdom:[186]

And all the thirsty drank of them,
And were filled with wisdom,
And their dwellings were with the righteous and holy and elect.
2And at that hour that Son of Man was named[187]
In the presence of the Lord of Spirits,
And his name before the Head of Days.

3Yea, before the sun and the signs were created,
Before the stars of the heaven were made,[188]
His name was named before the Lord of Spirits.

He Shall Be the Light of the Nations

4He shall be a staff to the righteous
whereon to stay themselves and not fall,
And he shall be the light of the Gentiles,[189] ☆
And the hope of those who are troubled of heart.

---

184 **"The blood of the righteous has been required"**; **Revelation 19:2**, His judgments are true and just; for he has judged the great prostitute who corrupted the earth with her immorality, and *has avenged on her the blood of his servants*.

185 ☆ **"I saw the fountain of righteousness which was inexhaustible"**; Jesus Christ is the fountain of inexhaustible righteousness.

186 **"Fountains of wisdom"**; **Proverbs 18:4**, The words of a man's mouth are deep waters; the *fountain of wisdom* is a bubbling brook.

187 **"That Son of Man was named"**; **Revelation 5:5**, And one of the elders said to me, "Weep no more; behold, the Lion of the tribe of Judah, the Root of David, has conquered, so that he can open the scroll and its seven seals."

188 **"Before the stars of the heaven were made"**; In Hebrew thought naming a thing speaks of a things existence. Here the pre-existent nature of the Son of Man is in view. **John 1:3**, All things were made through him, and without him was not any thing made that was made. **Hebrews 1:2**, In these last days he has spoken to us by his Son, whom he appointed the heir of all things, through whom also he created the world. **Enoch 48:3,6**

189 ☆ **"The light of the gentiles"**; the translator's choice to use the word "gentiles" here may seem anachronistic as the birth of the nation of Israel as distinct from the nations had not yet occurred in Enoch's time. There need not seem to be a problem here if the meaning of gentiles is understood as synonymous with "nations". **Luke 2:30-32**, My eyes have seen your

The Worldwide Worship of the Son of Man

[5]All who dwell on earth shall fall down and worship before him,[190] ✡
And will praise and bless and celebrate with song[191] the Lord of Spirits.

[6]And for this reason hath he been chosen and hidden before Him,
Before the creation of the world and for evermore.[186]

[7]And the wisdom of the Lord of Spirits
hath revealed him to the holy and righteous;[192]
For he hath preserved the lot of the righteous,
Because they have hated and despised this world of unrighteousness,[193]
And have hated all its works and ways[194] in the name of the Lord of Spirits:

In His Name They Are Saved

For in his name they are saved,[195] ✡
And according to his good pleasure[196] hath it been in regard to their life.

[8]In these days downcast in countenance
shall the kings of the earth have become,
And the strong who possess the land
because of the works of their hands,

For on the day of their anguish and affliction

---

salvation that you have prepared in the presence of all peoples, a *light for revelation to the Gentiles*, and for glory to your people Israel.

190 ✡ **"All shall fall down and worship before Him"**; **Philippians 2:9-11**, God has highly exalted him and bestowed on him the name that is above every name, so that at the name of Jesus every knee should bow, in heaven and on earth and under the earth, and every tongue confess that Jesus Christ is Lord, to the glory of God the Father. **Isaiah 45:23**, By myself I have sworn; from my mouth has gone out in righteousness a word that shall not return: 'To me every knee shall bow, every tongue shall swear allegiance.' **Enoch 10:21**

191 **"Will celebrate with song"**; **Revelation 14:3**, They were singing a new song before the throne and before the four living creatures and before the elders.

192 **"Revealed Him to the holy and righteous"**; **Matthew 11:25**, Jesus declared, "I thank you, Father, Lord of heaven and earth, that you have hidden these things from the wise and understanding and revealed them to little children; yes, Father, for such was your gracious will." **John 6:44**, No one can come to me unless the Father who sent me draws him.

193 **"This world of unrighteousness"**; **Galatians 1:4**, Who gave himself for our sins to deliver us from the present evil age. **Enoch 108:8**

194 **"Have hated all its works and ways"**; **1 John 2:15**, Do not love the world or the things in the world. If anyone loves the world, the love of the Father is not in him. **Enoch 108:8**

195 ✡ **"In his name they are saved"; 1 Cor. 6:11**, You were justified in the name of the Lord Jesus Christ and by the Spirit of our God. **Acts 4:12**, And there is salvation in no one else, for there is no other name under heaven given among men by which we must be saved. **John 1:12**, But to all who did receive him, who believed in his name, he gave the right to become children of God. **Enoch 48:7** and **50:3**

196 **Luke 12:32**, Fear not, little flock, for it is *your Father's good pleasure* to give you the kingdom. **Enoch 37:4, 39:9, 49:4**

they shall not be able to save themselves.
[9]And I will give them over into the hands of Mine elect:[197]
As straw in the fire so shall they burn before the face of the holy:[198]
As lead in the water shall they sink before the face of the righteous,
And no trace of them shall any more be found.

[10]And on the day of their affliction there shall be rest on the earth,
And before them they shall fall and not rise again:

And there shall be no one to take them with his hands and raise them:
✡ For they have denied[199] the Lord of Spirits and His Anointed.[200]
The name of the Lord of Spirits be blessed.

49 For wisdom is poured out like water,
And glory faileth not before him for evermore.

[2]For he is mighty in all the secrets of righteousness,
And unrighteousness shall disappear as a shadow,
And have no continuance;
Because the Elect One standeth before the Lord of Spirits,
And his glory is for ever and ever,
And his might unto all generations.

[3]And in him dwells the spirit of wisdom,[201]
And the spirit which gives insight,
And the spirit of understanding and of might,
And the spirit of those who have fallen asleep in righteousness.[202]

---

[197] **"I will give them over into the hands of Mine elect"**; **1 Corinthians 6:2-3**, Or do you not know that the saints will judge the world? And if the world is to be judged by you, are you incompetent to try trivial cases? Do you not know that we are to judge angels? How much more, then, matters pertaining to this life!

[198] **"They shall burn before the face of the holy"**; **Revelation 14:9-10**, And another angel, a third, followed them, saying with a loud voice, "If anyone worships the beast and its image and receives a mark on his forehead or on his hand, he also will drink the wine of God's wrath, poured full strength into the cup of his anger, and he will be *tormented with fire and sulfur in the presence of the holy angels* and in the presence of the Lamb."

[199] ✡ **"They have denied the Lord of Spirits and His Anointed"**; Jesus Christ is God's Anointed One; the terms Messiah and Christ mean "anointed one". Those who deny the Lord's Christ, deny God. **Luke 12:9**, The one who denies me before men will be denied before the angels of God. **Matthew 10:33**, Whoever denies me before men, I also will deny before my Father who is in heaven.

[200] **"His Anointed"** is another title for the Son of Man in Enoch's vision. "His Anointed" is synonymous for "His Messiah" in the *Book of Enoch*; the term occurs two times, only in the *Book of the Parables*. **Enoch 48:10** and **52:4**.

[201] **"The spirit of wisdom"**; **Isaiah 11:2**, And the Spirit of the LORD shall rest upon him, *the Spirit of wisdom* and understanding, the Spirit of counsel and might, the Spirit of knowledge and the fear of the LORD.

[202] **"Those who have fallen asleep"**; **1 Corinthians 15:20-21**, But in fact Christ has been raised from the dead, the first fruits of those who have fallen asleep. For as by a man came death, by a man has come also the resurrection of the dead.

[4]And he shall judge the secret things,[203]
And none shall be able to utter a lying word before him;
For he is the Elect One before the Lord of Spirits according to His good pleasure. [204]

We Shall Be Changed!

50 And in those days a change shall take place
for the holy and elect,[205]
And the light of days shall abide upon them,
And glory and honor shall turn to the holy,
[2]On the day of affliction on which
evil shall have been treasured up against the sinners.

And the righteous shall be victorious in the name of the Lord of Spirits:
And He will cause the others to witness this
That they may repent
And forgo the works of their hands.

[3]They shall have no honor through the name of the Lord of Spirits,
Yet through His name shall they be saved,[206]
And the Lord of Spirits will have compassion on them,
For His compassion is great.

[4]And He is righteous also in His judgment,
And in the presence of His glory
unrighteousness also shall not maintain itself:
At His judgment the unrepentant shall perish before Him.
[5]And from henceforth I will have no mercy on them,
saith the Lord of Spirits.

Sheol Will Give Back the Dead

51 And in those days shall the earth also give back

---

203 **"He shall judge the secret things"**; **Romans 2:16**, On that day when, according to my gospel, *God judges the secrets of men* by Christ Jesus.
204 **Luke 12:32**, Fear not, little flock, for *it is your Father's good pleasure* to give you the kingdom. **Enoch 37:4, 39:9, 48:7**
205 **"In those days a change shall take place for the holy and elect";** The sequence of prophetic events in Enoch 50, seems to line up quite well with the idea of a pre-tribulation rapture; first the saints are "changed", then the rest of the people enter "the day of affliction", in order "that they may repent". Thanks to Terrie Kolean for this insight. **1 Corinthians 15:52**, In a moment, in the twinkling of an eye, at the last trumpet. For the trumpet will sound, and the dead will be raised imperishable, and *we shall be changed.*
206 **"In his name they are saved"; 1 Corinthians 6:11**, You were justified in the name of the Lord Jesus Christ and by the Spirit of our God. **Acts 4:12**, And there is salvation in no one else, for there is no other name under heaven given among men by which we must be saved. **John 1:12**, But to all who did receive him, who believed in his name, he gave the right to become children of God. **Enoch 48:7, 50:3**

that which has been entrusted to it,
And Sheol also shall give back that which it has received,[207]
And hell shall give back that which it owes.

Salvation is Drawing Nigh

[2]And he shall choose the righteous and holy from among them:
For the day has drawn nigh[208] that they should be saved.

The Elect One Sits on God's Throne

✡ [3]And the Elect One shall in those days sit on My throne,[209]
And his mouth shall pour forth[210]
all the secrets of wisdom and counsel:
For the Lord of Spirits hath given them to him and hath glorified him.

[4]And in those days shall the mountains leap like rams,
And the hills also shall skip like lambs[211] satisfied with milk,
And the faces of all the angels in heaven shall be lighted up with joy.[212]

[5]For in those days the Elect One shall arise,
And the earth shall rejoice,
And the righteous shall dwell upon it,
And the elect shall walk thereon.

---

207 **"Sheol shall give back that which it has received"**; **Revelation 20:13**, And the sea gave up the dead who were in it, Death and Hades gave up the dead who were in them, and they were judged, each one of them, according to what they had done.

208 **"The day has drawn nigh that they should be saved"; Luke 21:28**, Now when these things begin to take place, straighten up and raise your heads, because *your redemption is drawing near.*

209 ✡ **"The Elect One shall sit on My throne"; Enoch 51:3** reveals the divine relationship between God the Father and God the Son, Jesus Christ; he sits on his Father's throne. For Enoch to have written of this divine relationship before the birth of Jesus is prophetic. **Revelation 7:17**, For the Lamb in the midst of the throne will be their shepherd, and he will guide them to springs of living water, and God will wipe away every tear from their eyes.

210 **"His mouth shall pour forth all the secrets of wisdom and counsel"**; **Isaiah 2:3**, Many peoples shall come, and say: "Come, let us go up to the mountain of the LORD, to the house of the God of Jacob, that he may teach us his ways and that we may walk in his paths."

211 **"The hills also shall skip like lambs"**; **Psalm 114:4**, The mountains skipped like rams, the hills like lambs.

212 **"The faces of all the angels in heaven shall be lighted up with joy"**; **Luke 15:10**, Just so, I tell you, there is joy before the angels of God over one sinner who repents.

Enoch's Second Sojourn
Seven Mountains Define Earth's History

52 And after those days in that place where I had seen all the visions of that which is hidden- for I had been carried off in a whirlwind and they had borne me towards the west- [2]There mine eyes saw all the secret things of heaven that shall be, a mountain of iron, and a mountain of copper, and a mountain of silver, and a mountain of gold, and a mountain of soft metal, and a mountain of lead. [3]And I asked the angel who went with me, saying, "What things are these which I have seen in secret?"

[4]And he said unto me: "All these things which thou hast seen shall serve the dominion[213] of His Anointed[214] that he may be potent and mighty ✡ on the earth."

[5]And that angel of peace answered, saying unto me: "Wait a little, and there shall be revealed unto thee all the secret things which surround the Lord of Spirits.

[6]And these mountains which thine eyes have seen,
The mountain of iron, and the mountain of copper,
and the mountain of silver,
And the mountain of gold, and the mountain of soft metal,
and the mountain of lead,
All these shall be in the presence of the Elect One
As wax before the fire,[215]
And like the water which streams down
from above upon those mountains,
And they shall become powerless before his feet.
[7]And it shall come to pass in those days that none shall be saved,
Either by gold or by silver,
And none be able to escape.
[8]And there shall be no iron for war,
Nor shall one clothe oneself with a breastplate.
Bronze shall be of no service,
And tin shall be of no service and shall not be esteemed,
And lead shall not be desired.
[9]And all these things shall be denied and destroyed

---

[213] **"All these... shall serve the dominion of His Anointed"**; Here the timeline of earth is laid out as a succession of seven mountains, or seven kingdoms. The seventh mountain is inferred in verse 4, when the angel states, "all these shall serve the dominion of His Anointed." The installation of Messiah's kingdom supplants all that came prior.

[214] ✡ **"His Anointed"** is another title for the Son of Man in Enoch's vision. "His Anointed" is synonymous for "His Messiah" in the *Book of Enoch* and occurs two times only in the *Book of the Parables*, in **Enoch 48:10** and **52:4**.

[215] **"As wax before the fire"**; **Psalm 97:5**, The mountains melt like wax before the LORD, before the Lord of all the earth. **Micah 1:4**, The mountains will melt under him, and the valleys will split open, like wax before the fire, like waters poured down a steep place. **Enoch 1:6**

from the surface of the earth,
When the Elect One shall appear before the face of the Lord of Spirits."

The Congregation of the Elect One Appears

53 There mine eyes saw a deep valley with open mouths, and all who dwell on the earth and sea and islands shall bring to him gifts[216] and presents and tokens of homage, but that deep valley shall not become full.

[2]And their hands commit lawless deeds,
And the sinners devour all whom they lawlessly oppress:
Yet the sinners shall be destroyed before the face of the Lord of Spirits,
And they shall be banished from off the face of His earth,
And they shall perish for ever and ever.

[3]For I saw all the angels of punishment abiding there and preparing all the instruments of Satan.

[4]And I asked the angel of peace who went with me: "For whom are they preparing these instruments?"

[5]And he said unto me: "They prepare these for the kings and the mighty of this earth, that they may thereby be destroyed."

[6]And after this the Righteous and Elect One[217] shall cause the house ✡ of his congregation[218] to appear: henceforth they shall be no more hindered in the name of the Lord of Spirits.

[7]And these mountains shall not stand as the earth before his righteousness,
But the hills shall be as a fountain of water,
And the righteous shall have rest from the oppression of sinners."[219]

---

[216] **"All who dwell on the earth and sea and islands shall bring to him gifts"**; **Rev. 21:26**, They will bring into it the glory and the honor of the nations.

[217] ✡ **"The Righteous One"**; the passage is both messianic as well as prophetic of Christ's ministry in establishing his Church. The title *"the Righteous One"* used for Messiah is found twice in the *Book of the Parables* and once in the *Book of the Preaching of Enoch*; it is also found in the Old and New Testaments. In **Enoch 92:3** the resurrection of *the Righteous One* is prophesied. **Isaiah 53:11**, By his knowledge shall *the Righteous One*, my servant, make many to be accounted righteous, and he shall bear their iniquities. **Acts 3:14**, You denied *the Holy and Righteous One*, and asked for a murderer to be granted to you. **Acts 7:52-53**, They killed those who announced beforehand the coming of *the Righteous One*, whom you have now betrayed and murdered. **Acts 22:14-15**, And he said, "The God of our fathers appointed you to know his will, to see *the Righteous One* and to hear a voice from his mouth; for you will be a witness for him to everyone of what you have seen and heard." **Enoch 38:2, 92:3**

[218] **"The house of His congregation", Enoch 38:1, 46:8, 62:8**

[219] **"The righteous shall have rest from oppression"**; **Daniel 7:22**, The Ancient of Days came, and judgment was given for the saints of the Most High, and the time came when the saints possessed the kingdom.

The Last Judgment

54 And I looked and turned to another part of the earth, and saw there a deep valley with burning fire. [2]And they brought the kings and the mighty, and began to cast them into this deep valley.[220] [3]And there mine eyes saw how they made these their instruments, iron chains of immeasurable weight. [4]And I asked the angel of peace who went with me, saying: "For whom are these chains being prepared?"

Leading Astray Those Who Dwell On Earth

[5]And he said unto me: "These are being prepared for the hosts of Azazel,[221] so that they may take them and cast them into the abyss of complete condemnation,[222] and they shall cover their jaws with rough stones as the Lord of Spirits commanded. [6]And Michael, and Gabriel, and Raphael, and Phanuel shall take hold of them on that great day, and cast them on that day into the burning furnace, that the Lord of Spirits may take vengeance on them for their unrighteousness in becoming subject to Satan[223] and leading astray those who dwell on the earth.[224] [7]And in those days shall punishment come from the Lord of Spirits, and He will open all the chambers of waters which are above the heavens, and of the fountains which are beneath the earth. [8]And all the waters shall be joined with the waters: that which is above the heavens is the masculine, and the water which is beneath the earth is the feminine. [9]And they shall destroy all who dwell on the earth and those who dwell under the ends of the heaven. [10]And when they have recognized their unrighteousness which they have wrought on the earth, then by these shall they perish."

Next Time the Fire

55 And after that the Head of Days repented and said: "In vain have I destroyed all who dwell on the earth." [2]And He swore by His great name:

---

[220] **"And began to cast them into this deep valley"**; **Isaiah 14:9**, Sheol beneath is stirred up to meet you when you come; it rouses the shades to greet you, all who were leaders of the earth; it raises from their thrones all who were kings of the nations.

[221] **"These are being prepared for the hosts of Azazel"**; Hell was not intended for mankind. **Matthew 25:41**, Then he will say to those on his left, "Depart from me, you cursed, into the eternal fire prepared for the devil and his angels."

[222] **"Cast them into the abyss of complete condemnation"**; **2 Peter 2:4**, God did not spare angels when they sinned, but cast them into hell and committed them to chains of gloomy darkness to be kept until the judgment. **Jude 1:6-7**, The angels who did not stay within their own position of authority, but left their proper dwelling, he has kept in eternal chains under gloomy darkness until the judgment of the great day.

[223] **"Becoming subject to Satan"**; this is the one verse in Enoch that connects the sin of the Watchers with the earlier rebellion of Satan. The Watchers, either simply in the act of sinning, or later, fell in league with Satan, becoming subject to him.

[224] **"Leading astray those who dwell on the earth"; Revelation 13:3**, The whole earth marveled as they followed the beast. **Revelation 13:12**, It makes the earth and its inhabitants worship the first beast. **Revelation 13:14**, By the signs that it is allowed to work in the presence of the beast it deceives those who dwell on earth. **Enoch 54:6, 67:7**

"Henceforth I will not do so to all who dwell on the earth, and I will set a sign in the heaven:[225] and this shall be a pledge of good faith between Me and them for ever, so long as heaven is above the earth. And this is in accordance with My command. [3]When I have desired to take hold of them by the hand of the angels on the day of tribulation and pain because of this, I will cause My chastisement and My wrath to abide upon them,[226] saith God, the Lord of Spirits. [4]Ye mighty kings who dwell on the earth, ye shall have to behold[227] Mine Elect One, how he sits on the throne of glory and judges[228] Azazel, and all his associates,[229] and all his hosts in the name of the Lord of Spirits."

56 And I saw there the hosts of the angels of punishment going, and they held scourges and chains of iron and bronze. [2]And I asked the angel of peace who went with me, saying: "To whom are these who hold the scourges going?"

[3]And he said unto me: "To their elect and beloved ones,[230] that they may be cast into the chasm of the abyss of the valley.

[4]And then that valley shall be filled with their elect and beloved,
And the days of their lives shall be at an end,
And the days of their leading astray shall not thenceforward be reckoned.

"The Angels Shall Return"

[5]And in those days the angels shall return
And hurl themselves to the east upon the Parthians and Medes:[231]

---

[225] **"I will set a sign in the heaven"; Genesis 9:13**, I have set my bow in the cloud, and it shall be a sign of the covenant between me and the earth.
[226] **"I will cause my wrath to abide upon them"; John 3:36**, Whoever believes in the Son has eternal life; whoever does not obey the Son shall not see life, but the wrath of God remains on him.
[227] **""Ye mighty kings shall have to behold Mine Elect One how He judges Azazel"**: In Enoch 10:12, the Watchers were forced to see the judgment of God carried out upon their offspring. In Enoch 55:4, this is reversed as the Watcher offspring have to behold the judgment of the Watchers.
[228] **"Behold Mine Elect One, how he sits on the throne of glory"; Matthew 19:28**, Jesus said to them, "Truly, I say to you, in the new world, when the Son of Man will sit on his glorious throne, you who have followed me will also sit on twelve thrones, judging the twelve tribes of Israel." **Enoch 10:21, 61:8**
[229] **"And all his associates"**, the rest of the angels who sinned.
[230] **"Their beloved ones"**; here refers to the same group Moses calls "the mighty men who were of old, the men of renown" (Genesis 6:4). They are also called "lawless ones" in Enoch 7:6; they are the offspring of the Watchers. In Enoch 10:12, the Watchers are imprisoned in the earth after witnessing their "beloved ones" killed by one another's hands through internecine warfare. In this passage the final judgment of the Watchers' offspring is in view. The final judgment brings an end to the activity of the demonic in the world, per Enoch 15:8-16:1. **Enoch 10:12, 12:6** and **56:3-4**.
[231] **"The Parthians and the Medes"**; here "Parthians and Medes" stand in as geographical place names. Apparently, at times, scribal copyists felt no reluctance in updating geographical place-names in a likely attempt to prevent locations in ancient writings from becoming lost and forgotten due to changes in location place-names over time. This passage envisions a

They shall stir up the kings,
so that a spirit of unrest shall come upon them,
And they shall rouse them from their thrones,[232]

That they may break forth as lions from their lairs,
And as hungry wolves among their flocks.

The City of My Righteous Shall Be a Hindrance

6And they shall go up and tread underfoot the land of His elect ones,
And the land of His elect ones shall be before them a threshing-floor and a highway:
7But the city of my righteous shall be a hindrance to their horses.[233]

Confusion in the Enemies' Ranks

And they shall begin to fight among themselves,
And their right hand shall be strong against themselves,

And a man shall not know his brother,
Nor a son his father or his mother,

Till there be no number of the corpses through their slaughter,
And their punishment be not in vain.

8In those days Sheol shall open its jaws,
And they shall be swallowed up therein,[234]

And their destruction shall be at an end;
Sheol shall devour the sinners in the presence of the elect."

---

prophecy yet future as there are no historical events which fit the details of this description; for instance, in the Parthian invasion of Israel in 40 B.C., Jerusalem was sacked and presented no "hindrance to their horses", as in verse 7, below.

232 **"They shall rouse them from their thrones"**; a couple of passages from Revelation seem to connect the future activity of the evil angels with the same geographical region; is the Euphrates River the region where the angels were bound in Enoch 10, verses 4 and 12? **Revelation 9:14**, Saying to the sixth angel who had the trumpet, "Release the four angels who are bound at the great river Euphrates." So the four angels, who had been prepared for the hour, the day, the month, and the year, were released to kill a third of mankind. **Revelation 16:12**, The sixth angel poured out his bowl on the great river Euphrates, and its water was dried up, to prepare the way for the kings from the east.

233 **"The city of my righteous shall be a hindrance to their horses"; Zechariah 12:2-4**, Behold, I am about to make Jerusalem a cup of staggering to all the surrounding peoples. The siege of Jerusalem will also be against Judah. On that day I will make Jerusalem a heavy stone for all the peoples. All who lift it will surely hurt themselves. And all the nations of the earth will gather against it. On that day, declares the LORD, I will strike every horse with panic, and its rider with madness. But for the sake of the house of Judah I will keep my eyes open, when I strike every horse of the peoples with blindness.

234 **"Sheol shall open its jaws"**; here Sheol is not giving back but swallowing up. **Revelation 20:13**, And the sea gave up the dead who were in it, Death and Hades gave up the dead who were in them, and they were judged, each one of them, according to what they had done. **Enoch 51:1**

57 And it came to pass after this that I saw another host of wagons, and men riding thereon, and coming on the winds from the east, and from the west to the south. [2]And the noise of their wagons was heard, and when this turmoil took place the holy ones from heaven remarked it, and the pillars of the earth were moved from their place, and the sound thereof was heard from the one end of heaven to the other, in one day. [3]And they shall all fall down and worship the Lord of Spirits.

And this is the end of the second Parable.

The Third Oracle: The Elect in the Light of Eternal Life

58 And I began to speak the third Parable[235] concerning the righteous and elect.[236]

[2]Blessed are ye, ye righteous and elect,
For glorious shall be your lot.

[3]And the righteous shall be in the light of the sun,
And the elect in the light of eternal life:[237]
The days of their life shall be unending,
And the days of the holy without number.

[4]And they shall seek the light
and find righteousness with the Lord of Spirits:
There shall be peace to the righteous in the name of the Eternal Lord.

[5]And after this it shall be said to the holy in heaven
That they should seek out the secrets of righteousness,
the heritage of faith:
For it has become bright as the sun upon earth,
And the darkness is past.[238]

[6]And there shall be a light that never endeth,
And to a number of days they shall not come,[239]
For the darkness shall first have been destroyed,
And the light established before the Lord of Spirits

[235] **"The third parable"**; the use of the word parable here and elsewhere in the book is uncommon and should be understood as synonymous with "oracle" or "prophecy". The Dead Sea Scrolls have "oracle" in **Enoch 1:3**. The three "parables" in the *Book of the Parables*, are found in **Enoch 38:1, 45:1, 58:1**

[236] **Enoch 1:3**

[237] **"The elect shall be in the light of eternal life"**; **John 1:4**, In him was life, and the life was the light of men. **John 8:12**, Again Jesus spoke to them, saying, "I am the light of the world. Whoever follows me will not walk in darkness, but will have the light of life."

[238] **"The darkness is past"**; **Romans 13:12**, The night is far gone; the day is at hand. **1 John 2:8**, The darkness is passing away and the true light is already shining.

[239] **"And to a number of days they shall not come"**, in other words, due to their longevity, their days cannot be numbered.

And the light of uprightness established
for ever before the Lord of Spirits.

Preview of the Geocentric Calendar Book

59 In those days mine eyes saw the secrets of the lightnings,[240] and of the lights, and the judgments they execute: and they lighten for a blessing or a curse as the Lord of Spirits willeth. [2]And there I saw the secrets of the thunder,[241] and how when it resounds above in the heaven, the sound thereof is heard, and he caused me to see the judgments executed on the earth, whether they be for well-being and blessing, or for a curse according to the word of the Lord of Spirits.

[3]And after that all the secrets of the lights and lightnings were shown to me, and they lighten for blessing and for satisfying.

The Book of Noah
Noah Completes the Book of the Parables

60 In the year 500, in the seventh month, on the fourteenth day of the month in the life of Enoch.[242] In that Parable[243] I saw how a mighty quaking made the heaven of heavens to quake, and the host of the Most High, and the angels, a thousand thousands and ten thousand times ten thousand, [244] were disquieted with a great disquiet.

[2]And the Head of Days sat on the throne of His glory,[245] and the angels and the righteous stood around Him.

---

[240] **"The secrets of the lightnings"**; **Job 36:29-30**, Can anyone understand the spreading of the clouds, the thunderings of his pavilion? Behold, he scatters his lightning about him and covers the roots of the sea. **Enoch 18:1** and **41:3**

[241] **"The secrets of the thunder"**; **Revelation 10:3-4**, He called out with a loud voice, like a lion roaring. When he called out, the seven thunders sounded. And when the seven thunders had sounded, I was about to write, but I heard a voice from heaven saying, "Seal up what the seven thunders have said, and *do not write it down.*"

[242] **"In the year 500...in the life of Enoch"**; the writer of **Enoch 60:1-71:17,** is identified as Noah in v. 8 below. Noah and Enoch were not contemporaries. "Year 500 in the life of Enoch" is 135 years after Enoch was translated, per Genesis 5:23-24, "Thus all the days of Enoch were 365 years. Enoch walked with God, and he was not, for God took him." Noah, the writer in this passage, is here measuring time from the birth of Enoch who is still alive though already translated to heaven. Noah was born after the translation of Enoch, and would have been in his mid-60's in the 500th year of Enoch.

[243] **"In that parable"**, in other words, the third parable, or oracle, of Enoch's *Book of the Parables*. The third parable of the book is completed by Noah himself. Enoch 68:1, relates the *Book of the Parables* was turned over to Noah by Enoch.

[244] **"A thousand thousands"**; **Daniel 7:10**, A thousand thousands served him, and ten thousand times ten thousand stood before him. **Revelation 5:11**, I heard around the throne and the living creatures and the elders the voice of many angels, numbering myriads of myriads and thousands of thousands. **Enoch 14:22, 40:1, 71:8, 71:12**

[245] **"The Head of Days sat on the throne of His glory"**; **Daniel 7:9**, As I looked, thrones were placed, and the Ancient of Days took his seat; his clothing was white as snow, and the hair of his head like pure wool; his throne was fiery flames; its wheels were burning fire.

[3]And a great trembling seized me,
And fear took hold of me,
And my loins gave way,
And dissolved were my reins,
And I fell upon my face.[246]

[4]And Michael sent another angel from among the holy ones and he raised me up, and when he had raised me up my spirit returned; for I had not been able to endure the look of this host, and the commotion and the quaking of the heaven. [5]And Michael said unto me: "Why art thou disquieted with such a vision? Until this day lasted the day of His mercy; and He hath been merciful and long-suffering towards those who dwell on the earth. [6]And when the day, and the power, and the punishment, and the judgment come, which the Lord of Spirits hath prepared for those who worship not the righteous law, and for those who deny the righteous judgment, and for those who take His name in vain-[247] that day is prepared, for the elect a covenant, but for sinners an inquisition."

Discourse On Leviathan and Behemoth

[7]And on that day were two monsters parted, a female monster named Leviathan,[248] to dwell in the abysses of the ocean over the fountains of the waters. [8]But the male is named Behemoth,[249] who occupied with his breast a waste wilderness named Duidain,[250] on the east of the garden where the elect and righteous dwell, where my grandfather[251] was taken up, the seventh from Adam,[252] the first man whom the Lord of Spirits created. [9]And I besought the other angel that he should show me the might of those monsters, how they were parted on one day and cast, the

---

[246] **"I fell upon my face"; Daniel 8:17-18**, So he came near where I stood. And when he came, *I was frightened and fell on my face*. But he said to me, "Understand, O son of man, that the vision is for the time of the end." And when he had spoken to me, *I fell into a deep sleep with my face to the ground*. But he touched me and made me stand up.
[247] **"Those who take His name in vain"; Exodus 20:7**, You shall not take the name of the LORD your God *in vain*, for the LORD will not hold him guiltless who takes his name in vain.
[248] **"A female monster named Leviathan"; Job 41:1**, Can you draw out Leviathan with a fishhook or press down his tongue with a cord?
[249] **"The male is named Behemoth"; Job 40:15**, Behold, Behemoth, which I made as I made you; he eats grass like an ox.
[250] **"A waste wilderness named Duidain"**; in the available manuscripts this place-name in Enoch 60:8, has various spellings. This is likely the same location as "Dudael" in Enoch 10:4; this is the locale for the abyss into which Azazel was cast. If so, Leviathan is in "the abysses of the ocean" (v.7), and Behemoth is in the abyss in a "waste wilderness" on land. It is interesting to note in this light that John in the *Book of Revelation* chapter 13, reports seeing a vision of two beasts which arise one from the sea and the other from the land which come up to cause trouble for those who dwell on earth in the last days. If we identify the beasts in Enoch 60, with those found in Revelation 13, then Leviathan could represent the political system from which the Antichrist will arise, and Behemoth would represent the religious system from which the False Prophet will arise.
[251] **"My grandfather was taken up"**; in both the *Book of Genesis* and the *Book of Enoch*, Enoch and Noah share characteristics in common. A quality unique to these men we are told is they both "walked with God" (Genesis 5:24 and 6:9). In the *Book of Enoch*, both Enoch and Noah share the experience of visiting heaven for the purpose of receiving revelation. See chapter 71 for Noah's visit to heaven.
[252] **"The seventh from Adam"; Jude 1:14**, Enoch, *the seventh from Adam*, prophesied.

one into the abysses of the sea, and the other unto the dry land of the wilderness.

[10]And he said to me: "Thou son of man,[253] herein thou dost seek to know what is hidden."

[11]And the other angel who went with me and showed me what was hidden told me what is first and last in the heaven in the height, and beneath the earth in the depth, and at the ends of the heaven, and on the foundation of the heaven. [12]And the chambers of the winds, and how the winds are divided, and how they are weighed, and how the portals of the winds are reckoned, each according to the power of the wind, and the power of the lights of the moon, and according to the power that is fitting: and the divisions of the stars according to their names, and how all the divisions are divided. [13]And the thunders according to the places where they fall, and all the divisions that are made among the lightnings that it may lighten, and their host that they may at once obey. [14]For the thunder has places of rest which are assigned to it while it is waiting for its peal; and the thunder and lightning are inseparable, and although not one and undivided, they both go together through the spirit and separate not. [15]For when the lightning lightens, the thunder utters its voice, and the spirit enforces a pause during the peal, and divides equally between them; for the treasury of their peals is like the sand, and each one of them as it peals is held in with a bridle, and turned back by the power of the spirit, and pushed forward according to the many quarters of the earth.

[16]And the spirit of the sea is masculine and strong, and according to the might of his strength he draws it back with a rein, and in like manner it is driven forward and disperses amid all the mountains of the earth.

[17]And the spirit of the hoar-frost is his own angel, and the spirit of the hail is a good angel. [18]And the spirit of the snow has forsaken his chambers on account of his strength- There is a special spirit therein, and that which ascends from it is like smoke, and its name is frost. [19]And the spirit of the mist is not united with them in their chambers, but it has a special chamber; for its course is glorious both in light and in darkness, and in winter and in summer, and in its chamber is an angel. [20]And the spirit of the dew has its dwelling at the ends of the heaven, and is connected with the chambers of the rain, and its course is in winter and summer: and its clouds and the clouds of the mist are connected, and the one gives to the other. [21]And when the spirit of the rain goes forth from its chamber, the angels come and open the chamber and lead it out, and when it is diffused over the whole earth it unites with the water on the earth. And whensoever it unites with the water on the earth... For the waters are for those who dwell on the earth; [22]for they are

[253] **"Thou son of man"**; here and elsewhere in ancient Jewish literature "son of man" is a title applied to the prophets of God, to emphasize their humanity and mortality. When used to describe Messiah, the term highlights the human nature of God incarnated as a man.

nourishment for the earth from the Most High who is in heaven: therefore there is a measure for the rain, and the angels take it in charge.

[23]And these things I saw towards the Garden of the Righteous.[254]

[24]And the angel of peace who was with me said to me: "These two monsters, prepared conformably to the greatness of God, shall feed... [25]When the punishment of the Lord of Spirits shall rest upon them, it shall rest in order that the punishment of the Lord of Spirits may not come in vain, and it shall slay the children with their mothers and the children with their fathers. Afterwards the judgment shall take place according to His mercy and His patience."

The Angels Measure Paradise

61 And I saw in those days how long cords were given to those angels, and they took to themselves wings and flew[255], and they went towards the north. [2]And I asked the angel, saying unto him: "Why have those angels taken these cords and gone off?"

And he said unto me: "They have gone to measure."[256]

[3]And the angel who went with me said unto me:
"These shall bring the measures of the righteous,[257]
And the ropes of the righteous to the righteous,
That they may stay themselves on the name of the Lord of Spirits for ever and ever.

[4]The elect shall begin to dwell with the elect,
And those are the measures which shall be given to faith
And which shall strengthen righteousness.

[5]And these measures shall reveal
all the secrets of the depths of the earth,
And those who have been destroyed by the desert,
And those who have been devoured by the beasts,
And those who have been devoured by the fish of the sea,

That they may return and stay themselves
On the day of the Elect One;

---

[254] **"The Garden of the Righteous"; Enoch 32:3, 60:8+23, 61:12, 77:3**
[255] **"And they took to themselves wings and flew"**; one is hard-pressed to find any reference in all the Jewish literature before the Christian era in which angels are portrayed as having wings. Instead, angels are universally seen as appearing as young men. Seraphim have wings as do Cherubim, angels however, are not portrayed as having wings. In fact, this passage leaves the impression this was only temporary when it says, "they took to themselves wings".
[256] **"They have gone to measure"**; what they measure is clearly described in **Enoch 70:3** as, "The angels took the cords to measure for me the place for the elect and righteous"; the final home of the righteous is in view. This is echoed in Revelation 21:15, below,
[257] **Revelation 21:15**, And the one who spoke with me had a measuring rod of gold to measure the city and its gates and walls.

For none shall be destroyed before the Lord of Spirits,
And none can be destroyed.

6And all who dwell above in the heaven received a command and power and one voice and one light like unto fire.

7And that One with their first words they blessed,
And extolled and lauded with wisdom,
And they were wise in utterance and in the spirit of life.

8And the Lord of Spirits placed the Elect One on the throne of glory.[258]
And he shall judge all the works of the holy above in the heaven,
And in the balance shall their deeds be weighed.[259]

9And when he shall lift up his countenance
To judge their secret ways according to the
word of the name of the Lord of Spirits,
And their path according to the way of the
righteous judgment of the Lord of Spirits,
Then shall they all with one voice speak and bless,
And glorify and extol and sanctify the name of the Lord of Spirits.

10And He will summon all the host of the heavens, and all the holy ones above, and the host of God, the Cherubin, Seraphin and Ophannin,[260] and all the angels of power, and all the angels of principalities,[261] 11and the Elect One, and the other powers on the earth and over the water. On that day shall raise one voice, and bless and glorify and exalt in the spirit of faith, and in the spirit of wisdom,[262] and in the spirit of patience, and in the spirit of mercy, and in the spirit of judgment and of peace, and in the spirit of goodness, and shall all say with one voice: "Blessed is He, and may the name of the Lord of Spirits be blessed for ever and ever."[263]

---

[258] **"The Lord of Spirits placed the Elect One on the Throne of Glory"; Enoch 55:4**
[259] **"In the balance shall their deeds be weighed"**; **1 Samuel 2:3**, The LORD is a God of knowledge, and by him actions are weighed.
[260] **"Cherubin, Seraphin and Ophannin"**; or, Cherubim, Seraphim and Ophanim; these are different classes of heavenly creatures. Ophanim, is a Hebrew loan word in Ethiopic, meaning wheels; these are the living wheels with eyes detailed in **Ezekiel 1:16-18**, As for the appearance of the wheels and their construction: their appearance was like the gleaming of beryl. See also **Enoch 71:7**
[261] **"Angels of power, and angels of principalities"; 1 Peter 3:21-22**, Jesus Christ, who has gone into heaven and is at the right hand of God, with angels, authorities, and powers having been subjected to him. **Ephesians 6:12**, For we wrestle not against flesh and blood, but against principalities, against powers, against the rulers of the darkness of this world, against spiritual wickedness in high places. (KJV)
[262] **"The Spirit of wisdom"**; **Isaiah 11:2**, And the Spirit of the LORD shall rest upon him, the Spirit of wisdom and understanding, the Spirit of counsel and might, the Spirit of knowledge and the fear of the LORD. **Enoch 49:3**
[263] **"Blessed for ever and ever"; Daniel 2:20**, Blessed be the name of God forever and ever, to whom belong wisdom and might.

[12]All who sleep not above in heaven shall bless Him:
All the holy ones who are in heaven shall bless Him.
And all the elect who dwell in the garden of life:

And every spirit of light who is able to bless,
And glorify, and extol, and hallow Thy blessed name,
And all flesh shall beyond measure glorify and bless Thy name for ever and ever.

[13]For great is the mercy of the Lord of Spirits, and He is long-suffering,
And all His works and all that He has created
He has revealed to the righteous and elect
In the name of the Lord of Spirits."

The Judgment of the "Mighty Men of Renown"

62 And thus the Lord commanded the kings and the mighty and the exalted, and those who dwell on the earth, and said: "Open your eyes and lift up your horns if ye are able to recognize the Elect One."[264]

[2]And the Lord of Spirits seated him on the throne of His glory,
And the spirit of righteousness was poured out upon him,
And the word of his mouth slays all the sinners,[265]
And all the unrighteous are destroyed from before his face.[266]
[3]And there shall stand up in that day all the kings and the mighty,[267]
And the exalted and those who hold the earth,
And they shall see and recognize
How he sits on the throne of his glory,

---

[264] **"Open your eyes"**; The judgment of the "the kings and the mighty and the exalted and those who rule the earth", (Enoch 62:9) is in view here; they're the ones who at a later date Moses will call the "mighty men who were of old, the men of renown". Their final judgment occurs after the 1,000-year reign of Christ on earth when all who are left in the Abyss are transferred to the lake of fire. Though we know there are many, many others who will be gathered around the great white throne for judgment, Enoch narrowly discusses the judgment of the Watchers' beloved ones on that day throughout the *Book of the Parables*. Altogether, the Watcher offspring pass through three phases of their condemnation and judgment: 1. In history they were judged by war. In Enoch 10:9-10, Archangel Gabriel incites them to civil war which decimated their ranks over a period of 120-years before the flood; 2. in the present time, they are condemned to be unclean spirits causing trouble in the world of mankind. (Enoch 15:8-16:1); 3. in the future, they will stand before the great white throne where final sentencing will take place at which time they will take their place in eternal flames. (Enoch 62:1-12)

[265] **"The word of his mouth slays the sinners"; Revelation 1:16**, From his mouth came a sharp two-edged sword. **Revelation 19:15**, From his mouth comes a sharp sword with which to strike down the nations, and he will rule them with a rod of iron. **Revelation 19:21**, And the rest were slain by the sword that came from the mouth of him who was sitting on the horse, and all the birds were gorged with their flesh.

[266] **"Destroyed from before his face"; 2 Thessalonians 2:8**, And then the lawless one will be revealed, whom the Lord Jesus will kill with the breath of his mouth and bring to nothing by the appearance of his coming.

[267] **"There shall stand up in that day all the kings"; Isaiah 24:21**, On that day the LORD will punish the host of heaven, in heaven, and the kings of the earth, on the earth.

And righteousness is judged before him,
And no lying word is spoken before him.

[4]Then shall pain come upon them as on a woman in travail,[268]
And she has pain in bringing forth
When her child enters the mouth of the womb,
And she has pain in bringing forth.

[5]And one portion of them shall look on the other,
And they shall be terrified,
And they shall be downcast of countenance,
And pain shall seize them,
When they see that Son of Man[269]
Sitting on the throne of his glory.[270]

[6]And the kings and the mighty and all who possess the earth shall bless and glorify and extol him who rules over all, who was hidden.

[7]For from the beginning the Son of Man was hidden,[271]
And the Most High preserved him in the presence of His might,
And revealed him to the elect.

The Congregation of the Righteous Vindicated

[8]And the congregation of the elect and holy[272] shall be sown.
And all the elect shall stand before him on that day.

[9]And all the kings and the mighty
and the exalted and those who rule the earth
Shall fall down before him on their faces,[273]
And worship and set their hope upon that Son of Man,
And petition him and supplicate for mercy at his hands.

---

[268] **"As on a woman in travail"; 1 Thessalonians 5:3**, While people are saying, "There is peace and security," then sudden destruction will come upon them as labor pains come upon a pregnant woman, and they will not escape.
[269] **"Pain shall seize them, when they see that Son of Man"**; **Revelation 6:15-16**, Then the kings of the earth and the great ones and the generals and the rich and the powerful, and everyone, slave and free, hid themselves in the caves and among the rocks of the mountains, calling to the mountains and rocks, "Fall on us and hide us from the face of him who is seated on the throne, and from the wrath of the Lamb!"
[270] **"Sitting on the throne of his glory"**; **Matthew 25:31**, When the Son of Man comes in his glory, and all the angels with him, then he will sit on his glorious throne.
[271] **"From the beginning the Son of Man was hidden"; Colossians 1:26-27**, The mystery hidden for ages and generations but now revealed to his saints. To them God chose to make known how great among the Gentiles are the riches of the glory of this mystery, which is Christ in you, the hope of glory. **Enoch 69:26**
[272] **"The congregation of the elect and holy", Enoch 38:1, 46:8, 53:6**
[273] **"Shall fall down before him"**; **Philippians 2:9-11**, God has highly exalted him and bestowed on him the name that is above every name, so that at the name of Jesus every knee should bow, in heaven and on earth and under the earth, and every tongue confess that Jesus Christ is Lord, to the glory of God the Father.

[10]Nevertheless that Lord of Spirits will so press them
That they shall hastily go forth from His presence,[274]
And their faces shall be filled with shame,[275]
And the darkness grow deeper on their faces.

[11]And He will deliver them to the angels for punishment,
To execute vengeance on them because
They have oppressed His children and His elect [276]
[12]And they shall be a spectacle for the righteous and for His elect:
They shall rejoice over them,
Because the wrath of the Lord of Spirits resteth upon them,
And His sword is drunk with their blood.[277]

[13]And the righteous and elect shall be saved on that day,
And they shall never thenceforward see the face of the sinners and unrighteous.

[14]And the Lord of Spirits will abide over them,[278]
And with that Son of Man shall they eat[279]
And lie down and rise up for ever and ever.[280]

[15]And the righteous and elect shall have risen from the earth,[281]
And ceased to be of downcast countenance.

Garments of Glory

And they shall have been clothed with garments of glory,[282]
[16]And these shall be the garments of life from the Lord of Spirits:[283]
And your garments shall not grow old,
Nor your glory pass away before the Lord of Spirits.

---

[274] **"They shall hastily go forth from His presence"**; **2 Thessalonians 1:9**, They will suffer the punishment of eternal destruction, away from the presence of the Lord and from the glory of his might.
[275] **"Faces filled with shame"**; **Enoch 63:11**
[276] **"They have oppressed His children"**; **Enoch 46:8, 53:6**
[277] **"His sword is drunk with their blood"; Isaiah 34:6**, The LORD has a sword; it is sated with blood.
[278] **"The Lord of Spirits shall abide over them"**; **Psalm 91:1**, He who dwells in the shelter of the Most High will abide in the shadow of the Almighty.
[279] **"With that Son of Man they shall eat"**; **Matthew 26:29**, I tell you I will not drink again of this fruit of the vine until that day when I drink it new with you in my Father's kingdom.
[280] **"And lie down and rise up for ever"; Psalm 23:1+6**, The LORD is my shepherd; I shall not want. *He makes me lie down* in green pastures. Surely goodness and mercy shall follow me all the days of my life, and I shall dwell in the house of the LORD forever.
[281] **"The righteous and elect shall have risen from the earth"**; **1 Thessalonians 4:17**, Then we who are alive, who are left, will be caught up together with them in the clouds to meet the Lord in the air, and so we will always be with the Lord.
[282] **"Clothed with garments of glory"**; **Revelation 3:5**, The one who conquers will be clothed thus in white garments. **Revelation 19:8**, It was granted her to clothe herself with fine linen, bright and pure— for the fine linen is the righteous deeds of the saints.
[283] **"The garments of life"; 2 Corinthians 5:1-2**, We know that if the tent that is our earthly home is destroyed, we have a building from God, a house not made with hands, eternal in the heavens. For in this tent we groan, longing to put on our heavenly dwelling.

Every Knee Shall Bow, Every Tongue Confess

63 In those days shall the mighty and the kings who possess the earth implore Him to grant them a little respite from His angels of punishment to whom they were delivered,[284] that they might fall down and worship before the Lord of Spirits, and confess their sins before Him. [2]And they shall bless and glorify the Lord of Spirits, and say:

"Blessed is the Lord of Spirits and the Lord of kings,
And the Lord of the mighty and the Lord of the rich,
And the Lord of glory and the Lord of wisdom,
[3]And splendid in every secret thing
is Thy power from generation to generation,
And Thy glory for ever and ever:

Deep are all Thy secrets and innumerable,
And Thy righteousness is beyond reckoning.

[4]We have now learnt that we should glorify
And bless the Lord of kings and Him who is king over all kings."[285]
[5]And they shall say:
"Would that we had rest to glorify and give thanks
And confess our faith before His glory!

[6]And now we long for a little rest but find it not:
We follow hard upon and obtain it not:

And light has vanished from before us,
And darkness is our dwelling-place for ever and ever:

[7]For we have not believed before Him
Nor glorified the name of the Lord of Spirits, nor glorified our Lord

But our hope was in the scepter of our kingdom,[286]
And in our glory.

[8]And in the day of our suffering and tribulation He saves us not,
And we find no respite for confession

---

[284] **"Implore Him to grant them a little respite"**; like their Watcher parents before them in Enoch 14:4, here the kings of the earth wish the opportunity to repent be granted them by God. Also like their parents before them, no repentance or forgiveness is given. As the Biblical record progressed, it would become apparent that the possibility of repentance would be a unique gift given only to the children of mankind.

[285] **"Him who is king over all kings"; Revelation 17:14**, He is Lord of lords and King of kings. **Revelation 19:16**, On his robe and on his thigh he has a name written, King of kings and Lord of lords.

[286] **"Our hope was in the scepter of our kingdom"; Jeremiah 17:5**, Thus says the LORD: "Cursed is the man who trusts in man and makes flesh his strength, whose heart turns away from the LORD."

That our Lord is true in all His works,
and in His judgments and His justice,
And His judgments have no respect of persons.[287]

[9]And we pass away from before His face on account of our works,
And all our sins are reckoned up in righteousness."

[10]Now they shall say unto themselves: "Our souls are full of unrighteous gain, but it does not prevent us from descending from the midst thereof into the burden of Sheol."

[11]And after that their faces shall be filled with darkness
And shame before that Son of Man,
And they shall be driven from his presence,[288]
And the sword shall abide before his face in their midst.

[12]Thus spake the Lord of Spirits: "This is the ordinance and judgment with respect to the mighty and the kings and the exalted and those who possess the earth before the Lord of Spirits."

64 And other forms I saw hidden in that place. [2]I heard the voice of the angel saying: "These are the angels who descended to the earth, and revealed what was hidden to the children of men and seduced the children of men into committing sin."

Noah Speaks with Enoch

65 And in those days Noah saw the earth that it had sunk down and its destruction was nigh. [2]And he arose from thence and went to the ends of the earth,[289] and cried aloud to his grandfather Enoch: and Noah said three times with an embittered voice: "Hear me, hear me, hear me."

[3]And I said unto him: "Tell me what it is that is falling out on the earth that the earth is in such evil plight and shaken, lest perchance I shall perish with it?"

[4]And thereupon there was a great commotion on the earth, and a voice was heard from heaven, and I fell on my face.

[5]And Enoch my grandfather came and stood by me, and said unto me: "Why hast thou cried unto me with a bitter cry and weeping? [6]And a

---

[287] **"No respect of persons" ; Romans 2:11**, There is *no respect of persons* with God. (KJV)
[288] **"Driven from his presence"; 2 Thessalonians 1:9**, They will suffer the punishment of eternal destruction, away from the presence of the Lord and from the glory of his might.
[289] **"He arose and went to the ends of the earth"**; This is one of two occasions on which Enoch visits the earth after his translation to heaven. Perhaps Noah's trip to the "ends of the earth" is idiomatic for traveling to the top of a tall mountain. Once there, Noah meets Enoch in similar fashion to when the Lord Jesus met with Moses and Elijah on the Mount of Transfiguration. In **Enoch 106:8**, we have what was a yet earlier occurrence when Methuselah too sought Enoch at the "ends of the earth".

command has gone forth from the presence of the Lord concerning those who dwell on the earth that their ruin is accomplished because[290] they have learnt all the secrets of the angels, and all the violence of the satans, and all their powers- the most secret ones- and all the power of those who practice sorcery, and the power of witchcraft, and the power of those who make molten images for the whole earth: 7And how silver is produced from the dust of the earth, and how soft metal originates in the earth. 8For lead and tin are not produced from the earth like the first: it is a fountain that produces them, and an angel stands therein, and that angel is pre-eminent."

9And after that my grandfather Enoch took hold of me by my hand and raised me up, and said unto me: "Go, for I have asked the Lord of Spirits as touching this commotion on the earth. 10And He said unto me: 'Because of their unrighteousness their judgment has been determined upon and shall not be withheld by Me for ever. Because of the sorceries which they have searched out and learnt, the earth and those who dwell upon it shall be destroyed.'

11"And these- they have no place of repentance for ever, because they have shown them what was hidden, and they are the damned: but as for thee, my son, the Lord of Spirits knows that thou art pure, and guiltless of this reproach concerning the secrets.

12"And He has destined thy name to be among the holy,
And will preserve thee amongst those who dwell on the earth,
And has destined thy righteous seed
both for kingship and for great honors,
✡ And from thy seed shall proceed a fountain of the righteous and holy without number for ever."[291]

66 And after that he showed me the angels of punishment who are prepared to come and let loose all the powers of the waters which are beneath in the earth in order to bring judgment and destruction on all who abide and dwell on the earth. 2And the Lord of Spirits gave commandment to the angels who were going forth, that they should not cause the waters to rise but should hold them in check; for those angels were over the powers of the waters.

3And I went away from the presence of Enoch.

---

290 **"Their ruin is accomplished because"**; The criticism is sometimes made that the *Book of Enoch* contradicts the Bible by stating the flood came as judgment for the sin of the angels and their offspring. However, this passage clearly shows that the *Book of Enoch*, like the Bible, states the flood is coming because of the sins of mankind. In this passage mankind has learned "violence, sorcery, witchcraft and idolatry" from the sinning angels. Here, as in the Bible, though Satan's part is clear, mankind is to be judged for their own guilt and responsibility for sin.

291 ✡ **"From thy seed shall proceed a fountain of the righteous"**; it is Jesus the Messiah, who is the fountain of the righteous, descended from Noah through Abraham, Isaac and Jacob.

The Judgment of Noah's Day Approaches

67 And in those days the word of God came unto me, and He said unto me: "Noah, thy lot has come up before Me, a lot without blame,[292] a lot of love and uprightness.

[2]"And now the angels are making a wooden building, and when they have completed that task I will place My hand upon it and preserve it, and there shall come forth from it the seed of life, and a change shall set in so that the earth will not remain without inhabitant. [3]And I will make fast thy seed before me for ever and ever, and I will spread abroad those who dwell with thee: it shall not be unfruitful on the face of the earth, but it shall be blessed and multiply on the earth in the name of the Lord."

[4]And He will imprison those angels, who have shown unrighteousness, in that burning valley which my grandfather Enoch had formerly shown to me in the west among the mountains of gold and silver and iron and soft metal and tin. [5]And I saw that valley in which there was a great convulsion and a convulsion of the waters. [6]And when all this took place, from that fiery molten metal and from the convulsion thereof in that place, there was produced a smell of sulphur, and it was connected with those waters, and that valley of the angels who had led astray mankind burned beneath that land. [7]And through its valleys proceed streams of fire, where these angels are punished[293] who had led astray those who dwell upon the earth.[294]

[8]But those waters shall in those days serve for the kings and the mighty and the exalted, and those who dwell on the earth, for the healing of the body, but for the punishment of the spirit; now their spirit is full of lust, that they may be punished in their body, for they have denied the Lord of Spirits and see their punishment daily, and yet believe not in His name. [9]And in proportion as the burning of their bodies becomes severe, a corresponding change shall take place in their spirit for ever and ever; for before the Lord of Spirits none shall utter an idle word. [10]For the judgment shall come upon them, because they believe in the lust of their body and deny the Spirit of the Lord.

[11]And those same waters will undergo a change in those days; for when those angels are punished in these waters, these water-springs shall change their temperature, and when the angels ascend, this water of the springs shall change and become cold.

---

[292] **"A lot without blame"; Genesis 6:9**, These are the generations of Noah. Noah was a righteous man, blameless in his generation. Noah walked with God.
[293] **"Where these angels are punished"; Matthew 25:41**, Then he will say to those on his left, "Depart from me, you cursed, into the eternal fire prepared for the devil and his angels."
[294] **"Who had led astray those who dwell upon the earth"; Revelation 13:12**, It makes the earth and its inhabitants worship the first beast. **Revelation 13:14**, By the signs that it is allowed to work in the presence of the beast it deceives those who dwell on earth. **Enoch 54:6, 67:1**

[12]And I heard Michael answering and saying: "This judgment wherewith the angels are judged is a testimony for the kings and the mighty who possess the earth. [13]Because these waters of judgment minister to the healing of the body of the kings and the lust of their body; therefore they will not see and will not believe that those waters will change and become a fire which burns for ever."

The Book of the Parables Preserved by Noah

68 And after that my grandfather Enoch gave me the teaching of all the secrets in the book in the Parables which had been given to him, and he put them together for me in the words of the *Book of the Parables.*[295]

[2]And on that day Michael answered Raphael and said: "The power of the spirit transports and makes me to tremble because of the severity of the judgment of the secrets, the judgment of the angels: who can endure the severe judgment which has been executed, and before which they melt away?"

[3]And Michael answered again, and said to Raphael: "Who is he whose heart is not softened concerning it, and whose reins are not troubled by this word of judgment that has gone forth upon them because of those who have thus led them out?"

[4]And it came to pass when he stood before the Lord of Spirits, Michael said thus to Raphael: "I will not take their part under the eye of the Lord; for the Lord of Spirits has been angry with them because they do as if they were the Lord.[296] [5]Therefore all that is hidden shall come upon them for ever and ever; for neither angel nor man shall have his portion in it, but alone they have received their judgment for ever and ever."

A Litany of the Angels' Sins

69 And after this judgment they shall terrify and make them to tremble because they have shown this to those who dwell on the earth.

[2]And behold the names of those angels and these are their names: the first of them is Samjaza, the second Artaqifa, and the third Armen, the fourth Kokabel, the fifth Turael, the sixth Rumjal, the seventh Danjal,

---

[295] **"The Book of the Parables"**; Here the origin and transmission history of the *Book of the Parables* is distinguished among the five books of Enoch. Books 3, 4 and 5 are explicitly stated to have been handed off by Enoch to his son Methuselah, and we can assume the same for book 1, though it is unstated. The *Book of the Parables*, however, is shown to have been written by Enoch after his translation and later given to Noah who then completed the book by writing chapters 60-71.

[296] **"They do as if they were the Lord"**, in other words the sinning angels act like gods. **Isaiah 14:13-14**, You said in your heart, "I will ascend to heaven; above the stars of God I will set my throne on high; I will sit on the mount of assembly in the far reaches of the north; I will ascend above the heights of the clouds; I will make myself like the Most High."

the eighth Neqael, the ninth Baraqel, the tenth Azazel, the eleventh Armaros, the twelfth Batarjal, the thirteenth Busasejal, the fourteenth Hananel, the fifteenth Turel, and the sixteenth Simapesiel, the seventeenth Jetrel, the eighteenth Tumael, the nineteenth Turel, the twentieth Rumael, the twenty-first Azazel.

[3]And these are the chiefs of their angels and their names, and their chief ones over hundreds and over fifties and over tens.

[4]The name of the first Jeqon: that is, the one who led astray all the sons of God, and brought them down to the earth, and led them astray through the daughters of men.

[5]And the second was named Asbeel: he imparted to the holy sons of God evil counsel, and led them astray so that they defiled their bodies with the daughters of men.

[6]And the third was named Gadreel: he it is who showed the children of men all the blows of death, and he led astray Eve, and showed the weapons of death to the sons of men the shield and the coat of mail, and the sword for battle, and all the weapons of death to the children of men. [7]And from his hand they have proceeded against those who dwell on the earth from that day and for evermore.

[8]And the fourth was named Penemue: he taught the children of men the bitter and the sweet, and he taught them all the secrets of their wisdom. [9]And he instructed mankind in writing with ink and paper,[297] and thereby many sinned from eternity to eternity and until this day. [10]For men were not created for such a purpose, to give confirmation to their good faith with pen and ink. [11]For men were created exactly like the angels, to the intent that they should continue pure and righteous, and death, which destroys everything, could not have taken hold of them, but through this their knowledge they are perishing, and through this power it is consuming me.

The Watchers Teach Abortion

[12]And the fifth was named Kasdeja: this is he who showed the children of men all the wicked smitings of spirits and demons, and the smitings of the embryo in the womb, that it may pass away, and the smitings of the soul the bites of the serpent, and the smitings which befall through the noontide heat, the son of the serpent named Tabaet.

[13]And this is the task of Kasbeel, the chief of the oath which he showed to the holy ones when he dwelt high above in glory, and its name is Biqa.

---

[297] **"He instructed mankind in writing with ink and paper"**; here and in other passages, an otherwise innocent technology is communicated to mankind for corrupt purposes. Enoch himself is contrasted with the misuse of writing in that he is referred to as a "scribe of righteousness", in Enoch 12:3 and 15:1. This is the only location in the book where writing with ink and paper is mentioned, and may be an apparent anachronism. All other references to the medium of writing in the *Book of Enoch* refer to writing on "tablets".

[14]This angel requested Michael to show him the hidden name, that he might enunciate it in the oath, so that those might quake before that name and oath who revealed all that was in secret to the children of men. [15]And this is the power of this oath, for it is powerful and strong, and he placed this oath Akae in the hand of Michael.

[16]And these are the secrets of this oath...
And they are strong through his oath:
And the heaven was suspended before the world was created,
And for ever.

[17]And through it the earth was founded upon the water,[298]
And from the secret recesses of the mountains come beautiful waters,
From the creation of the world and unto eternity.

[18]And through that oath the sea was created,
And as its foundation He set for it the sand
against the time of its anger,
And it dare not pass beyond it from the creation of the world
unto eternity.

[19]And through that oath are the depths made fast,
And abide and stir not from their place from eternity to eternity.

[20]And through that oath the sun and moon complete their course,
And deviate not from their ordinance from eternity to eternity.

[21]And through that oath the stars complete their course,
And He calls them by their names,
And they answer Him from eternity to eternity.

The Four Winds

[22]And in like manner the spirits of the water, and of the winds, and of all zephyrs, and their paths from all the quarters of the winds.[299] [23]And there are preserved the voices of the thunder and the light of the lightnings: and there are preserved the chambers of the hail and the chambers of the hoar-frost, and the chambers of the mist, and the chambers of the rain and the dew. [24]And all these believe and give thanks before the Lord of Spirits, and glorify Him with all their power, and their food is in every act of thanksgiving: they thank and glorify and extol the name of the Lord of Spirits for ever and ever.

---

[298] **"The earth was founded upon the water"**; **Psalm 24:1-2**, The earth is the LORD's and the fullness thereof, the world and those who dwell therein, for *he has founded it upon the seas and established it upon the rivers.*

[299] **"The quarters of the winds"**; **Revelation 7:1**, After this I saw four angels standing at the four corners of the earth, holding back the four winds of the earth.

25And this oath is mighty over them,
And through it they are preserved and their paths are preserved,[300]
And their course is not destroyed.

The Son of Man is Seated on His Glorious Throne

26And there was great joy amongst them,
And they blessed and glorified and extolled
Because the name of that Son of Man had been revealed unto them.[301] ✡

27And he sat on the throne of his glory,
And the sum of judgment was given unto the Son of Man,[302]
And he caused the sinners to pass away and be destroyed from off the face of the earth,
And those who have led the world astray.

28With chains shall they be bound,[303]
And in their assemblage-place of destruction shall they be imprisoned,[304]
And all their works vanish from the face of the earth.
29And from henceforth there shall be nothing corruptible;

For that Son of Man has appeared,
And has seated himself on the throne of his glory,
And all evil shall pass away before his face,
And the word of that Son of Man shall go forth[305]
And be strong before the Lord of Spirits.

This is the third Parable of Enoch.

---

300 **"Through it they are preserved"; Hebrews 1:3**, He upholds the universe by the word of his power.
301 ✡ **"That Son of Man had been revealed unto them"**; here the redeemed of earth rejoice before the throne that the name of the Son of Man *had been revealed to them.* They do not rejoice that the name of the Son of Man had been revealed at that moment before the throne, but that during the days of their earthly lives it had been revealed to each individually by God's Holy Spirit; no one comes to know Jesus as savior without the Father and the Holy Spirit revealing the truth and drawing them to Christ. They rejoice then, in their having been saved in life and now they will spend days without number in the joy of eternal life in the presence of God. **Proverbs 30:4**, Who has established all the ends of the earth? What is his name, and *what is his son's name*? Surely you know! **Enoch 62:7**
302 **"The sum of judgment was given unto the Son of Man"; John 5:22**, The Father judges no one, but has given all judgment to the Son. **John 5:27**, He has given him authority to execute judgment, because he is the Son of Man. **Enoch 41:9**
303 **"With chains shall they be bound"**; **Revelation 20:1**, Then I saw an angel coming down from heaven, holding in his hand the key to the bottomless pit *and a great chain.*
304 **"They shall be imprisoned"**; **Isaiah 24:21-22**, On that day the LORD will punish the host of heaven, in heaven, and the kings of the earth, on the earth. They will be gathered together *as prisoners in a pit*; they will be shut up in a prison, and after many days they will be punished.
305 **"The word of that Son of Man shall go forth"**; **Matthew 24:35**, Heaven and earth will pass away, but my words will not pass away.

Enoch is Raptured!

70 And it came to pass after this[306] that his name during his lifetime was raised aloft to that Son of Man and to the Lord of Spirits from amongst those who dwell on the earth.[307] [2]And he was raised aloft on the chariots of the spirit[308] and his name vanished among them. [3]And from that day I was no longer numbered amongst them: and he set me between the two winds, between the North and the West, where the angels took the cords to measure for me the place for the elect[309] and righteous. [4]And there I saw the first fathers and the righteous who from the beginning dwell in that place.

Noah Too Visits Heaven

71 And it came to pass after this that my spirit was translated[310]
And it ascended into the heavens:
And I saw the holy sons of God.[311]
They were stepping on flames of fire:[312]

---

306 **"It came to pass after this..."**; per Enoch 60:8, the translation of Enoch had already taken place at an earlier time. Chapter 70 then, amounts to a retelling of the translation of Enoch in greater detail.

307 This is the last time we are told Enoch is caught up into heaven; here in narrative flashback, we are given the details of how Enoch had been taken up. This is the event mentioned in Genesis 5:24 and Hebrews 11:5. Two earlier accounts of Enoch being caught up to heaven are detailed in **Enoch 14:8** and **39:3**, where Enoch is taken into heaven for the purpose of receiving revelation. In total, Enoch makes two excursions into heaven before his translation; after his translation, he makes two excursions back to earth in **Enoch 65** and **106**. **Hebrews 11:5**, By faith Enoch was taken up so that he should not see death, and he was not found, because God had taken him, and in **Genesis 5:24**, Enoch walked with God, and he was not, for God took him.

308 **"Chariots of the Spirit"**; here Enoch is said to be carried away on "chariots of the spirit"; at a later date, the Bible records, Elijah will be taken up on "chariots of fire". **2 Kings 2:11**, Behold, chariots of fire and horses of fire separated the two of them. And Elijah went up by a whirlwind into heaven.

309 **"Angels took the cords to measure for me the place for the elect"; Enoch 61:1-5** The place of the saved can be measured; this signifies the special blessing to which those who are numbered in that number are destined. The measuring of "the place for the elect" is recapitulated in, **Revelation 21:15**, The one who spoke with me had a measuring rod of gold to measure the city and its gates and walls.

310 **"My spirit was translated";** here Noah too is said to have visited heaven for the purpose of receiving revelation, some of which will be used by Noah to complete the *Book of the Parables*. Both Enoch and Noah have the unique attribution in the Genesis account as men who "walked with God", in the *Book of Enoch*, they share an additional connection, they both visit heaven as well.

311 **"I saw the holy sons of God"**; **Genesis 6:2-4**, The sons of God saw that the daughters of man were attractive. And they took as their wives any they chose. **Job 1:6**, Now there was a day when the sons of God came to present themselves before the LORD, and Satan also came among them. **Job 2:1**, Again there was a day when the sons of God came to present themselves before the LORD, and Satan also came among them to present himself before the LORD. **Job 38:7**, The morning stars sang together and all the sons of God shouted for joy.

312 **"Stepping on flames of fire"**; **Ezekiel 28:14**, You were an anointed guardian cherub. I placed you; you were on the holy mountain of God; *in the midst of the stones of fire you walked.* **Ezekiel 28:16**, I destroyed you, O guardian cherub, from the midst of the stones of fire.

Their garments were white and their raiment,[313]
And their faces shone like snow.

[2]And I saw two streams of fire,
And the light of that fire shone like hyacinth,
And I fell on my face before the Lord of Spirits.

[3]And the angel Michael one of the archangels
seized me by my right hand,
And lifted me up and led me forth into all the secrets,
And he showed me all the secrets of righteousness.

[4]And he showed me all the secrets of the ends of the heaven,
And all the chambers of all the stars, and all the luminaries,
Whence they proceed before the face of the holy ones.

Noah Sees What Enoch Saw

[5]And he translated my spirit into the heaven of heavens,
And I saw there as it were a structure built of crystals,[314]
And between those crystals tongues of living fire.

[6]And my spirit saw the girdle which girt that house of fire,
And on its four sides were streams full of living fire,
And they girt that house.

[7]And round about were Seraphin, Cherubin, and Ophannin:[315]
And these are they who sleep not
And guard the throne of His glory.[316]

[8]And I saw angels who could not be counted,
A thousand thousands, and ten thousand times ten thousand,[317]
Encircling that house.

---

[313] **"Their garments were white"**; **Revelation 15:6**, Out of the sanctuary came the seven angels with the seven plagues, *clothed in pure, bright linen*, with golden sashes around their chests.

[314] **"A structure built of crystals"; Enoch 14:9**

[315] **"Cherubin, Seraphin and Ophannin"**; or, Cherubim, Seraphim and Ophanim; these are different classes of heavenly creatures. Ophanim, is a Hebrew loan word in Ethiopic, meaning wheels; these are the living wheels with eyes detailed in **Ezekiel 1:16-18**, As for the appearance of the wheels and their construction: their appearance was like the gleaming of beryl. **Enoch 61:10**

[316] **"The throne of His glory"; Revelation 4:2**, At once I was in the Spirit, and behold, a throne stood in heaven, with one seated on the throne.

[317] **"A thousand thousands"**; **Daniel 7:10**, A thousand thousands served him, and ten thousand times ten thousand stood before him. **Revelation 5:11**, I heard around the throne and the living creatures and the elders the voice of many angels, numbering myriads of myriads and thousands of thousands. **Enoch 14:22, 40:1, 60:1, 71:12**

And Michael, and Raphael, and Gabriel, and Phanuel,[318]
And the holy angels who are above the heavens,
Go in and out of that house.[319]

9And they came forth from that house,[320]
And Michael and Gabriel, Raphael and Phanuel,[316]
And many holy angels without number.

10And with them the Head of Days,
His head white and pure as wool,[321]
And His raiment indescribable.

11And I fell on my face,
And my whole body became relaxed,
And my spirit was transfigured;
And I cried with a loud voice,
...with the spirit of power,
And blessed and glorified and extolled.

12And these blessings which went forth out of my mouth were well pleasing before that Head of Days. 13And that Head of Days came with Michael and Gabriel, Raphael and Phanuel, thousands and ten thousands of angels without number.[315] *{Lost passage wherein the Son of Man was described as accompanying the Head of Days, and [Noah] asked one of the angels, as in 46:3, concerning the Son of Man as to who he was.}*

The Son of Man is Born Unto Righteousness

14And he came to me and greeted me with His voice, and said unto me:
"This is the Son of Man who is born unto righteousness,[322] ✡
And righteousness abides over him,

---

[318] The "four presences" of **Enoch 40:1-10**

[319] **"The holy angels go in and out of that house"; Revelation 15:5-6**, After this I looked, and the sanctuary of the tent of witness in heaven was opened, and *out of the sanctuary came the seven angels* with the seven plagues, clothed in pure, bright linen, with golden sashes around their chests.

[320] **"They came forth from that house"**; **Revelation 14:15-18**, *Another angel came out of the temple*, calling with a loud voice to him who sat on the cloud, "Put in your sickle, and reap, for the hour to reap has come, for the harvest of the earth is fully ripe." So he who sat on the cloud swung his sickle across the earth, and the earth was reaped. Then *another angel came out of the temple in heaven*, and he too had a sharp sickle. And another angel came out from the altar, the angel who has authority over the fire, and he called with a loud voice to the one who had the sharp sickle.

[321] **"His head white and pure as wool"**; **Revelation 1:14**, The hairs of his head were white, like white wool, like snow. His eyes were like a flame of fire.

[322] ✡ **"The Son of Man who is born unto righteousness"**; here the earthly nativity of the coming messiah is in view, he will be born as a man in the normal human manner of birth. That Messiah Jesus is 'born unto righteousness', draws our attention to the fact that before Jesus had acted or spoken anything, righteousness was inherent to who he was from the beginning; in this sense the birth of Jesus, the Messiah, would be totally unlike any other human birth.

And the righteousness of the Head of Days forsakes him not."[323]
[15]And he said unto me:
"He proclaims unto thee peace in the name of the world to come;[324]
For from hence has proceeded peace since the creation of the world,
And so shall it be unto thee for ever and for ever and ever.

Nothing Shall Separate Us

[16]And all shall walk in his ways
since righteousness never forsaketh him:
With him will be their dwelling-places,[325] and with him their heritage,
And they shall not be separated from him for ever and ever and ever.[326]

[17]And so there shall be length of days with that Son of Man,
And the righteous shall have peace and an upright way
In the name of the Lord of Spirits for ever and ever."

---

[323] It should be mentioned here, there is a bit of controversy regarding Enoch 71:14. Baty has the angel saying, "Thou art the offspring of man". Lawrence's first edition had the same. Schodde has, "Thou art a son of man". These all place emphasis on the humanity of Enoch. Charles departed from this understanding as we see here placing emphasis on the earthly nativity of the heavenly Son of Man. Some later translators (Knibb, Nickelson, Olson, as well as Lawrence's later) depart from both positions and adopt the radical idea the verse should say, Enoch is "that Son of Man". This position is wrong. This novel interpretation of a single verse would seem to subvert the entire message of the *Book of the Parables*. If context means anything, Charles' take on the verse makes more sense to the integrity of the book, for in Enoch 48:3, the Son of Man exists before creation.
[324] **"The world to come"; Hebrews 2:5**, Now it was not to angels that God subjected *the world to come*, of which we are speaking.
[325] **"With Him will be their dwelling-places"**; **John 14:2-3**, In my Father's house are many rooms. If it were not so, would I have told you that I go to prepare a place for you? And if I go and prepare a place for you, I will come again and will take you to myself, that where I am you may be also.
[326] **"They shall not be separated from Him"**; **Romans 8:38-39**, For I am sure that neither death nor life, nor angels nor rulers, nor things present nor things to come, nor powers, nor height nor depth, nor anything else in all creation, *will be able to separate us from the love of God in Christ Jesus our Lord.* **Enoch 105:2**

Introduction to the Geocentric Calendar Book

Title ~ In modern times this book has usually been titled, "The Astronomical Book", or the "Book of the Luminaries." "The *Geocentric Calendar Book*" is a new title here, first suggested by Daniel Tavolieri of the UK. This title was chosen for this edition as a more accurate description of the book's contents. In this book, Enoch describes the phases of the calendar year as viewed from the earth.

Authorship ~ In Enoch 82:1, Enoch addresses his son in the first person. In it we read how Enoch entrusted the preservation of this and the rest of his books to his son Methuselah, who is instructed to, *"see that thou deliver them to the generations of the world."* Methuselah must ensure the preservation of Enoch's writings so that they will be available for all time. In this we see the first phase of what would become the phenomenal history of the preservation of the *Book of Enoch.*

Date ~ In Enoch 81:6, we read, *"One year we will leave thee with thy son, till thou givest thy last commands, that thou mayst teach thy children and record it for them, and testify to all thy children; and in the second year they shall take thee from their midst."* This book is being written during Enoch's final year on earth. This would place this book's composition in the 364th year of the life of Enoch, nearly seven centuries before the flood of Noah's day.

Major Theme ~ The book's major theme shows the importance of the proper reckoning of the times of the solar/lunar year from a geocentric or earthbound perspective. The book provides a model for how Enoch's descendants can and should calculate the phases of the calendar year.

Background ~ The *Geocentric Calendar Book* may be understood as a continuation of the *Book of the Watchers*. In the *Book of the Watchers,* Enoch had been given a celestial tour during which he briefly reported, in chapter 33, receiving another book in which were recorded the courses of the heavenly bodies. Chapters 72-82, can be seen as Enoch's report of this information.

Purpose ~ Among the five scrolls which were to become the *Book of Enoch,* this is perhaps the most difficult to understand and the most puzzling from today's perspective. However, from Enoch 82:7-9, we gather the book was apparently intended to be used by those wishing to properly calculate the appointed times for proper celebration of yearly festivals.

Synopsis ~ Though the book is described as being a revelation from heaven to Enoch, the perspective of the calendar portions of the book is thoroughly earthbound. From this terrestrial perspective, Enoch is instructed in the phases of the fixed order of the sun and moon throughout an earthly solar/lunar year. Lengthy descriptions of the yearly courses of the sun and moon are given to Enoch, so that future generations of Enoch's descendants may be able to more accurately mark the passage of time on earth.

~~~~~~~~~~~~~~~~~~~~~~~~~~~~~~

Outline ~

I. Introduction (72:1)
- A. Uriel gives Enoch the book (72:1)

II. The Portals of the Sun, Moon, Stars and Winds (72:2-78:17)
- A. The Portals of the Sun (72:2-37)
- B. The Portals of the Moon (73:1-74:17)
    1. The Lunar Year (74:1-17)
- C. The Portals of the Stars (75:1-9)
- D. The Portals of the Winds (76:1-14)
    1. The Four Corners of the World (77:1-8)
- E. The Waxing and Waning of the Moon (78:1-17)

VII. Conclusion (79:1-82:20)
- A. Instructions for Enoch's son Methuselah (79:1-82:20)
- B. Enoch will be translated within a year (81:5-6)
~~~~~~~~~~~~~~~~~~~~~~~~~~~~~~

The Geocentric Calendar Book

Time from Now Until the New Creation

72 The book[327] of the courses of the luminaries of the heaven, the relations of each, according to their classes, their dominion and their seasons, according to their names and places of origin, and according to their months, which Uriel, the holy angel, who was with me, who is their guide, showed me;[328] and he showed me all their laws exactly as they are,[329] and how it is with regard to all the years of the world and unto eternity, till the new creation[330] is accomplished[331] which dureth till eternity.

Portals of the Sun

2And this is the first law of the luminaries: the luminary the Sun has its rising in the eastern portals of the heaven, and its setting in the western portals of the heaven.

3And I saw six portals in which the sun rises, and six portals in which the sun sets: and the moon rises and sets in these portals, and the leaders of the stars and those whom they lead: six in the east and six in the west, and all following each other in accurately corresponding order: also many windows to the right and left of these portals.

4And first there goes forth the great luminary, named the Sun, and his circumference is like the circumference of the heaven, and he is quite filled with illuminating and heating fire. 5The chariot on which he ascends, the wind drives, and the sun goes down from the heaven and returns through the north in order to reach the east, and is so guided that he comes to that portal and shines in the face of the heaven. 6In this

---

[327] Perhaps the most puzzling of the five books of Enoch, is this, the *Geocentric Calendar Book*. I owe special thanks to Daniel Tavolieri of the U.K., for helping me understand the geocentric perspective of this book. Enoch 76:14 shows the book being initially entrusted to Methuselah, by Enoch. Enoch 75:2, 80:7 and 82:5, indicate the importance placed upon the proper reckoning of the times of the Solar and Lunar year in the Geocentric Calendar. The book was apparently intended to be used by those wishing to properly calculate the proper appointed times for celebration of yearly festivals. **Enoch 82:7-9**

[328] **"Uriel, the holy angel, who was with me, showed me"**; The *Geocentric Calendar Book* may be a record of what was given to Enoch in **Enoch 33:3-4**. Here we have it recounted in greater detail.

[329] **"He showed me their laws exactly as they are"**; The fixed order of creation is a theme throughout the book. This fixed order is contrasted with the sinning angels and mankind who routinely transgress God's laws. Enoch spends a great deal of effort detailing the fixed order of the heavenly bodies and meteorological phenomena. The development of a calendar so that future generations would be able to mark the seasons and properly observe the festival year was the apparent reason. **Enoch 2:1, 101:1**

[330] **The new creation is a theme found also in the Old and New Testaments.**

[331] **"Till the new creation is accomplished"**; **Revelation 21:1**, Then I saw a new heaven and a new earth, for the first heaven and the first earth had passed away, and the sea was no more.

way he rises in the first month in the great portal, which is the fourth those six portals in the east.

[7]And in that fourth portal from which the sun rises in the first month are twelve window-openings, from which proceed a flame when they are opened in their season.

[8]When the sun rises in the heaven, he comes forth through that fourth portal thirty mornings in succession, and sets accurately in the fourth portal in the west of the heaven. [9]And during this period the day becomes daily longer and the night nightly shorter to the thirtieth morning. [10]On that day the day is longer than the night by a ninth part, and the day amounts exactly to ten parts and the night to eight parts.

[11]And the sun rises from that fourth portal, and sets in the fourth and returns to the fifth portal of the east thirty mornings, and rises from it and sets in the fifth portal. [12]And then the day becomes longer by two parts and amounts to eleven parts, and the night becomes shorter and amounts to seven parts. [13]And it returns to the east and enters into the sixth portal, and rises and sets in the sixth portal one-and-thirty mornings on account of its sign.

[14]On that day the day becomes longer than the night, and the day becomes double the night, and the day becomes twelve parts, and the night is shortened and becomes six parts.

[15]And the sun mounts up to make the day shorter and the night longer, and the sun returns to the east and enters into the sixth portal, and rises from it and sets thirty mornings.

[16]And when thirty mornings are accomplished, the day decreases by exactly one part, and becomes eleven parts, and the night seven. [17]And the sun goes forth from that sixth portal in the west, and goes to the east and rises in the fifth portal for thirty mornings, and sets in the west again in the fifth western portal.

[18]On that day the day decreases by two parts, and amounts to ten parts and the night to eight parts. [19]And the sun goes forth from that fifth portal and sets in the fifth portal of the west, and rises in the fourth portal for one-and-thirty mornings on account of its sign, and sets in the west.

[20]On that day the day is equalized with the night, and becomes of equal length, and the night amounts to nine parts and the day to nine parts. [21]And the sun rises from that portal and sets in the west, and returns to the east and rises thirty mornings in the third portal and sets in the west in the third portal.

[22]And on that day the night becomes longer than the day, and night becomes longer than night, and day shorter than day till the thirtieth morning, and the night amounts exactly to ten parts and the day to eight

parts. [23]And the sun rises from that third portal and sets in the third portal in the west and returns to the east, and for thirty mornings rises in the second portal in the east, and in like manner sets in the second portal in the west of the heaven.

[24]And on that day the night amounts to eleven parts and the day to seven parts. [25]And the sun rises on that day from that second portal and sets in the west in the second portal, and returns to the east into the first portal for one-and-thirty mornings, and sets in the first portal in the west of the heaven.

[26]And on that day the night becomes longer and amounts to the double of the day: and the night amounts exactly to twelve parts and the day to six. [27]And the sun has therewith traversed the divisions of his orbit and turns again on those divisions of his orbit, and enters that portal thirty mornings and sets also in the west opposite to it. [28]And on that night has the night decreased in length by a ninth part, and the night has become eleven parts and the day seven parts.

[29]And the sun has returned and entered into the second portal in the east, and returns on those his divisions of his orbit for thirty mornings, rising and setting. [30]And on that day the night decreases in length, and the night amounts to ten parts and the day to eight.

[31]And on that day the sun rises from that portal, and sets in the west, and returns to the east, and rises in the third portal for one-and-thirty mornings, and sets in the west of the heaven. [32]On that day the night decreases and amounts to nine parts, and the day to nine parts, and the night is equal to the day and the year is exactly as to its days three hundred and sixty-four. [33]And the length of the day and of the night, and the shortness of the day and of the night arise- through the course of the sun these distinctions are made. [34]So it comes that its course becomes daily longer, and its course nightly shorter.

[35]And this is the law and the course of the sun, and his return as often as he returns sixty times and rises, that is the great luminary which is named the sun, for ever and ever. [36]And that which thus rises is the great luminary, and is so named according to its appearance, according as the Lord commanded. [37]As he rises, so he sets and decreases not, and rests not, but runs day and night, and his light is sevenfold brighter than that of the moon; but as regards size they are both equal.[332]

[332] From man's terrestrial perspective, both the sun and moon appear to be of similar size. For two minutes during a solar eclipse, viewers can safely look directly at the sun's corona while the moon neatly covers the totality of the disk of the sun. **Enoch 78:3**

Portals of the Moon

73 And after this law I saw another law dealing with the smaller luminary, which is named the Moon.

[2]And her circumference is like the circumference of the heaven, and her chariot in which she rides is driven by the wind, and light is given to her in definite measure. [3]And her rising and setting change every month: and her days are like the days of the sun, and when her light is full it amounts to the seventh part of the light of the sun. [4]And thus she rises.

And her first phase in the east comes forth on the thirtieth morning: and on that day she becomes visible, and constitutes for you the first phase of the moon on the thirtieth day together with the sun in the portal where the sun rises.

[5]And the one half of her goes forth by a seventh part, and her whole circumference is empty, without light, with the exception of one-seventh part of it, and the fourteenth part of her light. [6]And when she receives one-seventh part of the half of her light, her light amounts to one-seventh part and the half thereof. [7]And she sets with the sun, and when the sun rises the moon rises with him and receives the half of one part of light, and in that night in the beginning of her morning in the commencement of the lunar day the moon sets with the sun, and is invisible that night with the fourteen parts and the half of one of them. [8]And she rises on that day with exactly a seventh part, and comes forth and recedes from the rising of the sun, and in her remaining days she becomes bright in the remaining thirteen parts.

The Lunar Year

74 And I saw another course, a law for her, and how according to that law she performs her monthly revolution.

[2]And all these Uriel, the holy angel who is the leader of them all, showed to me, and their positions, and I wrote down their positions as he showed them to me, and I wrote down their months as they were, and the appearance of their lights till fifteen days were accomplished.

[3]In single seventh parts she accomplishes all her light in the east, and in single seventh parts accomplishes all her darkness in the west. [4]And in certain months she alters her settings, and in certain months she pursues her own peculiar course. [5]In two months the moon sets with the sun: in those two middle portals the third and the fourth. [6]She goes forth for seven days, and turns about and returns again through the portal where the sun rises, and accomplishes all her light: and she recedes from the sun, and in eight days enters the sixth portal from which the sun goes forth. [7]And when the sun goes forth from the fourth portal she goes forth seven days, until she goes forth from the fifth and turns back again

in seven days into the fourth portal and accomplishes all her light: and she recedes and enters into the first portal in eight days. [8]And she returns again in seven days into the fourth portal from which the sun goes forth.

[9]Thus I saw their position- how the moons rose and the sun set in those days.

[10]And if five years are added together the sun has an overplus of thirty days, and all the days which accrue to it for one of those five years, when they are full, amount to 364 days. [11]And the overplus of the sun and of the stars amounts to six days: in 5 years 6 days every year come to 30 days: and the moon falls behind the sun and stars to the number of 30 days.

[12]And the sun and the stars bring in all the years exactly, so that they do not advance or delay their position by a single day unto eternity; but complete the years with perfect justice in 364 days. [13]In 3 years there are 1,092 days, and in 5 years 1,820 days, so that in 8 years there are 2,912 days. [14]For the moon alone the days amount in 3 years to 1,062 days, and in 5 years she falls 50 days behind:[333] [15]And in 5 years there are 1,770 days, so that for the moon the days in 8 years amount to 2,832 days. [16]For in 8 years she falls behind to the amount of 80 days, all the days she falls behind in 8 years are 80. [17]And the year is accurately completed in conformity with their world-stations and the stations of the sun, which rise from the portals through which it the sun rises and sets 30 days.

75 And the leaders of the heads of the thousands, who are placed over the whole creation and over all the stars, have also to do with the four intercalary days, being inseparable from their office, according to the reckoning of the year, and these render service on the four days which are not reckoned in the reckoning of the year. [2]And owing to them men go wrong therein,[334] for those luminaries truly render service on the world-stations, one in the first portal, one in the third portal of the heaven, one in the fourth portal, and one in the sixth portal, and the exactness of the year is accomplished through its separate three hundred and sixty-four stations.

[3]For the signs and the times and the years and the days the angel Uriel showed to me, whom the Lord of glory hath set for ever over all the luminaries of the heaven, in the heaven and in the world, that they should rule on the face of the heaven and be seen on the earth, and be

[333] "i.e. to the sum of 1,770 there is to be added 1,000 and 62 days." (R.H. Charles)
[334] Per **Enoch 75:2, 80:7, 82:5 and 82:7-9**, the purpose of the *Geocentric Calendar Book* was to make it possible for correctly calculating the proper times for the festival year.

leaders for the day and the night,[335] and all the ministering creatures which make their revolution in all the chariots of the heaven.

[4]In like manner twelve doors Uriel showed me, open in the circumference of the sun's chariot in the heaven, through which the rays of the sun break forth: and from them is warmth diffused over the earth, when they are opened at their appointed seasons. [5]And for the winds and the spirit of the dew when they are opened, standing open in the heavens at the ends. [6]As for the twelve portals in the heaven, at the ends of the earth, out of which go forth the sun, moon, and stars, and all the works of heaven in the east and in the west, [7]there are many windows open to the left and right of them, and one window at its appointed season produces warmth, corresponding as these do to those doors from which the stars come forth according as He has commanded them, and wherein they set corresponding to their number.

[8]And I saw chariots in the heaven, running in the world, above those portals in which revolve the stars that never set.

[9]And one is larger than all the rest, and it is that that makes its course through the entire world.

Portals of the Winds

76 And at the ends of the earth I saw twelve portals open to all the quarters of the heaven, from which the winds go forth and blow over the earth. [2]Three of them are open on the face[336] of the heavens, and three in the west, and three on the right[337] of the heaven, and three on the left.[338] [3]And the three first are those of the east, and three are of the north, and three after those on the left of the south, and three of the west.

[4]Through four of these come winds[339] of blessing and prosperity, and from those eight come hurtful winds: when they are sent, they bring destruction on all the earth and on the water upon it, and on all who dwell thereon, and on everything which is in the water and on the land.

[5]And the first wind- from those portals, called the east wind, comes forth through the first portal which is in the east, inclining towards the south: from it come forth desolation, drought, heat, and destruction. [6]And through the second portal in the middle comes what is fitting, and from

---

[335] **"Leaders for the day and night"**; In other words, the sun, moon and stars. (Charles)
[336] i.e., the East
[337] i.e., the South
[338] i.e., the North
[339] **The four winds; Revelation 7:1-3**, After this I saw four angels standing at the four corners of the earth, holding back the four winds of the earth, that no wind might blow on earth or sea or against any tree. Then I saw another angel ascending from the rising of the sun, with the seal of the living God, and he called with a loud voice to the four angels who had been given power to harm earth and sea, saying, "Do not harm the earth or the sea or the trees, until we have sealed the servants of our God on their foreheads."

it there come rain and fruitfulness and prosperity and dew; and through the third portal which lies toward the north come cold and drought.

[7]And after these come forth the south winds through three portals: through the first portal of them inclining to the east comes forth a hot wind. [8]And through the middle portal next to it there come forth fragrant smells, and dew and rain, and prosperity and health. [9]And through the third portal lying to the west come forth dew and rain, locusts and desolation.

[10]And after these the north winds: from the seventh portal in the east come dew and rain, locusts and desolation. [11]And from the middle portal come in a direct direction health and rain and dew and prosperity; and through the third portal in the west come cloud and hoar-frost, and snow and rain, and dew and locusts.

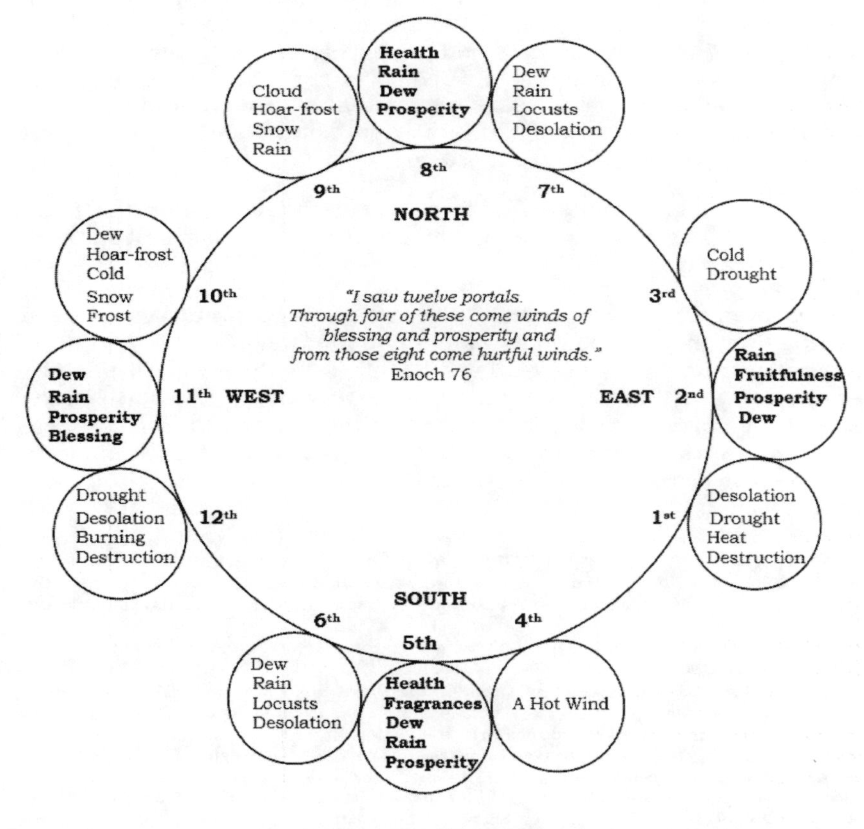

The Twelve Portals of the Quarters of the Heaven and Their Winds

[12]And after these four are the west winds: through the first portal adjoining the north come forth dew and hoar-frost, and cold and snow and frost.[340] [13]And from the middle portal come forth dew and rain, and prosperity and blessing; and through the last portal which adjoins the south come forth drought and desolation, and burning and destruction.

[14]And the twelve portals of the four quarters of the heaven are therewith completed, and all their laws and all their plagues and all their benefactions have I shown to thee, my son Methuselah.[341]

The Four Quarters of the Earth

77 And the first quarter is called the east, because it is the first: and the second, the south, because the Most High will descend there,[342] yea,✡ there in quite a special sense will He who is blessed for ever[343] descend. [2]And the west quarter is named the diminished, because there all the luminaries of the heaven wane and go down. [3]And the fourth quarter, named the north, is divided into three parts: the first of them is for the dwelling of men: and the second contains seas of water, and the abysses and forests and rivers, and darkness and clouds; and the third part contains the garden of righteousness.[344]

[4]I saw seven high mountains, higher than all the mountains which are on the earth: and thence comes forth hoar-frost, and days, seasons, and years pass away.

[5]I saw seven rivers on the earth larger than all the rivers: one of them coming from the west pours its waters into the Great Sea.[345] [6]And these two come from the north to the sea and pour their waters into the Erythraean Sea[346] in the east. [7]And the remaining four come forth on the side of the north to their own sea, two of them to the Erythraean Sea, and two into the Great Sea and discharge themselves there and some say: into the desert.

---

[340] **Job 38:22-23**, Have you entered the storehouses of the snow, or have you seen the storehouses of the hail, which I have reserved for the time of trouble, for the day of battle and war?

[341] Here we see Methuselah being entrusted with the preservation and transmission of the *Geocentric Calendar Book*.

[342] ✡ **"The Most High will descend there"**; here Enoch uses language similar to that in **Enoch 1:3-4**, "The Holy Great One will come forth from His dwelling, and the eternal God will tread upon the earth, even on Mount Sinai, and appear from His camp, and appear in the strength of His might from the heaven of heavens." Earth's final judgment will come about at the personal presence of God coming to earth. In Jude 1:14-15, we are told this is accomplished by the second coming of Jesus Christ. **Enoch 1:3, 25:3, 52:9, 77:1, 90:15,18,20, 91:7, 100:4 Hosea 5:15**, I will return again to my place, until they acknowledge their guilt and seek my face, and in their distress earnestly seek me.

[343] **"He who is blessed for ever"; Romans 9:5**, The Christ who is God over all, *blessed forever*. Amen.

[344] **"The Garden of Righteousness"; Enoch 32:3, 60:8+23, 61:12, 77:3**

[345] The Mediterranean Sea

[346] The Red Sea

[8]Seven great islands I saw in the sea and in the mainland: two in the mainland and five in the Great Sea.

The Waxing and Waning of the Moon

78 And the names of the sun are the following: the first Orjares, and the second Tomas.

[2]And the moon has four names: the first name is Asonja, the second Ebla, the third Benase, and the fourth Erae.

[3]These are the two great luminaries: their circumference is like the circumference of the heaven, and the size of the circumference of both is alike.[347] [4]In the circumference of the sun there are seven portions of light which are added to it more than to the moon, and in definite measures it is transferred till the seventh portion of the sun is exhausted.

[5]And they set and enter the portals of the west, and make their revolution by the north, and come forth through the eastern portals on the face of the heaven.

[6]And when the moon rises one-fourteenth part appears in the heaven: the light becomes full in her: on the fourteenth day she accomplishes her light. [7]And fifteen parts of light are transferred to her till the fifteenth day when her light is accomplished, according to the sign of the year, and she becomes fifteen parts, and the moon grows by the addition of fourteenth parts. [8]And in her waning the moon decreases on the first day to fourteen parts of her light, on the second to thirteen parts of light, on the third to twelve, on the fourth to eleven, on the fifth to ten, on the sixth to nine, on the seventh to eight, on the eighth to seven, on the ninth to six, on the tenth to five, on the eleventh to four, on the twelfth to three, on the thirteenth to two, on the fourteenth to the half of a seventh, and all her remaining light disappears wholly on the fifteenth.

[9]And in certain months the month has twenty-nine days and once twenty-eight.

[10]And Uriel showed me another law: when light is transferred to the moon, and on which side it is transferred to her by the sun. [11]During all the period during which the moon is growing in her light, she is transferring it to herself when opposite to the sun during fourteen days her light is accomplished in the heaven, and when she is illumined throughout, her light is accomplished full in the heaven. [12]And on the first day she is called the new moon, for on that day the light rises upon her. [13]She becomes full moon exactly on the day when the sun sets in the west, and from the east she rises at night, and the moon shines the

---

[347] From man's terrestrial perspective, both the sun and moon appear to be of similar size. For two minutes during a solar eclipse, viewers can safely look directly at the sun's corona while the moon neatly covers the totality of the disk of the sun. **Enoch 72:37**

whole night through till the sun rises over against her and the moon is seen over against the sun. [14]On the side whence the light of the moon comes forth, there again she wanes till all the light vanishes and all the days of the month are at an end, and her circumference is empty, void of light.

[15]And three months she makes of thirty days, and at her time she makes three months of twenty-nine days each, in which she accomplishes her waning in the first period of time, and in the first portal for one hundred and seventy-seven days. [16]And in the time of her going out she appears for three months of thirty days each, and for three months she appears of twenty-nine each.

[17]At night she appears like a man for twenty days each time, and by day she appears like the heaven, and there is nothing else in her save her light.

79 And now, my son, I have shown thee everything,[348] and the law of all the stars of the heaven is completed.

[2]And he showed me all the laws of these for every day, and for every season of bearing rule, and for every year, and for its going forth, and for the order prescribed to it every month and every week: [3]And the waning of the moon which takes place in the sixth portal: for in this sixth portal her light is accomplished, and after that there is the beginning of the waning: [4]And the waning which takes place in the first portal in its season, till one hundred and seventy-seven days are accomplished: reckoned according to weeks, twenty-five weeks and two days. [5]She falls behind the sun and the order of the stars exactly five days in the course of one period, and when this place which thou seest has been traversed.

[6]Such is the picture and sketch of every luminary which Uriel the archangel, who is their leader, showed unto me.

80 And in those days the angel Uriel answered and said to me: “Behold, I have shown thee everything[343] Enoch, and I have revealed everything to thee that thou shouldst see this sun and this moon, and the leaders of the stars of the heaven and all those who turn them, their tasks and times and departures.

The Sin of Mankind Affects the Heavenly Bodies

[2]And in the days of the sinners the years shall be shortened,
And their seed shall be tardy on their lands and fields,
And all things on the earth shall alter,

---

[348] **“I have shown thee everything”;** the *Geocentric Calendar Book*, having been transmitted to Enoch by Uriel, is now entrusted to Enoch’s son Methuselah, **Enoch 79:1, 80:1** and **81:6**

And shall not appear in their time:
And the rain shall be kept back
And the heaven shall withhold it.
[3]And in those times the fruits of the earth shall be backward,
And shall not grow in their time,
And the fruits of the trees shall be withheld in their time.

[4]And the moon shall alter her order,
And not appear at her time.
[5]And in those days the sun shall be seen and he shall journey in the evening on the extremity of the great chariot in the west
And shall shine more brightly than accords with the order of light.

[6]And many chiefs of the stars shall transgress the order prescribed.
And these shall alter their orbits and tasks,
And not appear at the seasons prescribed to them.

[7]And the whole order of the stars shall be concealed from the sinners,
And the thoughts of those on the earth shall err concerning them,[349]
And they shall be altered from all their ways,
Yea, they shall err and take them to be gods.

[8]And evil shall be multiplied upon them,
And punishment shall come upon them
So as to destroy all."[350]

Enoch Reads the Heavenly Tablets

81 And he said unto me:
"Observe, Enoch, these heavenly tablets,[351]
And read what is written thereon,
And mark every individual fact."

[2]And I observed the heavenly tablets, and read everything which was written thereon and understood everything, and read the book of all the deeds of mankind, and of all the children of flesh that shall be upon the earth to the remotest generations. [3]And forthwith I blessed the Great Lord the King of Glory for ever, in that He has made all the works of the world,

---

[349] Per **Enoch 75:2, 80:7, 82:5 and 82:7-9**, the purpose of the *Geocentric Calendar Book* was to make it possible for correctly calculating the proper times for the festival year. Here, the worship of the stars is seen as the ultimate perversion of the purpose of the heavens.
[350] **"So as to destroy all"; Isaiah 24:6**, Therefore a curse devours the earth, and its inhabitants suffer for their guilt; therefore the inhabitants of the earth are scorched, and few men are left.
[351] **"Observe, Enoch, these heavenly tablets"**; Enoch is shown heavenly records written upon tablets, in which he learns about the future of the world and the activities of mankind over time and the coming judgment. **Enoch 81:1-2, 93:2, 103:2, 106:19**

And I extolled the Lord because of His patience,
And blessed Him because of the children of men.

4And after that I said:
"Blessed is the man who dies in righteousness and goodness,[352]
Concerning whom there is no book of unrighteousness written,
And against whom no day of judgment shall be found."

Enoch Given One Year to Complete His Books

5And those seven holy ones brought me and placed me on the earth before the door of my house, and said to me: "Declare everything to thy son Methuselah, and show to all thy children that no flesh is righteous in the sight of the Lord,[353] for He is their Creator. 6One year we will leave thee with thy son,[354] till thou givest thy last commands, that thou mayst teach thy children and record it for them, and testify to all thy children; and in the second year they shall take thee from their midst.

7Let thy heart be strong,
For the good shall announce righteousness to the good;

The righteous with the righteous shall rejoice,
And shall offer congratulation to one another.

8But the sinners shall die with the sinners,
And the apostate go down with the apostate.

9And those who practice righteousness
shall die on account of the deeds of men,
And be taken away[355] on account of the doings of the godless."

10And in those days they ceased to speak to me, and I came to my people, blessing the Lord of the world.

Enoch's Charge to Methuselah

82 And now, my son Methuselah,[356] all these things I am recounting to thee and writing down for thee, and I have revealed to thee everything, and given thee books concerning all these: so preserve, my son

---

352 **"Blessed is the man who dies in righteousness"; Revelation 14:13**, I heard a voice from heaven saying, "Write this: Blessed are the dead who die in the Lord from now on. Blessed indeed," says the Spirit, "that they may rest from their labors, for their deeds follow them!"
353 **"No flesh is righteous in the sight of the Lord"; Romans 3:10**, As it is written: "None is righteous, no, not one." **Romans 3:23**, All have sinned and fall short of the glory of God.
354 One year before Enoch's translation (Enoch 81:6), Enoch entrusts the books he has written to his son Methuselah. The total number of books may have exceeded what we have in this volume. The *Book of the Parables*, however, was not given to Methuselah but to Noah at a later date in chapter 68.
355 This is a description of martyrdom.
356 **"And now, my son Methuselah"; Enoch 83:1, 91:1**

Methuselah, the books from thy father's hand, and see that thou deliver them to the generations of the world.

[2]I have given wisdom to thee and to thy children,
And thy children that shall be to thee,
That they may give it to their children for generations,
This wisdom namely that passeth their thought.
[3]And those who understand it shall not sleep,
But shall listen with the ear that they may learn this wisdom,
And it shall please those that eat thereof better than good food.

[4]Blessed are all the righteous, blessed are all those who walk in the way of righteousness and sin not as the sinners, in the reckoning of all their days in which the sun traverses the heaven, entering into and departing from the portals for thirty days with the heads of thousands of the order of the stars, together with the four which are intercalated which divide the four portions of the year, which lead them and enter with them four days. [5]Owing to them men shall be at fault and not reckon them in the whole reckoning of the year: yea, men shall be at fault, and not recognize them accurately.[357] [6]For they belong to the reckoning of the year and are truly recorded thereon for ever, one in the first portal and one in the third, and one in the fourth and one in the sixth, and the year is completed in three hundred and sixty-four days.

[7]And the account thereof is accurate and the recorded reckoning thereof exact; for the luminaries, and months and festivals, and years and days, has Uriel shown and revealed to me, to whom the Lord of the whole creation of the world hath subjected the host of heaven. [8]And he has power over night and day in the heaven to cause the light to give light to men- sun, moon, and stars, and all the powers of the heaven which revolve in their circular chariots. [9]And these are the orders of the stars, which set in their places, and in their seasons and festivals and months.

[10]And these are the names of those who lead them, who watch that they enter at their times, in their orders, in their seasons, in their months, in their periods of dominion, and in their positions. [11]Their four leaders who divide the four parts of the year enter first; and after them the twelve leaders of the orders who divide the months; and for the three hundred and sixty days there are heads over thousands who divide the days; and for the four intercalary days there are the leaders which sunder the four parts of the year. [12]And these heads over thousands are intercalated between leader and leader, each behind a station, but their leaders make the division.

[13]And these are the names of the leaders who divide the four parts of the year which are ordained: Milkiel, Helemmelek, and Melejal, and Narel. [14]And the names of those who lead them: Adnarel, and Ijasusael, and

---

[357] Per **Enoch 75:2, 80:7, 82:5 and 82:7-9**, it appears the purpose of this book was to make it possible to correctly calculate the proper times for the festival year.

Elomeel- these three follow the leaders of the orders, and there is one that follows the three leaders of the orders which follow those leaders of stations that divide the four parts of the year.

[15]In the beginning of the year Melkejal rises first and rules, who is named Tamaini and sun, and all the days of his dominion whilst he bears rule are ninety-one days. [16]And these are the signs of the days which are to be seen on earth in the days of his dominion: sweat, and heat, and calms; and all the trees bear fruit, and leaves are produced on all the trees, and the harvest of wheat, and the rose-flowers, and all the flowers which come forth in the field, but the trees of the winter season become withered. [17]And these are the names of the leaders which are under them: Berkael, Zelebsel, and another who is added a head of a thousand, called Hilujaseph: and the days of the dominion of this leader are at an end.

[18]The next leader after him is Helemmelek, whom one names the shining sun, and all the days of his light are ninety-one days.

[19]And these are the signs of his days on the earth: glowing heat and dryness, and the trees ripen their fruits and produce all their fruits ripe and ready, and the sheep pair and become pregnant, and all the fruits of the earth are gathered in, and everything that is in the fields, and the winepress: these things take place in the days of his dominion.

[20]These are the names, and the orders, and the leaders of those heads of thousands: Gidaijal, Keel, and Heel, and the name of the head of a thousand which is added to them, Asfael: and the days of his dominion are at an end.

Introduction to the Book of Dream-Visions

Title ~ Chapters 83-90 of the *Book of Enoch,* comprise the section called the *"Book of Dream-Visions."* This section gets its name from the contents of the book which contains descriptions of two dream-visions which Enoch received before he called to ministry.

Authorship ~ The book is written in the first-person by the Biblical Enoch to his son Methuselah.

Date ~ The composition of the *Book of Dream-Visions* continues where the previous book ended. Enoch is finishing up his writings in preparation for his departure within the year. This places the writing of this book in Enoch's 364th year and his son Methuselah's 300th. According to Enoch 83:1-2, these two dream-visions are said to have been received by Enoch before Enoch met his wife, and before he entered the office of prophet (which is found in Enoch 12).

Major Theme ~ *"For everything shall come and be fulfilled, and all the deeds of men in their order were shown to me."* (Enoch 90:41) The two visions give us a grand overview of the story of humanity from its beginning until the coming of the Messianic kingdom is fulfilled.

Background ~ The *"Book of Dream-Visions"* along with the final section "*The Book of the Preaching of Enoch*", are being written in view of the soon departure of Enoch, when he will be translated to heaven. With these last writings, Enoch is imparting to his son's care, a fuller picture of the revelations he has received from God during the course of his earthly life.

Purpose ~ The *Book of Enoch* belongs to that genre of ancient Jewish literature known as apocalypse. Apocalypses, like the *Book of Revelation,* record an unveiling of divine revelation to the reader. In order for Enoch's son Methuselah to possess a complete record of his father's revelations, Enoch here recounts his earliest two dream-visions, received years before Enoch was even called to the office of prophet.

Synopsis ~ The first and shorter of these two dream-visions previews the worldwide destruction destined to come during the flood of Noah's day. When Enoch awakes he is troubled by the dream-vision and prays to God to preserve a remnant of mankind through the flood so that a future righteous generation may come. The second, much longer dream-vision is often referred to as an "animal apocalypse", due to the fact that throughout the dream Enoch beholds the grand panorama of the history of salvation portrayed symbolically in the form of a variety of animals and their activities. At the vision's close, Enoch beholds the birth of Messiah who will bring about the future transformation of all humanity and the world he has foreseen in his vision.

~~~~~~~~~~~~~~~~~~~~~~~~~~~~~~

Outline ~

I. Introduction (83:1-2)
II. The First Vision: The Coming Cataclysm (83:3-84:6)
- A. Enoch sees the coming cataclysm (83:3-5)
- B. The Wise Counsel of Mahalalel (83:6-9)
- C. Enoch Intercedes for his posterity (83:10-84:6)
  1. "Establish the plant of the eternal seed."

III. The Second Vision: The Animal Apocalypse (85:1-90:39)
- A. From the Fall of the Watchers to Noah (86:1-89:1)
- B. From Noah to Abraham (89:1-10)
- C. From Abraham to Moses (89:10-15)
- D. From Moses to Joshua (89:15-36)
- E. From Joshua to Samuel (89:36-42)
- F. From Samuel to the Captivity (89:42-58)
- G. The Period of the Seventy Shepherds (89:59-90:13)
- H. The End of the Age and Last Judgment (90:14-31)
- I. The Messianic Kingdom (90:32-39)

IV. Enoch Weeps for the Future (90:40-42)
~~~~~~~~~~~~~~~~~~~~~~~~~~~~~~

The Book of Dream-Visions

Enoch Recalls Two Dream-Visions

83 And now, my son Methuselah,[358] I will show thee all my visions which I have seen, recounting them before thee.

[2]Two visions I saw before I took a wife, and the one was quite unlike the other: the first when I was learning to write: the second before I took thy mother, when I saw a terrible vision.[359]

[3]And regarding them I prayed to the Lord.

First Dream-Vision: Enoch Foresees the Cataclysm of Noah's Day

I had laid me down in the house of my grandfather Mahalalel, when I saw in a vision how the heaven collapsed and was borne off and fell to the earth. [4]And when it fell to the earth I saw how the earth was swallowed up in a great abyss, and mountains were suspended on mountains, and hills sank down on hills, and high trees were rent from their stems, and hurled down and sunk in the abyss. [5]And thereupon a word fell into my mouth,[360] and I lifted up my voice to cry aloud, and said: "The earth is destroyed."[361]

[6]And my grandfather Mahalalel waked me as I lay near him, and said unto me: "Why dost thou cry so, my son, and why dost thou make such lamentation?"

[7]And I recounted to him the whole vision which I had seen, and he said unto me: "A terrible thing hast thou seen, my son, and of grave moment is thy dream-vision as to the secrets of all the sin of the earth: it must sink into the abyss and be destroyed with a great destruction. [8]And now, my son, arise and make petition to the Lord of glory, since thou art a believer, that a remnant may remain on the earth, and that He may not

---

[358] **"My son Methuselah, I will show thee all my visions"**; the *Book of Dream-Visions* was initially entrusted to the custody and care of Methuselah, Enoch's son. **Enoch 82:1, 91:1**

[359] **"Two visions I saw before I took a wife"**; These two dream-visions comprise the content of the *Book of Dream-Visions*. These would appear to be the earliest of Enoch's dream-visions, coming before his initial call to the ministry of prophet which can be found in chapter 12.

[360] **"A word fell into my mouth"**; compare the language with Enoch 13:8, "Visions fell down upon me."

[361] In this, Enoch's earliest dream-vision, one can see a kind of foreshadowing of Enoch's still future call to the role of prophet. It is to the generation of those who will be living at the time of Noah's flood that Enoch will be called to prophesy at a later time. Given that this dream-vision is his earliest and first, the reaction of a younger Enoch is all the more understandable. Also of note is the fact that nowhere does Enoch's vision specify a flood of water as the manner by which judgment will come.

destroy the whole earth. [9]My son, from heaven all this will come upon the earth, and upon the earth there will be great destruction."

[10]After that I arose and prayed and implored and besought, and wrote down my prayer for the generations of the world, and I will show everything to thee, my son Methuselah.

[11]And when I had gone forth below and seen the heaven, and the sun rising in the east, and the moon setting in the west, and a few stars, and the whole earth, and everything as He had known it in the beginning, then I blessed the Lord of judgment and extolled Him because He had made the sun to go forth from the windows of the east, and he ascended and rose on the face of the heaven, and set out and kept traversing the path shown unto him.

Enoch's Prophetic Prayer Messiah ~ "The Eternal Seed"

84 And I lifted up my hands in righteousness and blessed the Holy and Great One, and spake with the breath of my mouth, and with the tongue of flesh, which God has made for the children of the flesh of men, that they should speak therewith, and He gave them breath and a tongue and a mouth that they should speak therewith:

[2]"Blessed be Thou, O Lord, King,
Great and mighty in Thy greatness,
Lord of the whole creation of the heaven,
King of kings and God of the whole world.

And Thy power and kingship and greatness abide for ever and ever,
And throughout all generations Thy dominion;
And all the heavens are Thy throne for ever,
And the whole earth Thy footstool for ever and ever.[362]

[3]For Thou hast made and Thou rulest all things,
And nothing is too hard for Thee,[363]
Wisdom departs not from the place of Thy throne,
Nor turns away from Thy presence.
And Thou knowest and seest and hearest everything,
And there is nothing hidden from Thee[364] for Thou seest everything.
[4]And now the angels of Thy heavens are guilty of trespass,
And upon the flesh of men abideth Thy wrath until the great day of

---

[362] **"The whole earth Thy footstool"**; **Isaiah 66:1**, Thus says the LORD: "Heaven is my throne, and *the earth is my footstool*; what is the house that you would build for me, and what is the place of my rest?

[363] **"Nothing is too hard for Thee"**; **Jeremiah 32:17**, Ah, Lord GOD! It is you who have made the heavens and the earth by your great power and by your outstretched arm! *Nothing is too hard for you.*

[364] **"There is nothing hidden from Thee"**; **Hebrews 4:13**, And *no creature is hidden from his sight*, but all are naked and exposed to the eyes of him to whom we must give account.

judgment.
[5]And now, O God and Lord and Great King,
I implore and beseech Thee to fulfill my prayer,
To leave me a posterity on earth,
And not destroy all the flesh of man,
And make the earth without inhabitant,
So that there should be an eternal destruction.
[6]And now, my Lord, destroy from the earth the flesh which has aroused Thy wrath,
☆ But the flesh of righteousness and uprightness establish as a plant of the eternal seed,[365]
And hide not Thy face from the prayer of Thy servant, O Lord."

Second Dream-Vision: An Animal Apocalypse

85 And after this I saw another dream, and I will show the whole dream to thee, my son.

[2]And Enoch lifted up his voice and spake to his son Methuselah: "To thee, my son, will I speak: hear my words- incline thine ear to the dream-vision of thy father.

[3]"Before I took thy mother Edna, I saw in a vision on my bed, and behold a bull[366] came forth from the earth, and that bull was white; and after it came forth a heifer,[367] and along with this latter came forth two bulls, one of them black[368] and the other red.[369] [4]And that black bull gored the red one and pursued him over the earth, and thereupon I could no longer see that red bull.

---

[365] ☆ **"The flesh of righteousness and uprightness establish as a plant of the eternal seed"**; After seeing in a dream-vision the coming destruction of the earth, Enoch cries out to God in distress concerning the judgment to come. In his prayer, Enoch implores, *"The flesh of righteousness and uprightness establish as a plant of the eternal seed, and hide not Thy face from the prayer of Thy servant, O Lord."* The plant metaphor "A Plant of the eternal seed" is a reference to the godly lineage traced from Noah, through whom will come Jesus Christ, who is the "the eternal seed". The term "eternal seed", is imagery that harks back to the promise given by God in Eden, that "the seed of the woman" will crush the head of the serpent. That a woman should possess seed is without parallel in ancient Jewish literature, and prophetically foreshadows the virgin conception and birth of Jesus the Messiah, who comes into the world to destroy the works of the devil. **Genesis 3:15**, I will put enmity between you and the woman, and between your seed and her seed; He shall bruise you on the head, and you shall bruise him on the heel. **Galatians 3:16**, The promises were spoken to Abraham and to his seed. He does not say, "and to seeds," as referring to many, but rather to one, "and to your seed," that is, Christ. **1 John 3:8**, The Son of God appeared for this purpose, to destroy the works of the devil. (NASB) **Enoch 10:16, 93:2+5+10**

[366] Adam; beginning with Adam the "bull" metaphor refers to the lineage of the early patriarchs.

[367] Eve

[368] Cain

[369] Abel

[5]"But that black bull grew and that heifer went with him, and I saw that many oxen proceeded from him which resembled and followed him.

[6]"And that cow, that first one, went from the presence of that first bull in order to seek that red one, but found him not, and lamented with a great lamentation over him and sought him. [7]And I looked till that first bull came to her and quieted her, and from that time onward she cried no more.

[8]"And after that she bore another white bull,[370] and after him she bore many bulls and black cows. [9]And I saw in my sleep that white bull likewise grow and become a great white bull, and from him proceeded many white bulls, and they resembled him. [10]And they began to beget many white bulls, which resembled them, one following the other, even many.

Descent of the Watchers

86 "And again I saw with mine eyes as I slept, and I saw the heaven above, and behold a star fell from heaven,[371] and it arose and ate and pastured amongst those oxen.[372]

[2]"And after that I saw the large and the black oxen, and behold they all changed their stalls and pastures and their cattle, and began to live with each other.

[3]"And again I saw in the vision, and looked towards the heaven, and behold I saw many stars descend and cast themselves down[373] from heaven to that first star,[374] and they became bulls amongst those cattle and pastured with them amongst them. [4]And I looked at them and saw, and behold they all let out their privy members, like horses, and began to cover the cows of the oxen, and they all became pregnant and bare elephants, camels, and asses.[375]

[5]"And all the oxen feared them and were affrighted at them, and began to bite with their teeth and to devour, and to gore with their horns. [6]And they began, moreover, to devour those oxen; and behold all the children of the earth began to tremble and quake before them and to flee from them.

---

[370] Seth

[371] **"Behold, a star fell from heaven"**; this is Biblical language for fallen angels. **Rev. 9:1,** And the fifth angel blew his trumpet, and I saw a star fallen from heaven to earth, and he was given the key to the shaft of the bottomless pit.

[372] The Fall of Semjaza, **Enoch 6:3**

[373] **"I saw many stars cast themselves down"**; **Revelation 12:4,** His tail swept down a third of the stars of heaven and cast them to the earth.

[374] The descent of the Watchers, **Enoch 6:6**

[375] **"They all became pregnant and bare elephants, camels, and asses"**, this verse indicates that giantism was not the only mutation in evidence among the Watcher offspring; there were apparently a variety of grotesqueries produced by these unions.

87 "And again I saw how they began to gore each other and to devour each other, and the earth began to cry aloud.

2"And I raised mine eyes again to heaven, and I saw in the vision, and behold there came forth from heaven beings who were like white men: and four[376] went forth from that place and three[377] with them. 3And those three that had last come forth grasped me by my hand and took me up, away from the generations of the earth, and raised me up to a lofty place, and showed me a tower raised high above the earth, and all the hills were lower.

4"And one said unto me: 'Remain here till thou seest everything that befalls those elephants, camels, and asses, and the stars and the oxen, and all of them.'

88 "And I saw one of those four who had come forth first,[378] and he seized that first star which had fallen from the heaven, and bound it hand and foot and cast it into an abyss: now that abyss was narrow and deep, and horrible and dark.

2"And one of them[379] drew a sword, and gave it to those elephants and camels and asses: then they began to smite each other, and the whole earth quaked because of them.[380]

3"And as I was beholding in the vision, lo, one of those four[381] who had come forth stoned them from heaven, and gathered and took all the great stars whose privy members were like those of horses, and bound them all hand and foot, and cast them in an abyss of the earth.

Noah and His Sons

89 "And one of those four[382] went to that white bull[383] and instructed him in a secret, without his being terrified: he was born a bull and became a man, and built for himself a great vessel and dwelt thereon; and three bulls dwelt with him in that vessel and they were covered in. 2And again I raised mine eyes towards heaven and saw a lofty roof, with seven water torrents thereon, and those torrents flowed with much water into an enclosure. 3And I saw again, and behold fountains were opened on the surface of that great enclosure, and that water began to swell and rise upon the surface, and I saw that enclosure till all its surface was

[376] **Enoch 40:1-10**
[377] **Enoch 20:1-8**
[378] Raphael (Enoch 10:4)
[379] Gabriel (Enoch 10:9)
[380] Consistent with the rest of the *Book of Enoch*, here the Watcher offspring are actually destroyed <u>before</u> the events of the flood.
[381] Michael (Enoch 10:11)
[382] Uriel (Enoch 10:1)
[383] Noah

covered with water. [4]And the water, the darkness, and mist increased upon it; and as I looked at the height of that water, that water had risen above the height of that enclosure, and was streaming over that enclosure, and it stood upon the earth. [5]And all the cattle of that enclosure were gathered together until I saw how they sank and were swallowed up and perished in that water. [6]But that vessel floated on the water, while all the oxen and elephants and camels and asses sank to the bottom with all the animals, so that I could no longer see them, and they were not able to escape, but perished and sank into the depths.

[7]"And again saw in the vision till those water torrents were removed from that high roof, and the chasms of the earth were leveled up and other abysses were opened. [8]Then the water began to run down into these, till the earth became visible; but that vessel settled on the earth, and the darkness retired and light appeared.

[9]"But that white bull which had become a man came out of that vessel, and the three bulls[384] with him, and one of those three was white like that bull, and one of them was red as blood, and one black: and that white bull departed from them.

Abraham and His Sons

[10]"And they began to bring forth beasts of the field and birds, so that there arose different genera: lions, tigers, wolves, dogs, hyenas, wild boars, foxes, squirrels, swine, falcons, vultures, kites, eagles, and ravens; and among them was born a white bull. [385] [11]And they began to bite one another; but that white bull which was born amongst them begat a wild ass[386] and a white bull[387] with it, and the wild asses multiplied. [12]But that bull which was born from him begat a black wild boar[388] and a white sheep;[389] and the former begat many boars, but that sheep begat twelve sheep.[390] [13]And when those twelve sheep had grown, they gave up one of them[391] to the asses,[392] and those asses again gave up that sheep to the wolves,[393] and that sheep grew up among the wolves. [14]And the Lord brought the eleven sheep to live with it and to pasture with it among the wolves: and they multiplied and became many flocks of sheep

---

[384] Noah's sons, Shem, Ham & Japheth
[385] Abraham
[386] Ishmael
[387] Isaac
[388] Esau
[389] Beginning here with Jacob, the godly lineage will be viewed through the "sheep" metaphor; only Jacob in this verse, and Messiah in 90:37-38, are referred to as both "bull" oxen as well as "sheep".
[390] The twelve patriarchs
[391] Joseph
[392] Midianites
[393] Egyptians

The Coming of Moses

[15]"And the wolves began to fear them, and they oppressed them until they destroyed their little ones, and they cast their young into a river of much water: but those sheep began to cry aloud on account of their little ones, and to complain unto their Lord. [16]And a sheep[394] which had been saved from the wolves fled and escaped to the wild asses; and I saw the sheep how they lamented and cried, and besought their Lord with all their might, till that Lord of the sheep[395] descended at the voice of the sheep from a lofty abode, and came to them and pastured them. [17]And He called that sheep which had escaped the wolves, and spake with it concerning the wolves that it should admonish them not to touch the sheep. [18]And the sheep went to the wolves according to the word of the Lord, and another sheep[396] met it and went with it, and the two went and entered together into the assembly of those wolves, and spake with them and admonished them not to touch the sheep from henceforth. [19]And thereupon I saw the wolves, and how they oppressed the sheep exceedingly with all their power; and the sheep cried aloud. [20]And the Lord came to the sheep and they began to smite those wolves:[397] and the wolves began to make lamentation; but the sheep became quiet and forthwith ceased to cry out.

The Exodus

[21]"And I saw the sheep till they departed from amongst the wolves; but the eyes of the wolves were blinded, and those wolves departed in pursuit of the sheep with all their power. [22]And the Lord of the sheep went with them, as their leader, and all His sheep followed Him: and His face was dazzling and glorious and terrible to behold. [23]But the wolves began to pursue those sheep till they reached a sea of water. [24]And that sea was divided, and the water stood on this side and on that before their face, and their Lord led them and placed Himself between them and the wolves. [25]And as those wolves did not yet see the sheep, they proceeded into the midst of that sea, and the wolves followed the sheep, and those wolves ran after them into that sea. [26]And when they saw the Lord of the sheep, they turned to flee before His face, but that sea gathered itself together, and became as it had been created, and the water swelled and rose till it covered those wolves. [27]And I saw till all the wolves who pursued those sheep perished and were drowned.

---

[394] **Though this passage certainly anticipates the coming of** Moses, nevertheless, it is a striking characteristic of the *Book of Enoch*, and unique among pre-Christian Jewish literature, that all reference to the Laws of Moses is conspicuously missing throughout. As one might expect from a book originating before the Law of Moses, notably missing from the *Book of Enoch* are references to Sabbath observance, dietary laws, and other laws and ordinances of Moses.

[395] **"Lord of the Sheep"**; this name for God is found in Enoch only in the *Book of Dream-Visions*, where it occurs 29 times.

[396] Aaron

[397] The 10 plagues

The Giving of the Law at Sinai

[28]"But the sheep escaped from that water and went forth into a wilderness, where there was no water and no grass; and they began to open their eyes and to see; and I saw the Lord of the sheep pasturing them and giving them water and grass, and that sheep going and leading them. [29]And that sheep ascended to the summit of that lofty rock,**[398]** and the Lord of the sheep sent it to them. [30]And after that I saw the Lord of the sheep who stood before them, and His appearance was great and terrible and majestic, and all those sheep saw Him and were afraid before His face. [31]And they all feared and trembled because of Him, and they cried to that sheep with them which was amongst them: "We are not able to stand before our Lord or to behold Him." [32]And that sheep which led them again ascended to the summit of that rock, but the sheep began to be blinded and to wander from the way which he had showed them, but that sheep wot not thereof. [33]And the Lord of the sheep was wrathful exceedingly against them, and that sheep discovered it, and went down from the summit of the rock, and came to the sheep, and found the greatest part of them blinded and fallen away. [34]And when they saw it they feared and trembled at its presence, and desired to return to their folds. [35]And that sheep took other sheep with it, and came to those sheep which had fallen away, and began to slay them; and the sheep feared its presence, and thus that sheep brought back those sheep that had fallen away, and they returned to their folds.

Joshua Leads the People Into Canaan

[36]"And I saw in this vision till that sheep became a man and built a house**[399]** for the Lord of the sheep, and placed all the sheep in that house. [37]And I saw till this sheep which had met that sheep which led them fell asleep: and I saw till all the great sheep perished and little ones arose in their place, and they came to a pasture, and approached a stream of water.**[400]** [38]Then that sheep, their leader which had become a man, withdrew from them and fell asleep, and all the sheep sought it and cried over it with a great crying. [39]And I saw till they left off crying for that sheep and crossed that stream of water, and there arose the two sheep**[401]** as leaders in the place of those which had led them and fallen asleep

[40]"And I saw till the sheep came to a goodly place, and a pleasant and glorious land,**[402]** and I saw till those sheep were satisfied; and that house stood amongst them in the Pleasant Land. [41]And sometimes their eyes

---

[398] Mount Sinai
[399] The Tabernacle in the wilderness
[400] The Jordan River
[401] Joshua and Caleb
[402] **"The pleasant land"**; the "pleasant land" is a title used for the land of Israel; **Psalm 106:24**, They despised *the pleasant land*, having no faith in his promise. **Zechariah 7:14**, I scattered them with a whirlwind among all the nations that they had not known. Thus the land they left was desolate, so that no one went to and fro, and *the pleasant land* was made desolate. **Enoch 90:20**

were opened, and sometimes blinded, till another sheep[403] arose and led them and brought them all back, and their eyes were opened.

The First Kings of Israel

[42]"And the dogs and the foxes and the wild boars began to devour those sheep till the Lord of the sheep raised up another sheep a ram[404] from their midst, which led them. [43]And that ram began to butt on either side those dogs, foxes, and wild boars till he had destroyed them all. [44]And that sheep whose eyes were opened saw that ram, which was amongst the sheep, till it forsook its glory and began to butt those sheep, and trampled upon them, and behaved itself unseemly. [45]And the Lord of the sheep sent the lamb to another lamb[405] and raised it to being a ram and leader of the sheep instead of that ram which had forsaken its glory. [46]And it went to it and spake to it alone, and raised it to being a ram, and made it the prince and leader of the sheep; but during all these things those dogs oppressed the sheep. [47]And the first ram pursued that second ram, and that second ram arose and fled before it; and I saw till those dogs pulled down the first ram. [48]And that second ram arose and led the little sheep. And that ram begat many sheep and fell asleep; and a little sheep[406] became ram in its stead, and became prince and leader of those sheep.

[49]"And those sheep grew and multiplied; but all the dogs, and foxes, and wild boars feared and fled before it, and that ram butted and killed the wild beasts, and those wild beasts had no longer any power among the sheep and robbed them no more of ought. [50]And that house became great and broad, and it was built for those sheep:[407] and a tower lofty and great was built on the house for the Lord of the sheep, and that house was low, but the tower was elevated and lofty, and the Lord of the sheep stood on that tower and they offered a full table before Him.

The People Led Captive

[51]"And again I saw those sheep that they again erred and went many ways, and forsook that their house, and the Lord of the sheep called some[408] from amongst the sheep and sent them to the sheep, but the sheep began to slay them. [52]And one of them was saved[409] and was not slain, and it sped away and cried aloud over the sheep; and they sought to slay it, but the Lord of the sheep saved it from the sheep, and brought it up to me, and caused it to dwell there. [53]And many other sheep He sent to those sheep to testify unto them and lament over them. [54]And after that I saw that when they forsook the house of the Lord and His tower

---

[403] Samuel
[404] King Saul
[405] David
[406] King Solomon
[407] Solomon's Temple
[408] The prophets of Israel and Judah
[409] Elijah

they fell away entirely, and their eyes were blinded; and I saw the Lord of the sheep how He wrought much slaughter amongst them in their herds until those sheep invited that slaughter and betrayed His place. 55And He gave them over into the hands of the lions and tigers, and wolves and hyenas, and into the hand of the foxes, and to all the wild beasts, and those wild beasts began to tear in pieces those sheep.[410] 56And I saw that He forsook that their house and their tower and gave them all into the hand of the lions, to tear and devour them, into the hand of all the wild beasts.[411]

57"And I began to cry aloud with all my power, and to appeal to the Lord of the sheep, and to represent to Him in regard to the sheep that they were devoured by all the wild beasts. 58But He remained unmoved, though He saw it, and rejoiced that they were devoured and swallowed and robbed, and left them to be devoured in the hand of all the beasts.

The Period of the Seventy Shepherds

59"And He called seventy shepherds,[412] and cast those sheep to them that they might pasture them, and He spake to the shepherds and their companions: "Let each individual of you pasture the sheep henceforward, and everything that I shall command you that do ye. 60And I will deliver them over unto you duly numbered, and tell you which of them are to be destroyed- and them destroy ye." And He gave over unto them those sheep.[413]

61"And He called another and spake unto him: 'Observe and mark everything that the shepherds will do to those sheep; for they will destroy more of them than I have commanded them. 62And every excess and the destruction which will be wrought through the shepherds, record namely

---

410 The Captivity of Israel

411 The Captivity of Judah

412 **"He called seventy shepherds"**, here, our normal expectation of the protective nature shepherds is turned upside down; these shepherds are destroyers, and they do not lead the sheep to pasture by streams of water, rather, they deliver them over into the hands of their enemies. These seventy "shepherds" are apparently evil angels who do God's bidding, but incur guilt by going beyond what they are instructed, see **Enoch 90:21,25.** Enoch's period of the seventy shepherds mirrors the same periods of time as the four gentile kingdoms Daniel saw in his vision in Daniel 7, once Israel had lost its monarchy. The period of the activity of the seventy shepherds begins with the Babylonian captivity and continues until the end of the age. This passage also shares some common features with Ezekiel 34, in which God finds fault with shepherds who act in an opposite fashion as that expected from good shepherds. **Ezekiel 34:7-10**, "Therefore, you shepherds, hear the word of the Lord: 'As I live', declares the Lord God, 'surely because my sheep have become a prey, and *my sheep have become food for all the wild beasts*, since there was no shepherd, and because my shepherds have not searched for my sheep, but the shepherds have fed themselves, and have not fed my sheep, therefore, you shepherds, hear the word of the Lord: thus says the Lord God, behold, I am against the shepherds, and I will require my sheep at their hand and put a stop to their feeding the sheep. No longer shall the shepherds feed themselves. I will rescue my sheep from their mouths, that they may not be food for them."

413 **"He gave over unto them those sheep"**; the phrase speaks of God's sovereignty even in calamity. A similar concept is reflected in **Romans 1:24,26,28**, "God gave them up." **John 19:11**, You would have no authority over me at all *unless it had been given you from above.* **Enoch 89:55**

how many they destroy according to my command, and how many according to their own caprice: record against every individual shepherd all the destruction he effects. [63]And read out before me by number how many they destroy, and how many they deliver over for destruction, that I may have this as a testimony against them, and know every deed of the shepherds, that I may comprehend and see what they do, whether or not they abide by my command which I have commanded them. [64]But they shall not know it, and thou shalt not declare it to them, nor admonish them, but only record against each individual all the destruction which the shepherds effect each in his time and lay it all before me.'

[65]"And I saw till those shepherds pastured in their season, and they began to slay and to destroy more than they were bidden, and they delivered those sheep into the hand of the lions. [66]And the lions and tigers eat and devoured the greater part of those sheep, and the wild boars eat along with them; and they burnt that tower and demolished that house.[414]

[67]"And I became exceedingly sorrowful over that tower because that house of the sheep was demolished, and afterwards I was unable to see if those sheep entered that house. [68]And the shepherds and their associates delivered over those sheep to all the wild beasts, to devour them, and each one of them received in his time a definite number: it was written by the other in a book how many each one of them destroyed of them. [69]And each one slew and destroyed many more than was prescribed; and I began to weep and lament on account of those sheep. [70]And thus in the vision I saw that one who wrote, how he wrote down every one that was destroyed by those shepherds, day by day, and carried up and laid down and showed actually the whole book to the Lord of the sheep- even everything that they had done, and all that each one of them had made away with, and all that they had given over to destruction. [71]And the book was read before the Lord of the sheep, and He took the book from his hand and read it and sealed it and laid it down.

[72]"And forthwith I saw how the shepherds pastured for twelve hours, and behold three of those sheep[415] turned back and came and entered and began to build up all that had fallen down of that house;[416] but the wild boars tried to hinder them, but they were not able. [73]And they began again to build as before, and they reared up that tower, and it was named the high tower; and they began again to place a table before the tower, but all the bread on it was polluted and not pure.[417] [74]And as touching all this the eyes of those sheep were blinded so that they saw not, and the eyes of their shepherds likewise; and they delivered them in large numbers to their shepherds for destruction, and they trampled the sheep with their feet and devoured them. [75]And the Lord of the sheep remained

---

[414] The destruction of the temple in 586 B.C.
[415] Zerubbabel, Joshua, and Nehemiah
[416] Rebuilding of the temple
[417] **"The bread on it was polluted"; Malachi 1:6-7**, You say, "How have we despised your name?" By offering *polluted food upon my altar.*

unmoved till all the sheep were dispersed over the field and mingled with them, and they did not save them out of the hand of the beasts.

76"And this one who wrote the book carried it up, and showed it and read it before the Lord of the sheep, and implored Him on their account, and besought Him on their account as he showed Him all the doings of the shepherds, and gave testimony before Him against all the shepherds.

77"And he took the actual book and laid it down beside Him and departed."

90 "And I saw till that in this manner thirty-five shepherds undertook the pasturing of the sheep, and they severally completed their periods as did the first; and others received them into their hands, to pasture them for their period, each shepherd in his own period.

2"And after that I saw in my vision all the birds of heaven coming, the eagles, the vultures, the kites, the ravens; but the eagles led all the birds; and they began to devour those sheep, and to pick out their eyes and to devour their flesh. 3And the sheep cried out because their flesh was being devoured by the birds, and as for me I looked and lamented in my sleep over that shepherd who pastured the sheep.

4"And I saw until those sheep were devoured by the dogs and eagles and kites, and they left neither flesh nor skin nor sinew remaining on them till only their bones stood there: and their bones too fell to the earth and the sheep became few.

5"And I saw until that twenty-three had undertaken the pasturing and completed in their several periods fifty-eight times.

6"But behold lambs were borne by those white sheep, and they began to open their eyes and to see, and to cry to the sheep. 7Yea, they cried to them, but they did not hearken to what they said to them, but were exceedingly deaf, and their eyes were very exceedingly blinded. 8And I saw in the vision how the ravens flew upon those lambs and took one of those lambs, and dashed the sheep in pieces and devoured them. 9And I saw till horns grew upon those lambs, and the ravens cast down their horns; and I saw till there sprouted a great horn of one of those sheep,[418] and their eyes were opened.

10"And it looked at them and their eyes opened, and it cried to the sheep, and the rams saw it and all ran to it. 11And notwithstanding all this those eagles and vultures and ravens and kites still kept tearing the sheep and swooping down upon them and devouring them: still the sheep remained silent, but the rams lamented and cried out. 12And those ravens fought and battled with it and sought to lay low its horn, but they had no power over it. 13And I saw till the shepherds and eagles and those vultures and

418 Judas Maccabaeus

kites came, and they cried to the ravens that they should break the horn of that ram, and they battled and fought with it, and it battled with them and cried that its help might come.[419]

The End of the Age

[14]"And I saw till that man, who wrote down the names of the shepherds and carried up into the presence of the Lord of the sheep came and helped it and showed it everything: he had come down for the help of that ram.

[15]"And I saw till the Lord of the sheep came unto them in wrath,[420] and all who saw Him fled, and they all fell into His shadow from before His face.

[16]"All the eagles and vultures and ravens and kites were gathered together, and there came with them all the sheep of the field, yea, they all came together, and helped each other to break that horn of the ram.

[17]"And I saw that man, who wrote the book according to the command of the Lord, till he opened that book concerning the destruction which those twelve last shepherds had wrought, and showed that they had destroyed much more than their predecessors, before the Lord of the sheep.

[18]"And I saw till the Lord of the sheep came unto them[421] and took in His hand the staff of His wrath, and smote the earth,[422] and the earth clave

---

[419] The "Animal Apocalypse" in Enoch 85-90, is a chronology of time beginning with the creation of Adam, and concluding with the eternal order; what is notable in this chronology however, is what's missing. The prophecy chronicles salvation history and brings the reader up to the time just before the coming of Christ in the 1st century AD; the prophecy then skips over Christ's public ministry, His death and His resurrection. The prophecy then picks up with God coming to earth in judgment. Fragments of this portion of the scroll are well documented among the Dead Sea Scrolls and have been dated to before the time of Christ. The effect this portion of Enoch would have had upon a reader in the early 1st century AD, could have been to give a sense that God could visit the world in judgment at any moment. In verses 37-38, the birth of Messiah *is* foreseen in summary flashback. The birth and kingship of Messiah come near the end of the vision and are divorced from any context within the chronology itself. Taken as a whole, the *Book of Enoch* reveals most of the pertinent details about the Messiah, except for aspects of chronology. Exactly how the advent and actions of Messiah fit into a larger chronology, is not revealed to Enoch in this book. Nor, for that matter, would these details be revealed to any of the prophets of Israel.

[420] **"Lord of the Sheep"**; this name for God is found in Enoch only in the *Book of Dream-Visions*, where it occurs 29 times.

[421] **"I saw till the Lord of the sheep came unto them"**; this theme first mentioned in Enoch chapter 1, and repeated throughout the book is reintroduced here. Justice will come to earth by reason of God Himself intervening in its history. This vision of Enoch echoes "The Holy Great One will come forth from His dwelling", is echoed in Enoch 1:3. The verse describes why it is the last generation who will inherit the special blessing promised in chapter 1; at the end of the age, the "Lord of the Sheep" will come to earth to deliver the last generation, by reason of the 2nd-Coming of Jesus Christ. **1 Peter 5:4**, When the *chief Shepherd* appears, you will receive the unfading crown of glory. **Enoch 1:3, 25:3, 52:9, 77:1, 90:15,18,20, 91:7, 100:4**

[422] **"The staff of His wrath"**; **Revelation 2:27,** He will rule them with a rod of iron, as when earthen pots are broken in pieces. **Revelation 12:5**, She gave birth to a male child, one who

asunder, and all the beasts and all the birds of the heaven fell from among those sheep, and were swallowed up in the earth and it covered them.[423]

[19]"And I saw till a great sword was given to the sheep, and the sheep proceeded against all the beasts of the field to slay them, and all the beasts and the birds of the heaven fled before their face.

The Last Judgment

[20]"And I saw till a throne was erected in the Pleasant Land,[424] and the Lord of the sheep[425] sat Himself thereon[427] and the other took the sealed books and opened those books before the Lord of the sheep.

[21]"And the Lord called those men the seven first white ones,[426] and commanded that they should bring before Him, beginning with the first star which led the way, all the stars whose privy members were like those of horses, and they brought them all before Him.

[22]"And He said to that man who wrote before Him, being one of those seven white ones, and said unto him: 'Take those seventy shepherds to whom I delivered the sheep, and who taking them on their own authority slew more than I commanded them.'

[23]"And behold they were all bound, I saw, and they all stood before Him. [24]And the judgment was held first over the stars, and they were judged and found guilty, and went to the place of condemnation, and they were cast into an abyss, full of fire and flaming, and full of pillars of fire. [25]And those seventy shepherds were judged and found guilty, and they were cast into that fiery abyss. [26]And I saw at that time how a like abyss was opened in the midst of the earth, full of fire, and they brought those blinded sheep, and they were all judged and found guilty and cast into this fiery abyss, and they burned; now this abyss was to the right of that house. [27]And I saw those sheep burning and their bones burning.

[28]"And I stood up to see till they folded up that old house; and carried off all the pillars, and all the beams and ornaments of the house were at the

---

is to rule all the nations with a rod of iron. **Revelation 19:15**, From his mouth comes a sharp sword with which to strike down the nations, and he will rule them with a rod of iron.

[423] **Verses 16-18** are doublets, retelling of the same events as verses 13-15.

[424] **"The pleasant land"**; the "pleasant land" is a title used for the land of Israel in **Psalm 106:24**, They despised the *pleasant land*, having no faith in his promise. **Zechariah 7:14**, I scattered them with a whirlwind among all the nations that they had not known. Thus the land they left was desolate, so that no one went to and fro, and *the pleasant land* was made desolate. **Enoch 89:40**

[425] **"The Lord of the sheep"**; **John 10:11**, I am the good shepherd. The good shepherd lays down his life for the sheep. **Hebrews 13:20-21**, May the God of peace who brought again from the dead our Lord Jesus, the great shepherd of the sheep, by the blood of the eternal covenant, equip you with everything good that you may do his will. **1 Peter 5:4**, And when the chief Shepherd appears, you will receive the unfading crown of glory. **Enoch 1:3, 25:3, 52:9, 77:1, 90:15,18,20, 91:7, 100:4**

[426] **"The seven first white ones"**; the seven archangels. **Enoch 87:2**

same time folded up with it, and they carried it off and laid it in a place in the south of the land.

[29]"And I saw till the Lord of the sheep brought a new house greater and loftier than that first, and set it up in the place of the first which had been folded up: all its pillars were new, and its ornaments were new and larger than those of the first, the old one which He had taken away, and all the sheep were within it.

[30]"And I saw all the sheep which had been left, and all the beasts on the earth, and all the birds of the heaven, falling down and doing homage to those sheep and making petition to and obeying them in everything.

[31]"And thereafter those three who were clothed in white and had seized me by my hand who had taken me up before, and the hand of that ram also seizing hold of me, they took me up and set me down in the midst of those sheep before the judgment took place.

The Blessings to Come

[32]"And those sheep were all white, and their wool was abundant and clean. [33]And all that had been destroyed and dispersed, and all the beasts of the field, and all the birds of the heaven, assembled in that house, and the Lord of the sheep rejoiced with great joy because they were all good and had returned to His house. [34]And I saw till they laid down that sword, which had been given to the sheep, and they brought it back into the house, and it was sealed before the presence of the Lord, and all the sheep were invited into that house, but it held them not. [35]And the eyes of them all were opened, and they saw the good, and there was not one among them that did not see. [36]And I saw that that house was large and broad and very full.

Messiah born to Rule the World

☼ [37]"And I saw that a white bull was born[427] with large horns, and all the beasts of the field and all the birds of the air feared him and made petition to him all the time. [38]And I saw till all their generations were transformed, and they all became white bulls; and the first among them became a lamb, and that lamb became a great animal and had great black horns on its head; and the Lord of the sheep rejoiced over it and over all the oxen.

[39]"And I slept in their midst: and I awoke and saw everything.

---

[427] ☼ **"And I saw that a white bull was born"**; The ensuing passage tells us something about the identity of the coming Messiah; Messiah is to be a bull and a lamb, in other words he will be born of human descent from the chosen people, from the chosen lineage. The fact that Messiah has large horns refers to his rulership; his rulership extends over the entire animal kingdom signifying Messiah's rulership over the nations. As a result of the rule of Messiah, all of humanity is transformed and becomes a source of rejoicing for God.

Enoch Weeps Because of What He has Seen

[40]"This is the vision which I saw while I slept, and I awoke and blessed the Lord of righteousness and gave Him glory. [41]Then I wept with a great weeping and my tears stayed not till I could no longer endure it: when I saw, they flowed on account of what I had seen; for everything shall come and be fulfilled, and all the deeds of men in their order were shown to me.

[42]"On that night I remembered the first dream, and because of it I wept and was troubled- because I had seen that vision."

Introduction to the Book of the Preaching of Enoch

Title ~ Chapters 91-108 of the *Book of Enoch*, is the section commonly referred to as *"The Letter of Enoch"*, or, *"The Epistle of Enoch"*. For this edition, we title this section, *"The Book of the Preaching of Enoch"*, since it is a more accurate description of the book's contents. Unlike all four previous sections of the *Book of Enoch*, the focus of this section is not primarily upon visions Enoch has received. Instead, the book's passionate sermons flow as from the heart of the man of whom the Bible says, he spent his life walking with God.

Authorship ~ In 91:1, as is evident throughout the rest of the book, the claim is made this is being written by the Biblical Enoch to his son Methuselah. Unlike the previous four sections, the contents of the *Book of the Preaching of Enoch*, were first given orally, then written down in book form.

Date ~ The book is a logical continuation of that long section of the *Book of Enoch* which begins in chapter 81, verses 5-6. This places the composition of this section one year before Enoch is translated to heaven, or about 670 years before the flood.

Major Theme ~ *"Methuselah went and summoned to him all his brothers and assembled his relatives. And Enoch spake unto all the children of righteousness and said, 'Hear, ye sons of Enoch, all the words of your father, and hearken aright to the voice of my mouth; for I exhort you and say unto you, beloved: Love uprightness and walk therein'" Enoch 91:2.*

Background ~ Enoch has had the hand of God on his life since a young age. Then when Enoch received God's call to the office of prophet, he delivered God's message of rebuke to the angels who sinned. Enoch has been given a tour of the cosmos, and has spent time in heaven where he has seen the vision the Holy One and the exalted Son of Man seated on God's throne. In this, the last of his writings, Enoch leaves his descendants an exhortation to righteousness.

THE BOOK OF THE PREACHING OF ENOCH

Purpose ~ Though the Watchers had already fallen by Enoch's time, the world will get much worse after Enoch's departure, and will continue to do so until the time of the flood, (Enoch 91:5). In this book Enoch preaches against the increasing evils of his time. It is in this context that Enoch startlingly reveals that the period of the last days will be even worse than the days before the flood. During the days of tribulation in the end times, *"transgression shall prevail in a twofold degree"*. The last of the last days will be twice as bad as the time before the flood. The *Book of the Preaching of Enoch* is to stand as a testimony not only to Enoch's own generation but also to the generation who will be living under similar circumstances at the end of the age.

Enoch has been told to record everything he has been shown. In this book Enoch dispatches this responsibility, teaching what he knows to his son Methuselah, who will in turn pass on his message and his books to later generations. Enoch's writings are to be deposited on earth as a testimony to the future generations of mankind.

Synopsis ~ The *Book of the Preaching of Enoch,* is a series of sermons contrasting the destinies of those who are God's people with those who are not. Though the unrighteous seem at ease and blessed and the righteous are suffering deprivation and injustice, the tables are set to turn. The righteous will be blessed forever and the unrighteous destroyed.

This book contains the Prophecy of Weeks. Though the Prophecy of Weeks is shorter than the Animal Apocalypse which we saw in the *Book of Dream-Visions,* it is no less grandiose in its scope covering human history from creation to the eternal order. Its special focus is the godly human lineage signified by the 'Plant of Righteousness'.

The end of the book recounts the unusual circumstances surrounding Noah's birth. Noah's birth closes out the *Book of Enoch,* which sets the stage for the story of the flood to be told in the *Book of Genesis.*

~~~~~~~~~~~~~~~~~~~~~~~~~~~~

Outline ~

I. The Testament of Enoch (91:1-108:15)
- A. Enoch calls a meeting of his family (91:1-3a)
- B. Enoch gives an overview (91:3b-11)
~~~~~~~~~~~~~~~~~~~~~~~~~~~~

a. Exhortation to love righteousness (91:4)
b. Earth will be destroyed twice (91:5-9)
1. Sin and sinners will be destroyed (91:5-9)
c. The righteous will resurrect to life (91:10-11)

II. The Prophecy of Weeks (91:12-93:14)
A. Weeks 8 through 10 (91:12-16)
B. The Eternal Order (91:17-19)
C. Narrative Interlude (92:1-93:2)
D. Weeks 1 through 7 (93:3-93:14)

III. Contrasting Two Destinies (94:1-104:13)
A. The righteous blessed, the godless cursed

IV. Narrative Concerning the Birth of Noah (94:1-105:2)

V. Epilogue Dedicated to the Final Generation (108:1-15)

Book of the Preaching of Enoch

"The Spirit is Poured Out Upon Me!"

91 "And now, my son Methuselah,[428] call to me all thy brothers
And gather together to me all the sons of thy mother;
For the word calls me,
And the Spirit is poured out upon me,[429]
That I may show you everything
That shall befall you for ever."

2And thereupon Methuselah went and summoned to him all his brothers and assembled his relatives. 3And he spake unto all the children of righteousness and said:

The Testament of Enoch

"Hear, ye sons of Enoch, all the words of your father,
And hearken aright to the voice of my mouth;
For I exhort you and say unto you, beloved:

4"Love uprightness and walk therein.
And draw not nigh to uprightness with a double heart,
And associate not with those of a double heart,

"But walk in righteousness, my sons.
And it shall guide you on good paths,
And righteousness shall be your companion.

Earth's First End

5"For I know that violence must increase on the earth,
And a great chastisement be executed on the earth,
And all unrighteousness come to an end:

"Yea, it shall be cut off from its roots,
And its whole structure be destroyed.

---

428 **"And now, my son Methuselah"**; here and elsewhere in the *Book of Enoch,* Methuselah is shown as the recipient of Enoch's writings. **Enoch 82:1, 83:1**
429 **"The Spirit is poured out upon me"**; similar language can be found throughout the Hebrew prophets. See **Isaiah 32:15, 44:3, Ezekiel 39:29, Joel 2:28-29, Acts 2:33, 10:45**

As in the Days of Noah

6"And unrighteousness shall again be consummated on the earth,
And all the deeds of unrighteousness and of violence
And transgression shall prevail in a twofold degree.[430]

7"And when sin and unrighteousness and blasphemy
And violence in all kinds of deeds increase,
And apostasy[431] and transgression and uncleanness increase,[432]

Earth's Second End

"A great chastisement shall come from heaven upon all these,
✡ And the Holy Lord will come forth with wrath and chastisement
To execute judgment on earth.[433]

8"In those days violence shall be cut off from its roots,
And the roots of unrighteousness together with deceit,
And they shall be destroyed from under heaven.

9"And all the idols of the heathen shall be abandoned,
And the temples burned with fire,
And they shall remove them from the whole earth,

"And they shall be cast into the judgment of fire,
And shall perish in wrath and in grievous judgment for ever.

The Righteous Shall Arise from Sleep

10"And the righteous shall arise from their sleep,[434]
And wisdom shall arise and be given unto them.

---

[430] **"Transgression shall prevail in a twofold degree"**; the shocking claim here is that the time of tribulation before the end of the age will be twice as bad as the days before the flood of Noah's day when, "the wickedness of man was great in the earth, and every intention of the thoughts of his heart was only evil continually" **Genesis 6:5**

[431] **Apostasy will increase; 1 Timothy 4:1,** The Spirit expressly says that in later times some will *depart from the faith* by devoting themselves to deceitful spirits and teachings of demons. **2 Thessalonians 2:3**, Let no one in any way deceive you, for it will not come unless *the apostasy* comes first, and the man of lawlessness is revealed, the son of destruction. (NASB)

[432] **Lawlessness will increase; Matthew 24:12**, And because lawlessness will be increased, the love of many will grow cold. **Matthew 24:21**, For then there will be great tribulation, such as has not been from the beginning of the world until now, no, and never will be. **2 Timothy 3:1**, But understand this, that in the last days there will come times of difficulty.

[433] ✡ **"The Holy Lord will come forth"**; here Enoch restates the language of **Enoch 1:3-4**, "The Holy Great One will come forth from His dwelling, and the eternal God will tread upon the earth, even on Mount Sinai, and appear from His camp, and appear in the strength of His might from the heaven of heavens." Earth's final judgment will come about at the personal presence of God coming to earth. In Jude 1:14-15, we are told this prophecy of Enoch is accomplished by the second coming of Jesus Christ. **Enoch 1:3, 25:3, 52:9, 77:1, 90:15,18,20, 91:7, 100:4**

[434] **"The righteous shall arise from their sleep"**; **Daniel 12:2**, And many of those who sleep in the dust of the earth shall awake. **1 Thessalonians 4:16**, The dead in Christ will rise first.

[11]"And after that the roots of unrighteousness shall be cut off, and the sinners shall be destroyed by the sword... shall be cut off from the blasphemers in every place, and those who plan violence and those who commit blasphemy shall perish by the sword.

The Prophecy of Weeks Part 2, Weeks 8-10 [435]

Week Eight: The Messianic Age

[12]"And after that there shall be another, the eighth week, that of righteousness, And a sword shall be given to it that a righteous judgment may be executed on the oppressors,
And sinners shall be delivered into the hands of the righteous.[436]

[13]"And at its close they shall acquire houses through their righteousness,
And a house shall be built for the Great King in glory for evermore,

Week Nine: Great White Throne Judgment

[14]"And after that, in the ninth week,
The righteous judgment shall be revealed to the whole world,
And all the works of the godless shall vanish from all the earth,
And the world shall be written down for destruction.[437]
And all mankind shall look to the path of uprightness.

Week Ten: New Heavens and New Earth

[15]"And after this, in the tenth week in the seventh part,
There shall be the great eternal judgment,
In which He will execute vengeance amongst the angels.

[16]"And the first heaven shall depart and pass away,[438]
And a new heaven shall appear,[439]
And all the powers of the heavens shall give sevenfold light.

---

[435] Verses 12-17 are possibly out of order. In this "Prophecy of Weeks", weeks 1 thru 7 are found in Enoch 93:3-10, weeks 8 thru 10 are found here in Enoch 91:12-17. I owe special thanks to Daniel Tavolieri's help in understanding the *Prophecy of Weeks*. Refer to appendix II: "Reordering the Prophecy of Weeks" for a fuller examination of this passage.

[436] **"Sinners shall be delivered into the hands of the righteous"**; **1 Corinthians 6:2-3**, Or do you not know that the saints will judge the world? And if the world is to be judged by you, are you incompetent to try trivial cases? Do you not know that we are to judge angels?

[437] **"The world shall be written down for destruction"; 2 Peter 3:7**, But by the same word the heavens and earth that now exist are stored up for fire, being kept until the day of judgment and destruction of the ungodly.

[438] **"The first heaven shall depart and pass away"**; **Revelation 21:1**, The first heaven and the first earth had passed away.

[439] **"A new heaven shall appear"; Revelation 20:11**, Then I saw a great white throne and him who was seated on it. From his presence earth and sky fled away, and no place was found for them. **Revelation 21:1**, Then I saw a new heaven and a new earth, for the first heaven and the first earth had passed away, and the sea was no more.

The Eternal Order

[17]"And after that there will be many weeks without number for ever,
And all shall be in goodness and righteousness,
And sin shall no more be mentioned for ever.

[18]"And now I tell you, my sons, and show you
The paths of righteousness and the paths of violence.
Yea, I will show them to you again
That ye may know what will come to pass.
[19]And now, hearken unto me, my sons,
And walk in the paths of righteousness,
And walk not in the paths of violence;
For all who walk in the paths of unrighteousness shall perish for ever."

Enoch Writes His Final Book

92 The book written by Enoch-[440] Enoch indeed wrote this complete doctrine of wisdom, which is praised of all men and a judge of all the earth for all my children who shall dwell on the earth. And for the future generations who shall observe uprightness and peace.

[2]Let not your spirit be troubled[441] on account of the times;
For the Holy and Great One has appointed days for all things.

Jesus, the Righteous One, Victorious Over Death

✡ [3]And the Righteous One[442] shall arise from sleep,[443]
Shall arise and walk in the paths of righteousness,
And all his path and conversation shall be in eternal goodness and grace.

---

[440] **"The book written by Enoch"; Enoch 1:1-2, 37:3, 108:1**
[441] **"Let not your spirit be troubled"; John 14:1**, Let not your hearts be troubled. Believe in God; believe also in me. **John 14:27**, Peace I leave with you; my peace I give to you. Not as the world gives do I give to you. Let not your hearts be troubled, neither let them be afraid.
[442] **"The Righteous One";** this title for Messiah is found twice in *The Book of the Parables* and once in *Book of the Preaching of Enoch*; it is also found in the Old and New Testaments. Here, in **Enoch 92:3** the resurrection of Jesus Christ, the Righteous One is prophesied. **Isaiah 53:11**, By his knowledge shall the *Righteous One*, my servant, make many to be accounted righteous, and he shall bear their iniquities. **Acts 3:14**, You denied the Holy and *Righteous One*, and asked for a murderer to be granted to you. **Acts 7:52-53**, They killed those who announced beforehand the coming of the *Righteous One*, whom you have now betrayed and murdered. **Acts 22:14**, The God of our fathers appointed you to know his will, to see the *Righteous One* and to hear a voice from his mouth. **Enoch 38:2, 53:6**
[443] ✡ **"The Righteous One shall arise from sleep"; Enoch 92:3**, a prophecy of the resurrection of the Righteous One, a Biblical name for Messiah. **1 Cor. 15:20-21**, But in fact Christ has been raised from the dead, the first fruits of those who have fallen asleep. For as by a man came death, by a man has come also the resurrection of the dead.

[4]He will be gracious to the righteous and give him eternal uprightness,
And He will give him power[444] so that
he shall be endowed with goodness and righteousness,
And he shall walk in eternal light.

[5]And sin shall perish in darkness for ever,
And shall no more be seen from that day for evermore.

93 And after that Enoch both gave and began to recount from the books. 2And Enoch said:

"Concerning the children of righteousness
and concerning the elect of the world,
And concerning the plant of uprightness,[445] I will speak these things,
Yea, I, Enoch will declare them unto you, my sons:

The Threefold Transmission of Revelation

	The Book of Enoch	***The Book of Revelation***
Visions	*"Which appeared to me in the Heavenly Vision"*	*"I saw the horses in my vision"*
Angels	*"I have known through the word of the Holy Angels"*	*"He made it known by sending his angel to his servant John"*
Books	*"Have learned from the Heavenly Tablets"*	*"So I went to the angel and told him to give me the little scroll"*

"According to that which appeared to me in the heavenly vision,[446]
And which I have known through the word of the holy angels,
And have learnt from the heavenly tablets."[447]

[444] **"He will give Him power"**; **John 17:2**, You have given him authority over all flesh, to give eternal life to all whom you have given him. **Matthew 28:18**, Jesus came and said to them, "All authority in heaven and on earth has been given to me."

[445] **"The Plant of uprightness", "plant of righteous judgment"** and **"plant of righteousness"** in verses 2,5 and 10, are references to the godly lineage to be traced from Noah to the patriarchs and beyond. The term is messianic in its implications because from the plant of righteousness sprung Jesus Christ the messiah; Jesus is the reason the plant inherits the quality of righteousness. **Enoch 10:16, 84:6, 93:2+5+10**

[446] **"The heavenly vision"**; **Acts 26:19**, Therefore, O King Agrippa, I was not disobedient to *the heavenly vision*.

[447] **"Vision, angels and heavenly tablets"**; here Enoch speaks of the three modes by which he received revelation. The same modes of communication can be seen in the *Revelation of John*, though in the Revelation, tablets have been replaced by scrolls. For more about these tablets, see footnote on Enoch 81:1-2

The Prophecy of Weeks Part 1, Weeks 1-7
Week One: Enoch's Era

[3]And Enoch began to recount from the books and said:
"I was born the seventh in the first week,[448]
While judgment and righteousness still endured. [449]

Week Two: Noah's Time and the Flood

[4]"And after me there shall arise in the second week great wickedness,
And deceit shall have sprung up;
And in it there shall be the first end.

"And in it a man shall be saved; [450]
And after it is ended unrighteousness shall grow up,
And a law shall be made for the sinners.[451]

Week Three: Abraham is Raised Up

[5]"And after that in the third week at its close
A man shall be elected as the plant of righteous judgment,[452]
And his posterity shall become the plant of righteousness for evermore.

Week Four: Moses' Law and the Tabernacle

[6]"And after that in the fourth week, at its close,
Visions of the holy and righteous shall be seen,
And a law for all generations and an enclosure shall be made for them.[453]

---

[448] In this "Prophecy of Weeks", weeks 1 thru 7 are found here in chapter 93:3-10, weeks 8 thru 10 are found in chapter 91:12-17. I owe special thanks to Daniel Tavolieri, for help in understanding the *Prophecy of Weeks*. Refer to appendix II: "Reordering the Prophecy of Weeks" for a fuller examination of this passage.

[449] **"While judgment and righteousness still endured"**; though the fall of the Watchers had occurred during Enoch's father's lifetime, during Enoch's day the world had not yet sunk down so low as the later time when the world became totally corrupt. Enoch's proclamation of judgment to the Watchers in Enoch 13, may have been as many as eight centuries prior to its having been carried out.

[450] **Noah**

[451] **"A law shall be made for the sinners"**; after having landed the ark in safety, Noah, through revelation, delivered a kind of universal law for his descendants which was in effect until the time of Moses. **Genesis 8. 1 Timothy 1:9-11**, Understanding this, that the law is not laid down for the just but for the lawless and disobedient, for the ungodly and sinners, for the unholy and profane.

[452] Here Abraham is the one "elected" or chosen as the plant of righteous judgment; from Abraham comes the "plant of righteousness", Abraham's offspring through Isaac then Jacob. The verse says the plant of righteousness is for evermore. God's plans for his people Israel, the descendants of Jacob, have never been set aside.

[453] **"A law for all generations and an enclosure"**; in other words, the Law of Moses and the tabernacle in the wilderness.

Week Five: Solomon's Temple

7"And after that in the fifth week, at its close,
The house of glory and dominion[454] shall be built for ever.

Week Six: Apostasy, Christ's Ascension, Temple Destroyed

8"And after that in the sixth week all who live in it shall be blinded,[455]
And the hearts of all of them shall godlessly forsake wisdom.

☼ "And in it a man shall ascend;[456]
And at its close the house of dominion shall be burnt with fire,[457]
And the whole race of the chosen root shall be dispersed.[458]

Week Seven: All Israel Will be Saved!

9"And after that in the seventh week shall an apostate generation arise,
And many shall be its deeds,
And all its deeds shall be apostate.

10"And at its close shall be elected[459]
The elect righteous of the eternal plant of righteousness,[439]
To receive sevenfold instruction concerning all His creation.
(See 91:12-17)

---

[454] **"The house of glory and dominion"**; in other words the temple in Jerusalem and the Davidic throne. It "shall be built forever"; despite temporary periods of time during which the temple is not standing (as in 93:8) or when there is no Davidic kingdom, the promise of their restoration remains unchanged. In our time, there is no earthly temple, and Christ the root and branch of David is enthroned in heaven; both the earthly temple and the throne will have restoration at the return of Christ.

[455] **"Shall be blinded"**; the sin of unbelief is highlighted here. Jesus Christ came to his own and his own did not recognize him.

[456] ☼ **"In it a man shall ascend";** the language is reminiscent of the catching away of Enoch, but here it is a prophecy of the ascension of Christ, followed by a prophecy of the destruction of the Jewish temple in 70 AD. **Acts 1:9**, And when he had said these things, as they were looking on, he was lifted up, and a cloud took him out of their sight.

[457] **"The house of dominion shall be burnt with fire"**; this is the house of dominion mentioned in 93:7. **Matthew 24:1-2**, Jesus left the temple and was going away, when his disciples came to point out to him the buildings of the temple. But he answered them, "You see all these, do you not? Truly, I say to you, there will not be left here one stone upon another that will not be thrown down." The stones were thrown down by the Romans in order to scrape the gold from between them which had melted and run down when the temple was burned.

[458] **"The whole race of the chosen root shall be dispersed"**; **Luke 21:24**, They will fall by the edge of the sword and be led captive among all nations, and Jerusalem will be trampled underfoot by the Gentiles, until the times of the Gentiles are fulfilled.

[459] **"At its close shall be elected the elect righteous of the eternal plant of righteousness"**; The nation who introduced Jesus Christ to the world will themselves be introduced to their Messiah. In this way the chosen people will be doubly chosen by reason of their election into Israel's Messiah. This earth-shattering event will set the stage for the return of Jesus to earth. The regeneration of Israel, long prophesied by the prophets, will signal the soon coming Messianic age, a golden age on earth and the end of Satan's rule over the affairs of humankind. **Romans 11:26**, "In this way all Israel will be saved."

Who Is Like God?

[11]"For who is there of all the children of men that is able to hear the voice of the Holy One without being troubled? And who can think His thoughts? And who is there that can behold all the works of heaven? [12]And how should there be one who could behold the heaven, and who is there that could understand the things of heaven and see a soul or a spirit and could tell thereof, or ascend and see all their ends and think them or do like them? [13]And who is there of all men that could know what is the breadth and the length of the earth, and to whom has been shown the measure of all of them? [14]Or is there anyone who could discern the length of the heaven and how great is its height, and upon what it is founded, and how great is the number of the stars, and where all the luminaries rest?"[460]

Further Exhortation to Righteousness

94 And now I say unto you, my sons,
love righteousness and walk therein;
For the paths of righteousness are worthy of acceptation,
But the paths of unrighteousness
shall suddenly be destroyed and vanish.

[2]And to certain men of a generation
shall the paths of violence and of death be revealed,
And they shall hold themselves afar from them,
And shall not follow them.

[3]And now I say unto you the righteous:
Walk not in the paths of wickedness, nor in the paths of death,
And draw not nigh to them, lest ye be destroyed.

[4]But seek and choose for yourselves righteousness and an elect life,
And walk in the paths of peace,
And ye shall live and prosper.

[5]And hold fast my words in the thoughts of your hearts,
And suffer them not to be effaced from your hearts;

For I know that sinners will tempt men to evilly-entreat wisdom,
So that no place may be found for her,[461]
And no manner of temptation may minish.

---

[460] **Who is like God?**; **Job 38:1-41**
[461] **Enoch 42**

The Litany of Woes

6Woe to those who build unrighteousness and oppression
And lay deceit as a foundation;
For they shall be suddenly overthrown,
And they shall have no peace.

7Woe to those who build their houses with sin;
For from all their foundations shall they be overthrown,
And by the sword shall they fall.
And those who acquire gold and silver in judgment suddenly shall perish.

8Woe to you, ye rich, for ye have trusted in your riches,[462]
And from your riches shall ye depart,
Because ye have not remembered the Most High
in the days of your riches.

9Ye have committed blasphemy and unrighteousness,
And have become ready for the day of slaughter,[463]
And the day of darkness and the day of the great judgment.[464]

10Thus I speak and declare unto you:
He who hath created you will overthrow you,
And for your fall there shall be no compassion,
And your Creator will rejoice at your destruction.

11And your righteous ones in those days shall be
A reproach to the sinners and the godless.

The Mournful Prophet

95 Oh that mine eyes were a cloud of waters[465]
That I might weep over you,
And pour down my tears as a cloud of waters:

---

462 **"Woe to you, ye rich"**; **Luke 6:24-26**, Woe to you who are rich. **James 5:1-3**, Come now, you rich, weep and howl for the miseries that are coming upon you. Your riches have rotted and your garments are moth-eaten. Your gold and silver have corroded, and their corrosion will be evidence against you and will eat your flesh like fire. You have laid up treasure in the last days.
463 **"You have become ready for the day of slaughter"**; **James 5:5**, You have lived on the earth in luxury and in self-indulgence. You have fattened your hearts in a *day of slaughter*.
464 **"The day of darkness and the day of the great judgment"**; **Joel 2:1-2**, The day of the LORD is coming; it is near, a *day of darkness* and gloom, a day of clouds and thick darkness!
465 **"Oh that mine eyes were a cloud of waters"; Jeremiah 9:1**, Oh that my head were waters, and my eyes a fountain of tears, that I might weep day and night for the slain of the daughter of my people! **Matthew 23:37**, O Jerusalem, Jerusalem, the city that kills the prophets and stones those who are sent to it! How often would I have gathered your children together as a hen gathers her brood under her wings, and you would not!

That so I might rest from my trouble of heart!
[2]Who has permitted you to practice reproaches and wickedness?

And so judgment shall overtake you, sinners.
[3]Fear not the sinners, ye righteous;

Further Woes

For again will the Lord deliver them into your hands,
That ye may execute judgment upon them according to your desires.
[4]Woe to you who fulminate anathemas which cannot be reversed:

Healing shall therefore be far from you because of your sins.
[5]Woe to you who requite your neighbor with evil;

For ye shall be requited according to your works.
[6]Woe to you, lying witnesses,

And to those who weigh out injustice,
For suddenly shall ye perish.
[7]Woe to you, sinners, for ye persecute the righteous;[466]

For ye shall be delivered up and persecuted because of injustice,
And heavy shall its yoke be upon you.

96 Be hopeful, ye righteous;
for suddenly shall the sinners perish before you,
And ye shall have lordship over them according to your desires.

Deliverance on Wings of Eagles

[2]And in the day of the tribulation of the sinners,
Your children shall mount and rise as eagles,[467]
And higher than the vultures will be your nest,
And ye shall ascend and enter the crevices of the earth,
And the clefts of the rock for ever as coneys before the unrighteous,
And the sirens[468] shall sigh because of you- and weep.

---

[466] **"Ye persecute the righteous"**; **Matthew 23:29-31**, Woe to you, scribes and Pharisees, hypocrites! For you build the tombs of the prophets and decorate the monuments of the righteous, saying, "If we had lived in the days of our fathers, we would not have taken part with them in shedding the blood of the prophets." Thus you witness against yourselves that you are sons of those who murdered the prophets. **Matthew 5:10**, Blessed are those who are persecuted for righteousness' sake, for theirs is the kingdom of heaven.
[467] **"Your children shall mount and rise as eagles"**; **Exodus 19:4**, You yourselves have seen what I did to the Egyptians, and how I bore you on eagles' wings and brought you to myself. **Revelation 12:14**, The woman was given the two wings of the great eagle so that she might fly from the serpent into the wilderness, to the place where she is to be nourished for a time, and times, and half a time.
[468] Nickelsburg-Vanderkam, lacks 'sirens', "...like conies, before the lawless. And they will sigh because of you and weep."

[3]Wherefore fear not, ye that have suffered;
For healing shall be your portion,
And a bright light shall enlighten you,
And the voice of rest ye shall hear from heaven.

Woe to the Unrighteous

[4]Woe unto you, ye sinners,
for your riches make you appear like the righteous,
But your hearts convict you of being sinners,
And this fact shall be a testimony against you
for a memorial of your evil deeds.

[5]Woe to you who devour the finest of the wheat,
And drink wine in large bowls,
And tread underfoot the lowly with your might.

[6]Woe to you who drink water from every fountain,[469]
For suddenly shall ye be consumed and wither away,
Because ye have forsaken the
Fountain of Life.[470]

[7]Woe to you who work unrighteousness
And deceit and blasphemy:
It shall be a memorial
against you for evil.
[8]Woe to you, ye mighty,
Who with might oppress the righteous;
For the day of your destruction is coming.

The Source of Life
Fresh running water flows from a spring, it is in constant motion, a fountain of "living water". God is the source, the origin, the refreshment of life.

The Coming Vindication of the Faithful

In those days many and good days shall come to the righteous- in the day of your judgment.

97 Believe, ye righteous, that the sinners will become a shame
And perish in the day of unrighteousness.
[2]Be it known unto you ye sinners,
that the Most High is mindful of your destruction,
And the angels of heaven rejoice over your destruction.[471]

---

[469] **"You who drink water from every fountain"**; **Jeremiah 2:13**, My people have committed two evils: they have forsaken me, the fountain of living waters, and hewed out cisterns for themselves, broken cisterns that can hold no water.
[470] **"The fountain of life"**; **Psalm 36:9**, For with you is *the fountain of life*; in your light do we see light.
[471] **"The angels of heaven rejoice over your destruction"**; **Revelation 19:1+3**, I heard what seemed to be the loud voice of a great multitude in heaven, crying out, "Hallelujah! The smoke from her goes up forever and ever."

[3]What will ye do, ye sinners,
And whither will ye flee on that day of judgment,
When ye hear the voice of the prayer of the righteous?

[4]Yea, ye shall fare like unto them,
Against whom this word shall be a testimony:
"Ye have been companions of sinners."

[5]And in those days the prayer of the righteous
shall reach unto the Lord,
And for you the days of your judgment shall come.
[6]And all the words of your unrighteousness shall be read out
before the Great Holy One,
And your faces shall be covered with shame,
And He will reject every work which is grounded on unrighteousness.

[7]Woe to you, ye sinners, who live on the mid ocean and on the dry land,
Whose remembrance is evil against you.

[8]Woe to you who acquire silver and gold in unrighteousness and say:[472]
"We have become rich with riches and have possessions;
And have acquired everything we have desired.[473]

[9]"And now let us do what we purposed:
For we have gathered silver,
And many are the husbandmen in our houses.
And our granaries are brim full as with water."

[10]Yea and like water your lies shall flow away;
For your riches shall not abide
But speedily ascend from you;

For ye have acquired it all in unrighteousness,
And ye shall be given over to a great curse.

98 And now I swear unto you, to the wise and to the foolish,
For ye shall have manifold experiences on the earth.

Prophecy Concerning Gender Confusion

[2]For ye men shall put on more adornments than a woman,
And colored garments more than a virgin:

---

[472] **"You who acquire silver and gold in unrighteousness"**; **James 5:3**, Your gold and silver have corroded, and their corrosion will be evidence against you and will eat your flesh like fire. You have laid up treasure in the last days.
[473] **"We have acquired everything we have desired"**; **Luke 12:19-21**, "I will say to my soul, Soul, you have ample goods laid up for many years; relax, eat, drink, be merry." But God said to him, "Fool! This night your soul is required of you, and the things you have prepared, whose will they be?" So is the one who lays up treasure for himself and is not rich toward God.

In royalty and in grandeur and in power,
And in silver and in gold and in purple,
And in splendor and in food they shall be poured out as water.

[3]Therefore they shall be wanting in doctrine and wisdom,
And they shall perish thereby together with their possessions;
And with all their glory and their splendor,
And in shame and in slaughter and in great destitution,
Their spirits shall be cast into the furnace of fire.

[4]I have sworn unto you, ye sinners,
as a mountain has not become a slave,
And a hill does not become the handmaid of a woman,
Even so sin has not been sent upon the earth,
But man of himself has created it,
And under a great curse shall they fall who commit it.

[5]And barrenness has not been given to the woman,
But on account of the deeds of her own hands she dies without children.

[6]I have sworn unto you, ye sinners, by the Holy Great One,
That all your evil deeds are revealed in the heavens,
And that none of your deeds of oppression are covered and hidden.[474]

[7]And do not think in your spirit nor say in your heart that ye do not know and that ye do not see that every sin is every day recorded[475] in heaven in the presence of the Most High. [8]From henceforth ye know that all your oppression wherewith ye oppress is written down every day till the day of your judgment.

The Coming Woes in the Day of Tribulation

[9]Woe to you, ye fools, for through your folly shall ye perish: and ye transgress against the wise, and so good hap shall not be your portion. [10]And now, know ye that ye are prepared for the day of destruction: wherefore do not hope to live, ye sinners, but ye shall depart and die; for ye know no ransom; for ye are prepared for the day of the great judgment, for the day of tribulation and great shame for your spirits.

[11]Woe to you, ye obstinate of heart, who work wickedness and eat blood.[476] Whence have ye good things to eat and to drink and to be filled? From all the good things which the Lord the Most High has placed in abundance on the earth; therefore ye shall have no peace.

---

[474] **"None of your deeds of oppression are covered and hidden"**; **Mark 4:22**, *Nothing is hidden* except to be made manifest; nor is anything secret except to come to light.
[475] **"Every sin is every day recorded in heaven"**; **Luke 12:3**, Whatever you have said in the dark shall be heard in the light, and what you have whispered in private rooms shall be proclaimed on the housetops. **Enoch 104:7-8**
[476] **Enoch 7:5**

[12]Woe to you who love the deeds of unrighteousness: wherefore do ye hope for good hap unto yourselves? Know that ye shall be delivered into the hands of the righteous, and they shall cut off your necks and slay you, and have no mercy upon you.

[13]Woe to you who rejoice in the tribulation of the righteous; for no grave shall be dug for you.

[14]Woe to you who set at naught the words of the righteous; for ye shall have no hope of life.

[15]Woe to you who write down lying and godless words;[477] for they write down their lies that men may hear them and act godlessly towards their neighbor. [16]Therefore they shall have no peace but die a sudden death.

99

Woe to you who work godlessness,
And glory in lying and extol them:
Ye shall perish, and no happy life shall be yours.

[2]Woe to them who pervert the words of uprightness,
And transgress the eternal law,
And transform themselves into what they were not:
They shall be trodden under foot upon the earth.

[3]In those days make ready, ye righteous, to raise your prayers as a memorial,[478]
And place them as a testimony before the angels,[479]
That they may place the sin of the sinners for a memorial before the Most High.

[4]In those days the nations shall be stirred up,
And the families of the nations shall arise on the day of destruction.[480]

[5]And in those days the destitute
shall go forth and carry off their children,
And they shall abandon them,
so that their children shall perish through them:

---

[477] **"Woe to you who write down lying and godless words"**; **2 Peter 2:1**, But false prophets also arose among the people, just as there will be false teachers among you, who will secretly bring in destructive heresies, even denying the Master who bought them, bringing upon themselves swift destruction.

[478] **"Raise your prayers as a memorial"**; **Acts 10:3-4**, He saw clearly in a vision an angel of God come in and say to him, "Cornelius." And he stared at him in terror and said, "What is it, Lord?" And he said to him, "*Your prayers and your alms have ascended as a memorial before God.*"

[479] **"Place them as a testimony before the angels"**; **Revelation 8:2-4**, Another angel came and stood at the altar with a golden censer, and he was given much incense to offer with the prayers of all the saints on the golden altar before the throne, and the smoke of the incense, with the prayers of the saints, rose before God from the hand of the angel.

[480] **"In those days the nations shall be stirred up"**; **Revelation 16:14**, They are demonic spirits, performing signs, who go abroad to the kings of the whole world, to assemble them for battle on the great day of God the Almighty.

Yea, they shall abandon their children that are still sucklings,
and not return to them,
And shall have no pity on their beloved ones.

[6]And again I swear to you, ye sinners, that sin is prepared for a day of unceasing bloodshed. [7]And they who worship stones, and grave images of gold and silver and wood and stone and clay, and those who worship impure spirits and demons,[481] and all kinds of idols not according to knowledge, shall get no manner of help from them.

[8]And they shall become godless by reason of the folly of their hearts,
And their eyes shall be blinded through the fear of their hearts
And through visions in their dreams.

[9]Through these they shall become godless and fearful;
For they shall have wrought all their work in a lie,
And shall have worshipped a stone:
Therefore in an instant shall they perish.

The Offer of Repentance is Still Open

[10]But in those days blessed are all they who accept
the words of wisdom, and understand them,
And observe the paths of the Most High,
and walk in the path of His righteousness,
And become not godless with the godless;
For they shall be saved.

More Woes in the End Times

[11]Woe to you who spread evil to your neighbors;
For you shall be slain in Sheol.

[12]Woe to you who make deceitful and false measures,
And to them who cause bitterness on the earth;
For they shall thereby be utterly consumed.

[13]Woe to you who build your houses through the grievous toil of others,
And all their building materials are the bricks and stones of sin;
I tell you ye shall have no peace.

[14]Woe to them who reject
the measure and eternal heritage of their fathers
And whose souls follow after idols;
For they shall have no rest.

---

[481] **"Those who worship impure spirits and demons"**; **Revelation 9:20**, The rest of mankind, who were not killed by these plagues, did not repent of the works of their hands nor give up worshiping demons and idols of gold and silver and bronze and stone and wood, which cannot see or hear or walk.

15Woe to them who work unrighteousness and help oppression,
And slay their neighbors until the day of the great judgment.

16For He shall cast down your glory,
And bring affliction on your hearts,
And shall arouse His fierce indignation
And destroy you all with the sword;
And all the holy and righteous shall remember your sins.

The Tribulation Drenched in Blood

100 And in those days in one place
the fathers together with their sons shall be smitten
And brothers one with another shall fall in death
Till the streams flow with their blood.

2For a man shall not withhold his hand
from slaying his sons and his sons' sons,
And the sinner shall not withhold his hand from his honored brother:
From dawn till sunset they shall slay one another.

Blood as High as a Horse's Bridle

3And the horse shall walk up to the breast in the blood of sinners,[482]
And the chariot shall be submerged to its height.

4In those days the angels shall descend into the secret places
And gather together into one place all those who brought down sin,
And the Most High will arise on that day of judgment[483]
To execute great judgment amongst sinners.

Angels on Assignment

5And over all the righteous and holy
He will appoint guardians from amongst the holy angels
To guard them as the apple of an eye,
Until He makes an end of all wickedness and all sin,

---

482 **"The horse shall walk up to the breast in the blood of sinners"**; the passage describes the aftermath of a future great war. That this is related to the end times is evident from the next verse which speaks of a coming day of God's judgment. There is a passage in the Book of Revelation in which the aftermath of a certain last days battle is described with strikingly similar terminology, with blood flowing "up to a horse's bridle". **Revelation 14:20**, The winepress was trodden outside the city, and blood flowed from the winepress, as high as a horse's bridle.

483 **"The Most High will arise"**. Per **Enoch 1:3,** and **91:7,** the manner in which God will arise at that time will be by His personal presence on earth. In the New Testament Epistle of Jude, we are informed this is fulfilled by the 2nd Coming of Jesus Christ. See footnote to Enoch 1:9. **Enoch 1:3, 25:3, 52:9, 77:1, 90:15,18,20, 91:7, 100:4**

And though the righteous sleep a long sleep,[484] they have naught to fear.

[6]And then the children of the earth shall see the wise in security,
And shall understand all the words of this book,
And recognize that their riches shall not be able to save them
In the overthrow of their sins.

[7]Woe to you, sinners, on the day of strong anguish,
Ye who afflict the righteous and burn them with fire:
Ye shall be requited according to your works.[485]

[8]Woe to you, ye obstinate of heart,
Who watch in order to devise wickedness:
Therefore shall fear come upon you
And there shall be none to help you.

[9]Woe to you, ye sinners, on account of the words of your mouth,
And on account of the deeds of your hands
which your godlessness has wrought,
In blazing flames burning worse than fire shall ye burn.[486]

[10]And now, know ye that from the angels He will inquire as to your deeds in heaven, from the sun and from the moon and from the stars in reference to your sins because upon the earth ye execute judgment on the righteous. [11]And He will summon to testify against you every cloud and mist and dew and rain; for they shall all be withheld because of you from descending upon you, and they shall be mindful of your sins. [12]And now give presents to the rain that it be not withheld from descending upon you, nor yet the dew, when it has received gold and silver from you that it may descend. [13]When the hoar-frost and snow with their chilliness, and all the snow-storms with all their plagues fall upon you, in those days ye shall not be able to stand before them.

The Coming End to Watcher Misrule

101 Observe the heaven, ye children of heaven,[487] and every work of the Most High, and fear ye Him and work no evil in His presence.

---

[484] **"Though the righteous sleep a long sleep, they have naught to fear"**; **1 Thessalonians 4:13**, We do not want you to be uninformed, brothers, about those who are asleep, that you may not grieve as others do who have no hope.
[485] **"Ye shall be requited according to your works"**; **2 Thessalonians 1:6-8**, God considers it just to repay with affliction those who afflict you, and to grant relief to you who are afflicted as well as to us, when the Lord Jesus is revealed from heaven with his mighty angels in flaming fire, inflicting vengeance on those who do not know God and on those who do not obey the gospel of our Lord Jesus.
[486] **"Blazing flames burning worse than fire"**; **Hebrews 10:27**, A fearful expectation of judgment, and a fury of fire that will consume the adversaries.
[487] **"Observe the heaven"**; in language reminiscent of **Enoch 2:1**, the Watchers are exhorted to observe the heavens which do not deviate from their assigned orders. This fixed order of

[2]If He closes the windows of heaven, and withholds the rain and the dew from descending on the earth on your account, what will ye do then? [3]And if He sends His anger upon you because of your deeds, ye cannot petition Him; for ye spake proud and insolent words against His righteousness: therefore ye shall have no peace.

[4]And see ye not the sailors of the ships, how their ships are tossed to and fro by the waves, and are shaken by the winds, and are in sore trouble? [5]And therefore do they fear because all their goodly possessions go upon the sea with them, and they have evil forebodings of heart that the sea will swallow them and they will perish therein.

[6]Are not the entire sea and all its waters, and all its movements, the work of the Most High, and has He not set limits to its doings, and confined it throughout by the sand? [7]And at His reproof it is afraid and dries up, and all its fish die and all that is in it; but ye sinners that are on the earth fear Him not.

[8]Has He not made the heaven and the earth, and all that is therein? Who has given understanding and wisdom to everything that moves on the earth and in the sea? [9]Do not the sailors of the ships fear the sea? Yet sinners fear not the Most High.

102 In those days when He hath brought a grievous fire upon you,
Whither will ye flee, and where will ye find deliverance?
And when He launches forth His word against you
Will you not be affrighted and fear?

[2]And all the luminaries shall be affrighted with great fear,
And all the earth shall be affrighted and tremble and be alarmed.[488]

[3]And all the angels shall execute their commands
And shall seek to hide themselves from the
presence of the Great Glory,[489]
And the children of earth shall tremble and quake;[490]
And ye sinners shall be cursed for ever,
And ye shall have no peace.

---

creation is contrasted with the sinning angels and sinful mankind who routinely transgress God's laws. This is not a call to repentance, but an indictment of their sin, and a sure promise of their coming judgment. **Enoch 72:1**

[488] **Isaiah 24:21-22**, On that day the LORD will punish the host of heaven, in heaven, and the kings of the earth, on the earth. They will be gathered together as prisoners in a pit; they will be shut up in a prison, and after many days they will be punished. **Enoch 1:5, 13:3**

[489] **Enoch 14:20, 102:3**

[490] **Enoch 1:5, 13:3**

The Consolation of the Righteous Dead

4Fear ye not, ye souls of the righteous,
And be hopeful ye that have died in righteousness.[491]

5And grieve not if your soul into Sheol has descended in grief,
And that in your life your body fared not according to your goodness,
But wait for the day of the judgment of sinners
And for the day of cursing and chastisement.

6And yet when ye die the sinners speak over you:
"As we die, so die the righteous,
And what benefit do they reap for their deeds?[492]

7"Behold, even as we, so do they die in grief and darkness,
And what have they more than we?
From henceforth we are equal.

8"And what will they receive and what will they see for ever?
Behold, they too have died,
And henceforth for ever shall they see no light."

9I tell you, ye sinners, ye are content to eat and drink, and rob and sin, and strip men naked, and acquire wealth and see good days. 10Have ye seen the righteous how their end falls out, that no manner of violence is found in them till their death? 11Nevertheless they perished and became as though they had not been, and their spirits descended into Sheol in tribulation.

103 Now, therefore, I swear to you, the righteous, by the glory of the Great and Honored and Mighty One in dominion, 2and by His greatness I swear to you.

"I Know a Mystery"

I know a mystery
And have read the heavenly tablets,[493]
And have seen the holy books,
And have found written therein and inscribed regarding them:

---

[491] **"Be hopeful ye that have died in righteousness"**; **Revelation 14:13**, And I heard a voice from heaven saying, "Write this: Blessed are the dead who die in the Lord from now on. Blessed indeed," says the Spirit, "that they may rest from their labors, for their deeds follow them!"

[492] **"What benefit do they reap for their deeds"?**; **1 Corinthians 15:32**, If the dead are not raised, "Let us eat and drink, for tomorrow we die."

[493] **"I have read the heavenly tablets"**; Enoch is shown heavenly records written upon tablets, in which he learns about the future of the world and the activities of mankind over time and the coming judgment. **Enoch 81:1-2, 93:2, 103:2, 106:19**

[3]That all goodness and joy and glory are prepared for them,
And written down for the spirits of those
who have died in righteousness,
And that manifold good shall be given to you
in recompense for your labors,[494]
And that your lot is abundantly beyond the lot of the living.[495]

[4]And the spirits of you who have died in righteousness
shall live and rejoice,
And their spirits shall not perish,
Nor their memorial from before the face of the Great One
Unto all the generations of the world:
wherefore no longer fear their contumely.

[5]Woe to you, ye sinners, when ye have died,
If ye die in the wealth of your sins,
And those who are like you say regarding you:
"Blessed are the sinners: they have seen all their days.

[6]And now they have died in prosperity and in wealth,
And have not seen tribulation or murder in their life;
And they have died in honor,
And judgment has not been executed on them during their life."

[7]Know ye, that their souls will be made to descend into Sheol
And they shall be wretched in their great tribulation.[496]

[8]And into darkness and chains and a burning flame
Where there is grievous judgment shall your spirits enter;
And the great judgment shall be for all the generations of the world.
Woe to you, for ye shall have no peace.

The Plight of the Persecuted

[9]Say not in regard to the righteous and good who are in life:
"In our troubled days we have toiled laboriously
and experienced every trouble,
And met with much evil and been consumed,
And have become few and our spirit small.

---

[494] **"Good shall be given to you in recompense for your labors"; Revelation 22:12-17**, Behold, I am coming soon, bringing my recompense with me, to repay everyone for what he has done.

[495] **"Your lot is abundantly beyond the lot of the living"; 2 Cor. 4:16-17**, We do not lose heart. Though our outer self is wasting away, our inner self is being renewed day by day. For this light momentary affliction is preparing for us an eternal weight of glory beyond all comparison.

[496] **"They shall be wretched in their great tribulation"; Mark 13:19**, For in those days there will be such tribulation as has not been from the beginning of the creation that God created until now, and never will be.

[10]And we have been destroyed
and have not found any to help us even with a word:
We have been tortured and destroyed,
and not hoped to see life from day to day.

[11]We hoped to be the head and have become the tail:[497]
We have toiled laboriously and had no satisfaction in our toil;
And we have become the food of the sinners and the unrighteous,
And they have laid their yoke heavily upon us.

[12]They have had dominion over us that hated us and smote us;
And to those that hated us we have bowed our necks
But they pitied us not.

[13]We desired to get away from them
that we might escape and be at rest,
But found no place whereunto we should flee and be safe from them.

[14]And we complained to the rulers in our tribulation,
And cried out against those who devoured us,
But they did not attend to our cries
And would not hearken to our voice.

[15]And they helped those who robbed us and devoured us and those who made us few; and they concealed their oppression, and they did not remove from us the yoke of those that devoured us and dispersed us and murdered us, and they concealed their murder, and remembered not that they had lifted up their hands against us.

Companions with Angels

104 I swear unto you, that in heaven the angels remember you for good before the glory of the Great One:[498] and your names are written before the glory of the Great One.[499] [2]Be hopeful; for aforetime ye were put to shame through ill and affliction;[500] but now ye shall shine as the

---

[497] **"We hoped to be the head and have become the tail"**; here the righteous complain that earthly prosperity has not been their lot. **Deuteronomy 28:13**, The LORD will make you the head and not the tail, and you shall only go up and not down, if you obey the commandments of the LORD your God, which I command you today, being careful to do them.

[498] **"In heaven the angels remember you for good"**; **Matthew 18:10**, See that you do not despise one of these little ones. For I tell you that in heaven their angels always see the face of my Father who is in heaven.

[499] **"Your names are written before the glory of the Great One"; Luke 10:20**, Nevertheless, do not rejoice in this, that the spirits are subject to you, but rejoice that your names are written in heaven.

[500] **"Be hopeful, for aforetime ye were put to shame through ill and affliction"**; **Matthew 5:10**, Blessed are those who are persecuted for righteousness' sake, for theirs is the kingdom of heaven.

lights of heaven, ye shall shine and ye shall be seen,[501] and the portals of heaven shall be opened to you.

[3]And in your cry, cry for judgment,[502] and it shall appear to you; for all your tribulation shall be visited on the rulers, and on all who helped those who plundered you.

[4]Be hopeful, and cast not away your hope;[503] for ye shall have great joy as the angels of heaven.[504] [5]What shall ye be obliged to do? Ye shall not have to hide on the day of the great judgment and ye shall not be found as sinners, and the eternal judgment shall be far from you for all the generations of the world.

[6]And now fear not, ye righteous, when ye see the sinners growing strong and prospering in their ways:[505] be not companions with them, but keep afar from their violence; for ye shall become companions of the hosts of heaven.[506]

Not So, the Wicked

[7]And, although ye sinners say: "All our sins shall not be searched out and be written down," nevertheless they shall write down all your sins every day.[507] [8]And now I show unto you that light and darkness, day and night, see all your sins.[508] [9]Be not godless in your hearts, and lie not and alter not the words of uprightness, nor charge with lying the words of the Holy Great One, nor take account of your idols; for all your lying and all your godlessness issue not in righteousness but in great sin.

---

501 **"Ye shall shine and ye shall be seen"; Daniel 12:3**, Those who are wise shall shine like the brightness of the sky above; and those who turn many to righteousness, like the stars forever and ever. **Romans 8:19**, The creation waits with eager longing for the revealing of the sons of God.

502 **"In your cry, cry for judgment"; Revelation 6:9-11**, I saw under the altar the souls of those who had been slain for the word of God and for the witness they had borne. They cried out with a loud voice, "O Sovereign Lord, holy and true, how long before you will judge and avenge our blood on those who dwell on the earth?" Then they were each given a white robe and told to rest a little longer, until the number of their fellow servants and their brothers should be complete, who were to be killed as they themselves had been.

503 **"Cast not away your hope"; Hebrews 10:35**, Do not throw away your confidence, which has a great reward.

504 **"Ye shall have great joy as the angels of heaven"; Luke 15:10**, Just so, I tell you, there is joy before the angels of God over one sinner who repents.

505 **"Fear not, ye righteous, when ye see the sinners prospering"; Psalm 37:7**, Be still before the LORD and wait patiently for him; fret not yourself over the one who prospers in his way, over the man who carries out evil devices!

506 **"Ye shall become companions of the hosts of heaven"**; God's people are destined to become friends of angels. **Enoch 39:5**

507 **"They shall write down all your sins every day"; Matthew 12:36**, I tell you, on the day of judgment people will give account for every careless word they speak. **Enoch 98:6-7**

508 **"Light and darkness, day and night, see all your sins"; Luke 12:3**, Whatever you have said in the dark shall be heard in the light, and what you have whispered in private rooms shall be proclaimed on the housetops.

Sinners Twist God's Word

[10]And now I know this mystery, that sinners will alter and pervert the words of righteousness in many ways,[509] and will speak wicked words, and lie, and practice great deceits, and write books concerning their words.

A Prophecy Concerning the Books of Enoch

[11]But when they write down truthfully all my words in their languages, and do not change or minish ought from my words but write them all down truthfully- all that I first testified concerning them. [12]Then, I know another mystery, that books will be given to the righteous and the wise to become a cause of joy and uprightness and much wisdom. [13]And to them shall the books be given, and they shall believe in them and rejoice over them, and then shall all the righteous who have learnt therefrom all the paths of uprightness be recompensed.[510]

105 In those days the Lord bade them to summon and testify to the children of earth concerning their wisdom: Show it unto them; for ye are their guides, and a recompense over the whole earth.

"I, and My Son, Will Be United With Them Forever"

[2]For I and My Son[511] will be united with them for ever[512] in the paths of ☼ uprightness in their lives; and ye shall have peace: rejoice, ye children of uprightness. Amen.

---

[509] **"Sinners will alter the words of righteousness"**; **Revelation 22:18-19**, I warn everyone who hears the words of the prophecy of this book: if anyone adds to them, God will add to him the plagues described in this book, and if anyone takes away from the words of the book of this prophecy, God will take away his share in the tree of life and in the holy city, which are described in this book.

[510] **"Books will be given to the righteous";** This incredible prophecy indicates a truthful record of Enoch's books has been preserved and awaits revealing in the last days. Either this has been fulfilled in the present text, or will be fulfilled with a more ancient, more trustworthy text(s) which remains to be discovered.

[511] ☼ **"I and my Son"**; In this passage using language which reminds us of Psalm 2:11-12, and Proverbs 30:4, the eternal God is said to have His Son by His side, which the New Testament identifies as Jesus Christ, the eternal Son of God. Here the writer of the *Book of Enoch* evidences the spirit of prophecy by his foreknowledge of the existence of the Son of God, the 2nd person of the Trinity, before the birth of Jesus Christ. **Psalm 2:11-12**, Serve the LORD with fear, and rejoice with trembling. Kiss the Son, lest he be angry, and you perish in the way. **Proverbs 30:4**, Who has established all the ends of the earth? What is His name, and what is His Son's name? Surely you know!

[512] **"I and my Son will be united with them forever"; John 14:23**, Jesus answered him, "If anyone loves me, he will keep my word, and my Father will love him, and we will come to him and make our home with him." **Revelation 21:3**, I heard a loud voice from the throne saying, "Behold, the dwelling place of God is with man. He will dwell with them, and they will be his people, and God himself will be with them as their God. **Enoch 71:16**

The Uncanny Birth of Noah

106 And after some days my son Methuselah took a wife for his son Lamech, and she became pregnant by him and bore a son.

2And his body was white as snow and red as the blooming of a rose, and the hair of his head and his long locks were white as wool, and his eyes beautiful. And when he opened his eyes, he lighted up the whole house like the sun, and the whole house was very bright.[513] 3And thereupon he arose in the hands of the midwife, opened his mouth, and conversed with the Lord of righteousness.

4And his father Lamech was afraid of him and fled, and came to his father Methuselah.

5And he said unto him: "I have begotten a strange son,[514] diverse from and unlike man, and resembling the sons of the God of heaven; and his nature is different and he is not like us, and his eyes are as the rays of the sun, and his countenance is glorious. 6And it seems to me that he is not sprung from me but from the angels, and I fear that in his days a wonder may be wrought on the earth. 7And now, my father, I am here to petition thee and implore thee that thou mayst go to Enoch, our father, and learn from him the truth, for his dwelling-place is amongst the angels."

A Visitation by Enoch to Methuselah

8And when Methuselah heard the words of his son, he came to me[515] to the ends of the earth;[516] for he had heard that I was there, and he cried

---

[513] **"The whole house was very bright"**; **Exodus 34:29**, Moses did not know that the skin of his face shone because he had been talking with God. **Matthew 17:1-2**, Jesus took with him Peter and James, and John his brother, and led them up a high mountain by themselves. And he was transfigured before them, and his face shone like the sun, and his clothes became white as light.

[514] **"I have gotten a strange son"**; The brightness coming from Noah's face was the kind of Shekinah glory which Moses had after meeting with God for 40 days. People were afraid of that brightness too and asked Moses to cover his face. Gradually the glory of Moses' face faded until it was gone. Apparently Noah was born with the Shekinah glory emanating from his face because this auspicious child was chosen by God to save humanity as a type of Christ, whose face also shone on the Mount of Transfiguration. Perhaps the Shekinah glory of God gradually faded from Noah's face as he grew. This isn't the only occurrence of a shining face in Scripture, nor the only occurrence of an unusual birth. John the Baptist jumped for joy in his mother's womb on hearing the voice of the mother of Jesus. That's pretty strange too. On a side note of interest, in the Dead Sea Scrolls, a book referred to as *The Genesis Apocryphon* also tells the story of the unusual circumstances of the birth of Noah.

[515] **Enoch 106:8-107:3**, purports to be the written by Enoch after he was translated.

[516] **"He came to me to the ends of the earth"**; This is one of two occasions on which Enoch visits the earth after his translation to heaven. Perhaps Methuselah's trip to the "ends of the earth" is idiomatic for traveling to the top of a tall mountain. Once there, Methuselah meets Enoch in similar fashion to our Lord's meeting with Moses and Elijah on the Mount of Transfiguration. In **Enoch 65:2**, we have a later event when Noah too sought Enoch at the "ends of the earth".

aloud, and I heard his voice and I came to him. And I said unto him: "Behold, here am I, my son, wherefore hast thou come to me?"

9And he answered and said: "Because of a great cause of anxiety have I come to thee, and because of a disturbing vision have I approached. 10And now, my father, hear me: unto Lamech my son there hath been born a son, the like of whom there is none, and his nature is not like man's nature, and the color of his body is whiter than snow and redder than the bloom of a rose, and the hair of his head is whiter than white wool, and his eyes are like the rays of the sun, and he opened his eyes and thereupon lighted up the whole house.

11"And he arose in the hands of the midwife, and opened his mouth and blessed the Lord of Heaven.

12"And his father Lamech became afraid and fled to me, and did not believe that he was sprung from him, but that he was in the likeness of the angels of heaven; and behold I have come to thee that thou mayst make known to me the truth."

The Lord Will Do a New Thing

13And I, Enoch, answered and said unto him: "The Lord will do a new thing on the earth, and this I have already seen in a vision, and make known to thee that in the generation of my father Jared[517] some of the angels of heaven transgressed the word of the Lord. 14"And behold they commit sin and transgress the law, and have united themselves with women and commit sin with them, and have married some of them, and have begot children by them. 15And they shall produce on the earth giants not according to the spirit, but according to the flesh, and there shall be a great punishment on the earth, and the earth shall be cleansed from all impurity.

16"Yea, there shall come a great destruction over the whole earth, and there shall be a deluge and a great destruction for one year.

17"And this son who has been born unto you shall be left on the earth, and his three children shall be saved with him: when all mankind that are on the earth shall die he and his sons shall be saved.

"Call His Name Noah"

18"And now make known to thy son Lamech that he who has been born is in truth his son, and call his name Noah; for he shall be left to you, and he and his sons shall be saved from the destruction, which shall

517 **"In the generation of my father Jared"**; Here Enoch indicates the events which occurred before his birth, were shown to him in a vision. Those events are recorded in chapters 6-8. **Enoch 6:6**

come upon the earth on account of all the sin and all the unrighteousness, which shall be consummated on the earth in his days.

There Shall Be More Unrighteousness than That

[19]And after that there shall be still more unrighteousness than that which was first consummated on the earth; for I know the mysteries of the holy ones; for He, the Lord, has showed me and informed me, and I have read them in the heavenly tablets."[518]

107 "And I saw written on them that generation upon generation shall transgress, till a generation of righteousness arises, and transgression is destroyed and sin passes away from the earth, and all manner of good comes upon it.

[2]"And now, my son, go and make known to thy son Lamech that this son, which has been born, is in truth his son, and that this is no lie."

[3]And when Methuselah had heard the words of his father Enoch- for he had shown to him everything in secret- he returned and showed them to him and called the name of that son Noah; for he will comfort the earth after all the destruction.

Time-Capsule to the Last Generation

108 Another book which Enoch wrote[519] for his son Methuselah and for those who will come after him, and keep the law in the last days.

[2]Ye who have done good shall wait for those days till an end is made of those who work evil, and an end of the might of the transgressors.[520] [3]And wait ye indeed till sin has passed away,[521] for their names shall be blotted out

The Book of Life

The *Book of Life* is mentioned here and throughout the Bible and early Jewish literature. Initially, all the living are enrolled in the *Book of Life*. However, *the soul that sins, shall die*, wrote Ezekiel, and when someone dies without the redemption that comes through Jesus Christ, their name is then blotted out of the book. At the end of time, the *Book of Life* will then be referred to as the *Lamb's Book of Life*, because the only names remaining in it will be those who have been redeemed by Christ, the Lamb of God. Will your name be listed in the book on that day?

---

[518] **"I have read them in the heavenly tablets"**; Enoch is shown heavenly records written upon tablets, in which he learns about the future of the world and the activities of mankind over time and the coming judgment. **Enoch 81:1-2, 93:2, 103:2, 106:19**

[519] **"Another book which Enoch wrote"**; The composite nature of the collection we now call the *Book of Enoch* is highlighted here. **Enoch 1:1-2, 37:3, 92:1**

[520] **"Wait for those days"**; the passage is an exhortation to those living in the time of the end. They are instructed to wait until an end is made of the transgressors which is accomplished by their deliverance from the transgressors by the return of Messiah Jesus.

[521] **"Till sin has passed away"; Daniel 9:24**, Seventy weeks are decreed about your people and your holy city, to finish the transgression, *to put an end to sin*, and to atone for iniquity,

of the Book of Life[522] and out of the holy books, and their seed shall be destroyed for ever, and their spirits shall be slain, and they shall cry and make lamentation in a place that is a chaotic wilderness,[523] and in the fire shall they burn; for there is no earth there.[524]

[4]And I saw there something like an invisible cloud; for by reason of its depth I could not look over, and I saw a flame of fire blazing brightly, and things like shining mountains circling and sweeping to and fro.[525]

[5]And I asked one of the holy angels who was with me and said unto him: "What is this shining thing? for it is not a heaven but only the flame of a blazing fire, and the voice of weeping and crying and lamentation and strong pain."

[6]And he said unto me: "This place which thou seest- here are cast the spirits of sinners and blasphemers, and of those who work wickedness, and of those who pervert everything that the Lord hath spoken[526] through the mouth of the prophets- even the things that shall be.

[7]"For some of them are written and inscribed above in the heaven, in order that the angels may read them and know[527] that which shall befall the sinners, and the spirits of the humble, and of those who have afflicted their bodies, and been recompensed by God; and of those who have been put to shame by wicked men: [8]Who love God and loved neither gold nor silver nor any of the good things which are in the world,[528] but gave over their bodies to torture.[529] [9]Who, since they came into being, longed not

---

to bring in everlasting righteousness, to seal both vision and prophet, and to anoint a most holy place.

522 **"Their names shall be blotted out of the book of life"**; **Exodus 32:33**, The LORD said to Moses, "Whoever has sinned against me, I will blot out of my book. **Psalm 69:28**, Let them be blotted out of the book of the living; let them not be enrolled among the righteous. **Revelation 3:5**, The one who conquers will be clothed thus in white garments, and I will never blot his name out of the book of life. I will confess his name before my Father and before his angels. **Revelation 20:15**, If anyone's name was not found written in the book of life, he was thrown into the lake of fire.

523 **"A chaotic wilderness"; Enoch 21:1-2**

524 **"There is no earth there"**; The Lake of Fire will be bottomless, as was the Abyss before it. **Revelation 20:15**, If anyone's name was not found written in the *Book of Life*, he was thrown into the lake of fire. **Enoch 10:13-14**

525 **"Things like shining mountains"**; here, and in Revelation 8:8, this imagery is idiomatic for fallen angels. **Revelation 8:8**, The second angel blew his trumpet, and something like a great mountain, burning with fire, was thrown into the sea, and a third of the sea became blood. See **Enoch 18:13-15, 21:3**

526 **"Those who pervert everything that the Lord hath spoken"**; **2 Peter 2:1**, False prophets also arose among the people, just as there will be false teachers among you, who will secretly bring in destructive heresies, even denying the Master who bought them, bringing upon themselves swift destruction.

527 **"That the angels may read them and know"**; in Enoch, angels are not all-knowing and desire to learn as we do. **1 Peter 1:12**, It was revealed to them that they were serving not themselves but you, in the things that have now been announced to you through those who preached the good news to you by the Holy Spirit sent from heaven, *things into which angels long to look*.

528 **1 John 2:15**, Do not love the world or the things in the world. If anyone loves the world, the love of the Father is not in him. **Enoch 48:7**

529 **"Gave over their bodies to torture"**; **Hebrews 11:35**, Some were tortured, refusing to accept release, so that they might rise again to a better life.

after earthly food, but regarded everything as a passing breath, and lived accordingly, and the Lord tried them much, and their spirits were found pure[530] so that they should bless His name.

[10]"And all the blessings destined for them I have recounted in the books. And He hath assigned them their recompense, because they have been found to be such as loved heaven more than their life[531] in the world, and though they were trodden under foot of wicked men, and experienced abuse and reviling from them and were put to shame, yet they blessed Me.[532]

"The Generation of Light"
The destiny of the "generation of light" is glorious. They will be rewarded with a jeweled "crown of life" (Rev. 2:10) and will share with Christ his royal status forever in eternal light.

[11]"And now I will summon the spirits of the good who belong to the generation of light,[533] and I will transform those who were born in darkness, who in the flesh were not recompensed with such honor as their faithfulness deserved. [12]And I will bring forth in shining light those who have loved My holy name, and I will seat each on the throne of his honor.[534] [13]And they shall be resplendent for times without number; for righteousness is the judgment of God; for to the faithful He will give faithfulness in the habitation of upright paths.

[14]"And they shall see those who were born in darkness led into darkness, while the righteous shall be resplendent. [15]And the sinners shall cry aloud and see them resplendent, and they indeed will go where days and seasons are prescribed for them."

---

[530] **"Their spirits were found pure"**; **Daniel 11:35**, Some of the wise shall stumble, so that they may be refined, purified, and made white, until the time of the end, for it still awaits the appointed time.

[531] **"Loved heaven more than their life"**; this is a euphemism for martyrdom. Those who love heaven more than life are those who are willing to die for love of God. **Revelation 12:11**, They have conquered him by the blood of the Lamb and by the word of their testimony, for they loved not their lives even unto death.

[532] **"Were put to shame, yet they blessed Me"**; **Matthew 5:10**, Blessed are those who are persecuted for righteousness' sake, for theirs is the kingdom of heaven.

[533] **"Who belong to the generation of light"**; **Ephesians 5:8**, At one time you were darkness, but now you are light in the Lord. Walk as *children of light.* **1 Thessalonians 5:5**, You are all *children of light,* children of the day. We are not of the night or of the darkness. **Colossians 1:13**, He has delivered us from the domain of darkness and transferred us to the kingdom of his beloved Son.

[534] **"I will seat each on the throne of his honor"; Ephesians 2:6-7**, God raised us up with him and seated us with him in the heavenly places in Christ Jesus, so that in the coming ages he might show the immeasurable riches of his grace in kindness toward us in Christ Jesus. **Matthew 19:28**, Jesus said to them, "Truly, I say to you, in the new world, when the Son of Man will sit on his glorious throne, you who have followed me will also sit on twelve thrones, judging the twelve tribes of Israel."

Who Really Wrote The Book of Enoch?

By
R. I. Burns

SageWorks Press
2017

Cover concept: P. Burns
Cover art: M. DeRaud

First KDP print edition, December 2017.
San Francisco, CA USA
ISBN: 978-057819869-9
ASIN: B0776K4TTN

www.TheBookofEnoch.info

Preface

Who really wrote the *Book of Enoch*? The standard answer to this question among scholars of ancient Jewish literature is to say the *Book of Enoch* was composed in Israel, by multiple authors, over a period of time between 100 to 300 BC.

Such a hypothesis should not surprise us. Textual scholars like these also tend to believe we do not have *any* Jewish books which were written before the time of the Babylonian captivity in the 6th century BC. So, according to that view, Moses could not have written Genesis. Did Isaiah write the book we have in his name? No, they say. It should not surprise us they disparage the Book of Enoch in the same way.

However, as we will see, there is a wealth of evidence both within the *Book of Enoch* as well as outside of it which points to a much more ancient time than current scholarship is willing to concede. Throughout the course of this book, we will examine aspects of history, archaeology, and the *Book of Enoch* itself, which indicate it was indeed written by its professed author, Enoch, the great-grandfather of Noah.

We about to uncover the evidence for the *Book of Enoch*'s great age. This great age continuing into our own era would not have been possible had the book not survived organized efforts to suppress and eliminate it from the libraries of the world. In the pages ahead we will discover this book's incredible history of survival over the millennia despite attempts by churchmen and rabbis to have it banned and/or destroyed. Does the survival of the *Book of Enoch* point to God's providential care to protect and ensure its continuation? Will this book indeed fulfill the promise within its own pages that the book itself would become a blessing to believers living in earth's last days?

We will also show in the pages to come that Enoch's book presents a thoroughly Biblical worldview. In fact, we will see how the *Book of Enoch* actually seems to clarify a number of ambiguous passages in our Bibles. When these puzzling passages are considered in the light of the *Book of Enoch* they present little or no problem at all.

The following pages will also demonstrate how the *Book of Enoch* portrays a very high view of the person and work of the Messiah, just like the New Testament says about Jesus Christ. On a related note, the book also contains a number of passages which claim to be prophetic, some of which have been fulfilled in history. Many of which are Messianic in character. We will also show that certain New Testament writers accepted the *Book of Enoch* as the authentic writings of Enoch.

Did the Biblical Enoch write the book which goes under his name? Come now, let us examine the evidence to help us answer this question....

Introduction

The *Book of Enoch* makes the claim for itself that it is the gathered writings of the pre-flood patriarch, Enoch. Enoch is mentioned briefly in the Book of Genesis, the first book of the Bible.

"Enoch walked with God and was not, for God took him."

Later, the *Letter of Jude* in the New Testament will quote from the *Book of Enoch*, prefacing it with the statement,

"Enoch, the seventh from Adam, prophesied."

In telling us this, Jude is revealing something about Enoch which the *Book of Genesis* does not. *Enoch was a prophet.*

From where did Jude discover that Enoch was a prophet? Under inspiration of the Holy Spirit, Jude quoted from the book bearing Enoch's name, a book which happens to contain many prophecies concerning the future of the world and the end of times. Both the *Letter of Jude* and the *Book of Enoch* share this idea in common. *Enoch prophesied.*

If the *Book of Enoch* truly was written by the Biblical Enoch, that makes it the oldest book in the world!

In that light the book's claims for itself are all the more astounding, for, in the first chapter of the book, the writer claims the purpose he wrote his book was to be a blessing to the final generation who will be alive on planet earth at the end of the age.

So, if the *Book of Enoch* was truly written by the Biblical Enoch, it means the *world's oldest book* has been preserved through time and circumstance with a message for the *world's last generation.*

It is the thesis of the following pages that the *Book of Enoch* was in fact written by the pre-flood Biblical patriarch, Enoch.

In the area of Biblical and para-Biblical literature, the *Book of Enoch* occupies a place unlike any other. The book's history has led it from intense popularity in the past... to being banned. The book eventually was thought to be lost. Then 1,000 years later, the book was rediscovered, and today it is regaining some of its former popularity among people around the world.

Any book which makes the claims for itself which this book makes, which is then quoted in holy Scripture, and which then has had the kind of history which this book has had, deserves a closer look. I hope this edition helps bring the kind of attention the *Book of Enoch* deserves, and that it will become a blessing to the lives of many who read it.

1
Rediscovering Enoch

The message in the *Book of Enoch* reads a lot like the Hebrew prophets in the Bible. Enoch's message is a mixture of rebuke for sin and exhortation to repentance. His message includes descriptions of God's coming judgment upon the wicked and the future blessings upon his people. Also like some, but not all of the Hebrew prophets, we are told Enoch wrote his message down.

There is an interesting parallel between the life of Enoch, related in his book, and the subsequent history of the book itself. We are told Enoch was secluded from mankind for a period of time. Then, after being called to become a preacher, Enoch reappeared as a powerful figure on the world scene. As we will see, the *Book of Enoch* has been through a similar process of reappearance in recent times.

Written for the Last Generation

For many centuries, the *Book of Enoch* was in a period of virtual seclusion. The book is now reemerging on the world stage with an important message undiminished by time. Amazingly, the course of the history of this book has nicely lined up with a prediction in the first few verses of its very first chapter. In the first chapter of the *Book of Enoch*, it is stated Enoch's book was not being written for the people living in his day, or even those who would immediately follow. No, from its beginning the *Book of Enoch* was purposed to have a much bigger impact. Enoch's book was written for the sake of the generation that would be living at the end of time. Like a kind of time-capsule set aside for the last generation, the *Book of Enoch* has again come to light in our day and is available for any who wish to discover its treasures.

To understand how all this happened we need to take a closer look at the amazing history of the *Book of Enoch*, as it has passed through distinct phases of popularity, seclusion, and finally reemergence.

Accepted in the Time of Christ

For many Jews in Israel at the time of Christ the *Book of Enoch* was held in high regard. This fact has been confirmed by the discovery of the Dead Sea Scrolls, in the late 1940's. At that time approximately 800 books and/or parts of books were discovered in caves near the Dead Sea in Israel. The top five most represented books in the Dead Sea Scrolls rank in this order, the books of *Psalms*, *Isaiah*, *Deuteronomy*, the *Book of Jubilees*, and the *Book of Enoch*. More copies of the *Book of Enoch* were stored in those caves than the first four books of Moses and most of the other books of the Old Testament! Scrolls of the *Book of Enoch* were stored with the books of the Hebrew Bible and treated with equal care and concern for their preservation. The recovery of these ancient copies of the *Book of Enoch* in the land of promise coincided with the rebirth of the nation of Israel in 1947.[535]

Before the destruction of the Jewish temple by the Romans in AD 70, the *Book of Enoch* is referred to in a positive way in the Jewish literature from that time. The *Book of Enoch* is even quoted in the New Testament in the *Letter of Jude,* the half-brother of Jesus, where we read,

> Enoch, the seventh from Adam, prophesied about these men: "See, the Lord is coming with thousands upon thousands of his holy ones to judge everyone, and to convict all the ungodly of all the ungodly acts they have done in the ungodly way, and of all the harsh words ungodly sinners have spoken against him." (Jude 1:14-15).

Though quoting Enoch 1:9, Jude does not say he was quoting the *Book of Enoch.* Jude says rather he is quoting Enoch the man, who descended the seventh from Adam. Though other books not considered Scripture are quoted in the New Testament, this quote from Enoch is different. Jude says in effect, *'when I quote from the Book of Enoch, I know I am in fact quoting Enoch himself'.* [536]

Both the Dead Sea Scrolls and the New Testament point to the high opinion of the book that was commonly known at that time. By the end of the first century this situation would begin to shift.

Rejected by Jewish Religious Leaders

Despite the popularity of the *Book of Enoch* before and during the first century, by the end of that period this situation would begin to reverse. The first phase in the book's decreasing popularity crystallized about a generation after the death and resurrection of Jesus Christ. External pressures caused by the destruction of the Jewish Temple in AD 70 and the growing Christian movement, motivated the spiritual leadership of Judaism to reform the religion. A strict canon of Scripture was standardized for all Jews. This canon eliminated Enoch and other well-used books and especially the books of the developing Christian movement which we now have in our New Testament.

The discovery of the Dead Sea Scrolls in the late 1940's has shown that many Jews of the first century had a special interest in the *Book of Enoch.* Fragments from at least 10 manuscript copies of the *Book of Enoch* have been found among the Dead Sea Scrolls recovered from caves in the desert of Judea.

Increasing communication by Westerners with the Falasha Jews and

---

[535] This subject is discussed in greater detail in chapter 10.
[536] In Chapter 8, we will show how the Epistle of Jude actually references the *Book of Enoch,* no less than seven times.

Christians of Ethiopia, who had historically been in considerable isolation from the rest of world, has also pointed out the importance given to the *Book of Enoch* in ancient times. The Old Testament of the Falasha Jews retained Enoch's book. When the Falasha Jews embraced Orthodox Christianity in Ethiopia, the book was brought into the Bible of the Ethiopian Orthodox Church, where it remains to this day.

Banned by Church Council

After the first century AD, the *Book of Enoch* continued for quite some time to be popular among early Christian writers and in the churches. Quotes, references, and allusions to Enoch's book can be found in the writings of Irenaeus, Clement, Tertullian, Athenagoras, Tatian, Lactantius, Methodius, Minucius Felix, Commodianus and Ambrose. At times the book was referred to as Scripture. Gradually, however, the book's popularity dimmed within Greek and Latin Christianity. Enoch's book started to fall into disfavor at the same time neo-platonic philosophy and Greek speculation about the purely spiritual nature of angels began to permeate Christian thought.

Ultimately, the *Book of Enoch* was forbidden by the Council of Laodicea near the beginning of the 5th century AD. Apparently, church leaders Augustine and Jerome were influential in further pushing the book into obscurity. Eventually, the *Book of Enoch* was removed from the libraries of the churches of the Mediterranean and gradually all existing copies were lost in that part of the Christian world. The *Book of Enoch* would become effectively lost in the Greek and Latin worlds for more than 1,000 years.

Preserved in Ethiopia

During this time, the world outside of Ethiopia was oblivious to the fact the *Book of Enoch* was being preserved by the Jews and Orthodox Christians there. It is undoubtedly fortunate for us today, that Ethiopian Christians and Jews were themselves in relative isolation from the people of the Mediterranean world throughout this period, for it resulted in the preservation of the book!

For most of the world the exclusion of the *Book of Enoch* was fully underway by the fifth century AD. Like the life of Enoch it was as if the book was being hidden for a time from the attention of the world at large. However, just as was anticipated within the book's pages, the book is currently on a trajectory from obscurity to prominence.

Reintroduced to the World

Since it was 'rediscovered' in the eighteenth century, the *Book of Enoch* has passed through several phases in its gradual reemergence. The following is a broad outline of the initial stages of the *Book of Enoch's* reemergence on the world scene.

- 1773 Rediscovery by James Bruce
- 1821 First English translation by Richard Laurence
- 1883 Revision by Richard Laurence
- 1893 Second major English translation by Robert H. Charles
- 1912 Revision by Robert H. Charles

The first step in this process occurred in the late 1700's. While searching for the source of the Nile River, explorer James Bruce acquired three complete copies of the *Book of Enoch* in the Ethiopic language Ge'ez (pronounced 'gi-is'). These were brought with him to Europe. It would be nearly 50 years before the first translation of the book into the English language would appear in 1821. It was translated by Archbishop Richard Laurence, Professor of Hebrew at Oxford. The translation was not well-received. Criticism of Laurence's translation work began. More than 60 years later, Laurence put forward a full revision in a failed attempt to address serious deficiencies in his work. Ten years later, Robert Henry Charles, Professor of Biblical Greek in Trinity College, Dublin, issued what would become the definitive English translation for the next 100 years. Charles corrected the problems with chapter and verse numbers introduced by Laurence. The version of Charles' translation included in this volume is his 1912 revision of his work.

Authenticated by the Dead Sea Scrolls

175 years after the *Book of Enoch* had been first rediscovered by the world at large, its authenticity was still doubted by many who believed it to be a forgery. After all, it would not be the first time someone had tried to recreate a 'lost book' and put it forth as original. The truth is without some sort of external corroboration, a legitimate cloud of doubt *could* have remained hanging over the book.

In the late 1940's, a discovery was made which removes all doubt that the version of Enoch preserved in Ethiopia is the same book which is quoted in the New Testament. The discovery of the Dead Sea Scrolls in caves in the desert of Judea included the discovery of a number of truly ancient copies of the *Book of Enoch.* Fragments from seven copies of Enoch in Aramaic had survived. These fragments have been positively dated to the three centuries before Christ, making them more than 2,000 years old. An additional three fragments of Enoch in Greek were also found in those caves.

These Dead Sea Scroll fragments of Enoch have been used to verify the reliability of our Ethiopian copies of Enoch. Since the Dead Sea Scroll copies of Enoch have been dated to two to three centuries before Christ. Modern readers can now be certain the complete copies of Enoch found in Ethiopia preserve the book that was quoted by Jude and is referred to by others in the New Testament.

Available on the World-Wide Web

For the first time in this phenomenal history of the book, the full text of the *Book of Enoch* can be freely read by anyone in the world with access to the Internet. This development has come about since the 1990's. As we have seen in this chapter, this has been just one more development in an on-going process by which the *Book of Enoch* has been gradually, but steadily, emerging as a known entity to the people of the world.

The Book of Enoch Today

Though there are those who say the *Book of Enoch* is 'pseudepigraphal' (a writing attributed to the wrong author), and though there are others who say it is 'apocryphal' (a writing of dubious origins), there are yet others who call it 'Scripture'. The Christians of Ethiopia believe it is the authentic writings of the Biblical Enoch, and a canonical part of their Bible.

They believe this in part because there is the ancient testimony of St. Jude in the New Testament. The reasonable question arises, would a New Testament writer under inspiration of the Holy Spirit quote the *Book of Enoch* if he discerned it was a false writing? One might also ask, would a New Testament writer who discerned the book to be a false writing, then say it contained legitimate sayings from the Biblical Enoch? Jude would have to have known it would not be hard for members of his flock to get ahold of or be exposed to rest of Enoch's book. No. Jude's manner of usage of the *Book of Enoch* indicates he believed its authorship was authentic indeed.

The *Book of Enoch* comes down to us today after two millennia of faithful copying and preserving by Jews and Christians. For the Ethiopian Orthodox Church, the *Book of Enoch* has been and is Scripture and therefore was treated with special care throughout the centuries. Modern scholarship has used the Dead Sea Scroll fragments of the *Book of Enoch* to spot-check the reliability of the Ethiopian text. The judgment has been that the *Book of Enoch* in the Ethiopic language is an essentially faithful literal translation of the original.

The question is often asked, *'why was the Book of Enoch left out of the Bible?'* The question really should be, to whose Bible are we referring? If we say it was left out of our own Bible, well and good, but we should realize it was not left out of everyone's Bible. The *Book of Enoch* has apparently always been on some groups' list of sacred books since before the time of Christ.

The preservation of the *Book of Enoch* over the millennia is testimony to the value which has been perceived in its pages. For generations the book has been a blessing to many. And no wonder as we look at its message it bears vivid, pre-Christian testimony to Jesus, the coming Messiah of Israel, as we shall see in the next chapter.

WHO REALLY WROTE THE BOOK OF ENOCH?

At the outset of this chapter, it was noted how Enoch had gone through a period of isolation away from mankind until his call to the office of prophet. Like Enoch, Enoch's book was hidden away for a time, and has been reentering the spotlight, and seems poised to soon fulfill the stated reason for its having been written and preserved. Enoch's book is *"not for [Enoch's] generation, but for a remote one which is for to come"* and for the *"righteous, who will be living in the day of tribulation."* (Enoch 1:1-2)

2
Enoch's Messianic Prophecies

I first read the *Book of Enoch* in September, 2006. I took note that St. Jude tells us *Enoch prophesied.* I remember reasoning if Enoch were indeed a prophet and if the *Book of Enoch* had in fact been written by him, one might well expect to find examples of prophetic insight in evidence in the book. Soon I began to make some striking discoveries.

The book which comes down to us titled the '*Book of Enoch*', is also sometimes called '*Ethiopian Enoch*', and '*1 Enoch*'. It is a composite book of five booklets attributed to the pre-flood patriarch.

It is good to keep this compiled nature of the book in mind when attempting to interpret its contents as apparently the five booklets were in circulation as independent units at some time past and do not relate a purely chronological narrative in their current arrangement.

The five smaller books comprising the *Book of Enoch* are called:

The Book of the Watchers ~ Chapters 1-36
The Book of the Parables ~ Chapters 37-71
The Geocentric Calendar Book ~ Chapters 72-81
The Book of Dream-Visions ~ Chapters 82-90
The Book of the Preaching of Enoch ~ Chapters 91-108

In each of these smaller books, we shall see that there can be found passages which seem to be prophetic in nature. What is especially prominent in this regard are the many Messianic prophecies contained in its pages.

Letter of Jude and Enoch's Messianic Prophecy

As we have seen, Enoch 1:9, is quoted in the New Testament *Letter of Jude*, verses 14-15, which read,

> Enoch, the seventh from Adam, prophesied, saying, "Behold, the Lord comes with ten thousands of his holy ones, to execute judgment on all and to convict all the ungodly of all their deeds of ungodliness that they have committed in such an ungodly way, and of all the harsh things that ungodly sinners have spoken against him."

In Enoch 1:1, the message of his book is to become applicable to those living in a future "day of tribulation." In Enoch 1:3, he also states his book is being written *not* for his own generation, but for "a remote one, which is for to come." According to Jude, the prophecy in Enoch chapter 1 concerning God coming to earth in judgment will be fulfilled by the

Second-Coming of Jesus Christ at the close of the age.

Despite whatever opinion one holds about the *Book of Enoch*, what the book claims for itself is incredible at face value. It presents itself as the oldest book in the world with a message for those living at the end of time!

Enoch's Messianic Theme: "The Eternal God will tread upon the earth."

A theme that runs throughout the five booklets that now comprise the *Book of Enoch*, is that God will come to earth to set up his kingdom.

In verses which come a little before the portion quoted by Jude we read in Enoch 1:3-4,

> The Holy Great One will come forth from His dwelling, and the eternal God will tread upon the earth, even on Mount Sinai, and appear from His camp and appear in the strength of His might from the heaven of heavens.

We can also find passages within our Bibles which contain language similar to this. On a surface level, this sort of language poses a slight problem-- how can it be said of God who fills all things and from whose presence we cannot go away, that He will, *"come forth from His dwelling"*, that He will *"tread upon the earth"*, and that He will *"appear"*? Old Testament commentators have traditionally called passages like this, a 'theophanies'. A theophany is a term for passages in the Old Testament where God is shown taking on a human appearance for a specific occasion or purpose. According to Jude, however, this problem does not exist because for Jude the passage refers to the second coming of Christ. According to Jude, God will indeed tread upon the earth at the personal return of the incarnate Christ, God the Son. In this way, the second coming of Jesus Christ will fulfill all the promises of God which say He will "personally" come and set up His kingdom on earth. This is because we believe God is quite literally in a human body due to the incarnation of God the Son, the second person of the Trinity.

Enoch chapter 1 is Messianic in character and remains to be fulfilled at the Second-coming of Jesus Christ.

There are other places in the *Book of Enoch* where God's personal presence coming to earth is prophesied and which the return of Christ will quite nicely fulfill.

"He shall come down to visit the earth with goodness."

> This high mountain which thou hast seen, whose summit is like the throne of God, is His throne, where the Holy Great One, the Lord of Glory, the Eternal King, will sit, when He shall come down to visit the earth with goodness. (Enoch 25:3)

The passage says, *"He shall come down."* Here Enoch uses language similar to chapter 1, where he wrote, *"The Holy Great One will come forth from His dwelling, and the eternal God will tread upon the earth."* A golden age on earth will come about when God in the flesh *"shall come down to visit the earth with goodness"*. This is the same sort of Enochan prophesy[537] Jude tells us will be fulfilled by the Second-coming of Jesus Christ.

"The Most High Will Descend There."

> The first quarter is called the east, because it is the first: and the second, the south, because the Most High will descend there, yea, there in quite a special sense will He who is blessed forever descend. (Enoch 77:1)

In this passage again we have language which nicely fits the picture of the Second coming of Christ.

"The Holy Lord Will Come Forth"

> A great chastisement shall come from heaven upon all these, and the Holy Lord will come forth with wrath and chastisement to execute judgment on earth. (Enoch 91:7)

By itself this passage does not seem to necessitate the arrival of God on earth for its fulfillment, but taken with the rest of the passages we've examined and due to the similarity of the language, the verse does seem to be talking about the same event at the end of the age when God will come to earth to establish justice, the theme first introduced in Enoch chapter 1.

Seventy Generations from Methuselah to Jesus

Until now we have been looking at Messianic prophecies in Enoch which are to be fulfilled at some as yet future time. There are fulfilled prophecies in Enoch as well.

---

[537] **Enoch 1:3,9, 25:3, 77:1, 90:15,18,20, 91:7** and **100:4**

In Enoch 10, we find perhaps the most amazing specific prophetic passage.

> The Lord said unto Michael: "Go, bind Semjaza and his associates who have united themselves with women so as to have defiled themselves with them in all their uncleanness. And when their sons have slain one another, and they have seen the destruction of their beloved ones, *bind them fast for seventy generations in the valleys of the earth*, till the day of their judgment and of their consummation, till the judgment that is for ever and ever is consummated. In those days they shall be led off to the abyss of fire: and to the torment and the prison in which they shall be confined forever. And whosoever shall be condemned and destroyed will from thenceforth be bound together with them to the end of all generations." (Enoch 10:11-15)

The passage states 70 generations will pass from Methuselah's time until the generation in which the judgment of the angels who sinned will occur.

If we look at the genealogy of Jesus Christ, in Luke 3:23-38, we count exactly 70 generations from the days of Methuselah, to the generation of Jesus. Here we have a specific intersection between the New Testament and a very precise prophecy found in the *Book of Enoch*.

Besides this, in Enoch 55:3-4, we are told that it is God's Elect One, the Messiah who will be the one to judge the sinful angels and their children.

> I will cause My chastisement and My wrath to abide upon them, saith God, the Lord of Spirits. *Ye mighty kings who dwell on the earth, ye shall have to behold Mine Elect One, how he sits on the throne of glory and judges Azazel, and all his associates, and all his hosts* in the name of the Lord of Spirits.

Taken together then, since it is to be 70 generations from Methuselah until the sinning angels will be judged, and since it is the Messiah who will be the one to do that judging, what we have in this prophecy, is a prediction of the exact generation in which Jesus the Messiah was to come.

The oft-repeated idea that some unnamed rabbi or scribe living between the Testaments is the real author of the *Book of Enoch* is extremely hard to justify. The passage evidences a foreknowledge of the actual time of Christ's birth. Prophesying and writing down specific events generations before they occur is solely reserved to the prophets, not to mere scribes.[538]

---

[538] The Dead Sea Scrolls fragment 4Q202, contains the text of Enoch 10:12, mentioning the passage of 70 generations until the judging of the angels. 4Q202 has been dated to about the

The prophecy states after 70 generations the judgment of the angels who had sinned would come. According to the New Testament, he who came *"to destroy the works of the devil"* **[539]** was born exactly 70 generations after Methuselah according to Luke's gospel. It was the life, death, and resurrection of Jesus Christ which signaled the defeat of Satan and his minions.

> God made [us] alive together with him, having forgiven us all our trespasses, by canceling the record of debt that stood against us with its legal demands. This he set aside, nailing it to the cross. He *disarmed the rulers and authorities and put them to open shame, by triumphing over them in him.* (Colossians 2:13-15)

It may be apparent then that the 'rulers and authorities' in heavenly places of which Paul writes were persuaded the condemnation of the sinning angels by someone born 70th from Methuselah was about to occur during the earthly lifetime of Jesus Christ. They wished to kill the Son of God in order to frustrate the prophecy in Enoch's book as well as other prophecies by the prophets of Israel. However, God had a hidden purpose in mind,

> But we impart a secret and hidden wisdom of God, which God decreed before the ages for our glory. None of the rulers of this age understood this, for if they had, they would not have crucified the Lord of glory. (1 Corinthians 2:7-8)

As it turned out, the very thing intended by the 'rulers of this age' to stop the plan of God was used to make God's plan come to completion.

The question may arise in the reader's mind, *why then hasn't the final judgment of the angels already occurred?* A portion of the ancient promise God made to the serpent in the Garden of Eden has indeed been fulfilled.

> I will put enmity between you and the woman, and between your seed and her seed; he shall bruise your head, and you shall bruise his heel. (Genesis 3:15, NASB).

Jesus, the "seed of the woman" had been "bruised in the heel", in other words, "hurt but recovered." By rising from the dead, Jesus triumphed over the powers of darkness. The time yet remains that Jesus, the 70th from Methuselah, will return, and then the remainder of that promise, "he will bruise your head" i.e., "hurt without recovery" will just as surely be fulfilled. Genesis 3:15 has been followed by John 3:16. Jesus has taken his seat at the right hand of the Majesty on high from where he shall come again. The 70th generation is the one in which the sinning angels *are in fact judged*, because *the One born* 70th *from Methuselah lives still!* We are even now within the generation in which the angels will be

---

middle of the 2nd century B.C. We can definitively say, this text was in existence before the birth of Christ.

[539] **1 John 3:8**, The reason the Son of God appeared was to destroy the works of the devil.

finally and utterly condemned. And His word of encouragement to us is true, for, *"The God of peace will soon crush Satan under your feet."* (Romans 16:20)

The 70 Generations from Methuselah to Jesus Christ (Enoch 10:15)

1 Methuselah	26 Obed	51 Rhesa
2 Lamech	27 Jesse	52 Joanan
3 Noah	28 David	53 Joda
4 Shem	29 Nathan	54 Josech
5 Arphaxad	30 Mattatha	55 Semein
6 Cainan	31 Menna	56 Mattathias
7 Shelah	32 Melea	57 Maath
8 Eber	33 Eliakim	58 Naggai
9 Peleg	34 Jonam	59 Esli
10 Reu	35 Joseph	60 Nahum
11 Serug	36 Judah	61 Amos
12 Nahor	37 Simeon	62 Mattathias
13 Terah	38 Levi	63 Joseph
14 Abraham	39 Matthat	64 Jannai
15 Isaac	40 Jorim	65 Melchi
16 Jacob	41 Eliezer	66 Levi
17 Judah	42 Joshua	67 Matthat
18 Perez	43 Er	68 Heli
19 Hezron	44 Elmadam	69 Joseph
20 Arni	45 Cosam	70 Jesus
21 Admin	46 Addi	
22 Amminadab	47 Melchi	(The Genealogy of Christ as recorded in Luke 3:23-38)
23 Nahshon	48 Neri	
24 Sala	49 Shealtiel	
25 Boaz	50 Zerubbabel	

Enter the Messiah

The section of the *Book of Enoch* called the *Book of the Parables* spends quite a few chapters describing a heavenly person whom Enoch sees. When we consider the descriptions Enoch uses for this individual, an astounding picture emerges. In Enoch, this heavenly person is said to 'accompany the Ancient of Days',[540] and is destined to become a light to the nations.[541] This person, portrayed in imagery as a heavenly

---

[540] **Enoch 46:2**
[541] **Enoch 48:4**

shepherd, is shown watering his flock by an *"inexhaustible Fountain of Righteousness."* [542] The name of this heavenly One is to be revealed only by God to His elect, and it is only in this name the elect will be saved.[543] It is also stated by Enoch this One existed before the creation of all things,[544] and is destined to take his seat on a glorious throne for the purpose of judging the world,[545] and it is God Himself who will seat this One on the throne of God's own glory.[546] Enoch states, ultimately the entire world will bow down before this heavenly One and worship him.[547]

Obviously, the only person who fits this description in all those ways is Jesus Christ, who lived, died, rose from the dead, and ascended to the right hand of the Father, from where he will come again to judge the living and the dead!

In Enoch, we also learn a lot about the identity of this heavenly person from the names or titles by which he is known. Enoch calls him the Righteous One,[548] the Elect One,[549] God's Anointed[550] and the Son of Man.[551]

"The Righteous One"

"The Righteous One" is a Messianic title used twice in *The Book of the Parables* and once in *The Book of the Preaching of Enoch.* This title is also used by various writers in the Old and New Testaments.

In the Book of Acts we see 'The Righteous One' was a favored title for Jesus Christ, used in the early Church. Peter says in Acts 3:14, *"You denied the Holy and Righteous One, and asked for a murderer to be granted to you."* In Acts 22:14, Ananias heals the blindness of Saul and prophesies, *"The God of our fathers appointed you to know his will, to see the Righteous One and to hear a voice from his mouth; for you will be a witness for him to everyone of what you have seen and heard."* In Acts 7:52-53, Stephen declares, *"Which of the prophets did your fathers not persecute? And they killed those who announced beforehand the coming of the Righteous One, whom you have now betrayed and murdered."* According to Stephen, Old Testament prophets suffered persecution for prophesying the coming of the Righteous One.

In Isaiah 53, the *Righteous One* is said to come as the sacrificial lamb of God. He is to be rejected and die, but in so doing he is foreseen as stricken by the Lord on behalf the people as a guilt offering for the

---

[542] **Enoch 48:1**
[543] **Enoch 48:6**
[544] **Enoch 48:3**
[545] **Enoch 45:3**
[546] **Enoch 51:3**
[547] **Enoch 48:5**
[548] **Enoch 38:2**
[549] **Enoch 39:6**
[550] **Enoch 48:10**
[551] **Enoch 46:2**

transgressions of the nation. But then, Isaiah tells us something very strange-- once Messiah has given his life for the sins of the people, Messiah will then "see his offspring", and he will "prolong his days." This is something which could only be made possible by Jesus rising from the dead. Because of the death and resurrection of Messiah, we are told in Isaiah 53:11, *"by his knowledge shall the Righteous One, my servant, make many to be accounted righteous, and he shall bear their iniquities."*

We find in Enoch 53:6, a picture of the last judgment at which time, *"the Righteous and Elect One shall cause the house of his congregation to appear: henceforth they shall be no more hindered in the name of the Lord of Spirits."* This verse foresees a Church which has prevailed against the gates of hell, and becomes triumphant through the power of Jesus Christ, the *Righteous One.*

"The Elect One"

> After this the Righteous and Elect One shall cause the house of his congregation to appear: henceforth they shall be no more hindered in the name of the Lord of Spirits. (Enoch 53:6)

"The Elect One" is a Messianic title found in Enoch only in *The Book of the Parables*, where it occurs 16 times. This title is synonymous with "Chosen One", and is echoed in Luke 9:35, *"a voice came out of the cloud, saying, 'This is my Son, my Chosen One; listen to him!'"* In that verse, God the Father is bearing witness that Jesus Christ is His Chosen, or Elect One, who was prophesied.

This title for Israel's Messiah is also found in Isaiah 42:1, *"Behold my servant, whom I uphold; mine Elect, in whom my soul delighteth."* (KJV)

The manner in which Luke 23:35 was rendered in the Douay-Rheims Bible also emphasizes this aspect of Jesus Christ's nature, *"the people stood beholding, and the rulers with them derided him, saying: 'He saved others; let him save himself, if he be Christ, the Elect of God.'"*

Jesus Christ is the eternally Elect One of God. It is due to Christ's 'choseness', that whoever places their faith in Him are also the chosen of God by reason of being considered 'in the Beloved',[552] and are therefore identified with God's Chosen One.

---

[552] **Ephesians 1:4-6,** *He chose us in him* before the foundation of the world, that we should be holy and blameless before him. In love he predestined us for adoption as sons through Jesus Christ, according to the purpose of his will, to the praise of his glorious grace, with which *he has blessed us in the Beloved.*

"God's Anointed"

> All these things which thou hast seen shall serve the dominion of His Anointed that he may be potent and mighty on the earth. (Enoch 52:4)

Another Messianic title assigned to the heavenly person in Enoch's vision is "God's Anointed." "His Anointed" is synonymous for "His Messiah" in the *Book of Enoch* and occurs two times, only in the *Book of the Parables,* (48:10 and 52:4). This is one of the most common titles applied to the Messiah in the Hebrew Scriptures. The "Anointed One" is the literal meaning of the Hebrew word for "Messiah."

In the Old Testament, persons were anointed by God through his messengers the prophets for specific purposes. Prophets, Priests, Kings and Judges were all anointed by God at the outset of their commissioning to their offices. Once anointed and commissioned, God's anointed became a minster in the affairs of men on behalf of God. God's anointing signified the Prophet, Priest, King or Judge was God's designated one and was to be respected as such. Many Jews believed that God would one day raise up an anointed one who would operate in all of the offices of God's anointed ones at the same time. This "Messiah", or anointed one, would operate on God's behalf among men as Prophet, Priest, King and Judge simultaneously.

Enoch, is identifying the Righteous and Elect One as God's Anointed One. Though Jesus Christ was baptized with water and the Holy Spirit at the river Jordan at the outset of his ministry, His anointing from God was from before the creation. He is God's eternally Anointed One.

"The Son of Man"

"The Son of Man" is a Messianic title used for the heavenly person in Enoch's vision. It is found in Enoch only in *The Book of the Parables,* where it occurs 16 times. This title is echoed throughout the four gospels in the New Testament, where Jesus Christ is the Son of Man.

Of the more than 100 places in the Hebrew Scriptures in which the term "son of man" is used, only one, in the Book of Daniel, is clearly referring to the Messiah,

> I saw in the night visions, and behold, with the clouds of heaven there came *one like a son of man,* and he came to the Ancient of Days and was presented before him. And to him was given dominion and glory and a kingdom, that all peoples, nations, and languages should serve him; his dominion is an everlasting dominion, which shall not pass away, and his kingdom one that shall not be destroyed. (Daniel 7:13-14)

Even in this, the single messianic use of the term "son of man" in the Hebrew Scriptures, the indefinite article "a" is used by translators to show the term is not so much a title but a description of how the Messiah looked in Daniel's vision. Daniel reports the Messiah appeared to be a human being in his vision. All the rest of the references to the term "son of man" in the Hebrew Old Testament *do not* refer to the Messiah, and more than 90 of these occur in the Book of Ezekiel and refer to Ezekiel himself.

If you ask your average Bible-believing Christian *to whom does the Bible refer when it uses the term 'the Son of Man'?* you will surely get the answer, *Jesus Christ*. Undoubtedly, this is because of the prevalent use of that term in the gospels. But this raises the question, how was it that a description of Israel's Messiah-to-come, which was only used once in the Hebrew Scriptures, came to be one of the most common titles used by Jesus Christ to describe himself. In Matthew's gospel the term is used nearly 30 times, in Luke's Gospel, more than 25 times. Mark's and John's gospels also use the term, but slightly less frequently. In total, the gospels refer to Jesus as "the Son of Man" more than 80 times. In almost every case, the term is used by Jesus to refer to himself. In this light then, it is striking that Jesus does not appear to make any effort to explain what the term means. From this we can assume, the term had some commonly shared meaning among his listeners.

This raises another question. How would Jesus' hearers have understood the term which Jesus was in the habit of using for himself, since Israel's Messiah is referred to as *"one like a son of man"* only once in the Hebrew Scriptures? Is it possible that both Jesus and his hearers shared *another* source by which they understood the term?

As it turns out, there was another source, a book containing many references to Israel's Messiah-Son of Man, a book which we now know was in fairly wide circulation in Jesus' day, and which is not currently found in the Old Testament of Western Bibles based upon the Hebrew Scriptures. Is it possible the widespread familiarity with this term among Jesus' audience was due to the popularity and circulation of the *Book of Enoch* at that time? Is this the reason Jesus did not need to explain His own use of the term?

Consider these amazing passages from the *Book of Enoch*:

> I asked the angel who went with me and showed me all the hidden things, concerning that Son of Man, who he was, and whence he was, and why he went with the Head of Days? And he answered and said unto me: this is the Son of Man who hath righteousness, with whom dwelleth righteousness, and who revealeth all the treasures of that which is hidden, because the Lord of Spirits hath chosen him, and whose lot hath the

> preeminence before the Lord of Spirits in uprightness for ever. (Enoch 46:2-3)
>
> At that hour that Son of Man was named in the presence of the Lord of Spirits, and his name before the Head of Days. Yea, before the sun and the signs were created, before the stars of the heaven were made, his name was named before the Lord of Spirits. He shall be a staff to the righteous whereon to stay themselves and not fall, and he shall be the light of the gentiles, and the hope of those who are troubled of heart. All who dwell on earth shall fall down and worship before him, and will praise and bless and celebrate with song the Lord of Spirits. And for this reason hath he been chosen and hidden before him, before the creation of the world and for evermore. (Enoch 48:2-6)
>
> The angel came to me and greeted me with his voice, and said unto me "this is the Son of Man who is born unto righteousness, and righteousness abides over him, and the righteousness of the Head of Days forsakes him not." And he said unto me: "he proclaims unto thee peace in the name of the world to come. For from hence has proceeded peace since the creation of the world, and so shall it be unto thee for ever and for ever and ever. And all shall walk in his ways since righteousness never forsaketh him: with him will be their dwelling-places, and with him their heritage, and they shall not be separated from him for ever and ever and ever. And so there shall be length of days with that Son of Man, and the righteous shall have peace and an upright way in the name of the Lord of Spirits for ever and ever." (Enoch 71:14-16)
>
> There was great joy amongst them, and they blessed and glorified and extolled because the name of that Son of Man had been revealed unto them. (Enoch 69:26)

Scattered throughout the *Book of the Parables*, are many passages concerning this heavenly person called the Righteous One, Elect One, Anointed One and Son of Man. Taken together, these terms give accurate pre-Christian testimony to the character of the person who would be revealed at the coming of Jesus of Nazareth.

The Birth of Messiah

In Enoch chapters 85-90, a lengthy passage is given in which the people of the nations of the earth are represented symbolically by different breeds of animals. In the passage, Adam, the first man is said to be a "bull", specifically an ox. In the passage "bull" oxen refer to the godly line traced from Adam until Jacob. As the story proceeds, Jacob who was initially identified as a bull is subsequently referred to as a "lamb". From him come countless sheep. From Jacob forward the terms "lamb" and "sheep" refer to the chosen people of God. The gentile nations are said to be various other species of animals which attack and devour sheep.

The passage culminates in telling us something about the identity of the coming Messiah. Messiah is to be a bull *and* a sheep, in other words he will be born as fully man descended from the line of Adam, but also from the chosen line of Jacob.

> I saw that a white bull was born, with large horns, and all the beasts of the field and all the birds of the air feared him and made petition to him all the time. And I saw till all their generations were transformed, and they all became white bulls; and the first among them became a lamb, and that lamb became a great animal and had great black horns on its head; and the Lord of the sheep rejoiced over it and over all the oxen. (Enoch 90:37-38)

The fact that Messiah has large horns refers to his rulership. That Messiah's rulership will extend over the entire animal kingdom signifies his rulership will be worldwide and over all the nations. As a result of the rule of Messiah, all of humanity is to be transformed and become a source of rejoicing to God.

The Resurrection of the Righteous One

> Let not your spirit be troubled on account of the times; for the Holy and Great One has appointed days for all things. And *the Righteous One shall arise from sleep*, and walk in the paths of righteousness, and all his path and conversation shall be in eternal goodness and grace. (Enoch 92:2-3)

In 1 Corinthians 15:20 we read,

> Christ has been raised from the dead, the first fruits of those who have fallen asleep.

In both passages, sleep is seen as a metaphor for death.

In Enoch 92:2-3, in language that anticipates the New Testament, God's people are encouraged to not be troubled in spirit for two reasons. First, God has appointed a time for all things, and second, the Righteous One will "arise from sleep." The disciples of Jesus were certainly troubled in spirit when they saw Jesus crucified. They did not realize God had appointed a time for Christ to die. Later, they would realize Jesus' death was necessary in God's plan to secure the forgiveness of sin for any who will believe in Jesus, the Righteous One. The day on which Christ died was appointed by God; it was also appointed that he would rise from the dead. This passage from Enoch is an exhortation to take courage because it is God's plan that though the Righteous One will die he will also rise from the dead.

The Plant of Righteousness

For two millennia, the Church has rightly pointed to the Messianic importance of God's promise to Abraham in Genesis 12:3, *"In you all the families of the earth shall be blessed."* It was through Abraham that Jesus Christ has come into the world and all the families of the earth have certainly been blessed by Him.

Enoch contains a number of passages with similar Messianic implications. Among these is the description of the *Plant of Righteousness.*

> Destroy all wrong from the face of the earth and let every evil work come to an end: and let *the plant of righteousness and truth* appear: and it shall prove a blessing; the works of righteousness and truth shall be planted in truth and joy for evermore. (Enoch 10:16)

This verse is followed by a description of the blessings of a future Messianic Kingdom. The prophecy is that once "the plant of righteousness" has taken root after the flood, it will eventually bear fruit and will introduce the world to a future golden Messianic age. The "plant of righteousness" here represents the genealogy of Noah through whom would come the patriarchs, the nation of Israel, and ultimately, Jesus Christ, the Messiah of Israel. The following passage from Enoch 10, will be fulfilled at the Second coming of Jesus Christ,

> Then shall the whole earth be tilled in righteousness, and shall all be planted with trees and be full of blessing. And all desirable trees shall be planted on it, and they shall plant vines on it: and the vine which they plant thereon shall yield wine in abundance, and as for all the seed which is sown thereon each measure of it shall bear a thousand, and each measure of olives shall yield ten presses of oil. And cleanse thou the earth from all oppression, and from all unrighteousness, and from all sin, and from all godlessness: and all the uncleanness that is wrought upon the earth destroy from off the earth. And all the children of men shall become righteous, and all nations shall offer adoration and shall praise Me, and all shall worship Me. And the earth shall be cleansed from all defilement, and from all sin, and from all punishment, and from all torment, and I will never again send them upon it from generation to generation and forever. (Enoch 10:18-22)

This language is very similar to what we are accustomed to in the Biblical prophets of Israel, as they describe the ideal earthly conditions that will prevail in the age of Messiah.

As with the prophecy mentioned earlier concerning the Messiah, the entire world is brought to a point of worshipping God in truth; *"all the children of men shall become righteous, and all nations shall offer adoration and shall praise Me, and all shall worship Me."*

The Plant of the Eternal Seed

We find more information about the plant of righteousness in Enoch chapter 84. After seeing in a dream-vision the coming destruction of the earth by devastation and flood, Enoch cries out to God in distress concerning the judgment to come. Enoch builds upon the earlier passage as he prays, *"The flesh of righteousness and uprightness establish as a plant of the eternal seed, and hide not Thy face from the prayer of Thy servant, O Lord".* (Enoch 84:6)

Here, it is no longer merely the "plant of righteousness" which comes in view. A new element has been introduced. The plant of righteousness, is to become "a plant of the eternal seed." The term "eternal seed", is imagery that harks back to the promise given to Eve by God in the Garden of Eden. God told Eve that one day "the seed of the woman" would come and crush the head of the serpent.

> I will put enmity between you and the woman, and between your seed and her seed; He shall bruise you on the head, and you shall bruise him on the heel. (Genesis 3:15, NASB)

That a woman should possess seed is without parallel in ancient Jewish literature, and prophetically foreshadows the virgin conception and birth of Jesus Christ, who comes into the world to destroy the works of the devil. The woman's material contribution to conception was not fully understood in ancient times. The man's contribution was said to be "seed" which was sown in the "field" of the woman's body. The resultant child was therefore viewed as the seed or offspring of the father. To speak of the "seed of the woman", as is done in Genesis 3:15, is to turn a basic assumption among people in ancient times upside-down. Thus the verse can truly be said to point to the virgin birth.[553] This concept is further developed in Enoch.

Though the use of the term "eternal seed" in Enoch 84:6, envisions the incarnation, it also infers the preexistence from eternity of the "eternal seed." As it turns out, this passage records Enoch's prophetic prayer,

---

[553] It may be of interest to the reader that a corollary passage regarding the Plant of Righteousness can be found in the *Book of Jubilees* 16:20, which says, Abraham "blesses his Creator who had created him in his generation, for according to his pleasure did he create him; for he knew and observed that from him would come the plant of righteousness for the generations of eternity, and that from him should also come the holy seed, like Him who made all things." (Schodde) The unique additional detail in the Jubilees passage is the "holy seed" is "like Him who made all things", inferring the divine nature of Christ.

alluding to both the incarnation as well as the preexistent nature of Jesus Christ. He is referred to as "the eternal seed", and Jesus Christ is indeed eternal by reason of His not having beginning or end. He is the eternally begotten Son of God.[554]

A Fountain of the Righteous and Holy

Enoch is addressing his great-grandson, Noah with the following prophecy:

> He has destined thy name to be among the holy, and will preserve thee amongst those who dwell on the earth, and has destined thy righteous seed both for kingship and for great honors, and from thy seed shall proceed a fountain of the righteous and holy without number for ever. (Enoch 65:12)

In the first part of the prophecy, Enoch speaks to Noah concerning what Noah will live to see. Noah is destined to be among the holy and will be preserved from the coming judgment of God on the whole earth. Then Enoch proceeds to prophesy concerning that which will occur after Noah's time on earth. According to Enoch, from Noah will come righteous kings and great honors. What's more, from Noah's descendants shall come a kind of fountain from which will proceed righteous and holy people that cannot be numbered. The blessings that will come from this fountain of blessing, from which those righteous and holy ones will proceed and from which they shall also drink will flow forth endlessly.

From Noah came the patriarchs of Israel, the nation, and the Davidic kingly line. To the descendants of Jacob were given the promises and the Abrahamic, Mosaic, Davidic and the New Covenants. The nation of Israel became God's "firstborn son" among the nations.[555] To the people were entrusted the tabernacle worship, and the written word of God. Also, from the nation of Israel came Jesus of Nazareth, King of the Jews and of the nations. From Jesus has arisen his Church and a steady procession of the righteous and holy still proceeds from him to this day and will forevermore.

Jesus is the fountain of blessing from whom the entire world receives the living waters of eternal life through faith in his name.

This prophecy of Enoch is having an on-going fulfillment in our day and no one can measure or has any idea how much of this blessing has been, is now, or will continue to proceed from that fountain of living water.

---

[554] In **Galatians 3:16**, we find similar language. "The promises were spoken to Abraham and to his seed. He does not say, 'and to seeds,' as referring to many, but rather to one, 'and to your seed,' that is, Christ. (NASB)

[555] **Exodus 4:22**, Thus says the LORD, Israel is my firstborn son.

"I and My Son"

The spirit of prophecy is also in evidence within the final section of the book, the *Book of the Preaching of Enoch.*

> In those days the Lord bade them to summon and testify to the children of earth concerning their wisdom: Show it unto them; for ye are their guides, and a recompense over the whole earth. For *I and My Son* will be united with them forever in the paths of uprightness in their lives; and ye shall have peace: rejoice, ye children of uprightness. Amen. (Enoch 105:1-2)

In this passage using language which reminds us of Psalm 2:11-12, and Proverbs 30:4,[556] the eternal God is said to have His Son by His side, who the New Testament identifies as Jesus Christ, the eternal Son of God. Here the writer of the *Book of Enoch* evidences prophetic insight by his knowledge of the existence of the Son of God, the 2nd person of the Trinity, prior to the incarnation of Jesus Christ.

"My Son" the Son of Man

Taking this passage together with what we know to this point, it may be apparent that the *Book of Enoch* anticipates the two natures of Messiah which we have come to know from the writings of the New Testament. It is the unified testimony of the New Testament writers that Jesus Christ is both fully God and fully man. This is shown in the *Book of Enoch* as well. The Messiah will be called the Son of Man, and he is also to be known as God's Son. Though Messianic prophecies abound in the Hebrew Scriptures, those that point to the two natures of Christ are less common. The *Book of Enoch* can be added to this somewhat rarer group of writings.

Future discoveries

There is much in the *Book of Enoch* which is prophetic in nature but which is not being discussed in this book. The purpose of this chapter is to show the Messianic character of many passages in the *Book of Enoch.* Other books could and should be written discussing other prophetic subjects within the *Book of Enoch.* The focus here is on Messianic prophecy in the *Book of Enoch.* I fully expect others will be able to dig deeper into this complex book which will no doubt yield further gems. Perhaps the most dramatic discoveries in this neglected book are yet to be found in the last days by the last generation, for whom this book is intended like a time-capsule with its message of hope in Jesus Christ, the Righteous One, Elect One, Anointed One, and Son of Man.

---

[556] **Psalm 2:11-12**, Serve the LORD with fear, and rejoice with trembling. Kiss the Son, lest he be angry, and you perish in the way. **Proverbs 30:4**, Who has established all the ends of the earth? What is His name, and what is His Son's name? Surely you know!

3
The Great Crisis: The Watchers Descend

Before proceeding to present more evidence for Enoch being the authentic author of the *Book of Enoch*, it seems important to first lay a foundation, and overview, for a general understanding of the contents of the book as a whole. This can seem a daunting task to some since the book is not laid out in a strictly chronological order. In this chapter we present a possible chronological outline of the book, putting in order the book's key events. (See also page 270 for a chronological overview).

Because the document we now call the *Book of Enoch* is in fact a composite work comprised of five smaller books which were combined into a single scroll at some point in ancient times, the chronology of events in the composite book can be a challenge to comprehend. Besides this, many parts of the book employ the story-telling devices of time-shifting, flashback, and the retelling of events with increasing detail. The following chapter is intended as a chronological framework for comprehending the events of the book as a whole. Relevant passages from the Biblical story will also be incorporated here as needed for clarification.

The Watchers Serve God in Heaven

According to the Bible, sometime before the earth was created, God's messengers, the angels, were created. In Job 38:4&7, God challenges Job with a question,

> Where were you when I laid the foundation of the earth? ...when the morning stars sang together and all the sons of God shouted for joy?

Despite this and other passages, the Bible gives us relatively little information about the angels. Today, much of what we assume we know about angels is theoretical based upon our theological assumptions. Much of what has been hypothesized by the Church about God's angels is now accepted as fact without much Biblical support. For example, it is often assumed that since the rebellion of Lucifer, those angels who remained faithful and did not follow Lucifer have been tested and are now impeccable or incapable of sin. Another assumption about the angels commonly held by Christians today is that the angels of God are somehow all-knowing concerning God's program for humanity and creation, and are therefore incapable of error. Also, it is assumed that angels are pure spirit without material bodies. All of these ideas were apparently not common among Christians in the first century before Greek ways of thinking began to dominate Christian theology. This subject is discussed in greater detail in chapter 5.

Our modern assumptions about angels were foreign not only to the writer of the *Book of Enoch*, but also apparently to all Jewish writers before the destruction of the Jewish temple in AD 70. Even the writers of the New Testament seem to corroborate this.

The Watchers Arrive on Earth

A central event of the *Book of Enoch* deals with a worldwide crisis which came about as a result of the sins of a group of 200 angels referred to as "Watchers". Watchers is a term referring to angels which is also found three times in the *Book of Daniel*.[557] Whether the term Watcher is meant to describe a particular class of angels, or if it is simply another term for all angels is not clarified in either the *Book of Enoch* or the *Book of Daniel*. The sin of these Watcher angels, which precipitates the crisis in the era before the flood, is said to have occurred "in the days of Jared"[558] the father of Enoch. That the Watcher angels who sinned already had occasion to visit earth prior to the crisis they caused can be inferred from the fact their temptation to sin precedes their fall.[559]

The term Watcher is also applied to certain angels who did not fall into sin. For instance, the archangels Michael and Gabriel as well as some others are referred to as Watchers in Enoch's book.[560]

The Watchers Desire the Daughters of Men

The chain of events which lead to the destruction of all the living on earth by the flood in Noah's day, began sometime between 1,194 and 1,033 years before the flood.[561] At that time a group of 200 Watcher angels became enticed by "the daughters of men" and desired to take them as wives.[562] At the juncture when the Watchers had not yet acted upon their desires, we may assume the opportunity for a change of mind and avoidance of sin was still a possibility for them.[563]

The Watchers Desire to Have Children

Enoch also tells us the Watcher angels wanted to have children.[564] After having acted as Watchers and apparently recorders[565] of events in the

---

557 **Daniel 4:13**, Behold, *a watcher*, a holy one, came down from heaven. **Daniel 4:17**, The sentence is by the decree of *the watchers*, the decision by the word of the holy ones, to the end that the living may know that the Most High rules the kingdom of men and gives it to whom he will and sets over it the lowliest of men. **Daniel 4:23**, The king saw *a watcher*, a holy one, coming down from heaven.

558 **Enoch 6:6**

559 **Enoch 6:2**

560 **Enoch 20:1-7**

561 These dates are based upon the genealogy found in Genesis chapter 5.

562 **Enoch 6:2**

563 **Enoch 6:3**

564 **Enoch 6:2**

565 **Enoch 89:76**, here and elsewhere in Enoch, angels are shown writing down the activities of humanity.

human realm, these Watchers became envious of the activities of humanity and wished to participate in taking wives and having children.

The Watchers Resolve to Act

Mount Hermon is the locale in the *Book of Enoch* reported as a gathering place for this group of Watcher angels. On one occasion, they were gathered there when discussion arose concerning the taking of human wives. After some discussion, a group decision was made to proceed to take wives as they wished from among humanity.[566]

The Watchers Swear an Oath

Before departing from Mount Hermon, a Watcher by the name Semjaza, challenged the others to take an oath to stick with the decision they had made. Semjaza's contention was the other angels may change their minds and Semjaza did not want to be the only one to experience any punishment that might result from this disobedient act. They all agreed. Semjaza and 199 other angels took an oath not to break with their plan to proceed with the taking of human wives.[567] Enoch tells us this is the way Mt. Hermon got its name, *"they called it Mount Hermon, because they had sworn and bound themselves by mutual imprecations upon it,"* (Enoch 6:6).

The Watchers Take "Wives"

The Watcher angels began acting on their plan. The relevant passages in Genesis and Enoch do not tell us the angels sought human co-operation with their actions.

When the angels began to take wives, our text reads, *"and each chose for himself one"*.[568] The language seems to imply the Watchers practiced monogamy. However, an Aramaic fragment from Dead Sea Scrolls gives us a clearer understanding of this verse. The fragment reads *"all took for themselves women, from all they chose."* Any hint the Watchers were monogamous is gone. The Watchers were polygamous.

The Watchers Are Defiled by Fornication

Genesis and Enoch say the angels were taking "wives". This indicates there was an effort on the part of the Watchers to lend an air of legitimacy to their actions. They were redefining the *meaning* of marriage by their actions. However, the *Book of Enoch* tells us God regarded their actions as fornication and their offspring as bastards.[569] No one can redefine marriage as God ordained it. Then, as now, redefining marriage can be

---

[566] **Enoch 6:4**
[567] **Enoch 6:5**
[568] **Enoch 7:1**
[569] **Enoch 10:9**

seen as a futile attempt to legitimize fornication.

It is at this point Enoch reports the Watchers became "defiled." The implication here is that until this point there remained the opportunity for the angels to change their minds and not go through with their intentions. However, once the Watchers had defiled themselves, their direction was determined. There would now be no turning back. Taking note the Watchers were polygamous, it is very likely each of the angels had innumerable "wives" and continued to take more throughout the following centuries. The stage was now set... the angels would cause the planet to be overrun with their grotesque offspring.

The Millennium of Watcher Misrule

As if turning their backs on God were not enough, the Watchers add to their guilt by placing themselves in that role which is reserved for God alone. The Watchers impose themselves over mankind.

According to Enoch, mankind was subjected to systematic misrule by the evil angels and their demonic offspring. Starting in the days of Enoch's father, Jared, and continuing until the flood, these terrible conditions persisted and increased on earth for more than a thousand years. It was during this time, we believe, that many of earth's puzzling megaliths were built by the Watchers and their children.

Over the course of the next ten centuries, the subjugation and degradation of mankind would pass through three distinct phases. In the book, each of these phases is introduced with a description of some form of evil angelic indoctrination followed by its immediate negative results. Enoch then culminates each phase with a summary of that period's ultimate disastrous outcome for mankind.

• *Phase One: Age of Monsters*

During the first phase,[570] the evil angels take any women they desire, effectively rape them, and begin to introduce them to occult doctrine and practice. Some have suggested the mention of *"cutting of roots"* [571] is a reference to genetic engineering. Indeed, the phrase is immediately followed by the birth of the giants. However, taken in context the cutting of roots likely refers to the magical use of the natural products of the earth.

The birth of the Watchers' offspring increases the subjugation and domination of mankind to a much greater degree. The oppression of humanity by the Watcher children is now layered on top of the abuse of the evil angels which is already well underway.

---

[570] **Enoch 7:1-6**
[571] **Enoch 7:1,8:3**

Both Genesis 6, and Enoch's book report the Watcher angels' offspring were called "Nephilim." The meaning of this word is subject to some debate. It is commonly assumed the word should be translated "giants." This is because the offspring of the Watchers were typified by mutations, one of the most common being gigantism. However, other types of mutations were apparently in evidence. In a later passage, using allegorical language Enoch refers to the women giving birth to Nephilim in this way, *"all of whom became pregnant, and brought forth elephants, camels, and asses"*.[572] Another ancient Jewish book from before the Christian era says, *"And they begat sons the Naphidim, and they were all unlike"*.[573]

The offspring of the Watchers begin to assert themselves in the world of humankind. Unlike Adam and Eve whom the Scriptures tell us fell from innocence, and unlike the Watchers, whom we are also informed fell from God's grace, the Nephilim were bad from birth. Being the offspring of both fallen humanity and fallen angelic beings, the Nephilim are never spoken of as having fallen from God's grace and are never given an opportunity to repent.

The Watcher children begin their oppression of humanity by consuming the fruit of mankind's labors[574] but soon this is not enough and they move to consuming humans themselves.[575] In the era before the flood, God had not as yet allowed mankind to eat the meat of animals,[576] but the Nephilim are unrestrained in consuming any and all of them. The Watcher children ultimately end up consuming each other as well as reveling in the drinking of blood.[577]

The outcome of this first phase is a world characterized by violence and bloodshed. The phrase *"the earth laid accusation against the lawless ones"* [578] is a manner of stating that much innocent blood is being shed on earth; it is as if the blood-soaked ground is crying out to heaven for justice.

As the age of monsters raged on, phase two was set to commence....

---

[572] **Enoch 86:4**
[573] **Jubilees 7:22**
[574] **Enoch 7:3**
[575] **Enoch 7:4**
[576] Before the flood we read in **Genesis 2:16**; The Lord God commanded the man, saying, "You may surely eat of every tree of the garden." After the flood we read in **Genesis 9:2-3**; "The fear of you and the dread of you shall be upon every beast of the earth and upon every bird of the heavens, upon everything that creeps on the ground and all the fish of the sea. Into your hand they are delivered. Every moving thing that lives shall be food for you. And as I gave you the green plants, I give you everything."
[577] **Enoch 7:5**
[578] **Enoch 7:6**

• *Phase Two: Thus Spoke Azazel*

During this phase[579] Azazel is credited with passing on to humanity the knowledge of certain technologies. In doing this, not only did Azazel cause human know-how to accelerate but he also made sure it was corrupted. Under the evil tutelage of Azazel the innocent knowledge of metallurgy was turned to warfare and personal beautification was turned toward evil purposes. We can surmise Azazel's motives in all this from the results he obtained. Because of the creation of weaponry and through certain uses of personal beautification, *"there arose much godlessness, and they committed fornication, and they were led astray, and became corrupt in all their ways."* Because of these outcomes, Azazel will be singled out for special punishment before the flood.

As the first two phases of this millennium of misery continued rolling on, phase three was about to erupt on the world stage....

• *Phase Three: Global Satanic Conspiracy*

In the third phase,[580] indoctrinating the human race in the occult arts became universal. What people believe matters, and as is always the case with occult beliefs, instead of educating, elevating, improving, and enlightening its adherents, mankind became further debased and further bloodshed spread over the face of the earth. It is about this situation that the Biblical record tells us, *"The Lord saw that the wickedness of man was great in the earth, and that every intention of the thoughts of his heart was only evil continually"* (Genesis 6:5).

Enoch's Calling and Ministry

Enoch having been born about 1033 years before the flood, had cause throughout his life to interact with Watcher angels, both those fallen and those who had not. While worshipping God in the presence of angels, Enoch receives his call to preach. The judgment of God against the Watchers and their children having been determined, Enoch is sent to preach God's decree to the sinning angels at Mount Hermon.[581] The call of Enoch has come nearly seven centuries before the flood.

Condemnation of the Watchers and Their Children

Enoch declares God's decree and pronounces God's judgment against the Watchers and their offspring. Enoch tells the Watchers, God has decreed Azazel will be first to be bound in chains and cast into an abyss in the desert.[582] After this, the Nephilim are to be judged. They will be

[579] **Enoch 8:1-2**
[580] **Enoch 8:3-4**
[581] **Enoch 12:1-6**
[582] **Enoch 10:4-8**

incited to civil war in order to destroy one another.[583] The remaining sinning angels are doomed to watch this slaughter and yet will be unable to stop it. Once the decimation of the Nephilim is complete and still fresh before the eyes of their fathers, the remaining Watchers are to be bound in chains and cast into the abyss, where Azazel will have already been imprisoned for the previous 120 years.[584] The sinning angels are to remain in chains, imprisoned in the abyss for a period of 70 generations, after this time, they will be removed from the abyss, finally judged, and cast into eternal flames.[585]

This is the decree from God which Enoch relates to the Watchers on Mount Hermon.[586]

Enoch Is Sent by the Watchers to Petition God

After hearing God's decree, the Watchers are greatly troubled and request Enoch to petition God on their behalf.[587] The Watchers request that God forgive their sins.[588]

The Watchers Ask God for the Lives of their Children

The Watchers also request mercy from God upon their offspring. They request the Nephilim not be judged but rather allowed to live out their full length of days.[589]

Enoch Receives a Vision from God

Enoch writes down the petition of the Watchers and sets out to speak to God on their behalf. Along his way, Enoch takes rest and reviews the Watchers' petition. Enoch falls asleep and is sent a dream-vision from God in which God responds to the Watchers' petition.[590]

The Watchers' Requests Are Denied by God

Aware of their requests, God informs Enoch in a dream-vision that the Watchers' requests will be denied.[591]

God's Decree of Judgment Is Sure

Once again, God informs Enoch of the sure condemnation and judgment of the Watchers and their children. Their requests for forgiveness for

[583] **Enoch 10:9-10**
[584] **Enoch 10:11-12**
[585] **Enoch 10:12-14**
[586] **Enoch 13:3**
[587] **Enoch 13:3-4**
[588] **Enoch 13:4**
[589] **Enoch 10:10, 14:7**
[590] **Enoch 13:7-8**
[591] **Enoch 10:10, 14:4**

themselves, and for leniency for their children, are denied.[592]

Enoch Returns to the Watchers

On Mount Hermon, Enoch returns to the angels who sinned. Upon arriving at the meeting Enoch finds the angels in a state of great agitation and regret, weeping for their fate and that of their children. Enoch declares his vision.... God's judgment is sure. The Watchers are not to be forgiven and the Nephilim are not to be granted an extension of their lives. Azazel is to be bound, the Nephilim are to be destroyed and the remaining Watchers are to be bound in the abyss until the last judgment.[593]

Enoch's message of judgment to the Watchers is now delivered. Enoch's assignment to deliver God's message of rebuke to the Watchers is complete. It will be centuries before the judgment pronounced against the Watchers and their children will be carried out.

The Book of Enoch Is Written

Enoch has been informed he will be taken from this world.[594] Enoch's remaining task is to write his message down as a witness to later generations. His book is especially intended to become a blessing and encouragement to the faithful who will be living during earth's final years, during the time of earth's last and greatest tribulation.[595]

For millennia, Enoch's books will be read, copied, preserved and passed down by the faithful, who will *"deliver them to the generations of the world."*[596]

Enoch is Raptured!

Sometime after these events, more than six centuries before the flood of Noah's time, Enoch is caught up. He is translated alive by God into heaven where he remains to this day.[597]

The Uncanny Birth of Noah

Noah is born about 175 years after Enoch's translation to heaven. The circumstances of Noah's birth are unusual and prompt Lamech, his father, to doubt whether Noah is his own child. Lamech is told Noah's unusual appearance is due to his unique calling as the savior of

---

592 **Enoch 16:2-4**
593 **Enoch 13:9-10**
594 **Enoch 81:5-6**
595 **Enoch 91:6-10**
596 **Enoch 82:1**
597 **Enoch 70:1-4**

humanity in God's soon-coming judgment of the world by flood.[598]

Noah Completes the Book of the Parables

Noah recounts that he received the *Book of the Parables* from Enoch himself.[599] The *Book of the Parables,* which was begun more than a century earlier, is now completed by chapters 60 through 71, written by Noah, Enoch's great-grandson.

Azazel Bound in the Abyss until Judgment

120 years before the flood, God's decree against the sinning Watchers begins to be carried out. The wretched condition of the world has sunken, having progressed for more than six centuries since Enoch initially pronounced God's judgment upon the Watchers. Azazel is now bound in chains and cast into darkness in an abyss in the desert and covered with rocks.[600] The implements of war, which had been one of Azazel's special contributions to the degradation of humanity, will now become the tool by which the children of the Watchers will be destroyed.

Watcher Offspring Are Incited to Civil War

With Azazel bound, and the remaining Watchers still free, Gabriel is able to incite the children of the Watchers to worldwide war. Civil war breaks out between the various clans of Nephilim, and the various monstrous races which have arisen from them over the course of the past nine centuries. For the next 120 years, war on a world scale will rage until the numbers of Nephilim and their children have been decimated upon the planet.[601]

The Watcher Offspring Are Stoned from Heaven

In order to speed the process of their destruction, angels hail stones from heaven upon the Nephilim on earth.[602]

Watchers Watch Their Offsprings' Destruction

Throughout the duration of the wars of the Nephilim, the Watchers who have not yet been bound in the abyss, witness the destruction of their offspring being powerless to stop it.[603]

Nephilim Condemned to Become Evil Spirits

---

[598] **Enoch 106**
[599] **Enoch 68:1**
[600] **Enoch 10:4-8**
[601] **Enoch 10:9-10**
[602] **Enoch 88:2-3**
[603] **Enoch 10:12, 14:6**

Once dead, the unique origin of the Nephilim, which made them angelic-human hybrids, leads as well to the pronouncement of a unique destiny for them after death. As disembodied spirits they are doomed to roam the earth as evil spirits. In this new role they will continue to experience their voracious hunger and thirst as formerly, but will be unable to satisfy those desires. They will serve as a source of trouble for sinful humanity from this time forward, until the final judgment when they will enter the final phase of their judgment, the eternal flames prepared for the angels who sinned.[604]

Remaining Watchers Are Bound in the Abyss

After the 120-years' war of the Watchers' offspring is complete, and with their deaths fresh in their parent's minds, the Archangel Michael begins to carry out the sentence against the Watchers. First Semjaza, who had led the initial rebellion of the 200 Watchers on Mt. Hermon, is bound and cast into the Abyss. The rest of the Watchers who sinned are now bound and cast into the Abyss with Azazel and Semjaza, who went before them.[605]

Arrival of the Flood

In the year the deluge comes, Methuselah, the son of Enoch, dies. Noah and his family enter the ark taking the writings of Enoch with them. These books were likely given to him by Noah's grandfather Methuselah, who in fact outlived Noah's father Lamech. The flood submerges the planet and destroys all life except for Noah and those saved from judgment with him in the ark. 1,000-years of the works of the Watchers and their children, is wiped from the face of the earth. The earth is cleansed and renewed.[606]

The Flourishing of the Plant of Righteousness

After the flood, the offspring of Noah through Shem take root just as Enoch prophesied. Their descendants are to be "the elect plant of righteousness", the people from whom will come the patriarchs, the Scriptures, and the Messiah.[607]

70 Generations Pass from Methuselah to Christ

According to Enoch 10:12, seventy generations will pass from the binding of the angels who sinned, until the birth of the Messiah, Son of Man. After the birth of Jesus, the 70th from Methuselah,[608] Satan sets out to destroy him in order to prevent God's plan to establish him as judge.

---

[604] **Enoch 15:8-16:1**
[605] **Enoch 10:11-12**
[606] **Enoch 10:1-3**
[607] **Enoch 10:16**
[608] **Luke 3:23-38**

Jesus will indeed be killed, but this serves to complete, rather than thwart, God's plan. Jesus, the prophesied Righteous One, rises from the dead and ascends victorious into heaven where he takes his seat on the right side of the throne of God.

Arrival of the Day of Tribulation

The world's last and greatest tribulation period suddenly springs upon the final generation of humanity. Two beasts arise from the earth in order to trouble mankind.[609] The first beast seen by John the Apostle, rises from the Mediterranean Sea and represents a leviathan of political and military oppression. This beast is epitomized in a man who is destined to be the Antichrist who the Bible has predicted for millennia. The second beast is seen rising from the land of Israel on the shore of the Mediterranean Sea. He represents a behemoth of religious deception and oppression. This beast is epitomized in the False Prophet who forces worship of the Antichrist upon the people of the world. Both beasts work together to wage war on the people of God who remain on earth.[610] Earth's days are now characterized by war, disasters in the natural realm, social upheaval, and increasing wickedness in the actions of men. Conditions on earth descend into an ever-worsening downward spiral, twice as bad as the times before the flood of Noah's day.[611] But as the days grow dark, the light begins to shine brighter for the increasing numbers of those who are coming to a saving knowledge of God in Christ.

Election of the Plant of Righteousness

During this tribulation period, the descendants of the 'elect plant of righteousness' will become doubly elect as they accept faith in Jesus Christ, the Messiah of Israel.[612] The people of Israel will call upon Jesus, as their Messiah, and ask him to deliver them. Their prayer will be heard and answered.[613]

The Holy Great One Comes from His Dwelling

That great event envisioned throughout the *Book of Enoch*, the prophets of Israel, and the writings of Christ's Apostles, is now at hand! Jesus Christ, comes to earth to deliver Israel and to trample the winepress of the wrath of God. Jesus returns from heaven[614] to set up his kingdom on earth, and to bring to fulfillment the majority of the prophecies of the

---

[609] **Revelation 13:1-18**

[610] **Revelation 13:7**

[611] **Enoch 91:6**

[612] **Enoch 93:9-10**

[613] **Zechariah 12:10**, I will pour out on the house of David and the inhabitants of Jerusalem a spirit of grace and pleas for mercy, so that, when they look on me, on him whom they have pierced, they shall mourn for him, as one mourns for an only child, and weep bitterly over him, as one weeps over a firstborn.

[614] **Hosea 5:15**, I will return again to my place, until they acknowledge their guilt and seek my face, and in their distress earnestly seek me.

Bible, including the one quoted in Jude's epistle from Enoch's book,

> And behold! He cometh with ten thousands of His holy ones, to execute judgment upon all, and to destroy all the ungodly: and to convict all flesh of all the works of their ungodliness which they have ungodly committed, and of all the hard things which ungodly sinners have spoken against Him, (Enoch 1:9).

The two beasts which have arisen from the earth are captured alive and are the first to be thrown alive into the lake of fire which burns forever and ever.[615] Satan is bound in the Abyss, with the angels who sinned.

Jesus Christ Rules on Earth

The righteous answer to the 1,000-year misrule of the Watchers is now realized. The earth is cleansed and justice is vindicated. Earth's promised golden age under the rulership of Messiah, has now come. Earth's golden age, envisioned since the Garden of Eden, is realized. God's plan for this earth is consummated. The world is finally delivered from all sin and misrule. The earth and its people experience their full potential and true peace is ushered in under the benevolent rule of the God-man Jesus, the Messiah of Israel.[616] At the close of the Millennium, Satan will be allowed to rise from there for a brief time to cause trouble once more. An attempt to overthrow the rule of Christ will fail, signaling the beginning of the last judgment.

The Son of Man Is Seated as Judge

The 1,000-years of the peaceful reign of Christ are now completed. With the Son of Man seated on his throne of glory, the final judgment now takes place. The last judgment of all who have died in sin has come. This includes the Watchers, and their beloved ones, the kings, the mighty, the exalted and those who ruled the earth for 1,000-years before the flood. They are removed from the Abyss and made to stand before the throne of the Son of Man and hear his just decrees. All knees bow, and all tongues confess, *"Jesus Christ is Lord"*, to the glory of God the Father.[617]

Watchers & Nephilim Thrown into the Lake of Fire

Satan, the Watchers, their children, and all who died following any of them in life are now thrown into the lake of fire forever.[618] There they join the two beasts who have been there now for 1,000 years.

The Chronicle of the Nephilim

After the final judgment of the Watchers' offspring, they will have passed

---

[615] **Revelation 19:20**
[616] **Enoch 10:17-22**
[617] **Enoch 62:1-16, 63:1-12**
[618] **Enoch 54:1-6**

through three phases of condemnation and judgment:

1. **In history**: they were judged by war (10:9-10).
2. **In the present**: they are condemned as unclean spirits (15:8-16:1).
3. **In the future**: they are punished in the lake of fire (54:1-6).

In history past, the Archangel Gabriel incited the children of the Watchers to war with one another. This decimated their ranks during the 120-years-war before the flood. In the present, they are condemned to be unclean spirits causing trouble in the world of mankind. In the future, they will stand before the great white throne where final sentencing will occur at which time they will take their place in eternal flames.

The Saga of the Watchers' Descent: The Four Abodes of the Watchers

When the saga of the Watchers' descent, sin, fall from grace, and their judgment has been completed, the Watchers will have passed through four abodes in descending order:

1. **H**eaven
2. **E**arth
3. **A**byss
4. **L**ake of Fire

> And on the day of the great judgment he shall be cast into the fire. And *heal* the earth which the angels have corrupted, and proclaim the *healing* of the earth, that they may *heal* the plague, and that all the children of men may not perish through all the secret things that the Watchers have disclosed and have taught their sons. And the whole earth has been corrupted through the works that were taught by Azazel. (Enoch 10:6-8)

Looking at the chronicle of the Nephilim and the abodes of the Watchers the curious role of the Abyss is highlighted. We also find it mentioned in Luke 8:31 when Jesus confronts the Gadarene demoniac. The unclean spirits beg Jesus not to send them to the Abyss. In Revelation 11:7 and 17:8, the Beast is said to rise from there. In Revelation 9:1-11, hundreds of millions of evil spirits will be released from the Abyss to cause trouble on earth during the Tribulation. The angels who sinned spend time there and the Devil will too. But the day is coming when the sinning angels and Satan will be taken from there and cast into the lake of fire. The Watchers' role in the human sphere is then ended. At that time the Abyss will be emptied and it too will come to an end, the reason for its existence being no longer needed. For now, the Abyss is a necessary reality.

4
A Brief History of the Bottomless Pit

If the Biblical Enoch is indeed the author of the book bearing his name, one might well expect the book's contents to be consistent with the books of the Bible. Not only do we find the *Book of Enoch* to be consistent with the Bible, but as it turns out, familiarity with the contents of the book aids in understanding certain difficult passages of the Bible. Does this intriguing fact point to a familiarity with the *Book of Enoch* on the part of the writers of the Bible? Or, does it demonstrate the writer of the *Book of Enoch* and the writers of the Bible both received divine revelation?

There are quite a number of subjects in the Old and New Testaments concerning which the Biblical writers seem to assume a certain level of prior knowledge on the part of their readers. It is the lack of this prior knowledge in our own day which creates problems for us in understanding these texts. There are a surprising number of these 'problem passages' of Scripture which knowledge of the contents of the *Book of Enoch* effectively erases. Here are a few examples:

- The nature of the sin of the "sons of God" in Genesis 6 [619]
- The curious origin of the Old Testament giants [620]
- The origin of demons not expressly explained in the Bible [621]
- The pervasive use by Christ of the term *Son of Man* [622]
- The nature of the angels' sin mentioned in 2 Peter 2 and Jude
- The reason the angels are imprisoned in 2 Peter and Jude
- The sending of the scapegoat to "Azazel" in Leviticus 16 [623]
- The identity of the seven angels in Ezekiel and Revelation
- Jude's classifying of Enoch as one of the prophets

If one is not familiar with the contents of the *Book of Enoch* each of the above-mentioned subjects poses questions which cannot be definitively answered from the 66 books of the Bible. If one is willing to refer to the *Book of Enoch* on these questions, however, none of these examples poses serious problems. Modern readers do well to bear in mind, at the time of Christ, the subject matter of the *Book of Enoch* was well-known and could have provided a well-spring of conceptual background for readers and hearers of the Scriptures in first-century Israel.

---

[619] Discussed at length in chapter 5 of this book.
[620] Discussed at length in chapters 5 and 6 of this book.
[621] Explained in Enoch 15:8-16:1
[622] Discussed in chapter 2 of this book.
[623] Explained in chapter 9 of this book.

BRIEF HISTORY OF THE BOTTOMLESS PIT

To this above-referenced list we can now add another curiosity from the New Testament:

- The *Book of Revelation's* unique mention of a "bottomless pit" is another example of how knowledge of the content of the *Book of Enoch* helps our understanding.

Out of nowhere, it seems, the *Book of Revelation* speaks of a curious region in the bowels of the earth called the "bottomless pit." The *Book of Revelation* refers to this bottomless pit six times, and in most English translations, the term "bottomless pit" does not appear in the other books of the Bible outside of the *Book of Revelation.*[624] In that light, it is all the more curious that when John wrote Revelation, he spent no time explaining the idea to his readers. John seems to assume prior knowledge of a place called the bottomless pit on the part of his readers.

The first mention of such a bottomless region inside the earth is found in Enoch.

> Bind Azazel hand and foot, and cast him into the darkness: and make *an opening in the desert,* which is in Dudael,[625] and cast him therein. (Enoch 10:4)
>
> Bind them fast for seventy generations *in the valleys of the earth.* (Enoch 10:12)

The sinning angels are bound and then cast into "an opening in the desert" also referred to as the "valleys of the earth." Though these passages do not speak of the *bottomless* nature of the pit into which the angels are cast they provide the basis for a developing concept. Later we read,

> I saw a place which had no firmament of the heaven above, and no firmly founded earth beneath it: there was no water upon it, and no birds, but it was a waste and horrible place. (Enoch 18:12)

Enoch sees a horrible place with no firmly founded earth beneath it. The angel informs Enoch, *"This place is the end of heaven and earth: this has become a prison for the stars and the host of heaven."* (Enoch 18:4) Elsewhere in the *Book of Enoch,* this locale in the heart of the earth is called the "Abyss."

On one occasion in Luke's gospel, the demons which Christ confronts seem to have prior knowledge of such an abyss.

> Jesus then asked him, "What is your name?" And he said, "Legion," for many demons had entered him. And *they begged*

[624] The New Living Translation uses the term "Bottomless Pit" in Luke 8:31
[625] The specific location of Dudael is lost to history.

> *him not to command them to depart into the Abyss.* (Luke 8:30-31)

What Enoch referred to as an abyss without firmly founded earth beneath, John calls the bottomless pit. It is interesting to note, the Greek word used by John, which most translations of the *Book of Revelation* render as the bottomless pit, is 'Abussos', or *abyss*.

In Enoch we discover this abyss is a temporary prison in the bowels of the earth in which some evil spirits and fallen angels are bound. As it turns out, this happens to be an apt description of how we see the bottomless pit functioning in the *Book of Revelation.* In the *Book of Revelation,* the bottomless pit is alternately shown being used to confine[626] or else release[627] evil beings upon the earth.

On closer examination, there are other references to the abyss besides those in Enoch and Revelation. Taking all these and other references together, we are ready to build a kind of timeline, or a brief history of the bottomless pit...

From the Beginning

The first mention of the Biblical Bottomless pit, the abyss, may actually be Genesis chapter 1.

In most of our English Bibles, the rendering of the Hebrew text of Genesis 1:2, reads like this, *"and darkness was over the face of the deep."* This is how modern translators of the Hebrew render it. However, Jewish scholars in ancient times have left us clues as to how the word was understood originally. Hundreds of years before the first Christians, while translating the Bible into Greek,[628] Jewish translators of Genesis translated the above passage like this, *"and darkness was over the abyss"* (NETS). What was destined to become an earthbound place of spiritual punishment was apparently being prepared right from the beginning.

"Chains of Gloomy Darkness"

The sinning angels in the *Book of Enoch* were placed in the abyss and its opening was subsequently covered over, thus obscuring its location.

> Bind Azazel hand and foot, and cast him into the darkness: and make an opening in the desert, which is in Dudael, and cast him therein. And *place upon him rough and jagged rocks, and cover*

---

[626] Revelation 20:1-3
[627] Revelation 9:1-10, 11:7, and 17:8
[628] The Septuagint is a translation of the Old Testament into Greek. It was made by Jews for Jews before the Christian era. Among the reasons the Septuagint is useful for Bible study today is because it can reveal how Jews in ancient times interpreted certain passages of Scripture.

> *him with darkness*, and let him abide there forever, and cover his face that he may not see light. (Enoch 10:4-5)

In the New Testament, Peter and Jude seem to be elaborating upon this same subject.

> God did not spare angels when they sinned, but cast them into hell and committed them to *chains of gloomy darkness* to be kept until the judgment. (2 Peter 2:4)

> The angels who did not stay within their own position of authority, but left their proper dwelling, he has kept in *eternal chains under gloomy darkness* until the judgment of the great day. (Jude 1:6)

The Abyss in Prophecy

The surface of our earth is pock-marked with crevices and abysses, some of which are man-made, and others which are naturally occurring. These can be seen as examples of the earth's ability to sustain and sometimes conceal deep holes, and these can help give us an idea what the opening to the Biblical abyss, or bottomless pit, may be like.

Something which can be observed from the behavior of sinkholes is that for millennia the earth can sustain huge holes in its mantle which are not visible from its surface. Without notice, suddenly, these can open up and wreak havoc. The abyss in Scripture is to have such a future in the sequence of prophetic events. Consider Revelation chapter 9:

> The fifth angel blew his trumpet, and I saw a star fallen from heaven to earth, and he was given the key to the shaft of the bottomless pit. He opened the shaft of the bottomless pit, and from the shaft rose smoke like the smoke of a great furnace, and the sun and the air were darkened with the smoke from the shaft. Then from the smoke came locusts on the earth, and they were given power like the power of scorpions of the earth. They were told not to harm the grass of the earth or any green plant or any tree, but only those people who do not have the seal of God on their foreheads. They were allowed to torment them for five months, but not to kill them, and their torment was like the torment of a scorpion when it stings someone. And in those days people will seek death and will not find it. They will long to die, but death will flee from them.

> In appearance the locusts were like horses prepared for battle: on their heads were what looked like crowns of gold; their faces were like human faces, their hair like women's hair, and their teeth like lions' teeth; they had breastplates like breastplates of iron, and the noise of their wings was like the noise of many chariots with horses rushing into battle. They have tails and stings like scorpions, and their power to hurt people for five

> months is in their tails. They have as king over them the angel of the bottomless pit. His name in Hebrew is Abaddon, and in Greek he is called Apollyon. (Revelation 9:1-11)

In the passage above, the bottomless pit is shown as a temporary holding place for unclean spirits and other kinds of spiritual evil. According to John, at some future time hordes of those evil creatures will be released to wreak havoc on earth under the guidance and direction of an evil angel.

At the Second-coming of Christ, the bottomless pit is to be employed yet again for the purpose of a temporary prison for evil.

> On that day the LORD will punish the host of heaven, in heaven, and the kings of the earth, on the earth. They will be gathered together as prisoners in a pit; they will be shut up in a prison, and after many days they will be punished. (Isaiah 24:21-22)

In Isaiah it is the world rulers and additional sinning angels who will be imprisoned at the time of Christ's return. John gives us more detail and discusses the coming imprisonment of Satan himself.

> I saw an angel coming down from heaven, holding in his hand the key to the bottomless pit and a great chain. And he seized the dragon, that ancient serpent, who is the devil and Satan, and bound him for a thousand years, and threw him into the pit, and shut it and sealed it over him, so that he might not deceive the nations any longer, until the thousand years were ended. After that he must be released for a little while. (Revelation 20:1-3)

> When the thousand years are ended, Satan will be released from his prison and will come out to deceive the nations that are at the four corners of the earth. (Revelation 20:7-8)

After the return of Christ, the bottomless pit will become the temporary holding cell of Satan himself. After 1,000 years of Christ's earthly rule, Satan will again be allowed to rise from the abyss and deceive mankind, according to Revelation 20. Then comes the last judgment. Satan and all those whose names are not found in the *Lamb's Book of Life* will be cast into the lake of fire which is neither temporary nor is it a place from which anyone can return.

Accepting what we have discussed to this point, the history of the bottomless pit can be viewed in the following seven stages, or epochs:

BRIEF HISTORY OF THE BOTTOMLESS PIT

The Seven Epochs of the Bottomless Pit

1. Created empty according to the *Book of Genesis* (Genesis 1:2).
2. Becomes a prison for sinning angels (Enoch 10:4).
3. Is also used as a prison for certain demons (Luke 8:30-31).
4. Will be opened in the last days to release demons, evil angels, and the Antichrist (Rev. 9:1-11, 11:7, and 17:8).
5. Will become a prison for Satan himself (Revelation 20:1-3).
6. Will be opened to release Satan for a time (Revelation 20:7-8).
7. All who are in it will be thrown into the lake of fire (Rev. 20:7-15).

Now that the time of final judgment has come, all those who remain in the Bottomless Pit are thrown into the lake of fire. The purpose for which the bottomless pit existed will no longer be needed. Having run its course its history is now finished. Just so ends the history of the bottomless pit. Enoch's message of judgment, which he had once delivered to the Watcher-angels so long ago, is now fulfilled, for the final condemnation of the Watchers who sinned has arrived.

5
Why Genesis 6:1-4 Puzzles Modern Readers

For many, one of the most debated and puzzling passages of Scripture in our Bible is Genesis 6:1-4. Yet, despite the seeming uncertainty about the meaning of this passage in our own day, in this chapter we will see how Judaism and Christianity before AD 70, were unanimous in their thinking about this passage. Both groups affirmed an understanding of Genesis 6:1-4 which was in agreement with the message of Enoch's book. The fact that this understanding was so prevalent may indicate the worldview of the *Book of Enoch* had been influencing both Jews and Christians from the earliest times. If so, that would be another indicator pointing to the great antiquity and influence of the book.

In Genesis 6, we read:

> When man began to multiply on the face of the land and daughters were born to them, the sons of God saw that the daughters of man were attractive. And they took as their wives any they chose. Then the LORD said, "My Spirit shall not abide in man forever, for he is flesh: his days shall be 120 years." The Nephilim were on the earth in those days, and also afterward, when the sons of God came in to the daughters of man and they bore children to them. These were the mighty men who were of old, the men of renown, (Genesis 6:1-4).[629]

Modern interpretations of Genesis 6:1-4, abound. One of the most common explanations is that the term "sons of God" in the passage refers to the righteous family line descending from the patriarch Seth. "The daughters of man", in the passage is then understood to be women who were of an unbelieving family line, perhaps that of Cain. In this view the sin of the sons of God is seen as intermarriage of God's people with unbelievers, leading to a spiritual decline among humanity.

This view, however, did not become widespread until long after AD 70, when the *Book of Enoch* began to be forbidden, first by the spiritual leaders of the Jews, then by the Christians.

Before the time of Christ, when the Jews who wrote and preserved the Old Testament Scriptures were the only interpreters of those Scriptures,

[629] The Septuagint Codex Vaticanus, reads, "And it happened, when humans began to become numerous upon the land, and [they had daughters], the angels of God, having seen the daughters of humans, that they were beautiful, took for themselves women from all whom they picked out."

the commonly held interpretation of Genesis 6:1-4, was as follows: the angels, the heavenly sons of God, also known as Watchers, lusted after the daughters of mankind and conspired to break God's law. They left their assigned abode in heaven, to take human wives and have children. They defiled themselves by sexual relations with women in order to give birth to children who turned out to be gigantic and monstrous. This was the unified Jewish/Christian understanding from the period when the Jewish temple was still standing and prior.

One is stricken with the sheer lack of controversy among early Jewish writers on this point. In fact, I have not yet found an example from the writings of the period of Second-Temple Judaism in which some writer disagrees with the Watcher/Nephilim saga, though many controversies can be noted in the writings of the period concerning other matters. In chapter 11, we will produce a list of the passages in ancient Jewish literature which touch on this subject.

The View during the Apostolic Era

This common view of early Judaism prevailed among New Testament writers too. Notice how the following quotes from the New Testament dovetail with the story we have earlier outlined from the *Book of Enoch*,

> If God did not spare angels when they sinned, but cast them into hell and committed them to chains of gloomy darkness to be kept until the judgment; if he did not spare the ancient world, but preserved Noah, a herald of righteousness, with seven others, when he brought a flood upon the world of the ungodly; if by turning the cities of Sodom and Gomorrah to ashes he condemned them to extinction, making them an example of what is going to happen to the ungodly; and if he rescued righteous Lot, greatly distressed by the sensual conduct of the wicked (for as that righteous man lived among them day after day, he was tormenting his righteous soul over their lawless deeds that he saw and heard); then the Lord knows how to rescue the godly from trials, and to keep the unrighteous under punishment until the day of judgment, and especially those who indulge in the lust of defiling passion and despise authority. (2 Peter 2:4-10)

> And angels who did not keep their own domain, but abandoned their proper abode, He has kept in eternal bonds under darkness for the judgment of the great day, just as Sodom and Gomorrah and the cities around them, since they *in the same way as these* indulged in gross immorality and went after strange flesh, are exhibited as an example in undergoing the punishment of eternal fire. (Jude 1:6-7 NASB)

When these two passages in Peter and Jude are explained by many today *without* reference to the *Book of Enoch*, they raise many unanswerable questions. However, when these are placed in the context of the Enochan storyline, they are easily explained. Here again we see an example of the *Book of Enoch*, helping to clarify two passages of Scripture which are hard to otherwise understand. Notice also, how both the passage in Peter and the one in Jude connect the sin of the angels with the sexual perversion of Sodom and Gomorrah. Once one realizes the *Book of Enoch* was known and read in Israel in the time of Christ, it seems almost impossible, to explain the Peter and Jude passages any other way than that laid out in Enoch's book.

Unfortunately, once the *Book of Enoch* became a forbidden text to Christians in the Greek and Latin worlds, the Enochan context of Peter and Jude was lost for many generations.

Certainly the idea that angels could interbreed with human women seems repugnant to our modern sensibilities, as it was also to the leaders of Greek and Latin Christianity from the end of the fourth century forward. This offense to our sensibilities and those of the Church fathers of the fifth century has more to do with our Greek philosophical assumptions about the nature of angels than it does with Scripture.

There are several areas in which the Church's ideas concerning angels are at major variance with the dominant view during the time of Christ and the Apostles.

Angelic Carnality

According to the prevailing ideas about angels among Christians of various stripes, angels are viewed as spirits, without materiality. Western ideas about the differences between human carnality and angelic spirituality make the idea of angelic-human copulation seem impossible. In all Jewish writings from the period of Second-Temple Judaism[630] no such problem can be detected. There is a consensus among Jewish writers from that period that angelic spirituality as well as angelic carnality were both possible, and not mutually exclusive. The writer of the *Book of Jubilees,* (another book from that period) even speaks of angels having been created in a circumcised state from the beginning. (This is mentioned here only as it reveals how Jews felt at the time on this subject).

---

[630] **2nd-Temple Judaism** generally refers to the period of history in Israel between the return from Babylon, and the destruction of the 2nd temple by the Romans in 70 AD. For simplicity however, the term can also be applied to all of the Jewish literature which survives from before the destruction of the temple. This would include the writings of Moses, David and Solomon and others written even earlier.

Angelic Fallibility

According to the current dominant thinking among Christians there seems to be somewhat of a consensus that long ago there occurred a rebellion among the members of the heavenly angelic hosts. Whatever the reasons for this rebellion, the result was certain angels aligned themselves with Lucifer, rebelled against God, sinned and fell. A seemingly assumed corollary to this view is the idea commonly held among Christians that those angels who did not fall, stood the test and are immune to further testing, temptation and the possibility of sinning. No such assumptions can be detected amongst Jewish writers from the period of Second-Temple Judaism. Not only did they believe angels fell during the time of Jared the father of Enoch, they also believed in previous fallings and allowed for the possibility of future fallings of angels as well.

An Angelic Learning Curve

There seems to be a rather pervasive idea among we Christians that angels are so aware of God's doings that they are fully informed of His plan for the ages. The prevailing view among the Jews and Christians in the first century and in earlier times seems to be different.

For instance, in Enoch we are given a picture that the angels, though they are in the presence of God, are *not* aware of the entire unfolding plan of God and are learners in much the same way as mankind though on a higher level. There is much they do not know. To certain angels who fell God says,

> You have been in heaven, but all the mysteries had not yet been revealed to you, and you knew worthless ones, and these in the hardness of your hearts you have made known to the women, and through these mysteries women and men work much evil on earth (Enoch 16:3).

In this passage, the sphere of angelic knowledge is seen as both incomplete as well as flawed.

In another passage we are given a picture of unfallen angels who are to read heavenly books so as to learn from them,

> For some of them [books] are written and inscribed above in the heaven, in order that the angels may read them and know that which shall befall the sinners. (Enoch 108:7)

According to Enoch, angels, like humans, are finite, growing, and capable of errors of thought and deed.

Isn't this the picture painted by certain parts of the New Testament too? That angels are learning is implied in the New Testament when we read,

> Concerning this salvation, the prophets who prophesied about the grace that was to be yours searched and inquired carefully, inquiring what person or time the Spirit of Christ in them was indicating when he predicted the sufferings of Christ and the subsequent glories. It was revealed to them that they were serving not themselves but you, in the things that have now been announced to you through those who preached the good news to you by the Holy Spirit sent from heaven, *things into which angels long to look.* (1 Peter 1:10-12)

Peter tells us the prophets who wrote about Jesus before the first advent wanted to know more about these things but were made aware the information they desired would be for a future generation yet to come. Then Peter says the prophets were not alone in their desire to know, and their intense interest about Christ. The angels *also* want to know!

These then are three ways in which our thinking about angels has drifted since the time of the Jews and Christians in the first centuries. Taken together the ancients had a very different angelology than that of which St. Augustine would have likely approved.

Does Jesus Contradict Enoch's View of Angels?

In the gospels there are a couple of passages which are often appealed to as apparent proof that angels could not commit the kind of sin the *Book of Enoch* mentions.

In Matthew 22:30, Jesus gives information about the relations of men and women in the world to come. He says, "in the resurrection they neither marry nor are given in marriage, but are like angels in heaven."

A parallel passage is found in Luke 20:34-36:

> The sons of this age marry and are given in marriage, but those who are considered worthy to attain to that age and to the resurrection from the dead neither marry nor are given in marriage, for they cannot die anymore, because they are equal to angels and are sons of God, being sons of the resurrection.

What is interesting about Christ's words in this passage is that they actually seem to allude to a relevant passage in the *Book of Enoch* in which God instructs Enoch what to say to reprimand the angels who sinned. Enoch is instructed to tell the Watchers,

> Wherefore have *ye left the high, holy, and eternal heaven, and lain with women, and defiled yourselves* with the daughters of men and taken to yourselves wives, and done like the children of earth, and begotten giants as your sons? And though ye were holy, spiritual, living the eternal life, you have defiled yourselves with the blood of women, and have begotten children with the blood of flesh, and, as the children of men, have lusted after flesh and blood as those also do who die and perish. Therefore have I given them wives also that they might impregnate them, and beget children by them, that thus nothing might be wanting to them on earth. But you were formerly spiritual, living the eternal life, and immortal for all generations of the world. And *therefore I have not appointed wives for you; for as for the spiritual ones of the heaven, in heaven is their dwelling.* (Enoch 15:5-7).

In the passages from Matthew and Luke, was Jesus alluding to this passage in Enoch? In Matthew's passage the emphasis is about there being no marriage in heaven. This is not instruction about whether angels can or cannot be carnal. Jesus' comment is concerning the normal state of affairs in heaven --in heaven angels are not given in marriage. The *Book of Enoch* does not state otherwise. In the Luke passage, it states that resurrected people "cannot die anymore" and this is tied to the end of the need for marriage. Enoch's passage also ties the need for marriage to human mortality. Therefore marriage is not for angels. Luke's passage does not invalidate the passage from Enoch. In fact, it seems as if Jesus is simply reiterating the point made in the passage from Enoch 15.

So, the quote from Jesus which some feel invalidates an aspect of the *Book of Enoch*, instead seems to allude to ideas in the book, which were current among the Jews of Jesus' day. Jesus goes on to say the Sadducees know neither the Scriptures nor the power of God and are thus wrong about the resurrection. In Jesus' view, was Enoch among the many books of Scripture which the Sadducees rejected and of which they were thus ignorant?

Contrasting Ideas

In ancient times Christian and Jewish thinking allowed that angels are individually capable of falling from grace, are capable of carnality, and are limited in their knowledge of God's plan. In a later era, the influence of Greek thinking and of Augustine on Christianity crystallized concepts that God's angels are pure spirit, impeccable and all-wise. The Bible neither supports this theology of angels which developed centuries after Christ, nor does the Bible contradict the views held in an earlier time which we find in the *Book of Enoch.*

To the Jews were given the lively oracles of God. Those oracles were in a language whose meanings were more immediate to them than to the Greeks or to us. The Jewish believers of the first century, living closer to the times of the actual composition of the books of the Bible, were thus more likely to be the inheritors of original traditions related to understanding, expounding upon, and interpreting their books.

When we consider the unanimous agreement among Jews in ancient times which held that Genesis 6:1-4 described the sin of angels, as well as the early agreement within the Church on this subject, we see one more fact pointing to the widespread influence the *Book of Enoch* once had. This is exactly what we would expect if the *Book of Enoch* had been around a long time and had been handed down for many generations.

But as we shall see in a moment, not only did Jews long ago believe angels could and had fallen into sin, they also expected it could happen and would happen again.

6
The Return of the Watchers

The *Book of Enoch* does not present a simple picture concerning the history of the angels who sinned. In addition to the fall of Satan in history past which is already assumed in the *Book of Enoch*,[631] there are least four separate times mentioned in the book in which angels are said to either have fallen in history or will fall in the future. The first occasion was discussed in the previous chapter, where according to Enoch 6, a group of angels descended to earth for the purpose of taking wives from among humans. But there are other occasions mentioned...

"Because They Did Not Come Forth"

In a dream-vision, Enoch sees a group of angels who fell even before the events of Enoch's day:

> I inquired regarding them. The angel said, "this place is the end of heaven and earth: this has become a prison for the stars and the host of heaven. And the stars which roll over the fire are they which have transgressed the commandment of the Lord in the beginning of their rising, *because they did not come forth at their appointed times*. And He was wroth with them, and bound them till the time when their guilt should be consummated (even) for ten thousand years." (Enoch 18:14-16)

We can see this group of angels who sinned is not the same group that fell by taking wives in Enoch 6. These angels are 7 in number, not 200. Their sin occurred "in the beginning of their rising", not in the "days of Jared." Their sin is described as "not coming forth at their appointed times", not lust. They are bound for 10,000 years, not 70 generations.

"Transgressed the Commandment of the Lord"

Later in his dream-vision, Enoch sees yet another group of fallen angels,

> I proceeded to where things were chaotic. And I saw there something horrible: I saw neither a heaven above nor a firmly founded earth, but a place chaotic and horrible. And there I saw seven stars of the heaven bound together in it, like great mountains and burning with fire. Then I said: "For what sin are they bound, and on what account have they been cast in hither?" Then said Uriel, one of the holy angels, who was with me, and was chief over them, and said: "Enoch, why dost thou ask, and why art thou eager for the truth? These are of the

[631] **Enoch 54:6**

> number of the stars of heaven, which have transgressed the commandment of the Lord, and are bound here till ten thousand years, the time entailed by their sins, are consummated." (Enoch 21:1-5)

This too is a another distinct group of angels which Enoch sees. This group of angels is also 7 in number. The angel speaking with Enoch does not answer his question as to *why* these are being punished. Instead he is simply told, "these have transgressed the commandment of the Lord." Like the previous group, these too are bound for 10,000 years.

Elect and Holy Children Will Descend

Enoch lived in the days when the world crisis created by the children of the Watchers was well underway. The following verse speaks of the future, however. Here Enoch predicts a repeat of the problem which existed in his day.

> It shall come to pass in those days that elect and holy children will descend from the high heaven, and their seed will become one with the children of men. And in those days Enoch received books of zeal and wrath, and books of disquiet and expulsion. And mercy shall not be accorded to them, saith the Lord of Spirits. (Enoch 39:1-2)

The seed of angels will become one with the children of men again. This may refer to an event which is still future, or it may simply be predicting the situation we see in the Old Testament after the days of Noah. There were other giants after the flood. Since the angels which had committed this misdeed the first time, had been bound in the abyss, the implication here is that other angels had fallen into the same sin. There had been another rebellion among the angels.

The Nephilim Were on the Earth in Those Days...

According to Genesis 6:4, Moses says there were giants who were born *after* the flood of Noah's day.

> The Nephilim were on the earth in those days, *and also afterward*, when the sons of God came in to the daughters of man and they bore children to them. These were the mighty men who were of old, the men of renown.

Moses wrote the Nephilim were before the flood *"and also afterward."* It is part of the Biblical record that the problem which arose before the flood regarding angelic offspring recurred to a lesser degree after the flood. This time the problem did not seem to be as widespread nor was it worldwide.

The following are other passages of Scriptures which refer to the giants who were born at a later time, after the flood.

> In the fourteenth year Chedorlaomer and the kings who were with him came and defeated *the Rephaim* in Ashteroth-karnaim, the Zuzim in Ham, the Emim in Shaveh-kiriathaim. (Genesis 14:5)

> There we saw the Nephilim (the sons of Anak, who come from the Nephilim), and we seemed to ourselves like grasshoppers, and so we seemed to them. (Numbers 13:33)

> The Emim formerly lived there, a people great and many, and tall as the Anakim. (Deuteronomy 2:10)

> A people great and many, and tall as the Anakim; but the LORD destroyed them before the Ammonites, and they dispossessed them and settled in their place. (Deuteronomy 2:21)

> For only Og the king of Bashan was left of the remnant of the Rephaim. Behold, his bed was a bed of iron. Is it not in Rabbah of the Ammonites? Nine cubits was its length, and four cubits its breadth, according to the common cubit. (Deuteronomy 3:11)

> Joshua came at that time and cut off the Anakim from the hill country, from Hebron, from Debir, from Anab, and from all the hill country of Judah, and from all the hill country of Israel. Joshua devoted them to destruction with their cities. (Joshua 11:21)

> There came out from the camp of the Philistines a champion named Goliath of Gath, whose height was six cubits and a span. He had a helmet of bronze on his head, and he was armed with a coat of mail, and the weight of the coat was five thousand shekels of bronze. And he had bronze armor on his legs, and a javelin of bronze slung between his shoulders. The shaft of his spear was like a weaver's beam, and his spear's head weighed six hundred shekels of iron. (1 Samuel 17:4-7)

> Ishbi-benob, one of the descendants of the giants, whose spear weighed three hundred shekels of bronze, and who was armed with a new sword, thought to kill David. But Abishai the son of Zeruiah came to his aid and attacked the Philistine and killed him. Then David's men swore to him, "You shall no longer go out with us to battle, lest you quench the lamp of Israel." After this there was again war with the Philistines at Gob. Then Sibbecai the Hushathite struck down Saph, who was one of the descendants of the giants. And there was again war with the Philistines at Gob, and Elhanan the son of Jaare-oregim, the Bethlehemite, struck down Goliath the Gittite, the shaft of whose spear was like a weaver's beam. And there was again war

> at Gath, where there was a man of great stature, who had six fingers on each hand, and six toes on each foot, twenty-four in number, and he also was descended from the giants. And when he taunted Israel, Jonathan the son of Shimei, David's brother, struck him down. These four were descended from the giants in Gath, and they fell by the hand of David and by the hand of his servants. (2 Samuel 21:16-22)

Again, what is inferred by these verses but never explicitly stated is the later giants came about as the result of other angels who sinned at a later time. Since the fallen angels from before the flood had been imprisoned in the abyss, who were the angelic parents of these gigantic offspring? One is led to conclude other angels had descended to earth and transgressed God's commands. They sinned as the Watchers had done before them.

If this has occurred in earth's past, can it happen again?

The Coming of the Lawless One

In the New Testament, the term "lawless one" is reserved uniquely for the coming the Antichrist. In Enoch, the term is used to describe the reprobate offspring of Watcher-human breeding.

> Then the earth laid accusation against *the lawless ones.* (Enoch 7:6)

When in Luke 17:26, Jesus said, *"Just as it was in the days of Noah, so will it be in the days of the Son of Man"*, does this include the unnatural birth of the final Antichrist as one of the illegitimate offspring of the angels? If so, the term "lawless one" may have been used by Paul as an idiom for offspring of angelic-human unions. In 2 Thessalonians 2:8-9, we read,

> Then *the lawless one* will be revealed, whom the Lord Jesus will kill with the breath of his mouth and bring to nothing by the appearance of his coming. The coming of the lawless one is by the activity of Satan with all power and false signs and wonders.

From the passages we have seen so far, it is now possible to recreate a kind of history of the angels who sinned. The complicated picture which develops, may well motivate us to reexamine certain passages of Scripture which up to now we have understood from our Western perspective. We should reexamine our assumptions about the nature and activity of angels. One passage we may wish to reevaluate is found in the *Book of Revelation*, chapter 12.

The War in Heaven

John's revelation records a vision of Satan, viewed as a dragon, bringing a third of the heavenly host to the earth with him. In interpreting this passage, it is often assumed the passage summarizes an historical event; the common belief is that ages ago Satan took an army of angels with him when he fell in the beginning. Even if we concede that such an event may have occurred, the passage in Revelation may not be describing it. In support of this view, consider the fact that in Scripture Satan is described as having some sort of access to heaven. We read,

> Now there was a day when the sons of God came to present themselves before the Lord, and Satan also came among them. (Job 1:6)

> A spirit came forward and stood before the Lord, saying, "I will entice [King Ahab]." 22 And the Lord said to him, "By what means?" And he said, "I will go out, and will be a lying spirit in the mouth of all his prophets." (1 Kings 22:21-22)

For some, these passages create more questions than answers. For instance, how could God allow someone so evil entrance into heaven? Some have reconciled this question by proposing that Satan's access is occasional, and only when he is summoned by God. However the reader chooses to answer this question, it should be conceded there are ways one might explain Satan having such access.

In this light, the passage we are examining in Revelation could be seen as a future event. From that perspective, at some point in the future, Satan's access to heaven will be ended, and he will be cast down to earth and limited to its sphere for his activities. In this light, it is possible to view the passage in Revelation as an event yet future. If so, "1/3 of the stars" will follow Satan in his warfare against the Messiah at some time future.

The Emerging Picture

Ancient Jewish understanding concerning the ability of angels to become corrupt, allowed for the possibility of occasional and recurring instances of angelic defections from God. Additionally, some have noted the sometimes human and sometimes supernatural Biblical descriptions of the Antichrist which are peppered throughout Scripture. Will the Antichrist be an angelic-human hybrid? How about the False Prophet? Will there be others as well?

The picture that is emerging is one in which the last generation living in the day of tribulation will face perilous times similar to those which existed before the flood when offspring from sinning angels will again wreak havoc on earth. In the day of tribulation, the conflict of the cosmos, the war of the ages, will be coming to the earth with unparalleled ferocity. In order to be a victor and not a victim, those living in the last generation will need to seek Him who has always been a shield to those who put their faith in Him. Those who place their faith in the Son of God will become more than victors at that time.

We are beginning to see a pattern here. The days before the flood and the time preceding the last days of planet earth share many characteristics in common. One might say the two periods are like the bookends of earthly history.

7
Bookends at the Ends of the World: Two Millennial Reigns

The prophets of Israel had long prophesied a future time of Messiah's rule on earth during which the world would be rejuvenated, injustice would be eliminated, and the world would be at peace. The lion will lay down with the lamb, Isaiah says. The New Testament indicates this will be fulfilled by a millennium of Christ's rule on earth.

In the *Book of Revelation,* there is the singular mention of the 1,000-year rule of Christ on earth. In just seven verses, in Revelation 20, John introduces and then sums up on this subject. The idea of a 1,000-year reign of Christ on earth has been viewed by some as having an element of strangeness to it. The 1,000-year-rule of Christ coming as it does before the reign of Christ throughout eternity can be viewed as seemingly redundant. Besides, some have noted the seeming incongruity of such a period of time in Scripture since "1,000 years" does not apparently correlate with any other similar time in the Bible.

After a careful examination of the *Book of Enoch,* however, another 1,000-year period of earthly rule does in fact come jumping off the pages for the reader. The world before the flood was ruled by the Watchers and by their offspring for 1,000 years. In this light, the 1,000-year rule of Christ does seem to have a corollary. The millennial reign of Christ can now be viewed juxtaposed to the earlier millennial rule of the Watchers and their children. In this context, the rule of Christ can be seen as a kind of repudiation of the 1,000-year dominion of the earth by the Watchers and their offspring.

"In the Days of Jared"

According to Enoch's book the descent of the Watchers occurred "in the days of Jared." Referring to the genealogy included in chapter 5 of the *Book of Genesis,* Jared was born about 1,194 years before the flood, and his son, Enoch, was born about 1,033 years before the flood. If we assume the fall of the Watchers in "the days of Jared" refers to the period after Jared's birth but before the life of Enoch, this would mean the descent of the Watchers occurred sometime between 1,194 and 1,033 years before the flood. This means the domination and rule of the Watchers and their children in the realm of humankind would have lasted for at least 1,000 years. It was a big surprise for me when I first realized how long a span of time the Watchers and their children held sway over this planet.

At the last judgment, we are told in Enoch 38:5, *"then shall the kings and the mighty perish".* Throughout Enoch 37-71, a specific group is particularly singled out for God's judgment. They are referred to as, *"the kings and the mighty and the exalted and those who rule the earth"*, (Enoch 62:9). They are a major focus of the *Book of the Parables*, and are described in various ways throughout it.[632] In Enoch 56:3-4, they are called the "beloved ones" of the Watchers, which identifies them as the Watcher offspring who oppress mankind as described in Enoch chapter 7.[633] This is the same group who Moses wrote about later, calling them, *"The mighty men, who were of old, men of renown."* (Genesis 6:4) In the *Book of the Parables*, Enoch informs us these Watcher children had ruled the earth of their time, but they were destined to be finally judged by the Son of Man, who will be seated on the throne of His glory. Their judgment is prophesied first in Enoch 10:12. That verse states the final judgment of the Watchers and their children would take place 70 generations from Methuselah. This will indeed occur when Jesus Christ, who was born 70 generations from Methuselah will sit in judgment on His throne of glory.

The rule of the Watchers and the Nephilim over the affairs of men is spelled out in chapters 7 and 8 of Enoch. In those chapters the Watchers assume the role of teachers to mankind. Watcher superiority in all areas of knowledge was assumed. As the children of the Watchers multiplied, the increasing corruption and oppression of mankind followed.

There seems now to be a kind of dark typology inherent in the Watcher-Nephilim saga. It would appear the millennial reign of the Son of God will be, at least in part, an answer to the millennial misrule of the Watchers and their offspring before the flood. These two millennia, one coming at the outset and the other coming at the close of earth's days can be seen as a kind of set of historical bookends to world history. Enoch 10:17-22, presents a lengthy description of the coming Messianic kingdom which in the passage is juxtaposed to the era of Watcher-Nephilim misrule. Here again we have encountered yet another Bible topic upon which the *Book of Enoch* sheds light and enhances our understanding of Scripture.

The following table serves to illustrate a wide range of points of similarity and contrast between the millennium of Watcher misrule and the coming 1,000-year reign of Jesus the Messiah:

---

[632] **Enoch 38:5, 46:4, 53:5, 54:2, 55:4, 62:1,3,6,9, 63:1,12**, and **67:8,12**
[633] **See also Enoch 10:12, 12:6** and **14:6**

Bookends at the Ends of the World: Two Millennial Reigns			
A comparison of the two Millennial reigns found in the Book of Enoch and the Books of Isaiah and Revelation			
Enoch	**Kingdom of the Watchers**	**Kingdom of Messiah**	**Isaiah and Revelation**
6:6	1,000-year rule of the angelic god-men	1,000-year rule of the God-man, Jesus	Rev. 20:6
6:2	Begins with fall of Angels to earth	Begins with descent of Jesus to earth	Rev. 19:11
7:1	Angels take wives at outset	Marriage supper of the Lamb at outset	Rev. 19:7
13:7-9	Rule from Mt. Hermon	Rule from Mount Zion	Is. 2:2-4
10:8	Azazel as chief	Jesus as king	Rev. 20:6
8:3	Dissemination of occult knowledge	Dissemination of the word of God	Is. 2:3
9:6	Knowledge of God suppressed	Knowledge of God fills the earth	Is. 11:9
8:3-4	Human longevity decreases	Human longevity increases	Is. 65:20
10:9	Nephilim judged and killed at end	Some Nephilim thrown in lake of fire at start	Rev. 19:20
10:12	Ends with Angels bound in Abyss	Begins with Satan bound in Abyss	Rev. 20:1-3
88:2	Finalized by world war	Finalized by world war	Rev. 19:21
12:5-6	Consummated by tribulation period	Preceded by tribulation period	Rev. 3:10
10:2	Ends with God's judgment by water	Ends with God's judgment by fire	Rev. 20:9
1:1	Occurred in earth's early days	Occurs in earth's latter days	Rev. 20:11
10:7	Earth renewed after	New earth after	Rev. 21:1
Relevant Events Between the Millennial Bookends			
The Book of Enoch prohibited and suppressed in the 4th century ~ Council of Laodicea		Belief in 1,000-year rule of Christ prohibited and suppressed in the 4th century ~ Council of Nicaea	

8
Enoch's Impact on the New Testament

When reading the *Book of Enoch*, one will notice there are many manners of expression which the book shares in common with the Bible in general and with the New Testament especially. Is it possible that the *Book of Enoch*'s rich language and imagery had influenced the concepts and phrases which would then become commonplace in the culture from which the Biblical writers emerged? If so, it could be seen as a kind of parallel to the lasting effect and influence the King James Bible and Shakespeare have exerted upon the English language since they were first written. Through the popularity of those 17th-century English works, innumerable forms of expression became commonplace and moved into general usage by English speakers and writers. If one were to say, everyone has 'a cross to bear', or that we should 'go the extra mile', or we should not 'throw pearls before swine', the meaning would be immediately understood even if one does not realize those phrases came from the King James Bible of 1611. Is this what happened with the *Book of Enoch*? Did the Biblical writers repeatedly use commonplaces which originated with the *Book of Enoch*?

Throughout the pages of the New Testament[634] are repeated references which seem to be allusions to and/or quotes from the demonstrably older *Book of Enoch*. To be sure, one can find similarities and parallels between the New Testament and the rest of the Jewish literature from the period of Second-Temple Judaism in general. There are similarities to the New Testament which can be found throughout the historical, apocalyptic, pseudepigraphal, and apocryphal literature from that tine-period. But, among all the Jewish literature which has been preserved from before AD 70, the *Book of Enoch* stands alone in terms of the sheer scope and number of parallels we find between it and the New Testament.

Many textual scholars explain this sort of thing by stating since the *Book of Enoch* was written centuries before the time of Christ, the New Testament writers simply referred to or relied upon it. This view, however, seems to present a problem for people of faith who view the Bible as a special revelation. If the *Book of Enoch* was not written by Enoch though that is its claim frequently throughout its pages, would the Apostles of Christ under inspiration of the Holy Spirit refer to it repeatedly in a positive way, without concern that the book was not authentic? The *Book of Enoch* uses imagery and terms which many of us believe are revealed truths unique to the New Testament. Would the New Testament writers, fresh from having been discipled and taught by Jesus Christ for three years, write under the inspiration of the Holy Spirit and yet see no

---

[634] For the purposes of this chapter, commonplaces from the *Book of Enoch* found in the Hebrew Scriptures (the Old Testament) will not be explored. Since the dominant theory of the book's origin is that it was composed in the 3rd and 2nd centuries B.C., Old Testament citations would not hold persuasive weight against this view.

problem in relying upon the terminology made popular by a book by an anonymous writer who lied claiming to be the prophet Enoch? Such an idea seems impossible from a perspective of faith. Instead, it seems clear the Apostles referred to the *Book of Enoch* precisely *because* they believed in the authenticity of the book.

The Apostolic Witness

The three most obvious New Testament references to the *Book of Enoch*, one being a direct quote, are the following:

Enoch Passage	**New Testament Passage**
Behold! He cometh with ten thousands of His holy ones to execute judgment upon all, and to destroy all the ungodly: and to convict all flesh of all the works of their ungodliness which they have ungodly committed, and of all the hard things which ungodly sinners have spoken against Him. Enoch 1:9	Behold, the Lord comes with ten thousands of his holy ones, to execute judgment on all and to convict all the ungodly of all their deeds of ungodliness that they have committed in such an ungodly way, and of all the harsh things that ungodly sinners have spoken against him. Jude 1:14-15
Bind them fast for seventy generations in the valleys of the earth, till the day of their judgment and of their consummation, till the judgment that is for ever and ever is consummated. Enoch 10:12	God did not spare angels when they sinned, but cast them into hell and committed them to chains of gloomy darkness to be kept until the judgment. 2 Peter 2:4
Wherefore have ye left the high, holy, and eternal heaven, and lain with women? Enoch 15:3	The angels who did not stay within their own position of authority, but left their proper dwelling, he has kept in eternal chains under gloomy darkness until the judgment of the great day. Jude 1:6

There is another perhaps slightly less obvious New Testament verse which seems to be referring to the Enochan storyline:

> For Christ also died for sins once for all, the just for the unjust, so that He might bring us to God, having been put to death in the flesh, but made alive in the spirit; in which also He went and made proclamation to the spirits now in prison, who once were disobedient, when the patience of God kept waiting in the days of Noah, during the construction of the ark, in which a few, that is, eight persons, were brought safely through the water. (1 Peter 3:18-20 NASB)

Here Peter refers to "spirits now in prison", who have been there since they were disobedient "in the days of Noah." Without the *Book of Enoch* as a point of reference it becomes a problem to figure out to what Peter could be referring. But if we include the *Book of Enoch* for consideration no such problem arises. In Enoch chapter 13, Enoch also preaches to the same group, years later these disobedient spirits are imprisoned in the abyss in the days of Noah, to await the yet future judgment of God.

New Testament Echoes

In addition to these examples, the New Testament is peppered throughout with what seem to be allusions, and manners of speaking which we find in the *Book of Enoch*. This is exactly what one would expect to see if Enoch were indeed a well-known, well-respected, ancient book from the pen of an acknowledged prophet.

Numerous parallels between the New Testament and the *Book of Enoch* have been suggested and many more could be added to this list. The following is a partial but representative sampling:

Enoch Quote	**New Testament Quote**
In the strength of his might En. 1:4	In the strength of his might Eph. 6:10
They shall inherit the earth En. 5:7	They shall inherit the earth Mat. 5:5
Bind Azazel hand and foot, and cast him into the darkness Enoch 10:4	Bind him hand and foot and cast him into the outer darkness Mat. 22:13
Then I went and spoke to them all together, and they were all afraid Enoch 13:3	Christ went and proclaimed to the spirits in prison, because they formerly did not obey 1 Peter 3:19-20
And His raiment shone more brightly than the sun and was whiter than any snow Enoch 14:20	His clothes became radiant, intensely white, as no one on earth could bleach them Mark 9:3
I have not appointed wives for you; for as for the spiritual ones of the heaven, in heaven is their dwelling Enoch 15:7	They neither marry nor are given in marriage, but are like angels in heaven Mat. 22:30
Those who were there were like flaming fire Enoch 17:1	His ministers a flame of fire Heb. 1:7
I saw the four winds Enoch 18:2	The four winds of the earth Rev. 7:1
The ends of all things Enoch 19:3	The end of all things 1 Pe. 4:7
Like great mountains and burning with fire Enoch 21:3	Like a great mountain burning with fire Rev. 8:8
A division has been made Enoch 22:9	A great chasm has been fixed Luke 16:26
Set apart in this great pain till the great day of judgment Enoch 22:11	Kept in eternal chains under gloomy darkness until the judgment of the great day Jude 1:6
The Lord of spirits Enoch 37:2	The Father of spirits Heb. 12:9

ENOCH'S IMPACT ON THE NEW TESTAMENT

The Righteous One shall appear Enoch 38:2	The coming of the Righteous One Acts 7:52
Good for them if they had not been born Enoch 38:2	Better for that man if he had not been born Mat. 26:24
Elect and holy children Enoch 39:1	Elect angels 1 Tim. 5:21
The righteous and elect shall be without number Enoch 39:6	A great multitude that no one could number Rev. 7:9
According to the good pleasure of the Lord Enoch 39:9	It is your Father's good pleasure to give you the kingdom Luke 12:32
Those who sleep not bless thee, they stand before thy glory and bless, praise and extol saying, Holy, holy, holy is the Lord Enoch 39:12	They rest not day and night saying Holy, holy, holy is the Lord Rev. 4:8
Those who inherit eternal life En 40:9	Will inherit eternal life Mat. 19:29
I saw the mansions of the holy Enoch 41:2	In my Father's house are many mansions John 14:2
The spirits of the righteous Enoch 41:8	The spirits of the righteous Heb. 12:23
He appoints a judge for them all Enoch 41:9	Hath committed all judgment unto the Son John 5:22
Shall try their works Enoch 45:3	Will test what sort of work each one has done 1 Cor. 3:13
The books of the living were opened before him Enoch 47:3	Great and small, standing before the throne, and books were opened. Then another book was opened, which is the book of life Rev. 20:12
In his name they are saved Enoch 48:7	There is salvation in no one else, for there is no other name under heaven given among men by which we must be saved Acts 4:12
They have denied the Lord of Spirits and His Anointed Enoch 48:10	Whoever denies me before men, I will also deny before my Father who is in heaven Mat. 10:33
Those who have fallen asleep in righteousness Enoch 49:3	Those also who have fallen asleep in Christ 1 Cor. 15:18
He shall judge the secret things Enoch 49:4	On the day when God judges the secrets of men by Christ Jesus Rom. 2:16
The day has drawn nigh that they should be saved Enoch 51:2	Your redemption is drawing near Luke 21:28
The faces of all the angels in heaven shall be lighted up with joy Enoch 51:4	There is joy before the angels of God over one sinner who repents Luke 15:10
I will cause my wrath to abide upon them Enoch 55:3	The wrath of God abides on him John 3:36
The darkness is past Enoch 58:5	The darkness is passing John 2:8

WHO REALLY WROTE THE BOOK OF ENOCH?

The angels of power, and all the angels of principalities Enoch 61:10	We wrestle not against flesh and blood, but against principalities, against powers, against the rulers of the darkness Eph. 6:12
The word of his mouth slays all the sinners Enoch 62:2	Whom the Lord Jesus will kill with the breath of his mouth and bring to nothing by the appearance of his coming 2 Thes. 2:8
And pain shall seize them, when they see that Son of Man sitting on the throne of his glory Enoch 62:5	All the tribes of the earth will mourn, and they will see the Son of Man coming on the clouds of heaven Mat. 24:30
That Son of Man has appeared, and has seated himself on the throne of his glory Enoch 69:29	When the Son of Man comes in his glory, and all the angels with him, then he will sit on his glorious throne Mat. 25:31
Where the angels took the cords to measure for me the place for the elect and righteous Enoch 70:3	The one who spoke with me had a measuring rod of gold to measure the city and its gates and walls Rev. 21:15
The holy angels who are above the heavens go in and out of that house Enoch 71:8	Out of the sanctuary came the seven angels Rev. 15:6
The world to come Enoch 71:15	The world to come Heb. 2:5
He who is blessed forever Enoch 77:1	Christ who is God over all, blessed forever Rom. 9:5
Blessed is the man who dies in righteousness Enoch 81:4	Blessed are the dead who die in the Lord Rev. 14:13
There is nothing hidden from thee Enoch 84:3	No creature is hidden from his sight Heb. 4:13
The eternal seed Enoch 84:6	To your seed, that is Christ Gal. 3:16
A star fell from heaven Enoch 86:1	A star fallen from heaven Rev. 9:1
The Lord of the sheep Enoch 90:18	The great shepherd of the sheep Heb. 13:20
Apostasy and transgression will increase Enoch 91:7	Lawlessness will be increased Mat. 24:12
The first heaven shall depart and pass away Enoch 91:16	The first heaven and the first earth had passed away Rev. 21:11
The heavenly vision Enoch 93:2	The heavenly vision Acts 26:19
Woe to you, ye rich Enoch 94:8	Woe to you who are rich Luke 6:24
You have become ready for the day of slaughter Enoch 94:9	You have fattened your hearts in a day of slaughter James 5:5
Ye persecute the righteous Enoch 95:7	Those who are persecuted for righteousness sake Mat. 5:10

ENOCH'S IMPACT ON THE NEW TESTAMENT

None of your deeds of oppression are covered and hidden Enoch 98:6	Nothing is hidden except to be made manifest Mark 4:22
Raise your prayers as a memorial before the angels Enoch 99:3	Your prayers have ascended as a memorial before God Acts 10:4
Who worship impure spirits and demons Enoch 99:6	Worshipping demons and idols of gold Rev. 9:20
The horse shall walk up to the breast in the blood of sinners Enoch 100:3	The blood flowed as high as a horses bridle Rev. 14:20
Though the righteous sleep a long sleep Enoch 100:5	Those who have fallen asleep in Christ 1 Cor. 15:18
In heaven the angels remember you for good before the glory of the Great One Enoch 104:1	In heaven their angels always see the face of my Father who is in heaven Mat. 18:10
Great joy as the angels of heaven Enoch 104:4	There is joy before the angels of God Luke 15:10
I and my Son will be united with them forever Enoch 105:2	My Father will love him, and we will come to him and make our home with him John 14:23
Who love God and loved neither gold nor silver nor any of the good things which are in the world Enoch 108:8	Do not love the world or the things in the world 1 John 2:15
Gave their bodies to torture Enoch 108:8	Some were tortured, refusing to accept release Heb. 11:35
Loved heaven more than life Enoch 108:10	Loved not their lives unto death Rev. 12:11
The generation of light. 108:11	Children of light. 1 Thessalonians 5:5
I will seat each on the throne of his honor Enoch 108:12	You who have followed me will also sit on twelve thrones Mat. 19:28

Allowing that apparent parallels of words and phrases can at times be superficial, accidental, and sometimes dependent upon conscious and unconscious choices made by translators, nevertheless, the sheer number of similarities and correlations of ideas and theological concepts between Enoch and the New Testament is astounding. However, we would expect nothing less if the *Book of Enoch* were indeed in wide use among the Jews over a protracted period of time. The *Book of Enoch* seems to have had a profound influence on the writers of the books of the New Testament.

The Book of Revelation

As it turns out, what is true of the New Testament in general can be seen as especially true of the *Book of Revelation* in particular. Among the books of the Bible, the *Book of Revelation* shares the most points in common with the *Book of Enoch*. For those of us who believe John's book was a fresh revelation from God received by the Apostle in the first century AD, the similarities his book shares with the demonstrably older *Book of Enoch* are all the more startling.

The following table demonstrates the uncanny similarities between the two books.

Things in Common: Similarities Between The Book of Revelation and The Book of Enoch	
Both writers receive revelation through angels	
Revelation 1:1-2	**Enoch 1:2**
Both John and Enoch write their books for people living in the end times	
Revelation 1:3	**Enoch 1:1-3**
Both Enoch and John report the Lord's head is 'white like wool'	
Revelation 1:14	**Enoch 71:10**
Both writers indicate that angels can receive information via books	
Revelation 2:1	**Enoch 108:7**
John and Enoch prophesy the righteous are to be clothed in glorious garments	
Revelation 3:5	**Enoch 62:15**
Both prophesy a time of tribulation upon the whole earth before the close of the age	
Revelation 3:10	**Enoch 1:2, 45:2**
Both writers report Christ sits on God's throne	
Revelation 3:21	**Enoch 51:3**
Both writers are caught up into heaven and behold God on His throne	
Revelation 4:2	**Enoch 14:20**
Both writers describe the Seraphim as those who never sleep day and night and who never stop praising God as the One who is Holy, Holy, Holy	
Revelation 4:8	**Enoch 39:12**
Both writers report Messiah's name is proclaimed in heaven	
Revelation 5:5	**Enoch 48:2**
John and Enoch both report seeing 10,000's times 10,000's angels in heaven	
Revelation 5:11	**Enoch 14:22**
Both see martyrs crying out for vengeance	
Revelation 6:10	**Enoch 22:7**

Each writer states Messiah will put down earth's kings	
Revelation 6:15-16	**Enoch 62:5**
Both Enoch and John report seeing the four winds of the earth.	
Revelation 7:1	**Enoch 18:2**
Both writers describe seeing an innumerable crowd of the righteous	
Revelation 7:9	**Enoch 39:6**
Each writer states the prayers of the righteous ascend like incense into heaven	
Revelation 8:3-4	**Enoch 47:1**
Both John's and Enoch's books prominently feature the activities of the 7 angels	
Revelation 8:6	**Enoch 15:1, 20:1, 21:9**
Both Enoch and John see fallen angels who they say are like 'mountains burning with fire'.	
Revelation 8:8	**Enoch 21:3**
Both Enoch and John describe a fallen angel as 'a star fallen from heaven'.	
Revelation 9:1	**Enoch 86:1**
Each writer reports seeing an abyss without a bottom	
Revelation 9:1-2	**Enoch 18:12**
Both foresee the rousing of evil angels near the great River Euphrates	
Revelation 9:14	**Enoch 56:5**
Both writers receive revelation by means of visions	
Revelation 9:17	**Enoch 1:2**
Both pronounce judgment on those who worship demons.	
Revelation 9:20	**Enoch 99:6**
Each writer says there are 'secrets of the thunders'	
Revelation 10:3-4	**Enoch 59:2**
Both receive revelation by means of heavenly books	
Revelation 10:8-10	**Enoch 81:1**
John and Enoch state God's adversaries accuse us to God	
Revelation 12:10	**Enoch 40:7**
Both Enoch and John praise those who do not love the world to the point of death	
Revelation 12:11	**Enoch 108:10**
Enoch and John predict the future deliverance of God's people on the 'wings of eagles'	
Revelation 12:14	**Enoch 96:2**
Each foresee the worldwide deception of those who dwell on earth	
Revelation 13:3	**Enoch 54:6**
Enoch and John state the wicked curse God's dwelling place in heaven	
Revelation 13:6	**Enoch 45:1**
Both writers report the righteous will sing in heaven.	
Revelation 14:3	**Enoch 48:6**

Theme	Revelation	Enoch
Each writer states the retribution of the Lord will be meted out before the angels of God	**Revelation 14:9-10**	**Enoch 48:9**
Both pronounce particular blessing on those who die in the Lord	**Revelation 14:13**	**Enoch 81:4**
The blood will flow up to the breast of the horses	**Revelation 14:20**	**Enoch 100:3**
John and Enoch report seeing angels coming out of the sanctuary in heaven	**Revelation 15:6**	**Enoch 71:8**
Both report heaven rejoices over the destruction of the wicked	**Revelation 19:1+3**	**Enoch 97:2**
Enoch and John both say the blood of the righteous will one day be required	**Revelation 19:2**	**Enoch 47:4**
The wicked are to be slain by the word of the Lord's mouth	**Revelation 19:21**	**Enoch 62:2**
The evil ones are to be bound with chains, imprisoned and covered over	**Revelation 20:1**	**Enoch 69:28**
Books of judgment will be opened before God seated on his glorious throne	**Revelation 20:11**	**Enoch 47:3**
Both John and Enoch report seeing the book of life opened.	**Revelation 20:12**	**Enoch 47:3**
Both say Sheol is going to give back its dead	**Revelation 20:13**	**Enoch 51:1**
The names of the wicked are not to be found in the Book of Life	**Revelation 20:15**	**Enoch 108:3**
A new heaven shall appear	**Revelation 21:1**	**Enoch 91:16**
The dwelling place of God is to be with man	**Revelation 21:3**	**Enoch 105:2**
Both predict an end to all sorrows	**Revelation 21:4**	**Enoch 25:6**
Both report the first heaven shall pass away.	**Revelation 21:11**	**Enoch 91:16**
Both report seeing angels who measure the heavenly habitations of the righteous	**Revelation 21:15**	**Enoch 70:3**
The wealth of the nations is to be presented to God	**Revelation 21:26**	**Enoch 53:1**

The righteous will receive the blessing of being able to partake of the Tree of Life	
Revelation 22:2	**Enoch 25:5**
Both writers issue warnings to anyone who would alter the contents of their books	
Revelation 22:18-19	**Enoch 104:10**

The point that is being made here is not that John copied Enoch. In the Bible there are places where one writer agrees with another yet we do not need to assume one writer copied the other. People of faith can explain such occurrences by noting that both writers were exposed to the same source of revelation, namely God. In the case of Enoch, such similarities seem to vouch for the authentic touch of someone for whom it was claimed by Jude, they are to be numbered among the prophets. Without making an argument that the *Book of Enoch* should be considered Scripture, suffice it to say, the *Book of Enoch* evidences the touch of a prophet's pen.

For someone who believes the *Book of Revelation* to be the revealed word of God to John, it seems impossible then to suggest the *Book of Enoch* was written by some anonymous rabbi or rabbis who purposely mislead their readers to believe the author was the Biblical Enoch when it was not.

The similarities between the *Book of Enoch* and the *Book of Revelation* are more evidence arguing for Enoch being the former book's real author.

Enoch and Jude ~ 7 Points of Connection

For obvious reasons, the *Letter of Jude* can be cited as a source lending support for the authenticity of the *Book of Enoch* as a genuine composition by the Biblical Enoch. What may not seem obvious is that Jude's letter contains more than just the one, obvious quote from the *Book of Enoch.*

I have often read statements to the effect that *just because the Letter of Jude quotes one passage from the Book of Enoch, does not mean Jude endorsed the whole book. The Apostle Paul also quotes from non-Biblical books without endorsing the whole books or their authors.*

This is perhaps the most common reason given for discounting the *Book of Enoch* as having any validity. The point is made that since The *Letter of Jude* merely cites a single passage from the *Book of Enoch,* Jude cannot be seen as endorsing the *Book of Enoch* as a whole.

Upon closer examination of Jude's letter, however, we can see there are at least seven places where Jude either directly quotes or refers to the contents of the book.

First, Jude calls Enoch a prophet despite the fact no explicit prophecy and no book of the prophecies of Enoch can be found in our 66-book Bible in the Western world. Jude alone, among the 40 or so writers of the Bible, mentions Enoch was a prophet. We could reason that Jude received this information about Enoch through direct revelation, however, the most obvious reason Jude makes this claim is found in the *Book of Enoch* itself which is purportedly filled with the prophecies of Enoch, including the prophecy which Jude quotes. So we can see the *Letter of Jude* and the *Book of Enoch* are in agreement on this point. Enoch is to be numbered among the prophets of old.

Consider too, Jude 1:6 refers to, "angels who did not stay within their own position of authority, but left their proper dwelling." This is a reference to Enoch 15:3, which says, "Wherefore have ye left the high, holy, and eternal heaven?" In Enoch, the sin of the angels is primarily in leaving their assigned place.

Further, Jude 1:6, relates these were angels which, "he has kept in eternal chains under gloomy darkness until the judgment of the great day" We see this outlined for us in the book in Enoch 10:12, "Bind them fast for seventy generations in the valleys of the earth, till the day of their judgment and of their consummation, till the judgment that is for ever and ever is consummated. In those days they shall be led off to the abyss of fire: and to the torment and the prison in which they shall be confined forever." In Enoch, the angels who sinned are temporarily bound until the day of judgment.

Jude also tells us in verse 6, the angels are bound, "...until the judgment of the *great day.*" The "great day" is the term used for the final day of judgment in Enoch 54:6, "Michael, and Gabriel, and Raphael, and Phanuel shall take hold of them on that *great day,* and cast them on that day into the burning furnace, that the Lord of Spirits may take vengeance on them for their unrighteousness in becoming subject to Satan and leading astray those who dwell on the earth."

Also, in verses 6-7, Jude says the sin of certain fallen angels was sexual immorality and that Sodom's sin was of the same class as those angels. We read,

> "Angels who did not keep their own domain, but abandoned their proper abode, He has kept in eternal bonds under darkness for the judgment of the great day, just as Sodom and Gomorrah and the cities around them, since they *in the same way as these* indulged in gross immorality and went after strange flesh, are exhibited as an example in undergoing the punishment of eternal fire." (NASB)

The four Greek words in this passage, τὸν ὅμοιον τρόπον τούτοις, which the translators of the New American Standard Bible render as *in the same way as these,* connects the "gross immorality" and the going "after strange flesh" of the people of Sodom and Gomorrah, as being of the same character as the sin of certain angels. There's no mistaking it, Jude believed the sin of these angels was sexual. The sexual nature of the angels' sin is described in Enoch 7:1, "All the others together with them took unto themselves wives, and each chose for himself one, and they began to go in unto them and to defile themselves with them."

Add to this Jude 1:14 which oddly calculates Enoch was the 7th from Adam, "It was also about these men that Enoch, in the seventh generation from Adam, prophesied." But to reckon it this way, Adam's generation has to be counted too. Enoch 60:8, reckons the generations in the identical fashion when Noah says, "my grandfather was taken up, the seventh from Adam"

Finally, in verses 14-15, Jude caps off his epistle by quoting the *Book of Enoch* directly as being the source of a prophecy regarding the Second-coming of Jesus Christ, "Behold, the Lord came with many thousands of His holy ones, to execute judgment upon all, and to convict all the ungodly of all their ungodly deeds which they have done in an ungodly way, and of all the harsh things which ungodly sinners have spoken against Him." This quote can be found in Enoch 1:9, "Behold! He cometh with ten thousands of His holy ones to execute judgment upon all, and to destroy all the ungodly: and to convict all flesh of all the works of their ungodliness which they have ungodly committed, and of all the hard things which ungodly sinners have spoken against Him."

For those keeping score, Jude alludes to and/or quotes from not just Enoch 1:9, but also 7:1, 10:12, 15:3, 54:6, and 60:8. Besides this, the *Letter of Jude* confirms the underlying thesis of the *Book of Enoch*, Enoch is to be numbered among the prophets. In this light then, it is no longer possible to state Jude did not accept the *Book of Enoch* as a whole. On the contrary, it appears the *Book of Enoch* was a favorite resource for the Apostle and half-brother of Jesus.

The following table is provided for reference purposes, in order to make the 7 points of contact between Jude and Enoch easily accessible to the reader.

Jude and Enoch: Seven Points of Connection	
Jude	**Enoch**
Enoch, the seventh from Adam, prophesied. **1:14**	The words of the blessing of Enoch... ...but not for this generation, but for a remote one which is for to come. **1:1-2**
...angels who did not stay within their own position of authority, but left their proper dwelling. **1:6**	Wherefore have ye left the high, holy, and eternal heaven? **15:3**
He has kept in eternal chains under gloomy darkness until the judgment. **1:6**	Bind them fast for seventy generations in the valleys of the earth, till the day of their judgment. **10:12**
...until the judgment of the great day. **1:6**	...take hold of them on that great day, and cast them on that day into the burning furnace. **54:6**
Angels who did not keep their own domain, but abandoned their proper abode, He has kept in eternal bonds under darkness for the judgment of the great day, just as Sodom and Gomorrah and the cities around them, since they in the same way as these indulged in gross immorality and went after strange flesh, are exhibited as an example in undergoing the punishment of eternal fire **1:6-7**	All the others together with them took unto themselves wives, and each chose for himself one, and they began to go in unto them and to defile themselves with them. **7:1**
Enoch, in the seventh generation from Adam... **1:14**	My grandfather was taken up, the seventh from Adam. **60:8**

Behold, the Lord came with many thousands of His holy ones, to execute judgment upon all, and to convict all the ungodly of all their ungodly deeds which they have done in an ungodly way, and of all the harsh things which ungodly sinners have spoken against Him. **1:14-15**	Behold! He cometh with ten thousands of His holy ones to execute judgment upon all, and to destroy all the ungodly: and to convict all flesh of all the works of their ungodliness which they have ungodly committed, and of all the hard things which ungodly sinners have spoken against Him. **1:9**

In this chapter we have explored the many parallels between the *Book of Enoch* and the New Testament. Doing this we have looked at the willingness on the part of the Apostles to either quote the *Book of Enoch,* or to refer to it for teaching purposes. We then noted the wide array of parallels between the *Book of Enoch* and the New Testament. This was followed by a deeper exploration of the large number of parallels which are concentrated in the *Book of Revelation.* Finally, we summed up with demonstrating that the *Letter of Jude* refers to the sum and substance of the *Book of Enoch* as a whole, not just the one quote usually discussed.

These parallels are being pointed out not only to show the thoroughly Biblical nature of *Book of Enoch,* but also to amass the evidence that the New Testament shows signs of being influenced by the contents of Enoch's book. The apparent influence of the *Book of Enoch* upon the writers of the New Testament seems to point to an pervasive, ancient, and on-going use of the book prior to and during that time period. The point is not being made that the New Testament copies Enoch. Rather, it seems, both sources were drinking deeply from the same revelatory source.

A chapter similar to this one could also be produced to show the many parallels between the *Book of Enoch* and the Old Testament. This is not being done here since demonstrating such parallels would not be inconsistent with current scholarly theories about how the *Book of Enoch* was authored. If the *Book of Enoch* were written by anonymous Jews living a few centuries before Christ, as is often asserted, the books of the Old Testament would have been available resources for those authors. To be honest, for people who do not believe the New Testament is a supernatural document, these parallels do not pose a problem either. For them, one ancient author borrows from another and so it goes.

However, since the *Book of Enoch* can be definitely shown to be older than the New Testament, the author of the *Book of Enoch* obviously could not have copied from it. So how does one explain the many parallels between Enoch and the New Testament? For those who believe the New Testament is the inspired word of God, these parallels add to the authenticity of the authorship and the credibility of the content of the older document. The evidence is there that not only did the Apostles *not* reject and contradict the *Book of Enoch*, they embraced it and used it for teaching purposes.

In this chapter, we have looked at evidence external to the *Book of Enoch* which highlights the book's great age. Is there evidence for this book's antiquity within the book itself? As we shall see, the answer to this is a definite, yes.

9
Enoch's Book: Older than We've Been Told

In the historical-critical view of The *Book of Enoch*, textual scholars generally agree sections of the book were written in the third century BC. Using the same historical-critical approach scholars also late-date the *Book of Daniel* because, after all, how else could the writer of the *Book of Daniel* record exact details of the history of Israel and the region before it occurred? Using the same logic, scholars late-date many other Biblical works as well, including the books of Moses and Isaiah. They use the same approach with Enoch. They believe it could not have been written by Enoch, and that possibility is not even considered or explored.

There is another reason scholars late-date Enoch. It is because as of the current time, the oldest fragments of Enoch that have been found have been dated to the third century BC. These are scroll fragments in Aramaic which were found in caves by the Dead Sea in Israel. Bear in mind the fragments of Enoch we have from the Dead Sea Scrolls are in fact older than most other copies of Biblical books we possess.

However, there is evidence internal to the *Book of Enoch* which indicates the book is much older however.

The Internal Evidence

Among the indicators of the great age of the *Book of Enoch* are concepts and terms which are *missing* from the book. When any book is written, the writer will include concepts and ideas common to their own time period. This happens in a mostly unconscious manner which makes it nearly impossible to prevent it or for a writer to thoroughly adopt the ideas and words from a time period different from their own. This is especially true if the author is attempting to write about an era very far removed from their own. For instance, it would be very difficult for you to write in the first person about living in the American colonies in the 1700's. All books tend to betray evidence of the true era of their composition by the ideas and words unconsciously included or excluded.

"Oh, Moses, Where Art Thou"?

Enoch is devoid of a number of items one would expect to find in a Jewish book written in the period after the Jewish return from Babylon but before the birth of Christ. Unlike other works from the time between the Testaments, Enoch is devoid of certain things associated with Judaism from this period. For instance, there is nothing specifically Mosaic in the *Book of Enoch*. There is no appeal to tradition, no mention of the Sabbath, and no concern for Jewish dietary laws. In its pages you will find no concern for ritual purity, no mention of the Jewish temple, no animal sacrifices, no "Jews" mentioned, and for that matter, no Israel. For a writer between the Testaments to create such a document without slipping up and introducing a single Mosaic assumption is an extreme feat indeed.

On a somewhat related note, it is interesting that even though Enoch speaks a lot about the yearly calendar, and many chapters are spent describing a solar/lunar calendar year divided into two sets of 6 "portals", Enoch does not state the names to the months. The Jewish calendar is nowhere in evidence in the book.

Readers should take note of the complete lack of mention of any of the controverted points of Judaism which were in vogue during the period before Christ. For instance, there is no evidence of the prevalent tension between tradition and Hellenization, which was an issue at that time. In fact, one cannot find any Greek ideas introduced, or any Greek influence within the book. There are, however, many examples of other Jewish books written between the Old and New Testaments which show a pronounced Greek influence.

There is a body of Jewish literature which was between the Old and New Testament time periods. As you read through any of these, elements of Judaism from the time period will be apparent to the reader. But try as one might, one will not find in Enoch anything specifically influenced by the Law of Moses. Enoch is bereft of any terminology remotely slightly in its tone or flavor. Even the books of the Christian New Testament betray Mosaic influence, but Enoch does not.

The Case of the Missing Covenants

The *Book of Enoch* is also unlike any other Biblical book in that it has no reference to the two major Jewish covenants. Enoch does not refer to the old covenant regarding the land of Israel, confirmed by God with Jacob and his descendants, *nor* does it refer to the new covenant, first promised in Jeremiah 31, to be made by God with the Jews and extended to any who will put their trust in the Jewish Messiah, which was realized in Jesus Christ.

The Enoch Seminars

Scholars have hypothesized how this lack of Old Testament influence upon the *Book of Enoch* may be explained.

Gabriele Boccaccini, Professor of Second-Temple Judaism at the

University of Michigan, is the organizer and chairperson of the biennial "Enoch Seminars", which have been meeting in Italy every other summer since 2001. The Enoch Seminar is an international gathering of scholars who meet and present papers and addresses regarding their findings based upon research into Enochan and related literature.

Boccaccini hypothesizes that among the various groups of religious Jews in ancient times, there was a previously unknown "Enochan" branch of Judaism. It was from within this community of Enochan Judaism that the *Book of Enoch* was composed, according to his theory. Boccaccini postulates Enochan Judaism was an alternative form of non-Mosaic Judaism which distinguished itself from the more well-known Mosaic forms such as Phariseeism, Sadduceeism and Essenism. In this light, Boccaccini proposes, the books attributed to Enoch, were written to promote a Judaism which had a more universal appeal being devoid of the trappings of Moses.

The main fault I find with this idea is it finds the evidence for the existence of a previously unknown Enochan Judaism entirely from within the Enochan literature it seeks to explain. The logic seems to rely upon a kind of circular reasoning. Besides, a Judaism without Moses? It seems unthinkable.

Instead, the entire problem of explaining the existence of the non-Mosaic, Enochan literature goes away completely, it seems, if the claims of that literature are accepted at face value, namely, that they were composed and completed before the time of Moses and the five books of Torah attributed to him.

Since many scholars insist the *Book of Enoch* was composed during the time between the Old and New Testaments, it seems only right they should explain how such a thing was accomplished that the book's author(s) do not reveal something of their own true situation in time. If Enoch is not the author of these books, scholars need to propose their reasons for believing Enoch was not involved. That there is a complete lack of any such an explanation in the scholastic literature is very apparent, however. To not consider worthy of exploration the idea that Enoch wrote the books attributed to him, indicates an unreasonable bias on the part of scholarship.

The Use of Tablets as Books

It's not just that the *Book of Enoch* is missing many features common to inter-testamental Jewish literature, there are also a number of elements which *are* included which indicate a greater antiquity for the book. One seeming archaic element included in the book is its repeated mention of the use of tablets as the medium of the writing.[635] There is no debate among historians that the oldest medium for writing was clay or other

[635] **Enoch 81:1-2, 93:2, 103:2, 106:19**

types of tablets. It is believed writing upon clay or other types of tablets predates the use of scrolls made from parchment and papyri. When in the *Book of Enoch* there are a number of mentions made of the medium upon which books are recorded, they are said to be on "tablets." Would a hypothetical scribe or group writing during the period between the Old and New Testaments think it necessary to include this sort of detail when noting the medium of writing simply to make the book's apparent timeframe more convincing? It seems unlikely.

Similarities with the Book of Job

The date of the original composition of the *Book of Job,* like that of Enoch, is debated. Like Enoch, the *Book of Job,* lacks all reference to Moses, the covenants of Israel, references to the Jewish calendar or Jewish controversies which persisted in the era before Christ. Regardless of its time of composition, there is no question that the ancient terminology Job uses has given translators trouble when attempting to render that book into other languages. This sort of difficulty exists in the *Book of Enoch* too. Consider the following archaic characteristics that the Books of Job and Enoch share in common.

1. Discourses on Leviathan and Behemoth

Both Job's and Enoch's books include lengthy discourses on the ancient creation of two creatures referred to as Leviathan and Behemoth. Attempts to explain the presence of these two creatures in the *Book of Job* have ranged a wide gambit. Some have attempted to equate these animals with the known crocodile and hippo, but when attempting to explain these creatures' seeming supernatural attributes as described in Job, the same commentators have resorted to referring to such language as "poetical extravagances."[636] Others have translated the proper names for these creatures into more descriptive words such as "serpent"[637] or "dragon"[638] for Leviathan, and "wild animals"[639] and "monsters"[640] for Behemoth. Sometimes an effort is made to equate the activities of these two creatures with the activities of Satan.[641] Whatever one believes about the essential reality of what Job and Enoch seek to describe, there must be an admitted tentativeness to our conclusions. It seems apparent some of the original understandings of these passages are lost to us due to the great antiquity of these original compositions.

---

636 See footnote on **Job 40:15** in the ESV Study bible
637 **Job 40:25,** Orthodox Study Bible
638 **Job 40:25,** New English Translation of the Septuagint
639 **Job 40:15**, Orthodox Study Bible
640 **Job 40:15,** New English Translation of the Septuagint
641 See footnote on **Job 40:15** in the Orthodox Study bible

2. An Older Cosmology

Both Job and Enoch use archaic language for the cosmos and natural phenomena.

> There I saw *closed chambers* out of which the winds are divided, the *chamber* of the hail and winds, the *chamber* of the mist, and of the clouds, and the cloud thereof hovers over the earth from the beginning of the world. (Enoch 41:4)

> Have you entered the *storehouses* of the snow, or have you seen the *storehouses* of the hail, which I have reserved for the time of trouble, for the day of battle and war? (Job 38:22-23)

Enoch describes the places from which winds, hail and clouds originate as "chambers" and "closed chambers." Job refers to them as "storehouses." Modern readers of the *Book of Job* often seek to explain this sort of language as poetic. The fact remains, this is the sort of language which we find in both Job and Enoch and which we associate with writings from very ancient times.

Enoch saw the "cornerstone" of the earth, and it is mentioned in Job as well,

> I saw the treasuries of all the winds: I saw how He had furnished with them the whole creation and the firm foundations of the earth. And *I saw the cornerstone of the earth.* (Enoch 18:1-2)

> Where were you when I laid the foundation of the earth? *Who laid its cornerstone*? (Job 38:4&6)

3. Referring to Angels as "sons of God"

In Job 1:6 and 2:1 we find the angels referred to as "the sons of God". *"There was a day when the sons of God came to present themselves before the LORD, and Satan also came among them."* and, *"Again there was a day when the sons of God came to present themselves before the LORD, and Satan also came among them to present himself before the LORD."* Job 38:7 is even clearer. In it God asks if Job were present at the creation of the earth *"when the morning stars sang together and all the sons of God shouted for joy?"* When we read the *Book of Enoch* we find, just as with the *Book of Job*, "the sons of God", are clear references to the angels.

Through its discourse on Leviathan and Behemoth, its use of ancient terminology for the cosmos and in its use of the term "sons of God" for the angels of God, Enoch shows itself to share a number of factors in common with the *Book of Job*, a book widely reputed to be very ancient.

Enoch Helps Us Understand Other Ancient Texts

Due to the *Book of Enoch*'s roots in ancient times, the book can help us in unlocking certain ideas found in the Bible, which initially may seem difficult to understand.

1. "The sons of God" in Genesis

> When man began to multiply on the face of the land and daughters were born to them, the sons of God saw that the daughters of man were attractive. And they took as their wives any they chose. Then the LORD said, "My Spirit shall not abide in man forever, for he is flesh: his days shall be 120 years." The Nephilim were on the earth in those days, and also afterward, when the sons of God came in to the daughters of man and they bore children to them. These were the mighty men who were of old, the men of renown, (Genesis 6:1-4).

In this passage it is striking that it seems as if Moses assumes his readers already know about the story he recounts. In what seems to be a rather off-the-cuff manner he remarks *"these were the mighty men of old"*, almost as if he is saying *"but you already know about those so I won't go into the details."* If Moses' audience did not already know the story, then Moses' inclusion of such little detail seems more confusing than helpful. But, if Moses' audience already knew all about it, from what source did they know it?

The first few words of both Genesis 6 and Enoch 6 are nearly word-for-word as they introduce this story. In very cursory fashion the passage in Genesis seems to be alluding to the passage in Enoch. In Enoch the angels who fell and their offspring are described with greater detail. The rest of Genesis chapter 6 also seems to incorporate abbreviated forms stories from other sources. In the *Book of Enoch*, however, chapter 6 is a section of the book that is straight narrative and does not seem abbreviated or compiled. Was Enoch's book Moses' source for Genesis 6:1-4?

2. "The other lot for Azazel" in Leviticus

Consider another enigmatic passage from Moses. In Leviticus 16, we find instruction concerning the scapegoat. A goat is drawn by lot for sending into the wilderness. Before sending the goat into the wilderness, the sins of the people are symbolically laid upon the goat.

There is then introduced in the passage from Leviticus a puzzling reference to "Azazel." Leviticus 16:8, says one goat is to be chosen for the LORD and the other lot for Azazel. *"Aaron shall cast lots over the two goats, one lot for the LORD and the other lot for Azazel."* Leviticus 16:10 and 26 then say the scapegoat is to be sent into the wilderness *to Azazel, "The goat on which the lot fell for Azazel shall be presented alive before the LORD to make atonement over it, that it may be sent away into the wilderness to Azazel,"* and *"He who lets the goat go to Azazel shall wash his clothes and bathe his body in water, and afterward he may come into the camp."* The question that arises quite normally in the mind of modern readers is who or what is Azazel? Moses gives the reader no explanation. Apparently, Moses' original audience did not need an explanation as we do today.

In the *Book of Enoch*, our question is apparently answered.

There Azazel is said be one of the angels who sinned and subsequently taught warfare to mankind, and to have encouraged promiscuity and fornication among the human race. Azazel's negative influence upon humanity is said to have been so notable, he is singled out for special judgment among the angels. He is the first to be bound in the abyss in the wilderness. There he is said to be helplessly imprisoned awaiting the last judgment as alluded to by Peter who wrote,

> God did not spare angels when they sinned, but cast them into hell and committed them to chains of gloomy darkness to be kept until the judgment. (2 Peter 2:4).

In this light, then, the choosing of a scapegoat *for Azazel* and symbolically placing of the sins of the people on the goat which is then sent into the wilderness to Azazel seems to paint a picture akin to sending the trash out to the garbage dump. In this way it is indicated the problem of sin among God's people, like Azazel himself, awaits a future time of judgment when those problems are settled for all time. The problem of the sin of God's people was settled by the death and resurrection of Christ, when He was judged in our place. The problem of the sinning angels, also stands to be remedied by the Son of Man. It will be dealt with in a final sense when He sits in judgment on the throne of His glory.

Enoch, a More Primitive Book

There is yet another element that should be considered which indicates a more ancient date for Enoch's book. Initially, this point may seem a bit hard to grasp.

Many have noted the abundance of rich parallels one can see between the *Book of Enoch* and the Old and New Testaments. In contrast to this, or perhaps in spite of this, one can see in these parallels subtle indicators that Enoch contains an original germ of a concept in a more undeveloped form than the Biblical writings of a later time. Though one can see in Enoch a spirit that is thoroughly of like kind with the Bible, there are indications that the ideas expressed in Enoch are more basic and less developed. In contrast, parallel ideas found in the Bible seem more concrete and more developed. If one accepts the idea that revelation is progressive this poses no problem for accepting both Enoch and the Bible as valid.

As an example, Enoch 49:3, describes the righteous dead as having *"fallen asleep in righteousness"*. This idea is made more concrete in the New Testament where the righteous dead are now seen as *"those who have fallen asleep in Christ"*, (1 Corinthians 15:18). In Enoch 70:3, we are told the angels measure the *"place for the elect and righteous"*. In the New Testament, this is again made more concrete in John's Revelation where we read the angels measure the New Jerusalem and its *"city and its gates and its walls"*, (Revelation 21:15). Another example can be found in Enoch 108:10, where we are told the righteous dead are those who *"loved heaven more than life"*. The New Testament again seems more explicit with describing the righteous dead as those who *"loved not their lives unto death"*, (Revelation 12:11). In these and in many other cases when comparing parallel passages from Enoch and the Bible, the Enoch passages seem more generic and less concrete, something one would expect to see regarding ideas which are being progressively revealed.

Widely Read in Israel

The evidence is there that by the time of Jesus, this ancient book was widely circulated, read, and highly esteemed in Israel. Numerous copies were apparently included in libraries across Jerusalem. Most current scholarship related to the Dead Sea Scrolls is leaning away from the hypothesis that the Essenes were the creators and depositors of the Dead Sea Scrolls. Since the scrolls became available to a much wider group of scholars in the late 1980's, a preponderance of evidence has been accumulating that indicates the scrolls were likely gathered from synagogues and libraries around Jerusalem and secreted in the caves during the period between the two sieges of Jerusalem by Vespasian and Titus in AD 68. It has been suggested this was done for the purpose of hiding and preserving the scrolls from the Romans. In that light then, it becomes more significant that the *Book of Enoch* was among the top five most represented documents recovered from the Dead Sea Scroll caves.

Additionally, the Enoch literature and its concepts are referred to numerous times in other ancient Jewish literature and the New Testament.

So why was this book eliminated by Judaism when it reorganized itself a generation after the destruction of Jerusalem? Why, centuries later, was the book banned within Christendom as well? Whatever chain of events one comes up with, we should attempt to see God's hand in those events. Banished by the religious leaders of Judaism and banned by an organized Christendom, Enoch's book was exiled but preserved and kept by God among a group of Jews who may have become part of the Diaspora in Ethiopia before the time of Christ.

In a sense, Enoch's book is like a comet on a wide elliptical orbit around the course of human history. At times this orbit brings it back into a closer relation to the course of human events on this globe as it has in these days. This seems to be in harmony with the book's internal claims that its purpose was to become a blessing to those who will be living in the day of tribulation.

The true value of Enoch's book is to be discovered in the last generation, by those who will find themselves living in the prophesied *day of tribulation.*

2,000-years ago copies of Enoch's book were literally entombed in caves by the Dead Sea, as if deposited for rediscovery in our day. Comparing the *Book of Enoch* to a kind of time-capsule seems to be very fitting when we consider the origin and discovery of the greatest archaeological find of the 20th century... the Dead Sea Scrolls.

10
They Found Enoch in Caves by the Dead Sea

Beginning in 1947 and continuing into the middle 1950's, a series of 11 caves were uncovered in Israel near the Dead Sea in which hundreds of books in scroll form had been deposited and hidden for almost 2,000 years.

When the Dead Sea Scrolls were discovered a hypothesis of their origin was put forward by two Dominican priests, Father Roland de Vaux and Father Josef T. Milik. They proposed the cache of books discovered were the product of an ascetic, monastic, celibate, sect of Judaism, the Essenes. They proposed the Qumran desert outpost located near the Dead Sea Caves was in fact a settlement of Essenes along the lines of a monastery complete with scriptorium-- a place set up for writing books.

Beyond the Essene Hypothesis

For nearly 40 years, de Vaux and Milik and a handful of other men maintained monopolistic control of all access to Enoch and other scrolls. During this time, scholarly requests for access to those scrolls would be mostly refused. During those years the Essene hypothesis dominated the scholarly landscape chiefly due to the lack of access to the scrolls by other researchers from other disciplines. That situation has changed.

Modern research is moving away from de Vaux's Essene hypothesis. Since 1989, when the scrolls were released to the public against the wishes of those who controlled them, a larger group of researchers with a more inter-disciplinary approach to the scrolls have been reevaluating the old assumptions.

Hidden on the Eve of Israel's Destruction

The movement today is toward the belief the scrolls do not represent the work of an ascetic sect of Jews, but rather, that the scrolls are more representative of a cross-section of what was in circulation among the Jews of the first century AD. It is now widely believed the scrolls represent a gathering together of books from synagogues and libraries across Jerusalem. Perhaps scrolls from the Jerusalem temple itself were also hidden there. The likely time period for the scrolls to have been hidden is the window of opportunity afforded to the Jews in AD 68, between the sieges of Jerusalem by first Vespasian and later Titus. When Vespasian's forces withdrew and before Titus' forces came, the Jews had the opportunity to gather and hide the books to protect them from the Romans, who they knew would return.

Further, a number of details have now come forward which seem to disprove the Essene hypothesis. For one, no evidence has been found at the Qumran outpost, for a scriptorium capable of producing the Dead Sea Scrolls. Also, the scrolls have been shown to have been produced by many hands over a period of centuries, not by a few persons dedicated as copyists at a single era and locale. A few scrolls even evidence a lack of skill in the scribal craft. Finally, the remains of women have been found in the cemetery at Qumran. That's not something one expects to find among celibate ascetics.

Revealed on the Day of Israel's Rebirth

The drama of the rebirth of the nation of Israel was unfolding simultaneously with the scrolls rediscovery at the Dead Sea. A nation which had ceased to exist nearly 2,000 years prior was being miraculously reborn. Simultaneous with that event books of the Bible as well as others which had remained hidden for 2,000 years were discovered by seeming happenstance.

More than seventy years have passed since those events. These days it is looking more and more as if the Essene hypothesis concerning the origin of the scrolls was the product of the imaginations of gentile-Christian monks, in which Christian monastic forms were insinuated into a first century Jewish context. The Jewish context of the scrolls is only now beginning to be fully appreciated. The theory that the settlement at Qumran was a community of ascetic, celibate, scribes still persists in some quarters, but it is gradually giving way to the findings of the new research.

Vindicated by the Dead Sea Scrolls

After James Bruce restored the *Book of Enoch* to the West in 1773, bringing back three copies of the book from Ethiopia, there were scholars who believed this Ethiopic *Book of Enoch* was a forgery. They did not believe it was the book from which the *Letter of Jude* quotes. They theorized its authorship was many centuries after Christ. This theory persisted in some quarters for nearly 200 years.

As time passed subsequent to the Dead Sea Scrolls discovery, and then subsequent to their general release to the public, there was a gradual realization that the form of the text of Ethiopic Enoch was in fact authenticated by the recovered Aramaic fragments.

In the Dead Sea Scroll caves were found multiple copies of all the books of the Old Testament, except for Esther, (which by the way, does not mean Esther *was not* there originally). Also found there were many other Jewish religious books. The five most represented books among the Dead Sea Scrolls are the *Book of Psalms, Isaiah, Deuteronomy,* the *Book of*

Jubilees and the *Book of Enoch.*[642] What this means is, more fragments of copies of Enoch were recovered in the Dead Sea Scrolls than of any of the books of the Old Testament except for *Isaiah*, *Psalms*, and *Deuteronomy*! This tells us something of the popularity of the *Book of Enoch* before and shortly after the time of Jesus Christ.

Scholars have determined that some of the materials used for the Enoch scrolls can be dated to between 200 and 300 BC.

By comparing these ancient scroll fragments with the Ethiopic translation of Enoch, it has now been demonstrated that Ethiopic Enoch is an essentially faithful, literal translation of the book that was in circulation at the time of Christ and the Apostles.

There is no doubt the *Book of Enoch* quoted in the New Testament is the *Book of Enoch* which has now been made available again in the West, which has been translated in English, and which we can read for ourselves.

Hidden on the eve of Israel's destruction and discovered again on the morning of her rebirth, the *Book of Enoch* is coming back into its former prominence. Like a deposit from millennia past, the *Book of Enoch* is seemingly being moved by world events to regain attention center stage. The prophecy related in the first few verses of the book is lining up as if to be fulfilled by the last generation of the descendants of Enoch's *"plant of righteousness"*. Enoch predicted the elect nation will become doubly elect at the end of the age.[643] This will occur only when they become elect and chosen in the salvation which comes only through faith in the name of Jesus of Nazareth, the Messiah of Israel.

---

[642] It is interesting to note, the top three most quoted books in the New Testament are also the top three most represented books in the Dead Sea Scrolls, Isaiah, Psalms and Deuteronomy.

[643] **Enoch 93:10**

FOUND IN CAVES BY THE DEAD SEA

This table shows the Enoch scroll fragments that have so far been identified among the Dead Sea Scrolls. The purpose here is to show how much of the *Book of Enoch* has been recovered from copies which were made before Apostolic times. These ancient fragments have been used to verify the version which has been used in the West for the past 100 years, is essentially the same as was used in New Testament times.

A Table of what was recovered from the Dead Sea Scrolls

Enoch Passage	DSS Scroll	Enoch Passage	DSS Scroll
1:1-6	4Q201	74:1-2 or 78:9-12	4Q209
1:9-5:1	4Q204	76:13-77	4Q209
2:1-5:6	4Q201	76:3-10	4Q210
5:9-6:4+6:7-8:1	4Q202	78:6-8	4Q210
6:4-8:1	4Q201	79:2-5	4Q209
6:7	4Q204	82:9-13	4Q209
8:2-9:4	4Q202	86:1-3	4Q207
8:3-9:3,6-8	4Q201	88:3-89:6	4Q206
10:13-19+12:3	4Q204	89:11-14	4Q205
10:21-11:1	4Q201	89:27-30	4Q206
10:3-4	4Q201	89:29 31	4Q205
10:8-12	4Q202	89:31-36	4Q204
13:6-14:16	4Q204	89:43-44	4Q205
14:4-6	4Q202	89:7-16	4Q206
18:8-12	4Q204	91:18-92:2	4Q212
22:13-24:1	4Q205	92:5-93:4	4Q212
22:3-7	4Q206	93:11-94:2	4Q212
25:7-27:1	4Q205	93:9-10+91:11-17	4Q212
28:3-29:2+31:2-32:3	4Q206	103:3-4 (Greek)	7Q12 + 7Q14
30:1-32:1	4Q204	104:13-106 2	4Q204
32:3-6+33:3-34:1	4Q206	106:13-107:2	4Q204
35:?+36:1-4	4Q204		

11
Ancient Mention of Enoch's Books

Now that we have seen the evidence internal to the *Book of Enoch* which indicates the book is very old, and we have also seen that the version of the book we are using today is essentially the same as was used in Apostolic times, a question remains.... Is it possible to find evidence of the existence of the *Book of Enoch* being referenced in other ancient books?

Before the invention of the printing press, the production and circulation of books required greater time and expense than today. For an ancient book to come to be quoted or mentioned in other ancient books required the passage of a great deal of time, as well as a widespread circulation. That the *Book of Enoch* had widespread popular usage over an expanse of time is evidenced by the many references we do find to the book in other ancient Jewish and literature.

In chapter 8, we spent a good deal of time pointing out references to the contents of the *Book of Enoch* in the books of the New Testament. In this chapter we will point out other ancient Jewish literature which either directly refers to the *Book of Enoch*, or the saga in its pages. This is being done *not* to make a case for these other books being authoritative in any way. Neither is the case being made that these books prove in and of themselves that the *Book of Enoch is true*. The following references to ancient Jewish literature are *for the sole purpose* of demonstrating that the *Book of Enoch* was widely known and revered among the Jews in very ancient times. The following quotations should demonstrate to the reader there was a high level of respect and usage accorded to the *Book of Enoch* before the time of Christ.[644] Unless otherwise noted the books mentioned in this chapter were written by Jews before New Testament times.

The Unusual Birth of Noah

There is an ancient Jewish book referred to by scholars as the "*Genesis Apocryphon.*" That title is probably not a good title for the book as it does not describe its contents well. A better title would probably be the "*Book of the Patriarchs.*" The book was quite long in its original form and consists of events from the lives of the patriarchs. Beginning with Noah, the book contains stories of each of the ancient patriarchs of Israel. Mostly, the stories are related in the first person, in turn, by each patriarch. The first part of the book relating the events from creation to

[644] Due to copyright issues not all of these sources will be quoted here, but enough information will be given for the reader to look into these further.

Enoch was lost in modern times, unfortunately. This book was not known to exist until the discovery of the Dead Sea Scrolls.

The earliest complete portion of the book which is preserved relates the story of the birth of Noah told in the words of Lamech his father. Lamech remarks that he was worried at the birth of Noah that he was not his child but that his wife might have had relations with a Watcher or one of the offspring of the Watchers.

Lamech questions his wife, telling her to speak the truth as to who Noah's real father truly is. Lamech's wife protests in anger and swears by God that she has been faithful and Noah is indeed Lamech's son. Lamech is not entirely convinced and seeks out his own father Methuselah and requests that Methuselah seek and ask Enoch for his judgment on the matter.

This is all of this segment of the book which survives. Readers may notice the similarity of this material to the same story of Noah's birth related in the *Book of Enoch* chapter 106. The *Genesis Apocryphon* version of the story gives greater detail than that we find in Enoch chapter 106.

Though the *Genesis Apocryphon* does not directly quote Enoch's writing, it does reveal a wider circulation of this story which, before the discovery of the Dead Sea Scrolls in the modern era, was only known from the *Book of Enoch.*

Abram Reads from the Book of the Words of Enoch

Further on into the *Genesis Apocryphon,* Abram relates events from his life and time in the first person. His traveling to Egypt during a time of famine is recounted by him. Fearful he may be killed by Pharaoh in order to steal Abram's wife, Sarai, Abram plans to ask his wife to say she is Abram's sister. Seemingly confirming his fears, officials from Pharaoh visit Abram, and while they are there they see Sarai who they decide to recommend to Pharaoh.

Before the officials return to Pharaoh, however, while fellowshipping with Abram over a meal, we are informed the Egyptian officials are expecting to receive some words of wisdom from Abram. Abram brings out the *Book of the Words of Enoch* and reads to them from it.

Here we have an ancient mention of the writings of Enoch outside of the writings of Enoch themselves. The *Genesis Apocryphon* is a composition demonstrably more ancient than New Testament times.

A Biblical Chronology

Another scroll preserved in the Dead Sea Scrolls is a genealogy of the patriarchs which states the relative ages of Abraham, Isaac, and Jacob when they each had children. In Jacob's case it is his child Levi upon whom the passage focuses. In the passage it is related that Levi is entrusted with the *Book of the Words of Enoch* for preserving and passing on.

> [. . .Abraham was] nin[ety-nine ye]ars old [when he fathered Isaac. Is]aac was [sixty years o]ld [when he fathered] [Jacob. Jacob was] sixty-five y[ears old when he fathered Levi.] [He gave to Levi the *Book of the Words of] Enoch* [to preserve and pass on][645]

In this fragmentary passage we have a story which suggests the generational transmission path of the writings of Enoch from Abraham to Jacob's son Levi.

The Testaments of the Twelve Patriarchs

The *Testaments of the Twelve Patriarchs* is an ancient book which purports to be the gathered sayings of the twelve sons of Jacob on their deathbeds. The book is a series of exhortations and prophecies delivered by each patriarch to his sons in similar fashion as is done by Jacob, in Genesis 49.

Though the book was of Jewish origin, the *Testaments of the Twelve Patriarchs* survives due to its preservation by Orthodox Christianity. There are some parts of the *Testaments* which are said by scholars to have been added by Christian scribes of a later date. Nevertheless the book is for the most part deemed by scholars to be a Jewish writing which originated before the Christian era. Five of the testaments in this book contain references to the *Book of Enoch*, and/or allusions to the Watcher-Nephilim saga. The passages which refer to the writings of Enoch, or the Enoch storyline are not among the sections of the book scholars have said were added by Christians at a later date.

In the *Testament of Simeon* 5:4-6, we read,

> I have seen it inscribed in the *writing of Enoch* that your sons shall be corrupted in fornication, and shall do harm to the sons of Levi with the sword. But they shall not be able to withstand Levi; for he shall wage the war of the Lord, and shall conquer all your hosts.[646]

---

[645] **4Q559 Col. 2,** Michael O. Wise, The Dead Sea Scrolls: A New Translation p. 564
[646] All quotations from the Testaments of the Twelve Patriarchs are from the R.H. Charles

The *Testament of Dan* 5:4-13, says,

> I know that in the last days ye shall depart from the Lord, and ye shall provoke Levi unto anger, and fight against Judah; but ye shall not prevail against them, for an angel of the Lord shall guide them both; for by them shall Israel stand. And whensoever ye depart from the Lord, ye shall walk in all evil and work the abominations of the gentiles, going a-whoring after women of *the lawless ones,* while with all wickedness the spirits of wickedness work in you. For I have read in the *Book of Enoch,* the righteous, that your prince is Satan, and that all the spirits of wickedness and pride will conspire to attend constantly on the sons of Levi, to cause them to sin before the Lord.

In the *Testament of Naphtali* 4:1-5, there is this passage,

> These things I say unto you, my children, for I have read in the *writing of Enoch* that ye yourselves also shall depart from the Lord, walking according to all the lawlessness of the gentiles, and ye shall do according to all the wickedness of Sodom.

From the *Testament of Benjamin* 9:1-5, we read,

> And I believe that there will be also evil-doings among you, from the *words of Enoch* the righteous: that ye shall commit fornication with the fornication of Sodom, and shall perish, all save a few, and shall renew wanton deeds with women.

The *Testament of Reuben* 5:5-7, alludes to the Watcher-Nephilim saga in the following passage,

> Thus they allured the Watchers who were before the flood; for as these continually beheld them, they lusted after them, and they conceived the act in their mind; for they changed themselves into the shape of men, and appeared to them when they were with their husbands. And the women lusting in their minds after their forms, gave birth to giants, for the Watchers appeared to them as reaching even unto heaven.

In the *Testament of Naphtali* 3:4-5, we find this similar allusion,

> But ye shall not be so, my children, recognizing in the firmament, in the earth, and in the sea, and in all created things, the Lord who made all things, that ye become not as Sodom,

---

translation, 1912.

> which changed the order of nature. In like manner the Watchers also changed the order of their nature, whom the Lord cursed at the flood, on whose account He made the earth without inhabitants and fruitless.

Readers will be interested to note that similar to Peter and Jude in the New Testament, the passage above compares the sin of the Watchers with the sin of Sodom and Gomorrah.

The Apocalypse of Baruch

The Apocalypse of Baruch is a Jewish book which some scholars believe was at least partly written in the first century AD.

> [Adam] became a danger to his own soul: even to the angels. For, moreover, at that time when he was created, they enjoyed liberty. And became he a danger some of them descended, and mingled with the women. And then those who did so were tormented in chains. But the rest of the multitude of the angels, of which there is (no) number, restrained themselves. And those who dwelt on the earth perished together (with them) through the waters of the deluge. (56:10-15, R.H. Charles)

The Book of Jubilees

The *Book of Jubilees* is a Jewish book which shares a closely similar path of transmission and preservation as the *Book of Enoch*. Like Enoch, it was widely used in Israel in Jesus' day, later fell into disuse and disappeared from the Jewish and Christian world throughout the Mediterranean. The *Book of Jubilees* has been preserved by Jews and Christians in Ethiopia. Among the Dead Sea Scrolls, copies of the *Book of Jubilees* are more plentiful than the *Book of Enoch*.

The *Book of Jubilees* retells human history in 49-year episodic increments, called "Jubilees", thus the book's modern title.

The *Book of Jubilees* contains an exceptional amount of material about Enoch and the Watchers.

> And in the second week of the tenth jubilee. Mahalalel took unto him to wife Dinah, the daughter of Barakiel the daughter of his father's brother, and she bare him a son in the third week in the sixth year, and he called his name Jared, for in his days the angels of the Lord descended on the earth, those who are named the Watchers, that they should instruct the children of men, and that they should do judgment and uprightness on the earth.

ANCIENT MENTION OF ENOCH'S BOOKS

(4:15, R.H. Charles)

Here we find information not offered in the *Book of Enoch.* According to the *Book of Jubilees,* the descent of the Watchers began as a benevolent mission. These angels on assignment came to earth to instruct humanity in God's ways.

And then we read,

> And in the eleventh jubilee Jared took to himself a wife, and her name was Baraka, the daughter of Rasujal, a daughter of his father's brother, in the fourth week of this jubilee, and she bare him a son in the fifth week, in the fourth year of the jubilee, and *he called his name Enoch.*
>
> And he was the first among men that are born on earth who learnt writing and knowledge and wisdom and who wrote down the signs of heaven according to the order of their months in a book, that men might know the seasons of the years according to the order of their separate months. And he was the first to write a testimony and he testified to the sons of men among the generations of the earth, and recounted the weeks of the jubilees, and made known to them the days of the years, and set in order the months and recounted the Sabbaths of the years as we made them, known to him.
>
> And what was and what will be he saw in a vision of his sleep, as it will happen to the children of men throughout their generations until the day of judgment; he saw and understood everything, and wrote his testimony, and placed the testimony on earth for all the children of men and for their generations. (4:16-19, R.H. Charles).

The *Book of Jubilees* says Enoch was the first man to learn the scribal art. We are also told Enoch the scribe *"wrote down the signs of heaven".* This is a reference to the sun, moon and stars which are given in Genesis 1, as "signs." We are told Enoch recorded these things so *"that men might know the seasons and the years."* That's a good description of what we have in Enoch's *Geocentric Calendar Book.*

We are also informed Enoch saw in a dream-vision *"what will happen to men throughout their generations until the day of judgment."* That is a good description of the contents of Enoch's *Book of Dream-Visions.*

There is another interesting statement at the end of the passage, we are told Enoch, *"wrote his testimony, and placed the testimony on earth for all the children of men and for their generations."* This passage says the testimony that Enoch left in writing would not be destroyed but would survive until the last generation, something which is specifically prophesied in the first chapter of *Book of Enoch*.

Later in the *Book of Jubilees* we have a description of Enoch's preaching ministry and his translation to heaven.

> He was moreover with the angels of God these six jubilees of years, and they showed him everything which is on earth and in the heavens, the rule of the sun, and he wrote down everything. And he testified to the Watchers, who had sinned with the daughters of men; for these had begun to unite themselves, so as to be defiled, with the daughters of men, and Enoch testified against them all.
>
> And he was taken from amongst the children of men, and we conducted him into the Garden of Eden in majesty and honor, and behold there he writes down the condemnation and judgment of the world, and all the wickedness of the children of men, (4:21-23, R.H. Charles).

This seems to be a reference to Enoch's preaching ministry as we have it in Enoch's *Book of the Watchers*. There is also a reference made to Enoch's translation to heaven which is related in Enoch's *Book of the Parables*.

The *Book of Jubilees* relates an extensive retelling of the nature of the sin of the angels, quoted here.

> And it came to pass when the children of men began to multiply on the face of the earth and daughters were born unto them, that the angels of God saw them on a certain year of this jubilee, that they were beautiful to look upon; and they took themselves wives of all whom they chose, and they bare unto them sons and they were giants.
>
> And lawlessness increased on the earth and all flesh corrupted its way, alike men and cattle and beasts and birds and everything that walks on the earth -all of them corrupted their ways and their orders, and they began to devour each other, and lawlessness increased on the earth and every imagination of the thoughts of all men (was) thus evil continually.
>
> And God looked upon the earth, and behold it was corrupt, and all flesh had corrupted its orders, and all that were upon the earth had wrought all manner of evil before His eyes. And He said that He would destroy man and all flesh upon the face of

> the earth which He had created. But Noah found grace before the eyes of the Lord.
>
> And against the angels whom He had sent upon the earth, He was exceedingly wroth, and He gave commandment to root them out of all their dominion, and He bade us to bind them in the depths of the earth, and behold they are bound in the midst of them, and are kept separate.
>
> And against their sons went forth a command from before His face that they should be smitten with the sword, and be removed from under heaven. And He said "My spirit shall not always abide on man; for they also are flesh and their days shall be one hundred and twenty years." And He sent His sword into their midst that each should slay his neighbor, and they began to slay each other till they all fell by the sword and were destroyed from the earth. And their fathers were witnesses of their destruction, and after this they were bound in the depths of the earth forever, until the day of the great condemnation, when judgment is executed on all those who have corrupted their ways and their works before the Lord. And He destroyed all from their places, and there was not left one of them whom He judged not according to all their wickedness. (5:1-11, R.H. Charles)

Then the *Book of Jubilees* adds even more detail,

> For owing to these three things came the flood upon the earth, namely, owing to the fornication wherein the Watchers against the law of their ordinances went a whoring after the daughters of men, and took themselves wives of all which they chose: and they made the beginning of uncleanness. And they begat sons the Naphidim, and they were all unlike, and they devoured one another: and the Giants slew the Naphil, and the Naphil slew the Eljo, and the Eljo mankind, and one man another. And every one sold himself to work iniquity and to shed much blood, and the earth was filled with iniquity. And after this they sinned against the beasts and birds, and all that moves and walks on the earth: and much blood was shed on the earth, and every imagination and desire of men imagined vanity and evil continually. And the Lord destroyed everything from off the face of the earth; because of the wickedness of their deeds, and because of the blood which they had shed in the midst of the earth He destroyed everything, (7:21-25, R.H. Charles).

The *Book of Jubilees* retells the story related in Enoch's book with all of its essential points. The angels sinned by disobeying God and taking human wives. Their children were monstrous and corrupt. As lawlessness in the earth increased among the Watchers, their offspring and mankind, God decided to bring it all to an end in the judgment of the flood. The Watcher children were killed first, then the Watchers were bound in the earth until the last judgment, and then the earth was cleansed and renewed by means of the flood.

The *Book of Jubilees* is an important witness to the existence of Enoch's book from ancient times. Since the *Book of Jubilees* came into wide usage over the passage of time, its witness to the existence of the *Book of Enoch*, demonstrates an even greater antiquity and wide usage for the *Book of Enoch*.

The Book of the Giants

A book which was known to have existed prior to the discovery of the Dead Sea Scrolls but for which no Aramaic or Hebrew originals were known, turned up in the caves by the Dead Sea. It has come to be called the *Book of the Giants*.

This strange book purports to preserve conversations between certain of the children of the Watchers. The document is in very fragmentary form so it is difficult to be certain of much beyond the following... In the book the story of the degradation of the world prior to Noah's day is reviewed. A number of the Watcher children's proper names are listed in the book; curiously, one of them is named Gilgamesh.[647]

There is a fragmentary portion of the book in which 200 each of various breeds of animals are brought before the Watchers. It is unclear if this is for the purpose of experimentation or some sort of unholy sacrifice.

The course of the book is then disrupted when certain of the Watcher offspring begin to receive troubling dream-visions. A vision is recounted of a clay tablet with the inscribed names of the giants being submerged in water. The clay tablet resurfaces with the names of the giants erased from its surface. Another dream has the roots of a tree being destroyed by fire and deluge. Another dream has the Holy One descend to earth for the purpose of judging all.

Certain Watcher children are deeply troubled about the visions and discuss what the dreams might mean. It is suggested that Enoch the scribe be sought to come and interpret the dream-visions for them.

---

[647] Gilgamesh is also a character found in the Sumerian *"Epic of Gilgamesh"*. The *Epic of Gilgamesh* was first discovered in the late 1800's on 4,000-year-old clay tablets. The Epic describes the story of a worldwide flood and the heroism of Gilgamesh, who survives the flood. The reader may be interested to know the *Book of the Giants* paints a very different picture of the Gilgamesh character. In the *Book of the Giants*, Gilgamesh is a bloodthirsty child of the Watchers who receives a vision in which the names of himself and other giants are erased from a clay tablet after being submerged in a flood.

Enoch comes and addresses the group.

The book obviously dovetails with key points of the Enochan saga.

The Damascus Document

The *Damascus Document* is a document written about the time of the early Church or slightly before. It is a series of instructions for Jews who are serious about the commitment to follow the Law.

In a section of the book[648] which warns against the sin of lust the writer informs us that lust of the mind and of the eyes has caused many to fall and has brought low even the brave and heroic. The writer tells us this is the reason why the Watchers fell. They failed to keep God's laws due to their own evil desires. And what is the outcome of their having fulfilled their lust? They and their children fell and have now become as if they never were since they have been removed from the earth.

A Sermon on the Flood

There is a book among the Dead Sea Scrolls which seems to be a kind of sermon on the subject of the flood of Noah's day. In it the writer mentions how the flood was sent upon the earth because people disobeyed the commandments of the Lord. The scroll mentions the giants also being removed from earth at that time.

The Aramaic Levi Document

This scroll was known to exist before the discovery of the Dead Sea Scrolls. In the 1800's a part of this book was found in storage in a synagogue in Cairo, Egypt. The book puzzled scholars due to its unique character and unknown origins. Since then, parts of the book have also turned up among the Dead Sea Scrolls. In the book Levi states he has learned from the words of Enoch that his descendants will apostatize.[649]

---

[648] **4Q266 Col. 2**
[649] **4Q213 8-10**

The Ages of Creation

In a book from the Dead Sea Scrolls referred to by translators as "The Ages of Creation", mention is made of the descent of the angels who took women in order to sire children who became giants. Azazel is singled out for God's punishment.[650]

The Deuterocanonicals [651]

Among the books of the Bible of the Eastern Orthodox Church, are four which also refer to the story-arc of Enoch's book. These four books refer to the giants of the *Book of Enoch*.

Each of these four books were written by Jews in the centuries before Christ. Though these books are absent from most Protestant Bibles, they are of value here because, like the other books mentioned in this chapter, they demonstrate that the story of the *Book of Enoch* had circulated widely in ancient times. These books bear witness to the prevalence of belief in the story which we find in the *Book of Enoch*.

> It is your will that works of your wisdom should not be without effect; therefore men trust their lives even to the smallest piece of wood, and passing through the billows on a raft they come safely to land. For even in the beginning, when arrogant giants were perishing, the hope of the world took refuge on a raft, and guided by your hand left to the world the seed of a new generation, (Wisdom 14:5-6, ESV).

> He did not forgive *the ancient giants* who revolted in their might, (Sirach 16:7, NRSV).

> *The giants were born there*, who were famous of old, great in stature, expert in war.[652] God did not choose them, or give them the way to knowledge; so they perished because they had no wisdom, they perished through their folly, (Baruch 3:26-28, ESV).

> You, the creator of all things and the governor of all, are a just Ruler, and you judge those who have done anything in

---

[650] **4Q180 Frag. 1**

[651] Deuterocanonicals: Scriptures found in the Greek Septuagint and Orthodox Bibles but not in the Jewish canon or Protestant Bibles.

[652] **"The giants were born there, who were famous of old, great in stature, expert in war"**; notice how similar this description is to Moses' words in Genesis 6:4, *"These were the mighty men who were of old, the men of renown."*

> insolence and arrogance. You destroyed those who in the past committed injustice, *among whom were even giants* who trusted in their strength and boldness, whom you destroyed by bringing upon them a boundless flood, (3 Macc. 2:3-4, ESV).

The purpose of this chapter has *not* been to prove the *Book of Enoch* or any of the books mentioned above are *correct* in the claims they make. The point being made here is simply this, the message of the *Book of Enoch* was well-known and widely accepted as true among Jews in ancient times. This demonstrates the *Book of Enoch* to be even more ancient than the books listed here.

It is a notable fact that the *Book of Enoch* was well known in the past, but then became scarce, and effectively lost to the churches in the Greek and Latin world. What is also notable is that it has survived and is again becoming well known in our day.

12
"Holy! Holy! Holy is the Lord!"

We've been looking at evidence, both external as well as internal to the *Book of Enoch*, which points to the possibility that the Biblical Enoch is in fact its author. We've explored the evidence for the book's great age as well as the book's incredible history of survival despite being banned by churchmen and rabbis of various religious groups. We've seen that the *Book of Enoch* is thoroughly Biblical in its world view. In fact, the *Book of Enoch* seems to clarify a number of puzzling passages in our Bibles. Also, the book contains a very high view of the identity and character of the Messiah, along the lines of what we find in what the New Testament says about Jesus. On a related note, the book also contains a number of passages which claim to be prophetic and seem to have come to pass, some of which are Messianic in character. We have also noted that certain New Testament writers seem to accept the *Book of Enoch* as the authentic writings of Enoch.

So what are we to make of all this? If the *Book of Enoch* was written by the Biblical Enoch, this would mean the book would have been in existence and preserved and passed along since the times of the Patriarchs of the Old Testament. Indeed, in the previous chapter we saw there are in fact ancient Jewish traditions which purport to record a kind of history of transmission of the *Book of Enoch* from Abraham to Jacob, and from Jacob to Levi.

If that is the case, were the writings of Enoch considered to be Scripture before Moses and before the prophets of Israel had written their books?

"Enoch Was the First to Write a Testimony"

In the *Book of Jubilees*, a book which can be found in the Bible of the Ethiopian Orthodox Church, an ancient Jewish tradition is preserved in which we read,

> Moses was on the Mount forty days and forty nights, and God taught him the earlier and the later history of the division of all the days of the law and of the testimony. (Jubilees 1:4)

In the above-referenced passage from Jubilees the phrase "the law and the testimony" refers to the body of work which has come down to us today variously referred to as Torah, the Pentateuch and the Law of Moses. Not only did Moses give the children of Israel the Law, but he also left them a testimony to their early history as the foundation for what was to develop and become the 'Tanach' for Jews and Old Testament for Christians.

According to the tradition as preserved in the passage quoted above, God taught Moses the earlier and later history. Part of the earlier history taught to Moses was that Enoch was the,

> First to write a testimony and he testified to the sons of men among the generations of the earth, and recounted the weeks of the jubilees, and made known to them the days of the years, and set in order the months and recounted the Sabbaths of the years as we made them known to him. And what was and what will be he saw in a vision of his sleep, as it will happen to the children of men throughout their generations until the day of judgment; he saw and understood everything, and wrote his testimony, and placed the testimony on earth for all the children of men and for their generations. (Jubilees 4:18-19)

So we are told Enoch did for an earlier generation what Moses was to do in his own. Enoch was the first to write a testimony. The claim is made that just as the five books of Moses comprised a testimony to the people of his day, what we have today in the *Book of Enoch*, a composite of five books penned by Enoch over the course of his earthly sojourn, were to comprise a testimony to the generations which were to come after him. If this is so, the five books of Enoch would have comprised the core of the "Bible" for Abraham, Isaac and Jacob. It is an interesting speculation.

What is sure however, is that the three groups of literature which make up the *Book of Enoch*, the Old Testament, and the New Testament uphold the same message throughout. God loves His creation and intends to restore it through His Son, who is appointed to be its savior.

That these three bodies of literature uphold one another can be demonstrated again from three passages which contain eye-witness accounts to the heavenly worship scene around God's throne. In each of these passages the veil is pulled back and we are given a view of God worshipped by the hosts of Heaven.

Isaiah Sees the Lord

In Isaiah 6, we find,

> In the year King Uzziah died, I saw the Lord sitting upon a throne, high and lifted up; and the train of his robe filled the temple. Above him stood the seraphim. Each had six wings: with two he covered his face, and with two he covered his feet, and with two he flew. And one called to another and said: "Holy, holy, holy is the LORD of hosts; the whole earth is full of his glory!" And the foundations of the thresholds shook at the voice of him who called, and the house was filled with smoke.

John Sees the Lord

In the Revelation to John chapter 4, we read,

> And around the throne, on each side of the throne, are four living creatures, full of eyes in front and behind: the first living creature like a lion, the second living creature like an ox, the third living creature with the face of a man, and the fourth living creature like an eagle in flight. And the four living creatures, each of them with six wings, are full of eyes all around and within, and day and night they never cease to say, "Holy, holy, holy, is the Lord God Almighty, who was and is and is to come!."

Enoch Sees the Lord

In Enoch 39:10-13, we are told,

> For a long time my eyes regarded that place, and I blessed Him and praised Him, saying: 'Blessed is He, and may He be blessed from the beginning and for evermore. And before Him there is no ceasing. He knows before the world was created what is for ever and what will be from generation unto generation. Those who sleep not, bless Thee: they stand before Thy glory and bless, praise, and extol, saying: "Holy, holy, holy, is the Lord of Spirits:[653] He filleth the earth with spirits." And here my eyes saw all those who sleep not:, they stand before Him and bless and say: 'Blessed be Thou, and blessed be the name of the Lord for ever and ever." And my face was changed; for I could no longer behold."

These three passages each claim to be revelation of the heavenly worship scene around the throne of God. Taken together, the three passages attest to the nature of God as revealed in the past, present and future.

The passage from Enoch celebrates He who is holy for *He fills the earth with spirits*. The phrase points to God's work of creation. God is the "Lord of spirits" because he has filled the world with living things in which is the spirit of life. The God of life has populated the earth with the living in which he placed the spirit of life. Here the work of God as creator is celebrated. Enoch celebrates God as creator.

The passage in Isaiah celebrates He who is holy for the whole earth has been filled with His Glory. Here the work of God as redeemer of creation is celebrated. In Solomon's Temple, Isaiah receives the vision of God glorified. God is glorified in the earth as His work of redemption is

---

[653] "Lord of Spirits", this title for God found throughout Enoch's "*Book of the Parables*", reminds us of similar titles used in **Numbers 16:22**, And they fell on their faces and said, 'O God, the God of the spirits of all flesh, shall one man sin, and will you be angry with all the congregation?', and **Hebrews 12:9**, Shall we not much more be subject to the Father of spirits and live?

exemplified by the sacrificial system and temple worship under the Mosaic Covenant. Isaiah celebrates God as redeemer.

The passage from the *Book of Revelation* celebrates He who is holy for He was and is and is to come. According to John, not only is God creator and redeemer, but he is the One who will bring his works of creation and redemption to completion in the Revelation of Jesus Christ, for He is He who was, who is, and who is to come. John celebrates God as he who will bring his creation and redemption to completion.

Holy Is the One Who Was and Is and Is to Come

Holy is the One who did not leave his people without a testimony in the days of Enoch. Holy is the One who did not leave his people Israel without testimony but they were entrusted with the lively oracles of God. Holy is the One who is to come who has given us His testimony of God made flesh.

Though it is not now possible to know whether the patriarchs considered the *Book of Enoch* as Scripture, nevertheless, it is an interesting question that remains unanswered. What *is* known however, is that for most of the past two thousand years, the *Book of Enoch* has been considered Scripture by one or more Christian communities.

13
Why is Enoch Missing from Your Bible?

Sometimes people ask the question, *'why isn't the Book of Enoch in the Bible'*, or *'why was the Book of Enoch removed from the Bible?'*

As it turns out both questions make incorrect assumptions about the history of the *Book of Enoch* and its relationship to the Bible.

Firstly, when we ask *why isn't the Book of Enoch in the Bible,* we are assuming it is not in the Bible.[654] The truth is the *Book of Enoch is* and as far as anyone can tell always has been in the Bible of the Ethiopian Orthodox Church. In fact, it is probable the *Book of Enoch* is the legacy of Falasha Jewry to Orthodox Christianity when the Jews of Ethiopia converted to Orthodoxy.

Secondly, when it is asked, *when was the Book of Enoch removed from the Bible,* one seems to be assuming that in ancient times there existed Bibles bound together which contained all the books, but later the *Book of Enoch* was taken out. In fact, the major churches around the world in the earliest times would have had a collection or library of books written on individual scrolls from which readings would be done for the edification of the people. Among these books would have been those we now have in our Bibles and others we don't. In situations like that, the *Book of Enoch* could not have been removed from Bibles which were not yet bound.

The bottom line is, the evidence indicates that in the first century the *Book of Enoch* was widely circulated and read among Jews as well as Christians. How then, could the book have gone from being so widespread to virtually non-existent in most regions of Christianity?

It's very likely Enoch's predictions gave people living in the first century, hope that theirs was the generation of the last days and that the end of sin was near and the inauguration of a new heavens and earth in which righteousness would reign was soon to come. Enoch chapter 10, had given the generation of Jesus as the time frame in which the angels would be judged, after all.

As time progressed the Second coming of Christ did not rapidly occur and the final judgment Enoch predicted did not speedily come to pass. In this light it is not hard to see how the book would have become of somewhat less interest. Then, long after the early days of the church, the *Book of Enoch* was officially rejected by the Jews when they developed a canon of the Hebrew Scriptures. Then, nearly 300 years later the book

---

[654] When it comes to 'what is in the Bible' one should realize there is not now nor has there ever been a single canonical list of books to which all Christians have agreed to abide. Some churches only decided over time which books were on their "list" due to the on-going usage of certain books in the life of their faith communion.

was also officially rejected by Christians in the Greek and Latin worlds. At the Council of Laodicea in 364 AD, the reading of books in the churches was forbidden unless the book was included in official canonical lists of the books of Scripture. This resulted in the *Book of Enoch* taking a long hiatus from Greek and Latin Christianity.

In those days when books were handwritten, those books which did not circulate were at risk of not being copied and thus not being preserved. That's precisely what happened to Enoch, but not entirely...

The Falasha Jews and later the Orthodox Christians of Ethiopia kept the *Book of Enoch* alive by copying it over the centuries. As a result, this book, thought lost for nearly 1,000 years could later be "rediscovered" by the West when it was found in Ethiopia in the late eighteenth century. Copies of the *Book of Enoch* in an ancient Ethiopian language are the only complete copies of the book in existence today.

Throughout history Ethiopia has had a long and important relationship with Israel. There is the well-known story in the Bible of the Queen of Sheba traveling with her retinue to Israel to hear the wisdom of Solomon. 400 years later we are told that Abimelech the Ethiopian was the one to save Jeremiah the prophet from a miry pit in which he had been imprisoned. In the New Testament the story is recounted of a Jewish Ethiopian eunuch, who was a court official to the queen of Ethiopia, who is visiting Jerusalem for the festival. While this eunuch is reading a personal copy of the *Book of Isaiah,* he is approached by Phillip, evangelized, baptized, and sent back to Ethiopia as a disciple of Jesus. In this way, apparently, Christianity arrived in Ethiopia during the time of the Apostles.

The capital city of Ethiopia was one of the cities of the ancient world, along with Babylon and Alexandria, which became a thriving center for Jews living outside of the land of Israel. It is likely the books of the Bible have been copied and preserved in Ethiopia from very early times, perhaps as early as the time of King Solomon. It was at that time we know the Queen of Sheba returned to Ethiopia carrying gifts she received while visiting Solomon in Jerusalem. It's not too much to say the *Book of Enoch* would have also been in their possession as early as that too.[655]

Praised in the Third Century

Outside of Ethiopia, in the Greek world, one can read quotes and allusions to the *Book of Enoch* in writings from the first centuries of the Church. Many of these speak of the book in a positive light. The following

[655] On a side note, it is interesting to realize, the Jews of Ethiopia today, believe themselves to be descendants of Jews who arrived there after the fall of the Northern kingdom of Israel in 722 BC. They refer to themselves as "Beta Israel", and are black, Jewish-Christians allowed Israeli citizenship when they immigrate to Israel. They include Enoch in their Scriptures.

quote by Tertullian is one example.[656]

> I am aware that the Scripture of Enoch, which has assigned this order (of action) to angels, is not received by some, because it is not admitted into the Jewish canon either...
>
> But since Enoch in the same Scripture has preached likewise concerning the Lord, nothing at all must be rejected by us which pertains to us; and we read that "every Scripture suitable for edification is divinely inspired." By the Jews it may now seem to have been rejected for that (very) reason, just like all the other (portions) nearly which tell of Christ. Nor, of course, is this fact wonderful, that they did not receive some Scriptures which spake of Him whom even in person, speaking in their presence, they were not to receive. To these considerations is added the fact that Enoch possesses a testimony in the Apostle Jude.

Tertullian wrote this in the late second century or early third century. He speaks positively of the *Book of Enoch* as a reliable text of Scripture.

Banned in the Fifth Century

The following quote by Augustine is an example of a negative perspective on the *Book of Enoch* which came to dominate centuries later.

> Let us omit, then, the fables of those scriptures which are called apocryphal, because their obscure origin was unknown to the fathers from whom the authority of the true Scriptures has been transmitted to us by a most certain and well-ascertained succession. For though there is some truth in these apocryphal writings, yet they contain so many false statements, that they have no canonical authority. *We cannot deny that Enoch, the seventh from Adam, left some divine writings*, for this is asserted by the Apostle Jude in his canonical epistle. But it is not without reason that these writings have no place in that canon of Scripture which was preserved in the temple of the Hebrew people by the diligence of successive priests; for *their antiquity brought them under suspicion*, and it was impossible to ascertain whether these were his genuine writings, and they were not brought forward as genuine by the persons who were found to have carefully preserved the canonical books by a successive transmission. So that the writings which are produced under his name, and which contain these fables about the giants, saying that their fathers were not men; are properly judged by prudent men to be not genuine.[657]

---

[656] Tertullian, "On Female Fashion" I, Chapter 2

[657] Augustine, "City of God", I, XV, XXIII

Of interest to the reader is the statement by Augustine that, *"We cannot deny that Enoch, the seventh from Adam, left some divine writings, for this is asserted by the Apostle Jude in his canonical epistle"*. After saying this, Augustine poses the strange justification for rejecting the *Book of Enoch* by saying, the *Book of Enoch* and other books were rejected by the Jews because "their *antiquity brought them under suspicion*". In effect Augustine says, the *Book of Enoch* is too old to verify its origin. It should be noted by the reader that if the rest of the books of the Old Testament were judged by the same standard they too would come under the same umbrella of suspicion. Also, it is well known we do not have an unbroken record of "succession" even now as to how each of the books of the Old Testament were preserved by the Jews.

It may be revealing that just a few sentences later, Augustine apparently reveals the real reason he finds the *Book of Enoch* objectionable, when he writes, *"fables about the giants, saying that their fathers were not men; are properly judged by prudent men to be not genuine."* It seems the old Jewish belief concerning the ability of angels to fall into sins of the flesh is the real reason Augustine rejects the *Book of Enoch*.[658]

The above quote by Augustine is included here to show the likely reason the *Book of Enoch* became a lost book in Greek and Latin Christianity. Influential clerics such as Augustine and Jerome won the day, in no small part it is certain, due to their position and power within Christendom.

So began the *Book of Enoch*'s long hiatus from the bookshelves of the Greek and Latin Churches. The book was removed from the lists of permissible books for reading in the churches within Greek and Latin Christianity.[659] Its scrolls were not copied and preserved and it became a book which was believed lost for more than 1,000 years.

Meanwhile in Ethiopia, where the succession of the text of the *Book of Enoch* was not held in question, and where the concerns of Augustine held little sway, the book was faithfully copied and preserved generation after generation.

After all, if the book was to have a purpose and serve for a blessing to the last generation living in the day of tribulation, it would not do if the book were to vanish entirely from off the world's stage.

---

[658] See chapter 5, "The Sons of God in Genesis 6:1-4" where this question is explored in greater detail.

[659] As an interesting note, there exists a copy of a list of the books of the Bible recognized within Armenian Orthodoxy in the 12th/13th centuries AD. The list includes the *Book of Enoch*. Unfortunately, a copy of the book in Armenian has not survived. Nersessian, Vrej., The Bible in the Armenian Tradition (London: The British Library, 2001), 81.

14
Time-Capsule to the Last Generation: "As It Was in the Days of Noah"

In chapter one of this book, a broad overview of the history of the *Book of Enoch* since the first century was outlined. It was noted that since its rediscovery in the West, there have been stages of increasing reemergence of the book.

- 1773 Recovery by James Bruce
- 1821 First English translation by Richard Laurence
- 1883 Revision by Richard Laurence
- 1893 Second major translation by Robert H Charles
- 1912 Revision by Robert H Charles

To this list we now add:

- 1947 Enoch's book recovered and corroborated by Dead Sea Scrolls
- 1989 Open access to the Dead Sea Scrolls for all researchers

As we have seen there has been a progressively increasing amount of attention paid to the *Book of Enoch* in our world. Is it possible that soon interest in the *Book of Enoch* will explode when a discovery is made which will demand our attention?

The Coming Restoration of the Book of Enoch?

Without a doubt the discovery of a complete, truly ancient copy of the *Book of Enoch* in either Aramaic of Hebrew would be a watershed event in the history of the book. Given the fragmentary state of the Enoch manuscripts we now have from the Dead Sea Scrolls, the discovery of a complete Enoch scroll in one of the languages of the Jews of ancient Israel would be revolutionary for Enoch studies.

In this light, readers may be shocked to know that it has been reported such a scroll has already been found.

In "Understanding the Dead Sea Scrolls", Avi Katzman wrote,

> Regarding the [Dead Sea] scrolls, [John] Strugnell claims at least four other scrolls have been found that have not yet come to light: 'I've seen, with my own eyes, two.' One of the two is *a*

> *complete copy of the Book of Enoch...* These scrolls, like the *Temple Scroll*, came from Cave 11 at Qumran, according to Strugnell. The manuscripts are now "somewhere in Jordan. Various people own them. Several of them have been sold to big bankers. They're investments for these people. There's no point in forcing a sale. If they really need cash- as one seems to now- I have the money."
>
> As for the other two scrolls- the ones Strugnell has not seen- '[Lankester] Harding [the director of Jordan's Department of Antiquities] on his death bed told me he'd seen three, only one of which I've seen- so that makes four.'
>
> Strugnell is not concerned that the scrolls may deteriorate before scholars can look at them: "They're all being kept very carefully; no one need worry about them. They're a better investment than anything on the Israeli or the New York stock exchanges," he added.[660]

Such a find, if and when it comes forward, could catapult the *Book of Enoch* to a renewed status as a legacy of Israel to the world. An ancient copy of the *Book of Enoch* in one of the languages of ancient Israel may pave the way for restoring the book's reputation in the eyes of many and to better poise the book to become a resource of blessing for the last generation living during the coming Great Tribulation period.

We find the following cryptic statement in the *Book of Enoch*,

> When they write down truthfully all my words in their languages, and do not change or minish ought from my words but write them all down truthfully- all that I first testified concerning them. *Then, I know another mystery, that books will be given to the righteous and the wise to become a cause of joy and uprightness and much wisdom. And to them shall the books be given, and they shall believe in them* and rejoice over them, and then shall all the righteous who have learnt therefrom all the paths of uprightness be recompensed. (Enoch 104:11-13)

In this passage is Enoch simply predicting his books' preservation and survival over the millennia, or, is Enoch saying that his books will have a startling restoration in the last days?

Until then, it is the sure message of the *Book of Enoch* that a time of crisis like that of Enoch's day will come upon everyone living on earth at the end of the age.

---

[660] Shanks, H., Understanding the Dead Sea Scrolls: a Reader from the Biblical Archaeology Review (New York: Random House, 1992), 262.

The First End

According to Enoch 93:4, the flood of Noah's day should be understood as "the first end" for planet earth. Also according to Enoch, *there will be a second end* on planet earth which will share many characteristics in common with earth's first end. Before the coming of Christ, earth will experience a time similar to the time before the flood of Noah's day.

In Enoch 91, the relation between earth's first and second "ends" is highlighted. After describing the flood of Noah's day as an event by which "all unrighteousness will come to an end", (v.5), Enoch says, "unrighteousness shall again be consummated on the earth", (v.6). He also says, "deeds of unrighteousness, violence and transgression shall prevail in a *twofold degree*." According to Enoch, the time just prior to earth's second end will be twice as bad as the time before earth's first end, a time when the Watchers and their offspring were wreaking havoc on earth. The difference between the time just before earth's first and second ends is essentially a difference in magnitude, not kind.

"As Were the Days of Noah... "

This similarity described by Enoch between the time before the flood and the time before the Second-coming of Christ, was restated by Jesus Christ when he said,

> As were the days of Noah, so will be the coming of the Son of Man. For as in those days before the flood they were eating and drinking, marrying and giving in marriage, until the day when Noah entered the ark, and they were unaware until the flood came and swept them all away, so will be the coming of the Son of Man. (Matthew 24:37-39)

On a superficial level, Jesus seems to call up a picture of a future time in which people are merely oblivious to coming judgment and continue with the commonplaces of life, the ordinary activities of eating, drinking, and marrying. In this case however, context means everything. Matthew 24:37-39, coming as it does in the middle of Christ's Olivet Discourse cannot imply a time of blissful ignorance on earth, rather, Christ has just finished painting a picture of that time in which the persecution of Christ's followers will be worldwide. It is also a time in which "lawlessness shall increase", and "the love of many will grow cold", (v.12). Christ's teaching about the time before the end of the age is not one in which people will be reveling in the ordinariness of the activities of life. As it turns out, Christ has given us a key to understanding the last days... it will be as it was "in the days of Noah."

When we consider that the story about the Watchers and their offspring was commonly known to folks living in Jesus' day, his words would have taken on a more ominous tone in the ears of his hearers than we might initially assume, *"as were the days of Noah, so will be the coming of the Son of Man. For as in those days before the flood they were eating and drinking, marrying and giving in marriage, until the day when Noah entered the ark."* In the Enochan saga all these commonplace activities of life had been perverted and corrupted. God's original ordination of marriage had been redefined by the Watchers, and their children were blood drinkers and cannibals.[661] The commonplaces of life had been defiled and turned diabolical. The consistent message of Enoch and Jesus is the last days will be a time of extreme trial for the faithful living in those days. However, as always is true during times of testing, the grace of God is available to those who will call upon it.

A Message of Deliverance in the Last Days

In Matthew 24:16, Jesus instructs believing Jews living in Jerusalem and Judea to flee to *the mountains* when they see the abomination of desolation in the temple in the end times. If Revelation 12:14, is to be understood as describing the same period of time, a remnant of Israel will be given "the wings of the eagle." In ancient Jewish literature, the phrase *"the wings of the eagle"* is used as a metaphor for God's supernatural deliverance from harm. The term is first used in Exodus 19:4, which describes God's deliverance of the Jews at the time of Exodus, "You yourselves have seen what I did to the Egyptians, and how I bore you on eagles' wings and brought you to myself.." In Revelation 12:14, a last days remnant of believing Jews is to be kept and protected in *"the wilderness."* Jesus' instruction in Matthew 24, says the place of protection will be in the mountains, and in Revelation 12 it is in the wilderness. At that time believing Jews in Israel will flee to mountains in the wilderness to a place which will become obvious to them at that time. There they will be protected and prepared. They will be protected from Satan's efforts to destroy them through the political system of earth's final Antichrist and False Prophet. They will be prepared to invite Christ to return to earth to be their deliverer. To this generation on the run, Enoch corroborates the broad details.

> On the day of the tribulation of the sinners, your children will mount up and ascend like eagles, and higher than the vultures will be your nest; you will climb up and enter the crevices of the earth and the clefts of the rock forever, like conies, before the lawless. And they will sigh because of you and weep. (Enoch 96:2 Nickelsburg-Vanderkam)

The blessing promised by Enoch to the righteous living under the conditions of that time, will be to encourage them that they *will* indeed survive this horrific time because God's assurance of this was recorded and passed down to them from many thousands of years in the past. They will have these assurances in the Bible and these assurances in

---

[661] **Enoch 7:1-6**

Enoch that theirs is the generation which will live to see the deliverance of Israel by means of the Second coming of Christ.

As we have seen the Dead Sea Scrolls are a kind of time-capsule. Some of those scrolls were packed in clay jars, and wrapped in linen like grave cloths. The Dead Seas Scroll discovery occurred simultaneously with the rebirth of Israel. The Dead Sea Scrolls have demonstrated the ancient existence of the *Book of Enoch* with its message of hope passed down to the last generation.

All Israel Will Be Saved

How is the *Book of Enoch* to become a blessing to the last generation, to those *"who will be living in the day of tribulation"*? What more of a blessing can there be than to become chosen by God in his Elect One, Yeshua the Messiah of Israel. There is in fact no greater blessing than coming to know God through His Elect Son. The *Book of Enoch* will undoubtedly be a factor contributing to this grand event at that time.

A curious passage from the *Book of Enoch* in a section we call the "Prophecy of Weeks" reads,

> At [the] close [of the seventh week] shall be elected the elect righteous of the eternal plant of righteousness, to receive sevenfold instruction concerning all His creation. (Enoch 93:10)

It is curious that the passage says the elect will become elected. How can those already chosen become chosen? The answer is startling.

The passage is from a lengthy section which refers to the Plant of Righteousness, which is a recurrent theme in Enoch's book. The Plant of Righteousness is a reference to the children who descended from Abraham, Isaac and Jacob, the elect or chosen people of God. The prophecy states the chosen people will become doubly chosen.

The Hebrew prophets foresaw a time when all the people of Israel from the greatest to the least will come to know God and to be in right relationship to him. In the New Testament the Apostle Paul also foresaw this event when he wrote, *"all Israel will be saved"* (Romans 11:26). At some time in earth's future the world will be rocked by an amazing event which is destined to occur... The Chosen people will also become chosen in the Beloved One of God, Jesus the eternal Son of the Father, and thus all Israel *will* be saved.

The nation who introduced Jesus Christ to the world will themselves be introduced to their Messiah, through in part, rediscovering Enoch's ancient witness to Yeshua the Messiah, the Elect Righteous One, the Son of Man. In this way the chosen people will be doubly chosen by reason of their election into Israel's Messiah. This earth-shattering event will set the stage for the return of Jesus to earth. *"Now if their trespass means riches for the world, and if their failure means riches for the Gentiles, how much more will their full inclusion mean!"* (Romans 11:12) The coming regeneration of Israel, long envisioned by the prophets, will signal the soon coming Messianic age, a golden age for earth and the end of Satan's rule over the affairs of humankind.

We can now say, the implication of the first few verses of the *Book of Enoch* is the *Book of Enoch itself* is destined to play a role in the coming spiritual rebirth of the people of Israel. By reason of their reading Enoch's book it will become a source of the greatest blessing of all upon the people of Abraham, Isaac and Jacob, who will also become the people of Jesus the Messiah.

In Hosea 5:15, God through the mouth of the prophet declared,

> I will return again to my place, until they acknowledge their guilt and seek my face, and in their distress earnestly seek me.

For God to return to his place necessitates that he had left it. When in history past did God ever come forth from his place? God came forth from his place in heaven when he came to earth as the Jewish man, Jesus of Nazareth. Jesus was not declared to be the promised Messiah of Israel by that generation of the religious leaders of the nation. When Jesus ascended back to his Father he returned again to his place in heaven. The sure promise of Hosea is Jesus will return as deliverer of Israel when at some time yet future *they acknowledge their guilt and seek his face, and in their distress earnestly seek him.* When all Israel turns to God's Son in faith, then all Israel will be saved and Jesus will come again to deliver them in their day of tribulation. The *Book of Enoch* is a time-capsule to the last generation of Israel who will find themselves faced with unparalleled evil in the embodiment of the Antichrist and False Prophet.[662] Both Old and New Testaments predict an attempt will be made to destroy all the people of Israel. In their distress they will turn to God in repentance and putting faith in Jesus their savior they will cry out to him for deliverance from evil.

Epilogue

In the grand scope of time and eternity outlined in the Bible and the *Book of Enoch*-- in the tragic aftermath of the sin of God's creatures, there has been given to no creature other than human beings the opportunity for repentance, faith and salvation. Neither cherub, nor angel nor any other fallen creature has ever been offered the opportunity for repentance, only humankind.

We should treasure, then, God's gift of repentance as a singular gift from our Creator. No matter how bad we've become, no matter how far we've wandered, no matter how deep we have sunk in our depravity, God will

---

[662] **Revelation 13**

welcome any and all who will lift their heart to Him and pray that ancient prayer, "Lord Jesus Christ, Son of God, have mercy on me, a sinner."

The Scripture teaches us when we move toward God, away from sin, in a spirit of repentance, the angels experience joy in God's presence. Their joy is no doubt due to the singular wonder in all God's creation which is a sinner recovered by the grace of God.

Because of the crucifixion of Jesus Christ, he has become our sacrificial lamb that turns aside the wrath of God when we put our trust in him. Yeshua HaMashiach, our Passover lamb has been sacrificed. Let us enter in his gates, therefore, with thanksgiving in our hearts, for Jesus is indeed the lamb of God who takes away the sin of all the world!

It is hoped that everyone who reads this book will be inspired to treasure this good gift given only to mankind among all God's creatures. Not to treasure this gift would be the highest tragedy of all if we should neglect so great a salvation.

This book is offered in prayer that all who read its pages will find the secret of this wonderful gift, and especially those who find themselves in the last generation, who will find God's promise is true when he said, *"I will return again to my place, until they acknowledge their guilt and seek my face, and in their distress earnestly seek me."*

Appendix I Objections Answered

Since 2006, I have been involved in quite a few online discussions concerning the *Book of Enoch*. Over this time I have heard a number of reasons people have put forward that the *Book of Enoch* should not be considered of value for today. It has been my uniform experience that most of these arguments arise due to incorrect information about the book which has circulated.

In a sense, the entire book, *"Who Really Wrote the Book of Enoch?"*, can be read as my response to the many objections I have seen over the years. This section is included to cover some points which deserve further clarifying. In the following few pages I will restate some of the most frequently recurring arguments as well as the responses I have often given to them.

Objection 1. "Just because the Letter of Jude quotes one passage from the Book of Enoch, does not mean Jude endorsed the whole book. In the New Testament, Paul too, quotes from non-Biblical books without endorsing the whole books or their authors."

This is true, but it should be noted that Jude does not simply quote Enoch, but rather says, *"Enoch prophesied"*. That Paul quotes some non-Biblical sources because they include valid statements is not the same. (For a much fuller response to this important objection, see page 214, in *Who Really Wrote the Book of Enoch?*)

Objection 2. "All of the copies of the Book of Enoch that have been found do not agree with the Jude quote exactly word for word."

It is the claim of this person that the copies of the *Book of Enoch* which survive have become so corrupt over time, that we cannot now know the contents of the original book. I do not think that is an accurate portrayal of the situation.

The English translation of Enoch's book included in this volume, was translated and revised by Robert Henry Charles in 1912. It is mainly based upon texts in Geez, a Semitic language of Ethiopia. Over the past 2,000-years, these Ethiopic texts followed the following transmission path:

From Aramaic > into Greek > into Geez

The text of Enoch which was used by Jude in the New Testament *Letter of Jude*, probably followed a transmission path like this:

From Aramaic > into Greek

How careful were the Ethiopian translators and copyists with the text of Enoch over the past 2,000 years? You be the judge. The following are both examples translated into English:

Enoch 1:9 (R. H. Charles):

> Behold! **He** cometh with ten thousands of His holy ones,[663] to execute judgment upon all, **and to destroy** all the ungodly: and to convict all **flesh** of all the works of their ungodliness which they have ungodly committed, and of all the hard **things** which ungodly sinners have spoken against Him.

Jude 1:14-15 (ESV):

> Behold, **the Lord** cometh with ten thousands of His saints, to execute judgment upon all, and to convince all that are ungodly **among them** of all their ungodly deeds which they have ungodly committed, and of all their hard **speeches** which ungodly sinners have spoken against him.

Two different transmission routes which diverged around 1,500-years ago and yet the resulting translations into English are remarkably close to one another. That's the sort of differences we see with the texts we use of the books of the Bible to create our modern translations. The Ethiopic texts which we have today deserve a high degree of respect as being reliable examples of the original book. After R. H. Charles' day, a truly ancient copy of the text of Enoch 1:9 was found in Aramaic in the Dead Sea Scrolls. The parchment upon which the above-referenced verse survives has been dated to the third century BC which is more than 1,000 years older than anything else we have. Not only that, it is more ancient than most other surviving texts of the books of the Bible.

These facts which have come to our attention over the past 30 or so years, debunk the old theory put forth by some scholars in an earlier era, that the entire Ethiopic *Book of Enoch* was a forgery written to provide a background for the one verse in Jude. Amazingly, some sites on the Internet (such as Blue Letter Bible at the time of this writing), still perpetuate this disproved view.

---

[663] **"Holy ones"**; the term "holy ones", is synonymous with "saints". The New Testament uses the term "saint" to describe the rank-and-file follower of Jesus; it does not apply to a special or elevated class of believer.

Jude and 1 Enoch as we have it are in fundamental agreement.

Current Misinformation

Many of the old ideas that place doubt in the trustworthiness of Ethiopic Enoch, continue to have an extended life on internet discussion boards. For instance, one person wrote the following,

> *"A number of somewhat different versions have been found including some with the Dead Sea Scrolls. The versions are different from one another and no one can agree which one is the original."*

The quote above is not an accurate portrayal of the facts. The only complete copies of the *Book of Enoch*, (also known as *1 Enoch, Ethiopic Enoch*, and the *Book of the Words of Enoch*), are in one Ethiopic language. The versions of the Ethiopic texts which we have are not widely different from each other. The process by which R. H. Charles arrived at a text for translation purposes is like the process which is used for the preparing the texts of the Bible.

Nevertheless, one continues to read the concerns of writers that the "versions" of Enoch that are out there are very different from one another. I have tried repeatedly to discover why this myth is so persistent. Usually I find people are simply repeating what they have heard or read somewhere. As it occurs to me, I can think of two reasons why this idea seems to have a life of its own and refuses to die.

Richard Laurence's Misfire

In the early 19th century, Richard Laurence was the first to publish a translation of the *Book of Enoch* into English. It was Laurence's conviction that the *Book of Enoch* was greatly disordered and would best be served if his translation reordered the passages to the proper sequence he envisioned. He also renumbered the chapters and verses throughout. The result of this as well as his translation work, was less than satisfactory.

The Laurence translation is still widely available and his chapter numbering and versification are widely different from most other translations that have been published since then. I have personally witnessed the confusion this can cause. If two persons are discussing and citing passages from Enoch, yet only one of them is using the Laurence translation the results can be confusing. The perception can be created that "there are different versions" of the *Book of Enoch*. This impression can be especially severe because those who refer to Laurence's translation often do not realize the versification problem exists.

Other "Books of Enoch"

There is another element that causes confusion for some. There are two other compositions in circulation which also bear Enoch's name. There is an entirely different book referred to by scholars as *2 Enoch*, also known as *Slavonic Enoch* and *The Book of the Secrets of Enoch*. The oldest texts of the book are only available in the Slavonic language. There exists no clear ancient mention of this book outside of itself, it was not found in the Dead Sea Scrolls, and it is not the book alluded to repeatedly in the New Testament.

There is also a *3 Enoch*. That book claims for itself to have been written by a Rabbi Ishmael, and it too is an entirely different book with no ancient mention outside of itself.

It is possible the contents of these other books have been read by some who thought they were reading the *Book of Enoch* referred to in the Bible. This could be the source of some misunderstandings.

Other Obstacles

Once it has been determined that we are discussing the correct *Book of Enoch* which was referred to by Jude, and once we've eliminated the versification problem introduced by the Richard Laurence translation, there sometimes can be resistance to accepting the book as being legitimate on any level. One person wrote me,

> *"Jude did not quote all of the material written in the Book of Enoch. Even a fraud may present some truth, and Jude recognized this. One quote does not mean Jude endorsed the entire Book of Enoch."*

There is an element of truth in that statement, however, there are some details not taken into account by this poster. It is true Jude did not quote the whole *Book of Enoch*. In fact, Jude didn't even say he *was* quoting the *Book of Enoch*. Jude says rather he is quoting Enoch the man, descended 7th from Adam. And where do we know Jude got that quote? Jude quoted Enoch 1:9. The idea that Jude under inspiration of the Holy Spirit would knowingly take one verse from a book written by someone other than Enoch, and quote that one verse as if it were the very words of Enoch, is a problem.

Also, Jude would have known the book to which he referred was very popular and in wide circulation. Enoch was widely known in Israel and among Jews in the 1st century. Jude quotes from the book to highlight a prophecy to be fulfilled at the Second coming of Jesus Christ. Jude says he is quoting the ancient patriarch and prophet Enoch, when he quotes that book. Many of Jude's readers would also no doubt be familiar with the book from which Jude was quoting. The unmistakable impression would be left by Jude, that the *Book of Enoch* was indeed a book written by the antediluvian patriarch, Enoch. There really is no way to wiggle out of it... Jude leaves his readers with the impression the *Book of Enoch* was written by the Biblical Enoch.

Further, it has been demonstrated that the book from which Jude quoted, survives to this day. The version of the *Book of Enoch* which has survived has been demonstrated by modern scholarship to be a faithful rendition of the original book which was circulated among the Jews in the days of Jesus and the Apostles.

Objection 3. "Jude is not quoting the Book of Enoch. Rather, both Jude and the Book of Enoch are quoting a common oral tradition."

This argument seems to ignore the context of the times of the Apostle Jude. By the time Jude wrote his epistle, the *Book of Enoch* had already been a popular widely-known book, and had been for centuries. For Jude to be quoting an oral tradition and not the book bearing Enoch's name, Jude would be negligent to warn his readers that he was not quoting the book they knew, but rather that Jude was referring to an entirely different Enochan source *which just happened to have identical words.*

In addition, when one considers that Jude actually refers to the *Book of Enoch* not once, but as many as seven times in the course of his tiny epistle, this argument seems even more improbable. This is dealt with in greater detail beginning on page 214.

These and many more objections to the *Book of Enoch* are in circulation. The number of objections I've heard seems endless. For many, there seems to be a vague fear of this book. These objections are included here since they seem to have a bearing on whether the *Book of Enoch* we have today can be seen as the same book used by Jude, and whether the Biblical person Enoch could have written it.

II
Reordering the Prophecy of Weeks

The Prophecy of Weeks in Enoch 91 and 93 is a prophecy that breaks down the whole of earth's history into a summary of ten epochs referred to as "weeks."

The Prophecy of Weeks specifically concerns itself with the "Plant of uprightness" (93:2), also known as the "plant of righteous judgment" (93:5) and the "plant of righteousness" (93:10); the Prophecy of Weeks is not exactly a history of the world or mankind then, but it is actually about the family line that passed through Abraham and Isaac to those descending from Jacob. From the time of Abraham, in week three, it is a history of the people of Israel over the entire time-span of the world.

A curious aspect of the Prophecy of Weeks is that it is disordered in the *Book of Enoch.* Weeks eight through ten are found in chapter 91, and weeks one through seven come later in chapter 93.

The following is the entire Prophecy of Weeks placed in its proper order with explanatory notes as appropriate.

93 And after that Enoch both gave and began to recount from the books. 2And Enoch said:

"Concerning the children of righteousness and concerning the elect of the world,
And concerning the plant of uprightness, I will speak these things,
Yea, I, Enoch will declare them unto you, my sons:

"According to that which appeared to me in the heavenly vision,
And which I have known through the word of the holy angels,
And have learnt from the heavenly tablets."

Week One: Enoch's Era

3And Enoch began to recount from the books and said:
"I was born the seventh in the first week,
While judgment and righteousness still endured.[664]

[664] **"While judgment and righteousness still endured"**; though the fall of the Watchers had occurred during Enoch's father's lifetime, during Enoch's day the world had not yet sunk down so low as the later time when the world became totally corrupt. Enoch's proclamation of judgment to the Watchers in Enoch 13, may have been as many as eight centuries prior to its having been carried out.

Week Two: Noah's Time and the Flood

4 "And after me there shall arise in the second week great wickedness,
And deceit shall have sprung up;
And in it there shall be the first end.

"And in it a man shall be saved;[665]
And after it is ended unrighteousness shall grow up,
And a law shall be made for the sinners.[666]

Week Three: Abraham Is Raised Up

5"And after that in the third week at its close
A man shall be elected as the plant of righteous judgment,[667]
And his posterity shall become the plant of righteousness for evermore.

Week Four: Moses' Law and the Tabernacle

6"And after that in the fourth week, at its close,
Visions of the holy and righteous shall be seen,
And a law for all generations and an enclosure shall be made for them.[668]

Week Five: Solomon's Temple

7"And after that in the fifth week, at its close,
The house of glory and dominion[669] shall be built for ever.

Week Six: Apostasy, Christ's Ascension, Temple Destroyed

8"And after that in the sixth week all who live in it shall be blinded,[670]
And the hearts of all of them shall godlessly forsake wisdom.

---

665 **Noah**

666 **"A law shall be made for the sinners"**; after having landed the ark in safety, Noah, through revelation, delivered a kind of universal law for his descendants which was in effect until the time of Moses. **Genesis 8**

667 Here Abraham is the one "elected" or chosen as the plant of righteous judgment; from Abraham comes the "plant of righteousness", Abraham's offspring through Isaac then Jacob. The verse says the plant of righteousness is for evermore. God's plans for his people Israel, the descendants of Jacob, have never been set aside.

668 **"A law for all generations and an enclosure"**; in other words, the law of Moses and the tabernacle in the wilderness.

669 **"The house of glory and dominion"**; in other words the temple in Jerusalem and the Davidic throne. It "shall be built forever"; despite temporary periods of time during which the temple is not standing (as in 93:8) or when there is no Davidic kingdom, the promise of their restoration remains unchanged. In our time, there is no earthly temple, and Christ the root and branch of David is enthroned in heaven; both the earthly temple and the throne will have restoration at the return of Christ.

670 **"Shall be blinded"**; the sin of unbelief is highlighted here. Jesus Christ came to his own and his own did not recognize him.

"And in it a man shall ascend;[671]
And at its close the house of dominion shall be burnt with fire,[672]
And the whole race of the chosen root shall be dispersed.[673]

Week Seven: The Church Age

9"And after that in the seventh week shall an apostate generation arise,
And many shall be its deeds,
And all its deeds shall be apostate.[674]

10"And at its close shall be elected[675]
The elect righteous of the eternal plant of righteousness,
To receive sevenfold instruction concerning all His creation.

Week Eight: Messianic Age

91 12"And after that there shall be another, the eighth week, that of righteousness, And a sword shall be given to it that a righteous judgment may be executed on the oppressors,
And sinners shall be delivered into the hands of the righteous.

13"And at its close they shall acquire houses through their righteousness,
And a house shall be built for the Great King in glory for evermore,

Week Nine: Great White Throne Judgment

14"And after that, in the ninth week,
The righteous judgment shall be revealed to the whole world,

---

[671] **"In it a man shall ascend";** the language is reminiscent of the catching away of Enoch, but here it is a prophecy of the ascension of Christ. **Acts 1:9**, And when he had said these things, as they were looking on, he was lifted up, and a cloud took him out of their sight.
[672] **"The house of dominion shall be burnt with fire"**; this is the house of dominion mentioned in 93:7. **Matthew 24:1-2**, Jesus left the temple and was going away, when his disciples came to point out to him the buildings of the temple. But he answered them, "You see all these, do you not? Truly, I say to you, there will not be left here one stone upon another that will not be thrown down." The stones were thrown down by the Romans in order to scrape the gold from between them which had melted and run down when the temple was burned.
[673] **"The whole race of the chosen root shall be dispersed"**; **Luke 21:24**, They will fall by the edge of the sword and be led captive among all nations, and Jerusalem will be trampled underfoot by the Gentiles, until the times of the Gentiles are fulfilled.
[674] **"Apostate"** here means a defection from the God of Israel. Because of the rejection of Jesus, the Messiah of Israel, by the religious leaders of the Jews, the God of Israel had been also rejected. Jesus said, "no one comes to the father but by me", John 14:6
[675] **"At its close shall be elected the elect righteous of the eternal plant of righteousness"**; The nation who introduced Jesus Christ to the world will themselves be introduced to their Messiah. In this way the chosen people will be doubly chosen by reason of their election into Israel's Messiah. This earth-shattering event will set the stage for the return of Jesus to earth. The regeneration of Israel, long prophesied by the prophets, will signal the soon coming Messianic age, a golden age on earth and the end of Satan's rule over the affairs of humankind. **Romans 11:26**, "In this way all Israel will be saved."

And all the works of the godless shall vanish from all the earth,
And the world shall be written down for destruction.
And all mankind shall look to the path of uprightness.

Week Ten: New Heavens and New Earth

15"And after this, in the tenth week in the seventh part,
There shall be the great eternal judgment,
In which He will execute vengeance amongst the angels.

16"And the first heaven shall depart and pass away,
And a new heaven shall appear,
And all the powers of the heavens shall give sevenfold light.

The Eternal Order

17"And after that there will be many weeks without number for ever,
And all shall be in goodness and righteousness,
And sin shall no more be mentioned forever.

III
Enoch's Names of God and of Christ

The number of names we apply to things tells us something of how important they are to us. The Bible records many names of God. The *Book of Enoch* also contains many names or titles for God. Some of these names can be found in the Bible also, some are unique to the *Book of Enoch.*

Eternal God	1:4
Eternal King	25:3, 25:5, 25:7, 27:3
Eternal Lord	58:4
Fountain of Life	96:6
Fountain of Righteousness	48:1
God of Glory	25:7
God of gods	9:4
God of the Ages	9:4
Great & Honored & Mighty One	103:1
Great Glory	14:20, 102:3
Great King	84:5, 91:13
Great Lord	81:3
Great One	14:2, 103:4, 104:1, 104:9
Head of Days	46:2, 47:3, 48:2, 55:1, 60:2, 71:10, 71:12, 71:13,
	71:14
Holy Great One	1:3, 10:1, 14:1, 25:3, 84:1, 92:2, 98:6
Holy One	1:2, 93:11
King of Glory	81:3
King of Kings	9:4, 84:2
King of the Ages	12:3
Lord of Glory	22:14, 25:3, 27:3, 27:5, 36:4, 40:3, 63:2, 75:3,
	83:8
Lord of Heaven	13:4, 106:11
Lord of Judgment	83:11
Lord of Kings	63:2, 63:4
Lord of Lords	9:4
Lord of Majesty	12:3
Lord of Righteousness	23:14, 90:40, 106:3
Lord of Spirits	84 times in chapters 37-71
Lord of the Ages	9:4
Lord of the Mighty	63:2
Lord of the Rich	63:2
Lord of the Sheep	29 times in chapters 37-71
Lord of Wisdom	63:2
Most High	9:3, 10:1, 46:7, 60:1, 60:22, 62:7, 77:1, 94:8,
	97:2, 98:7, 98:11, 99:3, 99:10, 100:4, 101:1,
	101:6, 101:8
His Anointed	48:10, 52:4
The Elect One	39:6, 40:5, 45:3, 45:4, 49:2, 49:4, 51:3, 51:5,
	52:6, 52:9, 53:6, 55:4, 61:5, 61:8, 61:11, 62:1
The Righteous One	38:2, 92:3
My Son	105:2
The Son of Man	46:2, 46:3, 46:4, 48:2, 60:10, 62:5, 62:7, 62:9,
	62:14, 63:11, 69:26, 69:27, 69:29, 70:1, 71:14,
	71:17

IV
A Chronological Book of Enoch

The fact the *Book of Enoch* is a compilation of five separate books, means it cannot be read from beginning to end as a chronology of the events it recounts. Add to this that the book employs a number of literary devices such as the use of flashbacks, time-compression and the retelling of events and the reader is faced with a real challenge in understanding the sequence of events of the book.

Nevertheless, it is possible to rearrange the book's contents in order to recreate a chronology of the events it relates. Here is one possible reordering of the *Book of Enoch* in chronological order.

The years indicated below are a possible reconstruction of the *Book of Enoch*'s timeline when taken in the context of the relative dates in Genesis 5. The dates below are listed in terms of the approximate years before the flood of Noah's day.

Years before Flood	**Event**	**Passage**
-1050 or so	The Descent of the Watchers	Enoch 6:1-7:2
-1050 thru 0	The Demoralization of Mankind	7:3-8:4
-1033	Birth of Enoch	Genesis 5
-650	Enoch receives 2 dream-visions before being called	83:1-90:42
-671	Enoch's call to ministry	12:1-6
-671	Enoch's first address to the Watchers	13:1-3
-671	Enoch sent to deliver the Watcher's petition to God	13:4-6
-671	Enoch receives God's response in a dream-vision	13:7-10
-671	Enoch receives the *Geocentric Calendar Book*	33:2-4, 72:1-81:4
-671	Enoch's second address to the Watchers	14:1-36:4
-670	Enoch given one year to wrap up his affairs	81:5-10
-670	Enoch gives charge to Methuselah	82:1-20
-670	Enoch gives charge to his family	91:1-105:2, 108:1-15
-670	Enoch recaps his taking up his oracle	1:1-3
-670	Enoch summarizes the burden of his message	2:1-5:9
-670	Enoch receives another dream-vision	37:1-59:3
-669	Enoch is translated	70:1-4
-600	The Uncanny birth of Noah	106:1-107:3
-120	The holy angels entreat God to act	9:1-11
-120	God commands the preparation of Noah's ark	10:1-3
-120	God commands the binding of Azazel	10:4-8
-120 thru 0	The Nephilim judged by war	10:9-10
-2	Noah visits heaven	71:1-17
-2	Noah receives the *Book of the Parables* from Enoch	68:1
-1	Noah completes the *Book of the Parables*	60:1-69:29
-1	Death of Methuselah	Genesis 5
-1	Noah Acquires Enoch's books	60:1-69:29
0	The remaining Watchers are bound	10:11-16
0	Noah's family enters ark, the flood arrives	Genesis 6
+?	The Second Coming of Christ	1:3-9
+?	The Messianic kingdom	10:17-11:2

V
Index of Scriptures Used in this Volume

Isaiah 42:1	.....	Enoch 40:5
42:1	.....	45:3
44:3	.....	91:1
45:23	.....	10:21
45:23	.....	48:5
53:11	.....	38:2
53:11	.....	53:6
53:11	.....	92:3
66:1	.....	84:2
66:24	.....	46:6
Jeremiah 2:13	.....	96:6
9:1	.....	95:1
10:13	.....	41:4
17:5	.....	63:7
32:17	.....	84:3
51:16	.....	41:4
Lamentations 4:13	.....	47:1
4:13	.....	47:2
4:13	.....	47:4
Ezekiel 1:16	.....	14:18
1:16-18	.....	61:10
1:16-18	.....	71:7
1:26	.....	18:8
28:14	.....	71:1
28:16	.....	71:1
34:7-10	.....	89:59
39:29	.....	91:1
Daniel 2:20	.....	61:11
4:13	.....	1:5
4:13	.....	11:3
4:17	.....	1:5
4:17	.....	11:3
4:23	.....	1:5
4:23	.....	11:3
5:27	.....	41:1
7:9	.....	46:1
7:9	.....	60:2
7:9-10	.....	47:3
7:10	.....	14:19
7:10	.....	14:22
7:10	.....	40:1
7:10	.....	60:1
7:10	.....	71:8
7:13	.....	46:2
7:22	.....	53:7
8:17-18	.....	60:3
9:24	.....	108:2
11:35	.....	108:9
12:1	.....	20:5
12:2	.....	91:10
12:3	.....	38:4
12:3	.....	104:2
12:13	.....	27:4
Hosea 5:15	.....	Enoch 1:3
5:15	.....	77:1
Joel 2:1-2	.....	94:9
2:28-29	.....	91:1
Micah 1:3-4	.....	1:6
1:4	.....	52:6
Zechariah 3:1	.....	40:7
7:14	.....	89:40
7:14	.....	90:20
12:2-4	.....	56:7
Malachi 1:6-7	.....	89:73
3:13	.....	1:9
3:17	.....	1:8
Matthew 5:5	.....	5:6
5:5	.....	5:7
5:5	.....	45:5
5:10	.....	95:7
5:10	.....	104:2
5:10	.....	108:10
8:29	.....	16:1
10:33	.....	48:10
11:25	.....	48:7
12:36	.....	104:7
12:43	.....	15:11
17:1-2	.....	106:2
17:2	.....	14:20
17:2	.....	39:14
18:10	.....	104:1
19:28	.....	55:4
19:28	.....	108:12
19:29	.....	40:9
22:13	.....	10:4
22:13	.....	22:11
22:30	.....	15:7
23:29-31	.....	95:7
23:35	.....	47:1
23:35	.....	47:2
23:35	.....	47:4
23:37	.....	95:1
24:1-2	.....	93:8
24:12	.....	91:7
24:21	.....	91:7
24:35	.....	69:29
25:31	.....	45:3
25:31	.....	62:5
24:36-37	.....	16:3
25:41	.....	10:14
25:41	.....	21:10
25:41	.....	38:1
25:41	.....	54:5
25:41	.....	67:7
26:24	.....	38:2
26:29	.....	62:14

THE BOOK OF ENOCH

Matthew 28:18	.....	Enoch 92:4
Mark 4:22	.....	98:6
9:47-48	.....	46:6
13:19	.....	103:7
Luke 1:52	.....	46:4
2:30-32	.....	48:4
3:23-38	.....	10:12
6:24-26	.....	94:8
8:30-31	.....	16:1
9:35	.....	39:6
9:35	.....	40:5
9:35	.....	45:3
10:20	.....	104:1
12:3	.....	98:7
12:3	.....	104:8
12:9	.....	48:10
12:19-21	.....	97:8
12:32	.....	37:4
12:32	.....	39:9
12:32	.....	48:7
12:32	.....	49:3
15:10	.....	51:4
15:10	.....	104:4
16:26	.....	22:9
17:26	.....	7:6
20:34-36	.....	15:7
21:24	.....	93:8
21:26	.....	1:5
21:28	.....	51:2
23:35	.....	39:6
23:35	.....	40:5
23:35	.....	45:3
John 1:3	.....	48:3
1:4	.....	58:3
1:12	.....	48:7
1:12	.....	50:3
1:14	.....	46:1
2:15	.....	48:7
3:36	.....	55:3
5:22	.....	41:9
5:22	.....	69:27
5:27	.....	41:9
5:27	.....	69:27
6:44	.....	48:7
8:12	.....	58:3
10:11	.....	90:20
14:1	...	92:2
14:2	...	39:5
14:2	...	41:2
14:2-3	...	71:16
14:23	...	105:2
14:27	...	92:2
17:2	...	92:4
19:11	...	89:60
Acts 1:9	.....	Enoch 93:8
2:33	.....	91:1
3:14	.....	38:2
3:14	.....	53:6
3:14	.....	92:3
4:12	.....	48:7
4:12	.....	50:3
7:52-53	.....	38:2
7:52-53	.....	53:6
7:52-53	.....	92:3
8:1	.....	46:8
10:3-4	.....	99:3
10:45	.....	91:1
13:2	.....	12:3
26:19	.....	93:2
Romans 1:24	.....	89:60
1:26	.....	89:60
1:28	.....	89:60
2:11	.....	63:8
2:16	.....	49:3
3:10	.....	81:5
3:23	.....	81:5
8:19	.....	38:1
8:38-39	.....	71:17
9:5	.....	77:1
11:26	.....	93:10
13:1	.....	46:5
13:12	.....	58:5
1 Corinthians 2:6	.....	38:4
3:13	.....	45:3
6:2-3	.....	48:9
6:2-3	.....	91:12
6:3	.....	13:10
6:11	.....	48:7
6:11	.....	50:3
10:20	.....	19:1
15:20-21	.....	49:3
15:20-21	.....	92:3
15:32	.....	102:6
15:52	.....	50:1
2 Corinthians 3:18	.....	38:4
4:16-17	.....	103:3
5:1-2	.....	62:16
Galatians 1:4	.....	48:7
Galatians 1:13	.....	46:8
3:16	.....	84:6
Ephesians 2:6-7	.....	108:12
5:8	.....	108:11
5:29-32	.....	7:1
6:10	.....	1:4
6:12	.....	61:10
Philippians 1:23	.....	39:8
2:9-11	.....	10:21
2:9-11	.....	48:5

Philippians 2:9-11	...	Enoch 62:9
Colossians 1:13	.....	108:11
1:26-27	.....	62:7
2:2-3	.....	46:2
1 Thess. 4:13	.....	100:5
4:16	.....	91:10
4:17	.....	62:15
5:3	.....	62:4
5:5	.....	108:11
5:9	.....	39:9
2 Thess. 1:6-8	.....	100:7
1:9	.....	41:2
1:9	.....	62:10
1:9	.....	63:9
2:3	.....	91:7
2:8	.....	62:2
2:8-9	.....	7:6
1 Timothy 1:9-11	.....	93:4
4:1	.....	91:7
5:21	.....	39:1
6:15-16	.....	14:21
2 Timothy 3:1	.....	91:7
Hebrews 1:2	.....	48:3
1:3	.....	69:25
1:7	.....	17:1
1:14	.....	15:2
1:14	.....	40:9
2:5	.....	71:15
4:13	.....	84:3
10:27	.....	100:9
10:35	.....	104:4
11:5	.....	14:8
11:5	.....	39:3
11:5	.....	70:1
11:35	.....	108:8
12:9	.....	37:2
12:22-23	.....	41:8
13:2	.....	17:1
13:20-21	.....	90:20
James 2:19	.....	13:3
5:1-3	.....	94:8
5:3	.....	97:8
James 5:5	.....	94:9
1 Peter 1:10-12	.....	1:2
1:12	.....	16:3
1:12	.....	108:7
3:18-20	.....	13:10
3:21-22	.....	61:10
4:7	.....	19:3
5:4	.....	90:20
2 Peter 2:1	.....	98:15
2:1	.....	108:6
2:4	.....	10:12

2 Peter 2:4		Enoch 14:5
2:4	.....	54:5
3:7	.....	91:14
1 John 2:8	.....	58:5
2:15	.....	108:8
3:8	.....	84:6
Jude 1:6	.....	15:3
1:6	.....	22:11
1:6-7	.....	10:12
1:6-7	.....	14:5
1:6-7	.....	54:5
1:14	.....	60:8
1:14-15	.....	1:9
1:14-15	.....	27:2
Revelation 1:1-2	.....	1:2
1:3	.....	1:1
1:14	.....	71:10
1:16	.....	62:2
2:7	.....	25:5
2:27	.....	90:18
3:5	.....	62:15
3:5	.....	108:3
3:10	.....	45:2
4:2	.....	14:20
4:2	.....	71:7
4:8	.....	39:12
4:8	.....	40:2
5:5	.....	48:2
5:11	.....	14:22
5:11	.....	40:1
5:11	.....	60:1
5:11	.....	71:9
6:9-10	.....	22:12
6:9-11	.....	47:1
6:9-11	.....	104:3
6:15-16	.....	62:5
7:1	.....	18:2
7:1	.....	69:21
7:1-3	.....	76:4
7:9-10	.....	39:6
7:17	.....	51:3
8:2-4	.....	99:3
8:3-4	.....	47:1
8:6	.....	20:1
8:8	.....	21:3
8:8	.....	108:4
9:1	.....	86:1
9:1-2	.....	18:12
9:11	.....	18:12
9:14	.....	56:5
9:20	.....	19:1
9:20	.....	99:6
10:3-4	.....	59:2

THE BOOK OF ENOCH

Revelation 11:7...Enoch 18:12
12:4 ..... 86:3
12:5 ..... 90:18
12:7 ..... 20:5
12:10 ..... 40:7
12:11 ..... 108:10
12:13 ..... 20:5
12:14 ..... 96:2
13:3 ..... 54:6
13:6 ..... 45:1
13:12 ..... 54:6
13:12 ..... 67:7
13:14 ..... 54:6
13:14 ..... 67:7
14:3 ..... 48:6
14:9-10 ..... 48:9
14:13 ..... 81:4
14:13 ..... 102:4
14:15-18 ..... 71:9
14:20 ..... 100:3
15:1 ..... 20:5
15:5-6 ..... 71:8
15:6 ..... 71:1
16:12 ..... 56:5
16:14 ..... 99:4
17:8 ..... 18:12
17:14 ..... 63:4
19:1+3 ..... 97:2

Revelation 19:2 Enoch 47:4
19:8 ..... 62:15
19:15 ..... 62:2
19:15 ..... 90:18
19:21 ..... 62:2
20:1 ..... 18:12
20:1 ..... 69:28
20:11 ..... 47:3
20:11 ..... 91:16
20:12 ..... 47:3
20:13 ..... 51:1
20:13 ..... 56:8
20:15 ..... 47:3
20:15 ..... 108:3
21:1 ..... 72:1
21:1 ..... 91:16
21:3 ..... 45:4
21:3 ..... 105:2
21:4 ..... 25:5
21:9 ..... 20:5
21:15 ..... 61:3
21:15 ..... 70:3
21:26 ..... 53:1
22:2 ..... 25:5
22:3 ..... 25:5
22:12-17 ..... 103:2
22:14 ..... 25:5
22:18-19 ..... 104:10

VI
Glossary of Terms

Second-Temple Judaism refers to the period of history in Israel between the return of the Jews from Babylon in the days of Ezra, until the destruction of the temple by the Romans in AD 70.
Anaginoskomena is the Eastern Orthodox term for that group of books referred to negatively by Protestants as "Apocrypha". The term was coined by Athanasius to describe these books. This term means "readable things".
Angel: The Biblical word for angel, means messenger. Angels are a type of heavenly creature created for the purpose of providing service for God on behalf of humankind. Though in art we portray them with wings, in Scripture they are never so portrayed but always appear as young men.
Apocalypse comes from the Greek word, *apocalyptos*. The word means "revelation" as when a curtain is drawn back to reveal what is behind it. The word is applied to prophetic books which contain visions, and messages describing what things are like in the spiritual world, heaven, or the afterlife. The *Book of Enoch* and the *Book of Revelation* are apocalypses. Angels usually figure prominently in apocalypses. The books of Daniel and Zechariah are also examples of books containing apocalypses.
Apocrypha means *hidden*. The term may mean something which is hidden from all but a select group. The word has also came to carry the connotation of that which is dubious or false. Protestants apply this term to a group of books which can be found in Orthodox and Catholic Bibles but which are usually not found in Protestant ones. The *Book of Enoch* is not found in most copies of the Apocrypha, but is regarded as Scripture in the Ethiopian Orthodox Church and is found in their Bibles. Even some Protestant Bibles in Ethiopia contain the *Book of Enoch*. The *Book of Enoch* is being included in the Apocrypha of some Evangelical Bibles published by the United Bible Societies in Eritrea.
Aramaic Enoch is the oldest form of the *Book of Enoch* in existence. Fragments of 11 copies of Aramaic Enoch were found among the Dead Scrolls in the 1940's and '50's. Aramaic Enoch has been used to corroborate that Ethiopian copies of Enoch represent a faithful translation of the same book quoted and alluded to in the New Testament. Aramaic Enoch does not contain a complete copy of the *Book of Enoch*.
Canon refers to a rule. Canons of Scripture concern which holy books are suitable for edification of the Church, and thus to be included in the Bible. Though canonical lists of the books of the Bible were published by various synods and councils of the Church over the centuries there never has been, nor is there now, universal agreement of the Church on this subject. There are at least five different lists of canonical books of the Old Testament in use in the Church on a worldwide basis in our day.

Cherubin, or Cherubim are a type of heavenly creature described in the Bible and other Jewish literature during Biblical times, which are portrayed carrying the chariot throne of God (like a divan), or in the role of guardians. Cherubim possess animal-like features with four wings. In Scripture a cherub is never portrayed as a baby with wings as medieval Christian mythology portrays them in art.

Dead Sea Scrolls are scrolls and fragments of scroll books which were found in the vicinity of the Dead Sea in the 1940's and '50's in Israel. Most of these scrolls have been dated as being older than the Christian era, some of them more than two centuries older. The oldest copies of the books of the Hebrew Bible are the Dead Sea Scroll copies. Many other books were also found along with these Biblical books. The *Book of Enoch* was one of the top five represented books in those caves. Current scholarship is moving away from the Essene hypothesis of their origin. Instead it is believed the books were secreted in the cave in AD 68 to prevent their destruction by the Romans.

Deuterocanon is the Catholic term applied to that group of books negatively referred to by Protestants as "Apocrypha". The term has to do with Scripture books found in Catholic and Orthodox Bibles, but not in Jewish and Protestant ones.

Essene Hypothesis was a theory posed by Dominican priests, Roland de Vaux, and Josef T. Milik to the effect that the Dead Seas Scrolls were the product of an ascetic monastic sect of Jews called the Essenes. Once those priests' monopolistic hold on the Dead Sea Scrolls which was in effect for nearly 40 years was broken in the late '80's, other scholars were able to study the scrolls, apply an interdisciplinary approach, and to demonstrate problems with the Essene hypothesis. As it turns out, the priests had likely inferred Catholic norms upon these ancient Jewish artifacts.

Ethiopian Orthodox Church is the form of Christian Orthodoxy in Ethiopia which preserved the *Book of Enoch*. Due to the large number of Ethiopian Jews who became a part of this Church, Ethiopian Orthodoxy preserves numerous Jewish traditional practices, which may help explain the reason for the *Book of Enoch*'s preservation in Ethiopia.

Ethiopic Enoch refers to the version of the *Book of Enoch* which was recovered by explorer James Bruce while searching for the source of the Nile River in Ethiopia, in the late eighteenth century. It is in an Ethiopic language (Geez) which is largely based upon Hebrew.

Falasha Jewry is the term applied to Ethiopian Jews. The majority of Falasha Jews also consider themselves Christians. When Ethiopia's Jews embraced Christianity, they did so in such large numbers that they retained many Jewish traditions. They represent a Jewish-Christian amalgamation in Ethiopian Orthodox Christianity. When Christians in the Latin and Greek worlds were destroying their copies of the *Book of Enoch*, the Ethiopians continued to believe it, copy it, and preserve it.

Ge'ez is the ancient Semitic Ethiopian language into which the only existing complete copies of the *Book of Enoch* have been found. Today Geez is not spoken but is the liturgical language of the Ethiopian Orthodox Church.

Head of Days is a name of God used in Enoch eleven times only in the *Book of the Parables.* In Richard Laurence's translation of Enoch the phrase is translated *"Ancient of Days"*. Ancient of Days is used three times in the *Book of Daniel.* The word "Head" is used to signify the source or origin point of a thing, such as a river head. God is the source or head of days, the creator of time.

Ophannin or Ophannim, is a Hebrew word meaning "wheels." In Ezekiel, the Ophanim are portrayed as wheels within wheels covered with eyes. In Enoch, the Ophanim are seen as a type of heavenly creature.

Pseudepigrapha is a term which in ancient times referred to a any book which came to have the wrong author's name written on the outside of the first leaf of the scroll. The term has come to mean any book which is erroneously attributed to an author. If the *Book of Enoch* were a "pseudepigraphon", it would mean it was not written by the Biblical Enoch. Textual scholars call Enoch a pseudepigraphon, as they do to Isaiah and to Daniel and to many other books of the Bible.

Scroll was the usual medium for books in Biblical times. During the early days of the Christian era, the scroll was replaced by the codex for books. The Codex is similar to the modern form of books.

Seraphin, or Seraphim, are a type of heavenly creature which possess animal-like features with six wings. Their function in the Bible and Enoch is to worship God day and night. The term Seraph, which is singular for Seraphim, means a fiery one. The Seraphim are portrayed in Enoch 39, Isaiah 6 and Revelation 5.

Tablet is the oldest medium for "books", some of which survive to our day. Tablets were usually made from soft clay, upon which writing was inscribed before the clay tablet hardened. Tablets were replaced by scrolls as the preferred medium for books.

Watcher is a descriptive term used for certain angels. Besides the *Book of Enoch,* the term can be found in the *Book of Daniel* and in a number Jewish books from the period of Second-Temple Judaism. It is unclear whether the term was meant to stand for a special class of angels, or simply another term for all angels in general.

VII
A World of Evidence

In chapter eight we look at the *Book of Enoch's* impact on the New Testament. In chapter nine we uncover evidence internal to the *Book of Enoch* that indicates it is older than we are usually told. In chapter eleven we examine the influence the book has exerted on other ancient writings. Another chapter, indeed, another book could be written about the evidence in our world that the events described by Enoch actually did transpire on this globe we call earth. The evidence is compellingly persuasive and it is global in breadth. Since this subject is a bit outside the scope of my book, it is only briefly mentioned in this appendix because of the subject's possible new direction for others to research and write upon. I will mention just two spheres in our world which lend believability that the events described in Enoch's book really happened on our globe before the flood.

Humanity's Worldwide Legacy of Lore

It is interesting to note how widespread in our world are the myths and stories concerning the arrival on earth of gods and deities instructing and intermingling with mankind. Are these stories corruptions introduced among the nations by centuries of elaboration and retelling of ancient events? In that case the *Book of Enoch* can be viewed as preserving an original pure narrative. Stories and myths including the same basic elements are worldwide. The ancient Greek versions of these are by far the best known.

Did the original *Book of Enoch's* version of the story about "Azazel" in which Azazel teaches warfare to mankind, morph over time into the Greek "Ares", the god of war? Did the original *Book of Enoch* version of the story about Semjaza as the leader of the angels who sinned, morph over time into the Greek "Zeus" the chief of the gods? Also, did the Enochan stories of the offspring of angels and human woman morph over time into the tales of the children of the gods in Greek mythology, like Hercules?

If this is true, this would have happened as the nations became divided by language after the Tower of Babel incident. All except the descendants of Shem, the son of Noah, who were preserving the scrolls of Enoch's book, would have been severed from access to the original pure version of the story.

It is intriguing to watch today in popular culture we seem to be witness to the birth of a new mythology in which pre-flood events are being explained in terms of ancient aliens and astronauts. These ideas might seem more palatable to people in a technological age, but they are mythology nonetheless.

Earth's Worldwide Legacy in Stone

Our planet is quite littered with hundreds if not thousands of archaeological sites which raise more questions than answers about the early days of human civilization on planet earth. The common understanding of the history of civilization is that man began the first cities a little earlier than 3,000 BC in Sumer and Egypt. However, many megalithic sites around this world overturn this view. Ancient megaliths which predate the rise of those two civilizations indicate humans were organizing themselves into civilizations much earlier. Ancient building projects such as that discovered at Gobekli Tepe, in Turkey is such a site. There are many others. Add to this the huge scale in which many of these building projects were created, the implication is that the builders had engineering skills which are phenomenal even by modern engineering standards. This is easily understood since Enoch explains among the sins of the angels was prematurely accelerating man's understanding of the physical world. For example, the expended effort needed to intricately carve and precisely place stones which weighed hundreds of tons is simply 'herculean'!

The reader may be interested to consider the sites of Super Henge, the Sea of Galilee's underwater cairn, the Nazca Lines, Malta's incredible Hypogeum, and Pumapunku's pre-Incan foundations to name just a few.

The purpose of the flood was to erase the works of the Watchers and their offspring from the earth, but the civilizations which grew up before the flood have left many puzzling artifacts preserved in stone. That puzzlement ends if we accept the claims of Enoch's book at face value.

An Enochan Nexus

How could pre-literate humanity be responsible for littering the face of the planet with extremely well-engineered megalithic structures? This presents a seemingly insoluble puzzle for traditional histories primarily because of this: in the traditional view it is believed that prior to the rise of civilization, pre-literate men, on a worldwide basis were able to build huge megaliths which still amaze even by modern engineering standards.

Many of these megaliths have been found to be calendars which predict the precise movement of the sun, moon and stars over the course of time. It seems clear now that while the Watchers were indoctrinating mankind into astrology and the workings of the heavens, and while the Nephilim were building these vast structures, Enoch was also recording in writing the observable operations of the sun and moon devoid of occult corruptions.

VIII
Bibliography

(2009). the English Standard Version Bible: Containing the Old and New Testaments With Apocrypha. Oxford; New York, Oxford University Press.

Avigad, Nahman and Yigael Yadin. (1956). A Genesis Apocryphon: a Scroll from the Wilderness of Judaea. Jerusalem, The Magnes Press.

Barker, M. (1988). The Lost Prophet: the Book of Enoch and Its Influence On Christianity. London, SPCK.

Baty, John (1839). The Book of Enoch the Prophet. London. Hatchard and Son.

Beale, G. K. and D. A. Carson (2007). Commentary on the New Testament use of the Old Testament. Nottingham, England, Grand Rapids, Mich., Apollos; Baker Academic.

Boccaccini, G. (1998). Beyond the Essene Hypothesis: the Parting of the Ways Between Qumran and Enochic Judaism. Grand Rapids, Mich., William B. Eerdmans Pub.

Boccaccini, G. (2005). Enoch and Qumran Origins: New Light On A Forgotten Connection. Cambridge, U.K.; Grand Rapids, Mich., William B. Eerdmans.

Boccaccini, G. (2007). Enoch and the Messiah Son of Man: Revisiting the Book of Parables. Cambridge, U.K.; Grand Rapids, Mich., William B. Eerdmans Pub.

Boccaccini, G. and J. J. Collins (2007). The Early Enoch Literature. Leiden; Boston, Brill.

Brannan, R., Et Al. (2012). The Lexham English Septuagint. Bellingham, WA, Lexham Press.

Brown, Ronald K. (2000). The Book of Enoch. San Antonio, TX, Guadalupe Baptist Theological Seminary Press.

Charles, R. H. (1912). The Book of Enoch: (1 Enoch). London, Society for Promoting Christian Knowledge.

Charles, R. H. (1908). The Testaments of the Twelve Patriarchs: Translated From the Editor's Greek Test and Edited, With Introduction, Notes, and Indices. London, Adam and Charles Black.

Charlesworth, J. H. (1983). The Old Testament Pseudepigrapha. Garden City, N.Y., Doubleday.

Collins, J. J. (1997). Apocalypticism in the Dead Sea Scrolls. London; New York, Routledge.

Eisenman, R. H. and M. O. Wise (1992). The Dead Sea Scrolls Uncovered: the First Complete Translation and Interpretation of 50 Key Documents Withheld For Over 35 Years. Shaftesbury, Dorset; Rockport, Mass., Element.

Eissfeldt, O. (1965). The Old Testament: An Introduction, Including the Apocrypha and Pseudepigrapha, and Also the Works of Similar Type From Qumran: the History of the Formation of the Old Testament. New York,, Harper and Row.

Fitzmyer, J. A. (2004). The Genesis Apocryphon of Qumran Cave 1 (1Q20) : a commentary. Roma, Editrice Pontificio Istituto Biblico.

Flint, P. W. and J. C. Vanderkam (1998). The Dead Sea Scrolls After Fifty Years: A Comprehensive Assessment. Leiden; Boston, Brill.

Fruchtenbaum, Arnold G. (2004). The Footsteps of the Messiah: A Study of the Sequence of Prophetic Events. Tustin, CA, Ariel Ministries.

García Martínez, F. (1996). The Dead Sea Scrolls Translated: the Qumran Texts in English. New York, Grand Rapids, Mich., E.J. Brill; W.B. Eerdmans.

García Martínez, F. and E. J. C. Tigchelaar. (2000). The Dead Sea Scrolls Study Edition.
Gaster, T. H. (1976). The Dead Sea Scriptures, in English Translation. Garden City, N.Y., Anchor Press.
Golb, N. (1995). Who Wrote the Dead Sea Scrolls?: the Search For the Secret of Qumran. New York, Scribner.
Grosseteste, R. and A. Gilby (1793). The Testament of the Twelve Patriarchs the Sons of Jacob. Falkirk, Printed and Sold By Patrick Mair,.
Johnson, Johnson. (2012). Ancient Book of Enoch. Bible Facts.
Knibb, M. A., E. Ullendorff, Et Al. (1978). The Ethiopic Book of Enoch: A New Edition in the Light of the Aramaic Dead Sea Fragments. Oxford New York, Clarendon Press; Oxford University Press.
Kugler, R. A. (2001). The Testaments of the Twelve Patriarchs. Sheffield, England, Sheffield Academic Press.
Ladd, John D. (2009). Commentary on the Book of Enoch: Commentary and Paraphrase. Canton, OH, Xeon Press.
Laurence, R. (1883). The Book of Enoch the Prophet. London, Kegan Paul, Trench.
Lumpkin, Joseph B. (2004). The Book of Enoch: a Comprehensive Transliteration of the Forgotten Book of the Bible. Blountsville, AL, Fifth Estate.
Mansoor, M. (1983). The Dead Sea Scrolls: A Textbook and Study Guide. Grand Rapids, Mich., Baker Book House.
May, H. G. and B. M. Metzger (1977). The New Oxford Annotated Bible With the Apocrypha: Revised Standard Version, Containing the Second Edition of the New Testament and An Expanded Edition of the Apocrypha. New York, Oxford University Press.
Nersessian, Vrej. (2001). The Bible in the Armenian Tradition. London, The British Library.
Nickelsburg, G. W. E. and K. Baltzer (2001). 1 Enoch 1: A Commentary on the Book of 1 Enoch, Chapters 1-36, 81-108. Minneapolis MN, Fortress Press.
Nickelsburg, G. W. E. and K. Baltzer (2011). 1 Enoch 2: A Commentary on the Book of 1 Enoch, Chapters 37-82. Minneapolis MN, Fortress Press.
Nickelsburg, G. W. E. and J. C. Vanderkam (2004). 1 Enoch: A New Translation. Minneapolis, Fortress Press.
Olson, D. C. and Melkesedek (2004). Enoch: A New Translation: the Ethiopic Book of Enoch, Or 1 Enoch. North Richland Hills, Tex., BIBAL Press.
O'Neill, J. C. (1995). Who did Jesus think he was? Leiden ; New York, E.J. Brill.
Peters, Dorothy M. (2008). Noah Traditions in the Dead Sea Scrolls: Conversations and Controversies of Antiquity. Atlanta, GA, Society of Biblical Literature.
Schiffman, L. H. (1990). Archaeology and History in the Dead Sea Scrolls: the New York University Conference in Memory of Yigael Yadin. Sheffield, New York, JSOT Press; Hagop Kevorkian Center For Near Eastern Studies At New York University.
Schiffman, L. H. (1994). Reclaiming the Dead Sea Scrolls: the History of Judaism, the Background of Christianity, the Lost Library of Qumran. Philadelphia, Jewish Publication Society.
Schodde, G. H. (1882). The Book of Enoch: Translated From the Ethiopic, With Introduction and Notes. Andover,, W. F. Draper.
Scott, W. Eugene. (1984). And Enoch Also Prophesied. Glendale, CA, Dolores Press, Inc.
Shanks, H. (1992). Understanding the Dead Sea Scrolls: A Reader From the Biblical Archaeology Review. New York, Random House.
Shanks, H., J. C. Vanderkam, Et Al. (1991). The Dead Sea Scrolls After Forty Years. Washington, D.C., Biblical Archaeology Society.

Sparks, H. F. D. (1984). The Apocryphal Old Testament. Oxford, New York, Clarendon Press; Oxford University Press.

St. Athanasius Orthodox Academy. (2008). The Orthodox Study Bible. Nashville, Tenn., Thomas Nelson.

Stone, M. E. (1991). Selected Studies in Pseudepigrapha and Apocrypha With Special Reference to the Armenian Tradition. Leiden; New York, E.J. Brill.

Swete, H. B. (1899). The Psalms of Solomon With the Greek Fragments of the Book of Enoch. Cambridge, University Press,.

Vanderkam, J. C. (1984). Enoch and the Growth of An Apocalyptic Tradition. Washington, D.C., Catholic Biblical Association of America.

Vanderkam, J. C. (1995). Enoch: A Man For All Generations. Columbia, S.C., University of South Carolina Press.

Vanderkam, J. C. (1998). Calendars in the Dead Sea Scrolls: Measuring Time. London; New York, Routledge.

Vanderkam, J. C. and P. W. Flint (2002). The Meaning of the Dead Sea Scrolls: Their Significance For Understanding the Bible, Judaism, Jesus, and Christianity. [San Francisco Calif.], Harper San Francisco.

Vermès, G. (2004). The Complete Dead Sea Scrolls in English. London; New York, Penguin.

Wise, M. O., M. G. Abegg, Et Al. (1996). The Dead Sea Scrolls: A New Translation. San Francisco, Harper San Francisco.

Wise, M. O., M. G. Abegg, Et Al. (2005). The Dead Sea Scrolls: A New Translation. San Francisco, Harper San Francisco.

IX
Topical Index

A

B

F

G

H

I

J

L

M

N

P

R

S

APPENDICES

ISBN 978-057819869-9